SUPPLY CHAIN DEVELOPMENT FOR THE LEAN ENTERPRISE

STRATEGIES IN
CONFRONTATIONAL
COST MANAGEMENT
SERIES

SUPPLY CHAIN DEVELOPMENT FOR THE LEAN ENTERPRISE

INTERORGANIZATIONAL COST MANAGEMENT

ROBIN COOPER

REGINE SLAGMULDER

PRODUCTIVITY
PORTLAND, OREGON

THE IMA FOUNDATION FOR APPLIED RESEARCH, INC.
MONTVALE, NEW JERSEY

Additional copies of this book and information about the Strategies in Confrontational Cost Management Series are available from the publishers. Discounts are available for multiple copies.

The IMA Foundation for Applied Research, Inc.
10 Paragon Drive, Montvale, NJ 07645-1760
Telephone: 800-638-4427, ext. 278; telefax: 201-573-9507
E-mail: jpirard@imanet.org.

Productivity, Inc.
P.O. Box 13390, Portland, OR 97213-0309
Telephone: 503-235-0600; telefax: 503-235-0909
Sales Department: 800-394-6868
E-mail: service@productivityinc.com

Book design by Bill Stanton, Stanton Design
Cover design by Mark Weinstein, Productivity, Inc.
Page composition by Susan Swanson, In Pages
Art creation by Lee Smith, Smith & Fredrick Graphics
Printed and bound by Edwards Brothers in the United States of America

Library of Congress Cataloging-in-Publication Data

Cooper, Robin, 1951–
    Supply chain development for the lean enterprise / Robin Cooper, Regine Slagmulder.
        p.   cm—(Strategies in confrontational cost management series)
    Includes bibliographical references and index.
    ISBN 1–56327–218–0 (hardcover)
    1. Cost control. 2. Industrial procurement—Cost control. 3. Contracting out—Cost control. I. Slagmulder, Regine. II. Title. III. Series.
HD47.3
658.15'52—dc21   99–19428
                                                                                                      CIP

IMA Publication Number 99338

05 04 03 02 01 00 99   10 9 8 7 6 5 4 3 2 1

Contents

PART 1
CONFRONTATIONAL COST MANAGEMENT

CHAPTER 1

CHAPTER 2

CHAPTER 3

PART 2
THE PRINCIPLES OF LEAN SUPPLY

CHAPTER 4

PART 4
CASE STUDIES

CHAPTER 17

CHAPTER 18

CHAPTER 19

CHAPTER 20

CHAPTER 21

PREFACE TO THE SERIES

INTRODUCTION

Lean enterprises have faster reflexes than their mass production counterparts. They have the ability to design and launch products very rapidly. These fast reflexes render the sustainable competitive advantages that mass producers have relied on virtually impossible to achieve. Instead, lean enterprises compete by repeatedly creating temporary competitive advantages. Because they do not have sustainable competitive advantages, lean enterprises are forced to seek out competition. They adopt a generic strategy of confrontation; that is, they compete head on by trying to sell equivalent products to the same customers.

When firms compete in this manner, three product-related characteristics play a critical role in strategy formulation. These characteristics, known as the survival triplet, have internal and external forms. Internally they are the product's cost, quality, and functionality. Externally, they are its selling price, perceived quality, and perceived functionality. While the selling prices of products can be disconnected from their costs temporarily, if the firm is to remain profitable in the long run, costs must be brought into line with selling prices. The survival zone of a product identifies the range of values of the three characteristics that a product must have to be successful.

Firms that compete in a confrontational environment must develop and integrate their total quality management, product development, and cost management systems. The objective of this integration is to create a manufacturing strategy based on developing products with the right level of functionality and quality at the right price. The key point is that firms must learn to view the process of managing the survival triplet as a total systems solution, not a collection of independent techniques, either across characteristics of the survival triplet or within them.

While the way Japanese firms manage quality and time to market has been documented in depth elsewhere, the way in which Japanese firms manage costs has not attracted anywhere near as much attention and represents the missing piece of the puzzle of how lean enterprises compete. In response to this situation, the Institute of Management Accountants, Robin Cooper, and Regine Slagmulder agreed to carry out a joint research project based on studies of actual Japanese lean enterprises that have implemented advanced cost management programs. The primary objective of the project was to research, synthesize, and document key design issues and results, based on these companies' experiences.

THE SERIES

The purpose of this series is to begin the process of filling in the gap in the literature about Japanese cost management practices. The first volume in the series, published August 1997, is *Target Costing and Value Engineering*. The seven cases in this volume document how firms use target costing and value engineering to design products that have the functionality and quality customers demand at a cost that allows the firms to make adequate profits when the products are sold at their target selling prices.

Target costing achieves its objectives by transmitting the competitive pressures faced by the firm to its product designers and suppliers. It creates a common language among the various functions involved in bringing products to market: production, product engineering, procurement, and marketing. It helps individuals in the various functions develop products that have the right functionality, quality, and cost. By decomposing the product-level target costs to the component level, firms can begin the process of transmitting the competitive pressures they face to their suppliers.

The second volume in the series, *Supply Chain Development for the Lean Enterprise,* contains nine cases documenting the way Japanese firms transfer cost management pressures across organizational boundaries. The pressure to become more efficient has caused many firms to try to increase the efficiency of supplier firms through interorganizational cost management systems. These systems have emerged because it is no longer sufficient to be the most efficient firm; it is necessary to be part of the most efficient supply chain. To achieve this objective, many Japanese firms blur their organizational boundaries. Organizational blurring occurs when information critical to one firm is possessed by another firm either further up or down the supply chain. The two or more firms then create relationships that share organizational resources, including information that helps improve the efficiency of the interfirm activities. Mechanisms for information sharing include supporting joint research and development projects, placing employees of one firm in other firms, and establishing interorganizational cost management systems.

These interorganizational cost management systems are designed to achieve three objectives:

- They create conduits that transmit the competitive pressures faced by the end producers to their suppliers.
- Through trade-offs in the survival triplet, these cost management systems create a way to modify the specifications that the end producer sets for the parts it purchases. These modifications allow the part to be sold at its target price while still generating an adequate return for all firms in the supply chain.
- The systems let the product engineers at all firms in a supply chain jointly design products that can be manufactured more cost efficiently than if the firms acted independently.

Through trade-offs in the survival triplet, these cost management systems create a way to modify the specifications that the end producer sets for the parts it purchases. These modifications allow the part to be sold at its target price while still generating an adequate return for all firms in the supply chain.

The third volume in the series explores kaizen costing, which is continuous improvement applied to cost reduction in the manufacturing stage of a product's life. The seven cases in *Kaizen Costing* document the rich variety of practices surrounding kaizen costing. Unlike target costing, kaizen costing does not concern itself with changing a product's functionality. Instead, it keeps functionality constant and tries to find ways to reduce costs.

Kaizen costing has two major approaches: general and specific. General kaizen costing sets out to reduce the costs of production processes in general, and specific kaizen costing seeks to reduce the cost of a given product, either by changing its design or by reducing the cost of the production processes involved in its manufacture. Kaizen costing systems typically merge seamlessly with the firm's target costing systems. Therefore, these two cost management systems are better viewed as a single program rather than two separate systems.

THE FIRMS

The material in this series was developed through observation and analysis of 25 innovative Japanese lean enterprises that have advanced cost management programs. We especially appreciate the cooperation from the companies we have worked with for allowing us to describe their cost management systems in depth. We were fortunate to receive permission to present the 31 cases, predominantly undisguised.[1] These firms were:

Citizen Watch Company, Ltd.
Higashimaru Shoyu Company, Ltd. (2)[2]
Isuzu Motors, Ltd. (2)
Jidosha Kiki Company
Kamakura Iron Works Company, Ltd.

---

[1] Firms in italics are disguised.

[2] The number in brackets identifies the number of cases written on the company.

Kirin Brewery Company, Ltd.
Komatsu, Ltd. (2)
Kyocera Corporation
Mitsubishi Kasei Corporation
Miyota Company, Ltd.
Nippon Kayaku
Nissan Motor Company, Ltd.
Olympus Optical Company, Ltd. (3)
Omachi Olympus Company, Ltd.
Shionogi & Co., Ltd.
Sony Corporation
Sumitomo Electric Industries, Ltd.
Taiyo Kogyo Company, Ltd. (The Taiyo Group)
Tokyo Motor Works Company
Topcon Corporation
Toyo Radiator Company, Ltd.
Toyota Motor Corporation
Yamanouchi Pharmaceutical Company, Ltd.
Yamatake-Honeywell Company, Ltd.
Yokohama Corporation, Ltd.

In summary, this series represents a state-of-the-art analysis of the cost management systems at 25 Japanese manufacturing companies. The findings will provide insights into the nature of those systems, the conditions under which the techniques are likely to be most beneficial, and the detailed operations of such systems. Hopefully, these insights will be valuable in helping managers at firms that want to implement such systems achieve their objectives.

PREFACE

In today's intensely competitive environments, firms must become experts at developing low-cost, high-quality products that have the functionality that customers demand. They must adopt integrated quality, functionality, and cost management systems that ensure that products are successful when launched. These systems must create a firm-wide discipline to design and produce products of high quality and functionality at low cost. Thus, the objective of the cost management program is to install in everyone in the firm a disciplined approach to cost reduction. This discipline must begin when products or services are first conceived, continue during manufacturing, and end only when they are discontinued. The cost management program must not limit its scope to just the four walls of the factory or even the boundaries of the firm. It must spread across the entire supplier network.

Effective cost management must start at the design stage of a product's life. Once a product is designed, most of its costs are fixed. For example, the number of components, the different types of materials used, and the time it takes to assemble are all determined primarily by the way the product is designed. Some authorities estimate that as much as 90% to 95% of a product's costs are designed in; that is, they cannot be avoided without redesigning the product. Consequently, effective cost management programs must focus on the design as well as the manufacturing phase of a product's life cycle.

The primary cost management method used by many Japanese firms to control costs during the product development stage is a combination of target costing and value engineering. These two techniques are extended across the supply chain through the use of *interorganizational cost management systems*. Target costing lies at the heart of interorganizational cost management. It has two primary objectives. The first is to identify the cost at which a given product must be manufactured if it is to earn its target profit margin at its expected or target selling price. The second is to decompose the target cost down to the component level. The firm's suppliers then are expected to find ways to deliver the components they sell at the target prices set by their customers while still making adequate returns. When the suppliers also use target costing to discipline their product development processes, *chained target costing systems* emerge. Chained target costing is an important element of interorganizational cost management because it transmits the competitive pressure faced by the firm at the top of the supply chain to the other firms within the chain. It aligns the cost management programs of the firms in the chain by indicating to the suppliers where the buyer expects cost reduction to occur.

Target costing systems, whether stand-alone or chained, operate at arm's length as the cost-reduction efforts of the buyer and supplier are undertaken in isolation. However, this isolation limits the effectiveness of the overall cost management process because each firm confines its analysis to local savings. Interorganizational cost management overcomes this limitation by creating formal mechanisms for the design teams of the firms in the supply chain to interact. These interactions enable the product and its components to be designed in ways that reduce costs throughout the supply chain. Value engineering, an organized effort to find ways to achieve the product's functions in a manner that allows the firms to meet their target costs, lies at the heart of these interactions. Three different mechanisms to coordinate the efforts of the design teams are documented in this volume:

functionality-price-quality (FPQ) trade-offs, interorganizational cost investigations, and *concurrent cost management.*

For these interactions to be effective, each firm in the supply chain must act in ways that benefit the others. The adversarial relationships that characterize most Western supply chains are replaced by interdependent, cooperative relationships. When firms act in this manner, supplier networks emerge in which all the firms operate in mutually supportive ways even if they are in direct competition with each other.

While interorganizational cost management is one of the cornerstones of Japanese cost management programs, it has not received much attention in the West. Some Western firms have developed such systems, but many lack a fully integrated approach to buyer-supplier cost management. The objective of this volume is to document and analyze how Japanese manufacturing firms use interorganizational cost management techniques for strategic advantage. We hope that Western managers can learn from these firms' experiences and adapt the techniques to the specific requirements of their firms.

The volume is structured as follows. An executive summary provides an overview of the findings of this portion of the research project. In Part One, the first chapter assists readers in understanding the terminology and concepts behind the confrontation strategy by describing confrontational principles and how to manage the survival triplet. Chapter 2 covers the role of cost management in a confrontation strategy. Chapter 3 describes the research method. The bulk of Chapters 1 to 3 are common to all volumes in the series.

The two chapters in Part Two (Chapters 4 and 5) describe the principles of lean supply and set the stage for the material that follows. The 11 chapters in Part Three concern the main topic of this particular volume, interorganizational cost management. Chapter 6 presents an overview and Chapters 7 to 14 summarize the process and outputs of interorganizational cost management, based on an in-depth examination of the practices observed at nine companies. The first five of these chapters are about interorganizational cost management in the product design stage. The next two chapters deal with the manufacturing stage and Chapter 14 deals with the efficiency of the buyer-supplier interface. Chapter 15 provides an example of interorganizational cost management in action. Chapter 16 concludes with lessons for adopters.

The final part of the book, Chapters 17 to 25, contains nine case studies of Japanese manufacturing companies that have implemented interorganizational cost management systems. These nine companies illustrate four supply chains. The case studies highlight the competitive context that led management to implement interorganizational cost management programs, the design of those programs, and their application.

ACKNOWLEDGMENTS

This volume would not have been possible without extensive time commitment from a large number of persons. Some of these people were involved in the underlying research, others were responsible for editing the cases, and some were involved in reviewing the draft manuscripts. Many of them donated their time despite busy schedules.

First and foremost, we owe an enormous debt to individuals at the nine Japanese firms whose interorganizational cost management practices form the basis for this volume. It is impossible to say how many people in those firms, some of whom we never even met, provided input to the research, but the number is well over 60. To give some idea of the effort required on their part it should be noted that we spent a total of 25 days visiting the nine companies. When the cases were written, over 600 outstanding questions had to be answered. At the end of the project, only a few remained unanswered, and none of them was considered important. Individuals at the companies read every case at least three times, and corrections and suggestions were made after each reading. These suggestions helped to ensure the accuracy of the cases and the richness of our understanding of Japanese practice. We would particularly like to thank Toshiro Shimoyama, chairman and CEO of Olympus Optical Co., Ltd., for spending considerable time with us discussing the theory of confrontational strategy and the role of cost management.

We also owe a debt of gratitude to Professor Takeo Yoshikawa of Yokohama National University, who coauthored the cases on Yokohama and Kamakura. Professor Michiharu Sakurai of Senshu University, to whom we express our thanks, identified Komatsu. We are particularly fortunate to have the opportunity to include Chapter 5, on lean supplier networks, written by Dr. Kathleen Gumbleton. To her we express our deepest thanks. We would like to thank John Deasy for his contributions to Chapter 14. Finally, we want to thank the reviewers who provided us with invaluable feedback. They include Shannon Anderson, Jitsuo Goto, Jim Reeve, and Takeo Yoshikawa.

We also would like to thank those who were actively involved in the process of writing the cases and this volume: Sarah Connor, Juliene Hunter, and Amy Wong. Each provided unflagging energy to keep the project on course. Sarah, a case editor at Harvard Business School case services, performed the invaluable and nearly endless task of editing the more than 700 pages of cases and teaching notes that make up the Japanese Cost Management Series. It was a delight to work with her. Amy and Juliene helped arrange the visits to the companies and assisted with editing the drafts of the analysis chapters of the volume. Without their help, the project would have taken much longer to complete.

In addition we would like to thank all those at IMA and Productivity who helped shape this manuscript and bring it to bound book form: Claire Barth, senior editor, IMA, who edited the manuscript and coordinated the many reviews and changes; at Productivity, Lorraine Millard for project management, Bill Stanton for text design, Mark Weinstein for cover design, Lee Smith for art creation, Susan Swanson for page composition, and Julie Nemer for proofreading and indexing.

Clearly, this volume could not have come about without the help of the institutions that supported the research. This was an extremely expensive undertaking, and we hope that all the institutions consider their money well spent. First, there are the academic institutions with which we have or had associations and, second, there are the sponsors of the series. For Robin Cooper, the first three years of the project were supported by the Harvard Business School, division of research. The last four years were supported by the Institute of U.S./Japan Relations in the World Economy and the Claremont Graduate University. Regine Slagmulder was supported by the Institute of U.S./Japan Relations in the World Economy and Tilburg University.

There are two sponsors of the series. First, the Institute of Management Accountants had the foresight to see the need for the series. Their support and guidance contributed greatly to this project's success. The Project Committee of the IMA's Foundation for Applied Research, composed of Robert Miller (chairman) and Hank Davis, provided sustained enthusiasm and invaluable guidance as to the content and direction of each of the analysis chapters. In addition, the Institute of U.S./Japan Relations in the World Economy provided financial support for the series.

ABOUT THE AUTHORS

ROBIN COOPER, DBA

Professor Robin Cooper has been a member of the faculty of the Peter F. Drucker Graduate School of Management, Claremont Graduate University, Claremont, California, since July 1992. Prior to that date he was on the Harvard Business School faculty, from 1982 until 1992. He is currently Visiting Professor at the Goizueta Business School at Emory University. In 1996, he was awarded an honorary doctorate from the University of Ghent, Belgium.

His major field of interest is strategic cost management systems. His current research focuses on the design and use of cost management systems to achieve competitive advantage and, in particular, on Japanese cost management systems and activity-based cost systems.

In 1990, Dr. Cooper was the recipient of the first Innovations in Accounting Education Award, presented by the American Accounting Association in recognition of his course development efforts in product costing. In 1991 and 1993, he was the recipient of the Notable Contributions to Management Accounting Literature award presented by the Management Accounting Section of the American Accounting Association.

Dr. Cooper is a regular contributor to several journals including *Advances in Management Accounting, The Journal of Cost Management, International Journal of Production Economics, Management Accounting* (U.S.), *Management Accounting* (U.K.), *Accountancy* (U.K.), *Management Accounting Research* (U.K.), *Accounting Horizons, Accounting* (Japan), and *Sloan Management Review.* In addition, he has had four articles published in the *Harvard Business Review.*

He is the author or coauthor of six books: *Cost and Effect* (Harvard Business School Press, 1998); *Target Costing and Value Engineering* (Institute of Management Accountants, 1997); *When Lean Enterprises Collide: Competing Under Confrontation* (Harvard Business School Press, 1995); *Cost Management in a Confrontation Strategy: Lessons from Japan,* a customizable case book containing 22 cases on 19 Japanese firms; *Implementing Activity-Based Cost Management: Moving from Analysis to Action* (Institute of Management Accountants, 1992); and *The Design of Cost Management Systems: Text, Cases, and Readings* (Prentice-Hall, 1999, 1991).

Dr. Cooper received his MBA with high distinction from Harvard in 1977 and was named a Baker Scholar. A recipient of a Deloitte Haskins & Sells Foundation Fellowship and an ITT International Fellowship, he earned his DBA from Harvard in 1982. Before beginning his graduate studies, he worked as an accountant for Coopers & Lybrand in its London and Boston offices from 1972 to 1976. He is a fellow of the Institute of Chartered Accountants in England and Wales. He received his bachelor of science degree in chemistry with first-class honors from Manchester University in 1972.

REGINE SLAGMULDER, PH.D.

Professor Regine Slagmulder is a member of the faculty of Tilburg University, The Netherlands, and Visiting Professor at the University of Ghent, Belgium. She is a research fellow of the Institute for the Study of U.S./Japan Relations in the World Economy at the Claremont Graduate University, Claremont, California.

Her current research focuses on strategic cost management systems and their applications in both Japanese and Western firms. She has had several articles published in international journals, including *Management Accounting Research* and *International Journal of Production Economics.* In addition, she is the coauthor of three books: *Target Costing and Value Engineering,* published by the Institute of Management Accountants; *Management Accounting in de Nieuwe Produktie-Omgeving* (Management Accounting in the New Production Environment); and *Beheerscontrole, Ein Stimulans Voor Doelgericht Management van Organisaties* (Management Control).

Dr. Slagmulder received her Ph.D. in management from the University of Ghent in 1995. Her doctoral research focused on the use of management control systems to align capital investment decisions with strategy. During her doctoral studies, she spent a year as visiting research fellow at Boston University School of Management. She earned a master's degree in electrical engineering in 1988 and a master's degree in industrial management in 1991, both from the University of Ghent.

ABOUT THE SPONSORS

INSTITUTE OF
MANAGEMENT ACCOUNTANTS

The Institute of Management Accountants (IMA) is the world's largest organization devoted exclusively to management accounting and financial management. IMA has approximately 80,000 members and more than 300 chapters and affiliates across the United States and abroad. The IMA contributes to advancements in financial management and management accounting practices through education and professional certification. The IMA:

- publishes research reports and monographs on a wide variety of management accounting topics through its research affiliate, IMA's Foundation for Applied Research (FAR);
- provides continuing education courses and seminars to members;
- disseminates knowledge by publishing a monthly magazine, *Strategic Finance;*
- awards the professional designations of Certified Management Accountant (CMA) and Certified in Financial Management (CFM).

Through such activities the IMA carries out its vision: *global leadership in education, certification, and practice of management accounting and finance.*

INSTITUTE FOR THE STUDY OF U.S./JAPAN RELATIONS IN THE WORLD ECONOMY

The Institute for the Study of U.S./Japan Relations in the World Economy is part of the Peter F. Drucker Graduate School of Management at Claremont Graduate University. Its mission is to advance Japanese and U.S. economic, political, and social relations through intensive research and educational programs. To carry out its mission the Institute is developing partnerships globally with universities, research institutes, and sponsoring corporate foundations.

The Institute serves as an "objective and nonpartisan" resource center for the exchange of information and cross-fertilization of ideas for researchers and practitioners who are looking for solutions to reduce the economic, political, and social tensions between the United States and Japan. It also is an information exchange resource for the development of teaching and educational materials that can be used to train and educate current and future leaders in industry, academe, and government. It depends on an international network of multidisciplinary researchers (academics, research institutes, consultants, and government policy makers) to increase the influence of its findings on corporate leaders and public policy makers.

The Institute is unique in that it uses balanced research teams from the United States and Japan and strives to achieve balanced funding from U.S. and Japanese transnational corporations. By building a positive relationship with Japan through an innovative educational program that serves a global constituency, this program will help prepare current and future leaders for the strategic challenges ahead.

Claremont Graduate University in Claremont, California, is dedicated exclusively to graduate study, awarding degrees in 19 disciplines through six academic centers. A member of the Claremont Consortium, CGU combines relevant human-scale instruction with the facilities and academic breadth of a medium-size university.

Executive Summary

Introduction

In today's highly competitive environment, firms must manage costs aggressively if they are to survive. Cost management must be applied across the entire life of the product by everyone involved in its design and manufacture. Successful cost management cannot be limited to the four walls of the factory or even to the boundaries of the firm. It must spread across the entire supply chain and cover all aspects of the value chain of the firm's products or services. It must create significant pressure on individuals throughout the supply chain to reduce costs.

Interorganizational cost management is a *structured approach to coordinating the activities of firms in a supplier network so that total costs in the network are reduced*. Interorganizational cost management, that is, cost management that crosses the organizational boundary between buyer and supplier, is particularly important to lean enterprises for two primary reasons. First, lean enterprises typically outsource more of the value-added of their products than their mass producer counterparts. Second, they usually compete more

1

aggressively and therefore have to manage costs more effectively. Taken together, these two reasons mean that it is not sufficient for lean enterprises to be highly efficient; rather they must be part of a highly efficient supplier network. To achieve this objective lean enterprises have developed sophisticated cost management programs that spread across their entire supplier networks.

However, it is more than just cost management that must extend across the interorganizational boundaries between buyers and suppliers. Suppliers are a major source of innovation for lean enterprises. Consequently, the most successful supplier networks have mechanisms that encourage every firm in the network to innovate and compete more aggressively. The key point is that the supply chain must be managed for competitive advantage, not just to reduce costs. As will be seen, cost management should not be practiced in isolation. The competitive advantages from more effective management of the supply chain focus on improved quality and functionality of the components supplied, and hence of the end products, as well as on reduced costs. Interorganizational cost management thus plays a critical role in developing competitive advantages for lean enterprises.

Interorganizational cost management can reduce costs in three ways. The first way to reduce costs across organizational boundaries is during product design. Here, interorganizational cost management is a structured approach to coordinating the product development activities of firms in supplier networks so that the products and components those firms produce can be manufactured at their target costs. It is of particular importance to lean enterprises because usually they outsource as much as 70% of the value-added of their products. With such a high degree of outsourced value, coordinating product development throughout the supplier network is critical to the firm's success. In contrast, mass producers outsource considerably less, particularly product design. Therefore, such firms derive less benefit from interorganizational cost management. As firms become lean and undergo vertical disaggregation, they discover that it is no longer adequate for each firm in the supplier network to undertake cost management independently. Instead, they discover that product development programs have to become coordinated across the buyer-supplier interfaces.

The second way to apply interorganizational cost management is during product manufacture. Here interorganizational kaizen costing is used to coordinate the production activities of firms in the supplier network so that the products and components produced by those firms can be manufactured at their kaizen costs. The buyer uses kaizen costing to set cost-reduction objectives for its suppliers. These objectives should, like their target costing counterparts, reflect the competitive pressure that the buyer is facing in the marketplace. The aim of interorganizational kaizen costing is to ensure that all the firms in the supplier network are reducing the costs of their existing products at the rate demanded by the market.

The final way to apply interorganizational cost management is for buyers and suppliers to find ways to make the interfaces between their firms more efficient. Two types of improvements can be undertaken. First, techniques to reduce the costs of transaction processing are implemented. These techniques include electronic data interchange and bar coding. Second, ways to reduce uncertainty are developed. Uncertainty is reduced by increased information sharing and reduced cycle times. Reduced uncertainty is importance because it allows both the buyer and the supplier to keep less buffer inventory.

Four questions determine if a firm is using interorganizational cost management.

- Does your firm set specific cost-reduction objectives for its suppliers?
- Does your firm help its customers and/or suppliers find ways to achieve their cost-reduction objectives?
- Does your firm take into account the profitability of its suppliers when negotiating component pricing with them?
- Is your firm continuously making its buyer-supplier interfaces more efficient?

If the answer to any of the above questions is no, your firm is not taking full advantage of interorganizational cost management. It risks introducing products that cost too much and are not competitive.

Moreover, for interorganizational cost management to be effective, it is not sufficient for just one firm and its direct suppliers to practice it. Rather, most, if not all, of the firms in the supplier network must adopt it. Only when the entire network adopts interorganizational cost management practices is the full potential of the network realizable.

The Confrontation Strategy

Cost management and, in particular, interorganizational approaches to cost management have become more important in recent years because of the emergence of the lean enterprise. At the heart of the lean enterprise is the belief that single-piece flow is more efficient than batch-and-queue. The removal of all the queues and other inefficiencies associated with batch-and-queue systems enables lean enterprises to react faster, to enjoy economies of scale at lower production volumes, and to be inherently more efficient than their mass producer counterparts. They can produce products with higher quality and functionality, at lower cost, more quickly. These improved abilities are natural outcomes of the single-piece flow philosophy. Near-perfect quality is necessary because without the inventories inherent in batch-and-queue systems, the just-in-time production processes must stop when a defect is encountered until its cause is identified and corrected. In contrast, in a batch-and-queue system, the defective parts are put aside, attention switches to a different product, and high levels of defects can be tolerated.

Applying the same single-piece philosophy to product design enables firms to reduce significantly the time it takes to develop and launch new products. This objective is achieved by creating multifunctional teams, each responsible for the development of a single product, instead of splitting the product development process into a number of distinct steps, each managed by a different department. The result is an enhanced ability to compete on functionality. A firm that can develop new products every 18 months will compete on functionality in significantly different ways than one that takes a decade to develop a new product.

The emergence of the lean enterprise dramatically changed the way firms compete, but this fact was hidden by the slow rate of adoption of the new, single-piece manufacturing philosophy. This lag between the adoption of an innovation and a change in the competitive environment allowed managers to find other reasons for the intensified competition they faced. New theories of competition emerged to describe how to compete in the new environment, but these theories did not identify the change from a batch-and-queue to a single-piece philosophy as the primary driving force behind the new order.

The competitive environment of mass producers supports the generic strategies of cost leadership and product differentiation. Both these strategies are based on the assumption that a firm can develop and sustain competitive advantages and so avoid competition. By developing a sustainable cost advantage, the cost leader can offer products that are low in price and functionality. In essence, the cost leader avoids competition by saying, "Don't compete with me. If you do, I'll drop prices even lower and render you unprofitable."

In contrast, product differentiators develop a sustainable advantage in product development. Their products have higher functionality but sell at higher prices. They develop unique products or services that closely satisfy customers' requirements. In essence, they isolate a section of the main market and state, "This is my territory. I'm so good at what I do that attempting to compete with me is pointless."

With the emergence and spread of lean production, the competitive environment has undergone a slow, steady transformation from competition between mass producers to competition between lean producers. New theories of competition emerged during the late 1980s and early 1990s. Competition between lean enterprises is based on the assumption that sustainable, product-related competitive advantages are unlikely to be developed. Since in the eyes of these firms there is no mechanism to avoid competition, they confront it and compete head on. Confrontation is necessary because lean enterprises can react fast enough to make product-related competitive advantages too fleeting to be considered sustainable. There is not enough time to educate the customer to the positive attributes of the new product before other firms have me-too versions. Unlike occasional head-on competition between mass producers, head-on competition between lean producers, once they have become confrontational, is continuous. This difference in the attitude of lean producers toward competition makes obsolete many of the lessons learned about competition between mass producers.

THE SURVIVAL TRIPLET AND THE SURVIVAL ZONE

To understand when it is appropriate to adopt each of the three generic strategies—cost leadership, differentiation, and confrontation—it is helpful to introduce the concept of the survival triplet (see Figure 1). The survival triplet consists of the three dimensions that define a product, which are cost/price, quality, and functionality.

Only products with values along each of these three dimensions that are acceptable to the customer stand a chance of being successful. To identify a product's survival zone, the survival range for each characteristic in the survival triplet must be determined. The survival range is defined by determining the minimum and maximum values that each characteristic can have for a product to be successful. The survival zone is the volume created by connecting the three minimum values and the three maximum values (see Figure 2).

Cost leadership and differentiation strategies are successful when the survival zones for a firm's products are large. Large survival zones occur when the difference between the minimum and maximum ranges is significant for at least two of the characteristics. As the gap between the minimum and maximum levels widens, the ability of firms to create distinguishable products that have high values on one characteristic and low values on the others increases. When the gap becomes sufficiently large, it becomes possible to split the zone into at least two new survival zones, one based on low price and the other on enhanced functionality and quality. When

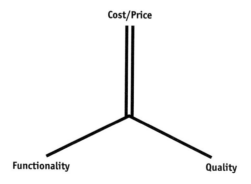

FIGURE 1. THE SURVIVAL TRIPLET

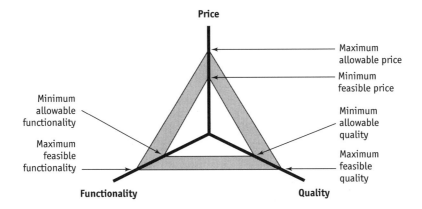

FIGURE 2. THE SURVIVAL ZONE FOR A PRODUCT

this situation emerges, firms must choose to compete on either the price characteristic or on the other two. Firms competing on the price characteristic are vying for the cost leadership position, while firms competing on functionality and quality characteristics have adopted differentiation strategies.

When lean enterprises compete, survival zones become very narrow and becoming a differentiator is no longer possible. The bulk of customers in the industry are unwilling to make significant trade-offs among the three dimensions: there is simply not enough leeway for a firm to be able to differentiate its products and sell them at a sufficient price premium to justify the increased costs. All firms offer products that have similar high quality and functionality at a low price, which requires the products to be produced at a low cost. Thus, confrontation strategies apply when, in effect, multiple firms compete for the same customers by developing equivalent products. Since the firms are evenly matched on all three dimensions, they have no choice but to compete head on and adopt a confrontational strategy.

COST MANAGEMENT IN A
CONFRONTATION STRATEGY

With the emergence of the lean enterprise and global competition, firms face ever-increasing levels of competition. As competition becomes more intense, firms are forced to learn to be more proactive in the way they manage costs. For many of these firms, survival depends on their ability to develop sophisticated cost management systems that create intense pressures to reduce costs over the entire life of the product and across the entire value chain. This increased importance of cost management is a central theme of *When Lean Enterprises Collide*:

> Firms that adopt a confrontation strategy must become experts at developing low cost, high quality products that have the functionality customers demand....A firm that fails to reduce costs as rapidly as its competitors will find its profit margins squeezed and its existence threatened....Cost management, like quality, has to become a discipline practiced by virtually every person in the firm. Therefore, overlapping systems that create intense downward pressures on all elements of costs are required.[1]

These systems manage costs in three ways. The first way is to manage the cost of future products, the second is to manage the cost of existing products, and the third is to harness the entrepreneurial spirit of the workforce. Japanese firms have developed three specific cost management techniques to manage the costs of future products: target costing, value engineering, and interorganizational cost management systems. Target costing is a structured approach to determine the cost at which a proposed product with specified functionality and quality must be produced to generate the desired level of profitability over its life cycle when sold at its anticipated selling price. Value engineering is used in the product design stage to find ways to achieve the specified functionality at the required standards of quality and reliability and at the target cost. To achieve the target cost without making sacrifices in product functionality and quality, interorganizational cost management systems are designed to create downward cost pressures on the entire supplier chain. The objective of these interorganizational systems is to identify innovative ways to reduce the cost of the components supplied by the chain.

Three cost management techniques are used to help manage the costs of existing products: kaizen costing, product costing, and operational control. Kaizen costing systems focus on making

---

[1] Robin Cooper, *When Lean Enterprises Collide: Competing Through Confrontation,* Boston: Harvard Business School Press, 1995, p. 7.

improvements to the production process of existing products. These improvements are designed either to increase the effectiveness of the production process in general or to reduce the costs of a specific product without altering its functionality.

Product costing systems are used to report the cost of existing products so that their profitability can be monitored. Using reported product costs, the firm can begin the process of identifying products that require redesign or discontinuance or that should be the focus of a specific kaizen program.

Operational control systems are used to monitor performance on the shop floor. They include techniques such as identifying responsibility centers, calculating variances, and providing feedback on performance.

A firm can lower the costs of its products in at least one other way: by harnessing the entrepreneurial spirit of its workforce. This method focuses on the workforce, not the products or production processes. The first technique used to accomplish this objective creates pseudo micro profit centers from cost centers, and the second converts the firm into multiple real micro profit centers.

The objective of the cost management programs in many Japanese manufacturing firms is to create continuous pressure for cost reduction over the entire life of the product and across the entire value chain. This pressure must begin when products or services are first conceived, continue during manufacturing, and end only when the product or service is discontinued. Furthermore, this pressure must be transmitted throughout the supplier network. Interorganizational cost management is the primary mechanism lean enterprises use to manage supplier costs.

INTERORGANIZATIONAL COST MANAGEMENT

The two major elements of interorganizational cost management are the environment in which it occurs and the effective use of its various mechanisms to reduce costs. Interorganizational cost management can be undertaken successfully only when the buyer-supplier relationships are lean—that is, cooperative, stable, and mutually beneficial. In addition, these relationships should be disciplined across the entire supply chain. Such discipline is created by the protocols characteristic of lean supplier networks.

An effective interorganizational cost management program requires careful integration of both disciplining and enabling mechanisms to reduce costs throughout the supplier network (see Figure 3). The purpose of the disciplining mechanisms is to transmit the cost-reduction pressures throughout the network by setting cost-reduction objectives for every aspect of buyer-supplier interactions. The objective of the enabling mechanisms is to help the firms in the network find ways to pool their skills and coordinate their design

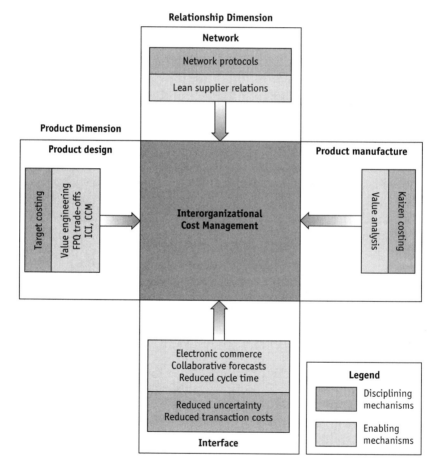

FIGURE 3. THE INTERORGANIZATIONAL COST MANAGEMENT PROCESS

and manufacturing efforts and the way they interact so they can collectively achieve their cost-reduction objectives.

The Environment of Interorganizational Cost Management

The lean enterprise typically outsources a high percentage of the value-added of its products. Seventy percent outsourcing is not unusual. When lean enterprises face highly competitive environments, they must as become efficient as possible. However, when a high percentage of the value-added of products is outsourced it is not sufficient to be the most efficient firm; rather it is necessary to be part of the most efficient supplier network.

Lean supply differs from mass supply because the single-piece flow that is characteristic of the lean enterprise is extended to the supply chain. Unlike their mass counterparts, lean supply chains do not rely on large inventories to buffer against stock-outs. Instead, the buyer's and supplier's production systems are tightly integrated. The buyer's demand creates the pull on the supplier's production system. This tight integration, coupled with the high level of outsourcing, leads to a greater reliance on suppliers than is typical for mass producers. This greater reliance forces the lean producer to develop richer relationships with its suppliers because the firms are tightly connected through their production processes.

Lean Buyer-Supplier Relations

Lean buyer-supplier relations have four major characteristics. The first deals with the reduced supplier base. Lean enterprises rely on a smaller number of suppliers than their mass production counterparts and so can create tighter linkages with their suppliers. Sustaining these tighter linkages requires rich relationships with the suppliers, relationships that play an important role in supporting interorganizational cost management.

The second characteristic deals with the level of the relationships. Buyer-supplier relationships depend heavily on the degree of reliance that the buyer is placing on the supplier for design innovation. When virtually no reliance is placed on the supplier for design innovation, the supplier is either a common supplier of commodities (such as nuts and bolts) or a subcontractor for simple components designed by the buyer (such as fan blades). When design innovation is required, the supplier is either a major supplier or a family member. Major suppliers design and manufacture group components (such as starter motors), and family members produce major functions (such as engine cooling systems). As the level of supplier shifts from common to family member, their number typically drops. Most firms identify only a limited number of family members while typically they interact with numerous common suppliers. The highly limited number of these high-level suppliers allows the most sophisticated of the enabling mechanisms of interorganizational cost management to be practiced.

The third characteristic captures the nature of lean buyer-supplier relationships. In particular they are characterized by interdependence—the buyer depends on the supplier for its design expertise, and the supplier depends on the buyer for both business and technical support. The outcome of this interdependence is buyer-supplier relations that are stable over time, have a high degree of cooperation, and operate for mutual benefit. While interdependence is the glue that holds the lean buyer-supplier relationship together, it is trust that enables the buyer and supplier to interact in the sophisticated and mutually beneficial ways that enable interorganizational cost management to reduce costs so effectively while simultaneously increasing functionality and quality (see Figure 4). Trust is created primarily through the stability of the buyer-supplier relationship. It is also created because there is a high level of cooperation between the two firms.

The final characteristic of buyer-supplier relations looks at the way that organizational boundaries are blurred as the firms begin to

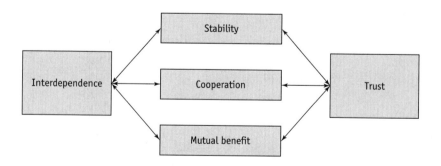

FIGURE 4. NATURE OF BUYER-SUPPLIER RELATIONS

share resources dynamically. Once the right types of relationships have been developed, the two firms can take advantage of the relationships and can begin to manage costs interorganizationally. In particular, three practices make it difficult to define where one firm's responsibilities begin and the other's end. The first of these practices is employee sharing, in which the buyer and supplier lend each other employees. In particular, from an interorganizational cost management perspective, the two firms share engineers and hence design skills. Second, the two firms share research and development, the buyer often outsourcing non-core competencies to its suppliers. Finally, the two firms are willing to make dedicated investments specifically designed to benefit the other firm. These dedicated investments lead to lower costs and/or increased functionality and quality.

The advantage of these lean buyer-supplier relationships lies in the increased ability and willingness to share information about product design, manufacturing processes, and product costs. This shared information enables the two firms to increase their degree of innovation, leading to products that have higher functionality and lower cost. It is within the context of these rich, highly cooperative, stable relationships that interorganizational cost management systems thrive. However, simply taking a narrow buyer-supplier perspective is not sufficient. Competitive markets based on these types of supplier relationships can be described as undertaking network sourcing. In network sourcing, the interactions between multiple buyers and multiple suppliers, not just a single buyer and supplier, create another dimension that shapes the interorganizational cost management process.

Lean Supplier Networks

The emergence of lean supply is the first step in the larger process of creating a lean supplier network. The high degree of outsourcing that characterizes lean enterprises means that every firm in a supply chain is responsible only for a small percentage of the total value-added of a product. To achieve the full advantages of lean design and production, all the firms in the supply chain have to adopt lean buyer-supplier relations. When they do, the whole turns out to be larger than the sum of the parts because the individual lean supply chains form a network of suppliers. These lean supplier networks function in many respects as a single entity dedicated to producing low-cost products with the high functionality and quality that end customers demand.

Two major aspects of lean supplier networks shape the environment for interorganizational cost management: the type of network and the existence of network protocols. The type of network is important because it shapes the power balance between buyers and suppliers. Network protocols are critical because they moderate the behavior of all the firms in the network to ensure that buyer-supplier relationships retain the characteristics of lean supply. It is the existence of a disciplined, lean supplier network that enables cost to be managed in a coordinated manner across the entire network.

The number of core firms in the network determines the first major characteristic of networks, namely their type. There are three types of networks: kingdoms, baronies, and republics. In kingdoms, there is only one core firm, the king, which dominates the network. Baronies contain several core firms. These firms dominate the network, but no single core firm is sufficiently powerful to dominate the others. In addition, the suppliers have greater relative power than in a kingdom because they can say no to an individual baron without suffering a major loss. In the final type of network, republics, there are no core firms. Here, firms form loose alliances to achieve their objectives. All the firms in a republic have essentially the same level of power. Interorganizational cost management is particularly effective in kingdoms and baronies. In these network forms, the core firms give direction to the cost management process. In republics, the loose nature of buyer-supplier relationships makes the discipline of interorganizational cost management more difficult to maintain. Instead, these firms typically rely on the discipline of the internal market of the network to create pressure to reduce costs.

The second major characteristic of lean supplier networks lies in the establishment of network protocols or "rules of conduct." These protocols are designed to mitigate negative repercussions from excessive competition and to encourage cooperation when coordination of activities across firm boundaries is required. To be effective, they must be operative throughout the supplier network. The way in which the protocols are established and enforced differs across the three network types. In a kingdom, the protocols are developed top-down and enforced by the king. In a barony, the protocols are negotiated but with the barons dominating the process. Finally, in a republic the protocols are developed by mutual agreement.

Once a lean supplier network has been established, the next step is to take advantage of the opportunities it offers. From a cost management perspective, being part of a supplier network provides three major benefits. The first derives from the ability to structure the interfirm linkages. This ability enables the core firms to structure the network in ways that provide external economies of scale and scope. The second benefit lies in the increased level of technology sharing possible among competitors. The core firms foster such sharing by rewarding innovative suppliers with extra business and then, as part of the deal, sharing the innovation with the suppliers' competitors. This technology sharing increases the spread of innovation and cost reduction throughout the network. The third benefit derives from managing the terms of interdependence. This ability enables the core firms to encourage their noncompeting suppliers to share innovations by mechanisms such as supplier associations. This type of cooperation enhances the network's ability to innovate and reduce costs.

It is within the context of lean supplier networks that interorganizational cost management is especially effective. The network has a focused objective (e.g., take advantage of external economies of scale) and protocols that ensure mutually supportive behavior and cooperation. This setting enables the firms to undertake cost management programs that spread across entire supply chains and, hence, the supplier network. For example, the design teams of all the firms in the chain can jointly identify ways to produce the product more efficiently in all the firms, not just one. Such interventions are not possible when buyer-supplier relationships are based on an "every firm for itself" mentality.

The Mechanisms of Interorganizational Cost Management

Once the network has been established and the protocols are in place, the firms that compete within it can begin to manage costs across their supply chains. The first aspect of interorganizational cost management deals with product design. The objective is to coordinate the product design processes in the network firms so that products and the components they contain are manufactured at their target costs. The second aspect deals with identifying ways to reduce the costs of existing products and the components they contain by coordinating the manufacturing cost-reduction efforts of the buyer and supplier. The final aspect deals with improving the efficiency of the interface between buyer and supplier. Only if that interface is highly efficient will the firms be able to compete effectively.

Cost Management During Product Design

At the heart of interorganizational cost management for product design lie two disciplining techniques and three enabling ones. The disciplining techniques are target costing and chained target costing. The objective of the disciplining mechanisms is to transmit the cost-reduction pressure faced by the end firms to the other firms in the supplier network. The objective of the enabling mechanisms—functionality-price-quality (FPQ) trade-offs, interorganizational cost investigations, and concurrent cost management—is to stimulate the design teams to interact and use value engineering techniques in ways that enable them to find lower-cost solutions than would be possible if they acted in isolation.

Target costing is primarily a technique for profit management (see Figure 5). Its objective is to ensure that future products generate the profits identified in the firm's long-term profit plan.[2] This objective can be achieved only if products satisfy the demands of the firm's customers and can be manufactured at their target costs. It is the establishment of component-level target costs that gives target costing its interorganizational capabilities. The buyer's component-level target costs essentially establish the supplier's selling prices and thereby transmit the competitive pressure faced by the buyer to its suppliers. Since this pressure is transmitted component by component, it helps the supplier to identify where to focus its cost-reduc-

---

[2] Target costs should include any costs that are driven by the number of units sold. For example, if the firm accepts responsibility for disposing of a product at the end of its useful life, these costs would be included in the target cost.

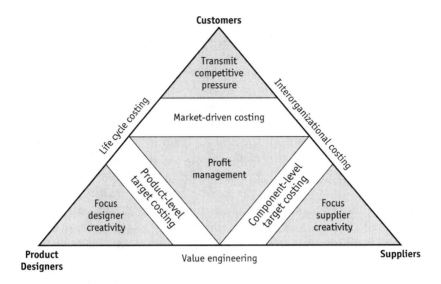

FIGURE 5. THE TARGET COSTING TRIANGLE

tion efforts. The result is a coordination of the buyer and supplier's cost management programs. It is this coordination that is so critical to the effectiveness of interorganizational cost management.

Target costing systems become especially effective when they are linked together to form a chain. Chained target costing systems are created when the output of a buyer's target costing system becomes an input to a supplier's target costing system. Component-level target costing at the buyer establishes the target selling prices used by the market-driven costing section of the supplier's target costing system to set the allowable cost of the components. This allowable cost becomes the basis for setting the product-level target costs and hence the component-level target costs for the supplier. These component-level target costs then establish the selling prices of the next firm in the supply chain. Thus, the primary benefit of chained target costing systems lies in their ability to transmit the competitive pressure faced by the firm at the top of the chain to the other firms down the chain.

When the disciplining mechanisms show that firms in the chain will encounter problems in achieving their target costs, the enabling mechanisms are used to initiate different levels of interaction among the design teams involved in the new product. At the heart of these interactions lies value engineering (VE). In VE, there are two ways to increase the value of a product. The first is to increase its functionality without a concomitant increase in its costs and the second is to decrease its costs without a concomitant decrease in functionality. Under FPQ trade-offs suppliers explore ways to provide their buyers with products that have functionality and quality below the levels originally requested, but still acceptable to the end customer. Successfully achieving this trade-off allows these suppliers to find solutions to a customer's product requirements while generating adequate returns. Lowering the functionality and quality of a component without decreasing the functionality or quality of the final product allows the suppliers' manufacturing costs to be reduced. Since the selling price remains unchanged, the firms increase their profits. Thus, for many firms in the middle or at the end of a target costing chain, the ability to remain profitable is determined, in part, by their ability to manage the survival triplet for their products.

Interorganizational cost investigations can be more effective than FPQ trade-offs because of the increased scope of the design changes that can be made to both the end product and the components it contains. Under chained target costing, the specifications of the end product are essentially fixed. While FPQ trade-offs allow some relaxation of the quality and functionality specifications of components, the buyer must essentially be indifferent to these changes. In particular, the functionality and quality of the buyer's product must remain unchanged in the eyes of its customers. However, more fundamental changes, such as redesigning a component in a way that requires the buyer to modify other aspects of the end product, call for an interorganizational cost investigation. The increased scope of the design changes and the interaction between product designers from both buyers and suppliers allows parts to be designed so that all the steps from raw material to finished product are more cost efficient. Put more formally, products and components can be designed so that they reflect global, not local, production economics. Costs can be reduced through interorganizational cost investigations, first, by changing the location where activities are performed so that they can be performed more efficiently. Second, the need to perform activities can be reduced or avoided by redesigning the product and the components it contains to take full advantage of the manufacturing skills throughout the target costing chain.

Concurrent cost management achieves even greater cost reduction than interorganizational cost investigations by involving the suppliers earlier in the design process (than the other two enabling techniques) and thus allows even more fundamental changes in the specifications of the product and the major functions it contains. There are two major approaches to concurrent cost management: parallel engineering and simultaneous engineering. In parallel engineering the two teams work in isolation but communicate frequently with each other. The primary advantage of parallel engineering to the supplier is that it can separate its product development programs from those of its customers. This decoupling gives it more time to introduce new technologies and find ways to reduce costs. In simultaneous engineering, the buyer's and supplier's design teams work together to identify mutually beneficial designs for both the product and the outsourced major function. The choice between the two approaches is driven by the perceived benefits from close interactions of the buyer's and supplier's design teams. If the value of such interaction is considered low, then parallel engineering is used. If the benefit is thought to be high, then simultaneous engineering is used.

The three enabling mechanisms differ, first, in the degree of modification possible in the outsourced item and the product that contains it, second, in the timing of the intervention, and, third, in the cost. The degree of modification is least for FPQ trade-offs and greatest for concurrent cost management. FPQ trade-offs and interorganizational cost investigations occur during the product design phase of product development, while concurrent cost management occurs much earlier, during the product conceptualization phase.

The cost of these interventions climbs from FPQ trade-offs, which are relatively inexpensive, to concurrent cost management interventions that consume considerable resources. Consequently, while FPQ trade-offs can be applied to outsourced items that represent quite modest percentages of the total value-added of the final product, concurrent cost management is applied only to major functions that represent a significant portion of the total value-added.

It is the way the disciplining mechanisms interact with the enabling ones that creates an effective interorganizational cost management program. Target costing and chained target costing identify the outsourced items that should be the focus of interventions that require interactions among the design teams in a supply chain. It is the magnitude of the problem and the enabling mechanism chosen that determine the scope and timing of those interventions. Target costing, the primary disciplining mechanism, has interorganizational implications that have to be addressed before interorganizational cost management can be practiced effectively.

Cost Management During Manufacturing

Kaizen costing is predominantly a feed-forward cost management technique that focuses on the manufacturing stage of a product's life. It operates in feed-forward mode by setting cost-reduction objectives in anticipation of the need to reduce costs rather than reacting to cost overruns. Kaizen costing is primarily a technique for profit management. Its objective is to help ensure that each product earns an adequate profit across its life. It complements target costing by extending the discipline it creates in the design stage to the manufacturing stage. In well-designed cost management programs, target and kaizen costing operate seamlessly together to ensure that cost-reduction pressures are in place across the entire life cycle of the firm's products.

The three different types of kaizen costing intervention are period, product, and overhead specific. Each of these types of intervention has a different objective. The objective of period-specific kaizen costing is to reduce the cost of production processes by a predetermined amount in the current period. In most firms, the level of this cost reduction is set to maintain the profitability of the firm. The objective of a product-specific kaizen costing intervention is to reduce the cost of a specific product so that it achieves its long-term profit objectives. Such interventions can be applied to either a new product whose costs on launching are too high or a mature product whose selling price is falling faster than its costs. Finally, overhead-specific kaizen costing has the objective of reducing overhead costs though programs to reduce product mix complexity.

Interorganizational kaizen costing starts when the buyer transmits the cost-reduction pressure it faces in the marketplace to its suppliers through the application of period kaizen costing. This pressure is transmitted when the buyer identifies kaizen cost-reduction objectives that tell its suppliers how rapidly it expects their selling prices to fall over time. These kaizen cost-reduction objectives can be set as a flat rate for all suppliers, or specific kaizen costing objectives can be set depending on the outsourced item.

Interorganizational kaizen costing extends the pressure established by target costing into the manufacturing phase of the product life cycle. Kaizen costing systems do not chain in the same manner as target costing systems. A given supplier will often sell its products to several buyers, each applying a potentially different overall kaizen cost-reduction rate. These various rates will be averaged by the supplier's kaizen costing system to develop an appropriate kaizen cost-reduction rate for its suppliers. It is only if the buyer sets specific cost-reduction objectives for a high-value component that true chaining might take place. For this reason, kaizen costing systems can be said to link but not chain.

Like many interorganizational cost management techniques, kaizen costing interventions can be initiated by either the buyer or the supplier (see Figure 6). For buyer-led interventions, the buyer is either augmenting the cost-reduction capabilities of the supplier or giving it access to cost-reduction opportunities that the supplier cannot access on its own. In supplier-led initiatives, the supplier finds new ways to manufacture components that lead to overall lower costs in the supply chain. All the interactions involve the application of value analysis (VA), the primary enabling mechanism of kaizen costing. Unlike VE, in VA the functionality of the product cannot be changed. Therefore, the only way to increase value is to decrease costs.

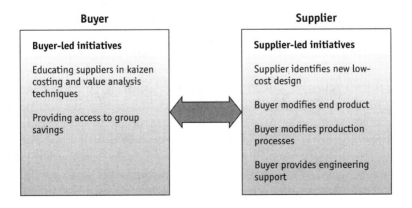

FIGURE 6. INTERORGANIZATIONAL KAIZEN COSTING

Improving the Efficiency of the Buyer-Supplier Interface

The buyer-supplier interface includes all activities and processes associated with the transfer of goods or services from one firm to another. It includes order placement, billing and payment, inventory management of finished goods at the supplier and purchased parts at the buyer, and transportation and external logistics. Increasing the efficiency of the buyer-supplier interface, the final aspect of interorganizational cost management, deals with reducing the costs associated with these activities and processes. The primary ways that the interface can be made more efficient are by lowering transaction processing costs and by reducing uncertainty (see Figure 7).

Transaction processing costs can be reduced in four ways. First, activities can be eliminated. The primary candidates for elimination are those activities that are duplicated at both locations. Second, some processes can be simplified so that they consume fewer resources. Processes that trigger common activities at both firms are prime candidates for simplification. Third, activities and processes can be standardized. Standardization is particularly effective when the activities and processes are both high-volume, routine, and common to all buyer-supplier interfaces. Finally, activities can be automated. Repetitive, high-volume, standardized activities are prime candidates for automation.

The improvements aimed at reducing uncertainty lead to lower inventory levels at both firms. The buyer uses inventory to buffer against failure on the part of the supplier to deliver goods to the line on time, and the supplier uses inventory to buffer against unexpected demands from the buyer. If these two sources of uncertainty can be eliminated, then the buffer inventories can be reduced. These uncertainties can be reduced in two ways. The two firms can increase the amount of information they share, and they can reduce the time it takes to process transactions that bridge the interface.

Improving the efficiency of the interface requires both firms to make changes in the way they interact. Some of these changes are joint projects that require close cooperation and coordination, while other are initiated primarily by either the buyer or the supplier. Joint improvements are those that require both the buyer and supplier to take cooperative and coordinated actions to increase the efficiency of their interface. Three major initiatives are typically undertaken.

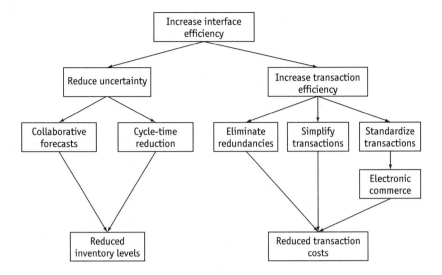

FIGURE 7. BUYER-SUPPLIER INTERFACE

One is electronic commerce, which uses information technology to automate the information transfer between the two firms. The second is improvement of the order-delivery process to reduce its standardized cycle times. The last is the development of collaborative forecasts to lessen uncertainty in the demand quantities.

Buyer-initiated improvements require that the buyer change its behavior in ways beneficial to the supplier. They also sometimes require minor changes at the supplier. The buyer can adopt seven major initiatives to improve the efficiency of the buyer-supplier interface. Four of these—managing demand, providing adequate order lead time, reducing special ordering, and sharing forecasts—primarily reduce uncertainty. The other three—the use of purchase contracts, payment on receipt, and improved accuracy of communications with suppliers—reduce transaction processing costs.

Supplier-initiated improvements require that the supplier change its behavior in ways that are beneficial to the buyer. They also sometimes require minor changes at the buyer. The supplier can adopt eight major initiatives to improve the efficiency of the buyer-supplier interface. Six of them—reducing delivery cycle time, increasing the ratio of on-schedule deliveries, reducing production cycle time, sharing performance metrics, sharing forecasts, and giving the buyer access to order status information—primarily reduce uncertainty. The other two—extended supplier control over inventories and improved accuracy of its communications with the buyer—reduce transaction processing costs.

LESSONS FOR ADOPTERS

The eight steps to adopting interorganizational cost management can be undertaken only in the environment of a lean or emerging lean enterprise. The first step is to *identify the parts of the product that are going to be externally sourced*. This step requires identifying the core technologies that have to be protected. If the technology is to be protected, then only noncritical components can be outsourced. In contrast, if the technology is not strategic, the associated research and development might be a candidate for outsourcing. For non-core technologies, the manufacture of the associated group components and major functions can be outsourced.

Once the appropriate sourcing decisions are made, the second step is to determine the *appropriate level of the buyer-supplier relationship* for each externally sourced item. This decision is shaped by the degree to which the buyer is reliant on the supplier's design skills and the importance of joint design. As the degree of reliance increases, richer relationships are required. When joint design is valuable, then the richest form of relationship is required as the two design teams must work closely together for extended periods of time.

The next step is part of the process of going lean. It requires that the firm *rationalize its supplier base* as the rich interactions that characterize lean supply and interorganizational cost management can be undertaken only with a relatively small supplier base. Once the supplier base has been rationalized, the next step is to *develop the appropriate supplier relationships*. Lean supply is characterized by cooperative, stable, and mutually beneficial relationships. Such relationships are very different from the adversarial buyer-supplier relations that characterize many Western mass producers. Without the appropriate relationships, interorganizational cost management will not function effectively.

The act of developing lean buyer-supplier relations does not lead automatically to full efficiency. The next two steps deal specifically with helping achieve that objective. The first step, *increasing the efficiency of the buyer-supplier interface*, deals with the way the two firms order and deliver the products that flow between them. The aim of this step is to reduce transaction costs as much as possible. The second step is then to *develop the necessary skills in the techniques of interorganizational cost management*. Interorganizational cost management is not simply extending internal cost management processes beyond the boundaries of the firm. Instead, it requires that a rich set of skills be developed by both buyers and suppliers. Without the necessary skill sets in place, the process will not be successful.

The final two steps extend the process throughout the supplier network and into the firm's subsidiaries. The first of these steps, *extending lean supply and interorganizational cost management both upstream and downstream into the firm's supply chains* transmits the process throughout the supplier network. It is a necessary step to ensure that an effective lean supplier network emerges. The last step, *extending lean supply and interorganizational cost management to internal suppliers,* completes the migration of the firm to full leanness and interorganizational cost management. The techniques of interorganizational cost management can be successfully used as intraorganizational techniques.

IMPLICATIONS FOR WESTERN MANAGERS

Under the confrontation strategy, it is not necessary or advisable to expend equal effort on all three characteristics of the survival triplet. One characteristic usually dominates the other two. The most important of the three characteristics of the survival triplet to the firm's customers, and hence to the firm, frequently changes over time. When the Japanese economy went into severe recession in the early 1990s, many Japanese firms changed their most important characteristic from functionality to cost.

The key to success lies in selecting the appropriate rate of improvement for each characteristic. In a market where the customer is demanding increased functionality and is willing to pay for it, for example, the most important characteristic is functionality. The firm that can increase the functionality of its products fastest (subject to cost-price and quality constraints) will develop a temporary competitive advantage.

Unfortunately, many Western managers have failed to understand the role of the survival triplet in confrontation strategy and have adopted a rallying call of highest quality, lowest cost, and first-to-market products. No firm can reasonably expect to be number one in all three elements of the survival triplet. Any firm that actually achieved this distinction for any length of time would dominate its competitors. Indeed, if it could sustain this advantage, it would become a monopoly because all its competitors would be bankrupt. Western firms have adopted this "best in all three" approach because they have encountered Japanese competitors that are superior to them on all three counts. To survive, these firms have had to improve simultaneously on all three characteristics. The resulting struggle for survival has caused many Western managers to lose sight of the critical fact that in most markets one element of the triplet is more important than the others. Once a product is inside its survival zone, the firm no longer has to improve its performance along all three elements equally aggressively. Instead, it has to learn to compete intelligently and to select the rate at which it improves performance on each element of the survival triplet.

Western managers who do not adjust their mode of competition will risk their firms. Firms that cling to the concept of sustainable competitive advantages and invest resources only in businesses that they believe have sustainable advantages will discover investment opportunities decreasing over time. Firms that cling to the traditional strategies of cost leadership and differentiation will discover that their ability to maintain these strategies is eroding. They will be forced to retreat from their markets as lean competitors outmaneuver them. Niche players may find themselves maneuvered into low-growth niches, as lean competitors launch products directly at them.

A similar fate awaits firms that try to cling to their historical profit margins. Competition between lean enterprises is fiercer than competition between mass producers, and overall profit margins are smaller. Retreating from products that have lower profit margins will be successful only if other, higher-margin products can be identified. However, in a confrontational environment high profits typically signify products that are in low-volume or dead-end niches. Therefore, there is a significant risk that chasing high-margin products will lead to an unacceptable long-term strategic position.

To survive the low margins, firms that adopt a confrontation strategy must become experts at developing low-cost, high-quality products with the functionality customers demand. The cost, quality, and functionality expertise required for this result must be used to form a coherent strategy based on developing products with the right level of functionality and quality at the right price. Consequently, firms adopting a confrontation strategy must develop integrated quality, functionality, and cost management systems. In addition, they must extend these systems to the entire supplier network.

It is the integration of these systems and their extension throughout the supplier network that allows many Japanese firms to respond so quickly to changes in economic conditions and to match the innovative products of their competitors. If these systems were stand-alone systems, a fast response rate would not be possible. Unfortunately, in Western literature the systems that have evolved to manage quality (typically described as "total quality management systems") and functionality (typically described as "time to market systems") have been described in isolation, and the systems that have emerged in Japanese firms to manage costs have been almost ignored. In a world of unsustainable competitive advantage, however, costs have to be managed both aggressively and intelligently. A firm that fails to reduce costs as rapidly as its competitors will find its profit margins squeezed and its existence threatened. It is no longer good enough to say "reduce costs by 10 percent across the board." Cost management, like quality, has to become a discipline practiced by nearly every person in the firm. Therefore, integrated systems are required that create intense downward pressures on all elements of cost across the entire supplier network.

PART 1

CONFRONTATIONAL
COST MANAGEMENT

CHAPTER 1

How Firms Compete Using the Confrontation Strategy

Introduction

Manufacturing in the 20th century has experienced two major revolutions. The first was the development of mass production, best exemplified by Henry Ford's Model T, and the second was the development of lean production by Toyota. Although it took both innovations only 10 years to evolve and mature—mass production from approximately 1915 to 1925 and lean production from 1951 to 1961—their spread to other countries and industries occurred more slowly. Indeed, it is still possible to identify firms that are lean but have yet to adapt to all the implications of being lean.

The slow spread of these innovations made subsequent evolution in the competitive environment appear independent of the changes in production philosophy. Firms that adopted one or the other of the innovations saw the nature of competition shift only as other firms in the industry changed their production philosophy. That is, lean competition occurs only when a sufficient percentage of the entire industry has converted to lean production. Until that time, the lean producers compete as if they were mass producers and thus make higher profits. This lag between the adoption of an innovation and any associated changes in the competitive environment allowed managers to find other reasons for the intensified competition they faced. New theories of competition emerged in the late 1980s and early 1990s to describe how to compete in the new environment, but these theories did not identify the change in production philosophy as the primary driving force behind the new order. Thus, the slow spread of these innovations obscured the result of their adoption—change in the nature of competition. Mass producers compete differently from craft producers; lean producers compete differently from mass producers.

The competitive environment of mass producers supports the generic strategies of cost leadership and product differentiation.[1] Both these strategies are based on the assumption that a firm can develop and sustain competitive advantages and therefore can avoid competition.[2] In theory, in their purest forms cost leadership and product differentiation strategies create zones of no competition. Consequently, it is unusual to see the best firms in an industry dominated by mass producers engaged in head-on competition.

With the emergence and spread of lean production, the competitive environment has undergone a slow, steady transformation from competition between mass producers to competition between lean producers. Consequently, before managers can determine how their firms should evolve over the next decade, they need to understand that lean enterprises do not compete in the same ways as mass producers.

LEAN PRODUCTION, LEAN PRODUCT DEVELOPMENT, AND LEAN SUPPLY[3]

At the heart of the lean enterprises is the central premise that single-piece processing is more efficient than batch-and-queue processing. In single-piece flow systems, an individual or a group manufactures

---

[1] Michael E. Porter, *Competitive Strategy: Techniques for Analyzing Industries and Competitors,* New York: The Free Press, 1980.

[2] Pankaj Ghemawat, "Sustainable Advantage," *Harvard Business Review,* September-October 1986, pp. 53–58.

[3] This section draws heavily from James P. Womack and D.T. Jones, *Lean Thinking,* New York: Simon & Schuster, 1996.

or designs only one product at a time. In addition, the individual or group is typically responsible for the entire process. In the single-piece approach, there are no meaningful queues between each operation—the next operation in the sequence "pulls" the product through the previous operation (see Figure 1–1). Thus, as soon as

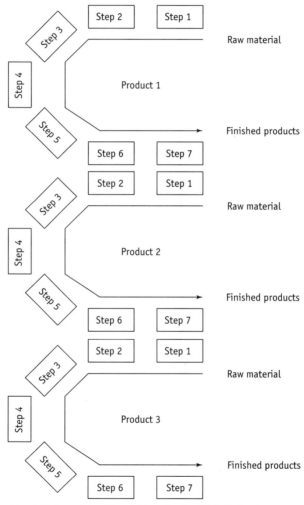

Adapted with the permission of Simon & Schuster from *Lean Thinking* by James P. Womack and Daniel T. Jones. Copyright © 1996 by James Womack and Daniel Jones.

FIGURE 1–1. SINGLE-PIECE PRODUCTION

the previous operation is completed, the next operation is by definition ready to receive it.

In contrast, in a batch-and-queue process products are produced or designed in batches. Each individual or group is responsible for only a part of the overall process. When that part is completed, the batch is sent to the next operation, where it waits in a queue until that individual or group is ready to start their portion of the overall process on the batch (see Figure 1–2). The product is pushed, not pulled, through the process. Hence, there is no guarantee that the next operation in the process will be ready, and extensive queues typically result.

The firms in the sample have applied single-piece principles wherever possible throughout the value chain of the product. They all use lean production philosophies, producing products one at a time. They also have adopted lean product development philosophies. At the heart of lean product development is an individual responsible for the entire development of the new product and sometimes for the product over its entire life. This directly responsible person, usually called the chief engineer, is supported by a multifunctional design team. The design team frequently includes people from marketing, engineering (often several branches), purchasing, production, and major suppliers. These teams are co-located and frequently have no other responsibilities than developing the product for which they were created (see Figure 1–3). The objective of creating these design teams is to enable the product development process to flow as rapidly as possible. Simultaneous engineering also is frequently used to speed up the product development process.

As the complexity of the product increases, it becomes beneficial to break the product into its major functions and create teams that are each responsible for one major function (see Figure 1–4). These teams are also co-located and again have no other responsibilities. The major function design teams report to the product design team and in some of the firms also to the head of the division responsible for designing that major function for all the firm's products. Thus, the entire product design process is single-piece with each team dedicated to the entire product or a major function of it.

In firms with complex product mixes, it is often helpful to identify product families. Each family consists of a number of similar products that can be produced interchangeably in a single produc-

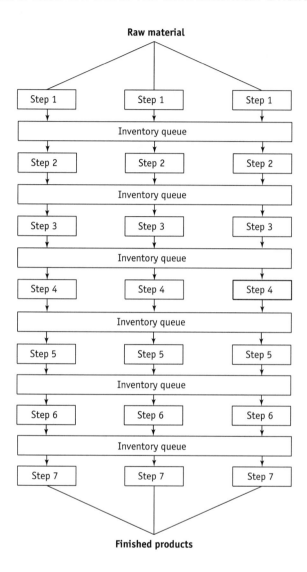

Figure 1–2. Batch-and-Queue Production

tion cell. It is useful to identify such families at the design stage, since they can usually be designed to share a large percentage of common components. To achieve this objective, product design is often managed at the product-family level. Each product family has its own design team led by a senior chief engineer who provides

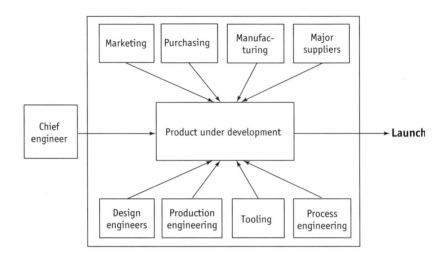

FIGURE 1–3. LEAN PRODUCT DEVELOPMENT

	Design team product A	Design team product B	Design team product C	...	Design team product M
Major function 1 division	Design team A1	Design team B1	Design team C1		Design team M1
Major function 2 division	Design team A2	Design team B2	Design team C2		Design team M2
Major function 3 division	Design team A3	Design team B3	Design team C3		Design team M3
				⋮	
Major function n division	Design team An	Design team Bn	Design team Cn		Design team Mn

FIGURE 1–4. MAJOR FUNCTION DESIGN TEAMS

common guidance to the chief engineers responsible for the individual products in the family (see Figure 1–5).

Lean product development can be contrasted to conventional product development, in which the development process is not the responsibility of a single team but is distributed across multiple

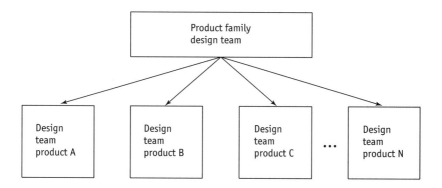

FIGURE 1-5. MANAGING THE DESIGN OF PRODUCT FAMILIES

departments (see Figure 1–6). This departmentalized approach leads to batch-and-queue product development. The product definition is developed by the marketing department and transferred to engineering, where it is converted into engineering specifications. These specifications are then converted into blueprints and, when the design is complete, handed over to production and tooling engineering. When these departments have completed their work, the final design is handed to process engineering for final review.

On the surface, this process sounds highly efficient. However, it hides a multitude of sins. First, the specialization and location of skills means that at each new stage, the design often has to be reworked to make it more feasible.

Second, the design typically undergoes a steady transformation during the product development process, as the market-based knowledge provided by marketing becomes more and more remote. This transformation occurs in two ways: through redesign requests to departments earlier in the process and through "secret redesign of earlier stages" by departments later in the process to make the product design feasible. These redesigns can lead to products that do not satisfy the customer because they lack critical functionality, have excess functionality, or cost too much to be sold profitably at an acceptable price.

Finally, each department may have a backlog of work so that there might be considerable queuing time between each step. This queuing time can add considerable delays to the product development process and lead to an inability to launch new products on a timely basis.

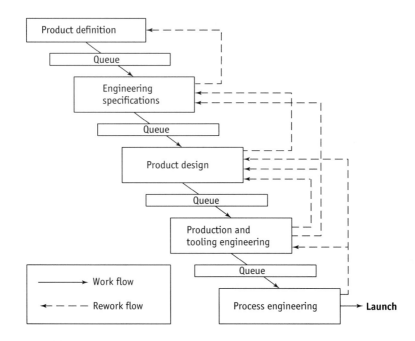

FIGURE 1–6. CONVENTIONAL BATCH-AND-QUEUE
PRODUCT DEVELOPMENT

In contrast, lean product development streamlines the entire product design process by removing all the redesign steps and the queues between departments. The single-piece design team works much like a lean production cell. All the members can see the entire design process and monitor its progress. The marketing representative ensures that the product meets customer specifications throughout the design process, and the production and supplier representatives ensure that it can be produced at a reasonable cost. The entire process is much faster, consumes fewer resources, and has a higher chance of success.

In highly competitive environments where product functionality plays a critical role in the way firms compete, it is essential to launch new products on time. In such environments, the short product life cycles mean that firms do not have the luxury of designing products, discovering that they cost too much, and then redesigning them. They must design the product right the first time. The intense discipline that target costing and interorganizational cost management bring to the product development process is critical because it helps increase the probability that the cost of new products will be acceptable when they are launched.

Lean enterprises outsource a considerable percentage of the value-added of their products, sometimes more than 70%. The rationale behind this high level of outsourcing derives from a focus on core competencies and the extension of single-piece flow to the supply chain. Since single-piece flow demands a high level of coordination with suppliers, lean enterprises rely on a smaller number of suppliers than their mass producer counterparts. The primary way that lean enterprises reduce the number of suppliers, without decreasing the level of outsourcing, is through outsourcing larger value-added parts such as group components and major functions. The outcome of this decision is the creation of a tiered supply network. The first tier provides both manufacturing and design skills (for example, they sell completed seats to the end producers). The second tier produces parts for the first-tier suppliers. Some of these parts require design skills and contain parts that are sourced from the third tier. Additional tiers can exist, but four is the usual maximum.

The structure of a lean supply chain differs significantly from that of a mass producer. Mass producers produce in-house a higher proportion of the value-added of their products (they are more vertically integrated) and almost all design engineering. Suppliers provide predominately simple components, not complex assemblies. The result is reliance on a greater number of direct suppliers and virtually no second- and third-tier suppliers.

The key difference between the two approaches is the development of interdependence between lean buyers and suppliers. It is this interdependence that allows the stable, cooperative, and balanced relationships between buyers and suppliers characteristic of lean supply. These relationships form the basis for interorganizational cost management because they enable the rich sharing of information and design and manufacturing skills across the interorganizational barrier.

One outcome of the adoption of single-piece flow philosophies in product design is a considerable reduction in the time it takes to bring products to market. Product development cycles at Olympus, for example, have dropped from 10 years to 18 months. The outcome of this contraction is that it is harder for firms to develop sustainable, product-related competitive advantages, and this fact shapes the way lean enterprises compete. Competition between lean enterprises is based on the assumption that sustainable, product-related competitive advantages are extremely difficult to develop. These firms do not expect to be able to create mechanisms to avoid competition. Instead, they are forced to confront it and compete head on.

Confrontation is necessary because the fast reaction times of lean enterprises, the sophistication of the customer, and the rapid diffusion of technology inherent in the supply chains operate together to render product-related competitive advantages too fleeting to be considered sustainable. There is not enough time to educate customers to the positive attributes of the new product before other firms have me-too versions. This difference in the attitude of lean producers toward competition makes many of the lessons learned about competition between mass producers obsolete. Firms competing in industries dominated by lean enterprises must adopt the generic strategy of confrontation to survive. Unfortunately, confrontation is inherently expensive and therefore typically less profitable than strategies that manage to reduce or avoid competition.

THE THREE GENERIC STRATEGIES OF COMPETITION

Most of the existing literature on competition is based on the assumption that firms can develop sustainable, product-related competitive advantages and avoid competition by adopting the generic strategies of cost leadership and product differentiation. For example, the cost leader is able to offer products that are low in price and functionality by developing a sustainable cost advantage. This ability allows the cost leader to avoid competition by saying, "Don't compete with me. If you do, I'll drop prices even lower and render you unprofitable."

Similarly, differentiators offer products that have higher functionality than the cost leader's but that sell at higher prices. They develop unique products or services that closely satisfy customers' requirements, thereby isolating a section of the main market. This ability allows the product differentiators to avoid competition by saying, "This is my territory. I'm so good at what I do that attempting to compete with me is pointless."

The importance of competitive avoidance in Western strategic thinking is highlighted by its codification into the concept of strategic portfolio planning.[4] In this concept a firm tries to identify its "stars," that is, divisions that have successfully differentiated themselves or have become cost leaders. These divisions earn above-average returns that reflect their success at achieving a sustainable competitive advantage. To nurture new stars the firm protects fledgling units, the question marks, as they try to develop their sustainable competitive advantage. The ones that fail to create such an advantage, the "dogs," are either sold or liquidated. Those that have created a competitive advantage no longer considered sustainable are treated as "cash cows."

The contrary assumption—that competition is unavoidable—leads to the emergence of the generic strategy of confrontation. Firms that adopt this strategy do not attempt to become either cost leaders or differentiators. Instead, they try to keep their products ahead of those of their competitors. It is important to understand that while these firms still try to differentiate their products, they do not expect to achieve sustainable competitive advantages; rather, they expect to achieve transitory ones. It is through transitory advantages that lean enterprises compete.

The Survival Triplet and Survival Zone

Three product-related characteristics, known as the survival triplet, play a critical role in the success of firms that have adopted the confrontation strategy. The survival triplet has an internal form that reflects the perspective of the producer and an external form that reflects the perspective of the customer (see Figure 1-7). Internally, the three characteristics are the product's cost, quality, and functionality. Externally, the characteristics are selling price, perceived quality, and perceived functionality. In the rest of this book the term "cost" will be used if the phenomenon being discussed is internal to the firm. If the phenomenon is external to the firm, the term "price" will be used for the cost/price characteristic. In addition, quality and functionality will be used to represent both internal and external views of those characteristics.

---

4 B. Heldey, "Strategy and the Business Portfolio," *Long Range Planning,* February 1977, p. 12.

FIGURE 1–7. THE SURVIVAL TRIPLET

While the selling prices of products can be disconnected from costs temporarily, if the firm is to remain profitable in the long run, costs must be brought into line with selling prices. Therefore, the survival triplet can be represented as cost/price, quality, and functionality. Here, cost/price is used to acknowledge that a long-term relationship exists between cost and price.

In the survival triplet, price is defined as the amount at which the product is sold in the marketplace in arm's-length transactions. In the highly competitive markets in which most Japanese firms compete, the market sets selling prices, and cost is the value of the resources consumed to get the product into the hands of the customer. Cost includes all investment costs (such as research and development), all production costs, and all marketing and selling costs. Unlike price, it is not set externally but, like quality and functionality, has to be managed.

Quality is defined as performance to specifications. This definition of quality is narrower than the definition often used in literature on quality, in which quality is defined to include the ability to design a product that meets customer requirements (quality of design). This narrower definition allows quality and functionality to be treated as two separate characteristics.

Functionality is defined by the specifications of the product. It is not a single dimension but rather is multidimensional. When managers model competition using the survival triplet, they may find it beneficial to decompose functionality into a number of characteristics. For example, the firm may want to differentiate between the fundamental functionality of the product, such as the ability of a bulldozer to move earth, and the service functionality, such as the ability to guarantee 48-hour delivery of spare parts anywhere in the world. These two dimensions might be called product focus and customer focus. Such a differentiation will permit a richer modeling of the competitive environment and allow management to better understand the nature of the competition they face. Similarly, differentiating between the status that a product conveys (psychological functionality) and its pure performance (physical functionality) can be useful in explaining the success of products such as Rolex watches.

Each product a firm sells has distinct values for each of these three dimensions. Only products with values acceptable to the customer stand a chance of being successful. It is useful to define a survival zone for each product, identified by the gaps between the feasible and allowable values of the three dimensions of the survival triplet (see Figure 1–8).

For quality and functionality, the minimum allowable level is the lowest value of each characteristic that the customer is willing to accept regardless of the values of the other two characteristics. Below a certain level of functionality, for example, few customers are willing to buy a product no matter how low the price or how high the quality.

The capabilities of the firm determine the maximum feasible values for quality and functionality. The maximum values are the highest values the firm can achieve without inducing significant

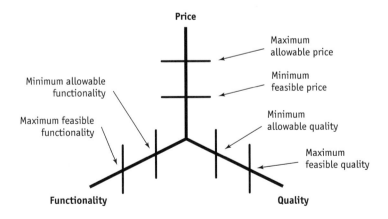

FIGURE 1–8. THE SURVIVAL TRIPLET FOR A PRODUCT

penalties in the other characteristics. For example, above a certain functionality level, products will have quality problems and will need to be priced very high to make adequate profits. Low quality and high prices will result in too few customers being willing to buy the products. The maximum feasible value then represents the highest value the characteristic can have with respect to the other two characteristics and still have customers purchase the product.

The price characteristic is slightly different from the other two in that the customer determines the maximum allowable price and the firm determines the minimum feasible price. The maximum allowable price is the highest price the customer is willing to pay regardless of the values of the other two characteristics. The minimum feasible price is the lowest price the firm is willing to accept for the product if it is at its minimum allowable quality and functionality levels. While the customer views the critical characteristic as price, the firm views it as cost. The minimum acceptable profit at any price level transforms cost to price. The survival zone of a product can be identified by connecting maximum and minimum values (see Figure 1–9).

The Survival Zones for Mass and Lean Producers

In a market where only mass producers are competing, one mass producer occupies the cost leader position and the others occupy differentiator positions (see Figure 1–10). Theoretically there is no

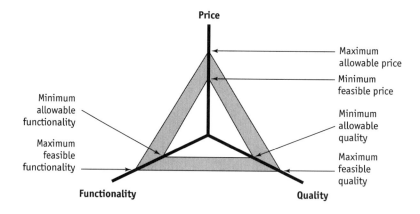

FIGURE 1–9. THE SURVIVAL ZONE FOR A PRODUCT

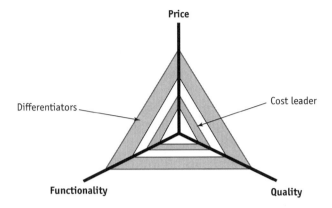

Price

Differentiators

Cost leader

Functionality

Quality

FIGURE 1–10. THE SURVIVAL ZONES OF THE COST LEADER
AND DIFFERENTIATORS

competition between the cost leader and differentiator as long as the quality and functionality gaps are sufficiently large to support the price gap. Thus, the cost leader launches products that are as close to the origin as possible but still inside their survival zones.

In contrast, the differentiator sells products that deliver higher quality and/or functionality than those of the cost leader, at a premium price. The differentiator launches products that are as far away from the origin as possible but still inside their survival zones. Since in practice functionality is not a single dimension, multiple differentiation strategies are possible; each designed to satisfy a different group of customers. It is this multidimensionality that allows multiple differentiators to coexist.

The emergence of the lean enterprise changes the shape of the survival zone. It increases the frontiers of functionality and quality considerably, but it simultaneously reduces their ranges (see Figure 1–11). The functionality improvements come about because the lean enterprise learns faster than its mass producer equivalent so it can increase the functionality of its products faster. However, the other lean enterprises with which it is competing catch up quickly, hence the reduced range. The same holds true for the other two dimensions of the survival triplet. In the narrow survival zones of the lean enterprise, becoming a differentiator is no longer possible. The bulk of the customers in the industry are unwilling to make significant trade-offs among the three dimensions, so there is simply

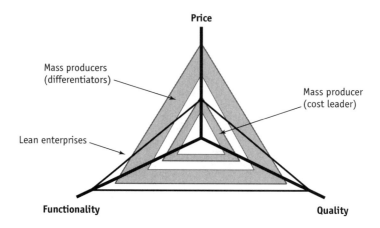

FIGURE 1-11. THE COLLAPSE OF THE COST LEADER AND DIFFERENTIATOR SURVIVAL ZONES

not enough leeway for a firm to differentiate its products and sell them at a sufficient price premium to justify the increased costs.

All the firms offer products with similar high quality and functionality at a low cost. Thus, confrontation strategies apply when, in effect, all firms occupy the same competitive position. They are trying to attract the same customers with equivalent products. One of the outcomes of multiple firms offering customers similar products is increased sophistication of the firm's customers. As customers learn to differentiate among products on relatively minor differences, they become more sensitive to such differences and take them into account when choosing between products. The result is to force competing firms to expend more effort in trying to differentiate their products from those of their competitors. The apparently contradictory outcome of these increased efforts is to make all the products on offer even more similar. In other words, the survival zone narrows even further as customers become sophisticated (see Figure 1–12).

MANAGING THE SURVIVAL TRIPLET

Firms that adopt a confrontation strategy must become experts at developing low-cost, high-quality products that have the function-

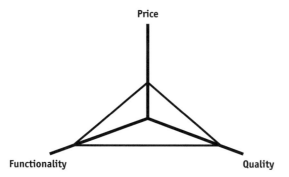

Price

Functionality

Quality

Figure 1-12. A Confrontation Survival Zone

ality customers demand. The cost, quality, and functionality expertise required for this result must be used to formulate a coherent
strategy based on developing products with the right level of functionality and quality at the right price. Firms adopting the confrontation strategy must develop integrated quality, functionality,
and cost management systems. It is the integration of these systems
that allows many Japanese firms to respond so quickly to changes
in economic conditions and to match the innovative products of
their competitors.

Managing Functionality

A firm can compete in several ways using product functionality. It
can, for example, accelerate the rate at which it introduces increased
functionality. Olympus reduced the time it took to design a camera
from 10 years for the OM10 to 18 months for a compact camera.
Second, the firm can change the way it differentiates its products.
For example, a firm that has historically differentiated its products
based on higher functionality and quality for a higher price might
suddenly launch products that offer different features for the same
price. Olympus used this approach to increase market share when it
introduced numerous products into the same price point using characteristics such as size and technical functionality. While horizontally differentiated products cost the same, they attract different customers. Finally, a firm can change the nature of the functionality of
a product. For example, Swatch changed the functionality of its

watches by making them a trendy fashion statement instead of just a way (attractive or otherwise) to tell the time.

Managing Quality

Quality is managed via the firm's total quality management (TQM) program. These programs have been well documented.[5] In many Japanese firms, the TQM programs have been so successful at increasing the maximum achievable levels for the quality characteristic that any additional improvements are unlikely to be considered of value to the customer. When defects are measured in parts per million, individual customers are unlikely to encounter defects, let alone detect improvements in the defect rate! At the same time, the Japanese consumer demands such a high level of quality that even minimum acceptable levels are high by traditional standards. Consequently, the survival range for the quality characteristic is extremely small for most products, and quality has become a hygiene factor that can be ignored as long as it is under control. This does not mean that these firms have abandoned their TQM programs. Quality enhancements still result in internal benefits such as the ability to reduce the number of workers on the line, introduce new technologies faster, and reduce costs.

Managing Costs

Firms competing under confrontation must also manage costs aggressively. Lean enterprises reduce costs in three primary ways. The first is to manage the cost of future products, the second is to manage the cost of existing products, and the third is to harness the entrepreneurial spirit of the workforce. While a number of factors determine the amount of energy a firm expends on each of these methods of cost reduction, three appear dominant. These factors are the competitive environment (in particular how the firm competes using the survival triplet), the maturity of the product's technology, and the length of the product's life cycle.

---

[5] See, for example, P. B. Crosby, *Quality Is Free*, New York: McGraw-Hill, 1979; P. Hauser and D. Clausing, "The House of Quality," *Harvard Business Review*, Vol. 66, No. 3, May-June 1988, pp. 63–73; and K. Ishikawa, *What Is Quality Control? The Japanese Way*, Englewood Cliffs, NJ: Prentice-Hall, 1985.

Managing All Three Dimensions Simultaneously

Typically, it is not necessary or advisable to expend equal effort on all three dimensions of the survival triplet. One dimension typically dominates the other two. The key to success is to select the appropriate rate of improvement for each of the three dimensions. For example, in a market where the customer is demanding increased functionality and is willing to pay for it, the most important dimension is functionality. In such a market, the firm that can increase the functionality of its products fastest (subject to price and quality constraints) will develop a competitive advantage. If, in contrast, the market is price driven, then the critical skill is cost reduction.

Failure to understand how to compete using the survival triplet brings the risk of expending too much effort on one element of the triplet and not enough on the others. At the limit, the firm will fall outside the survival zone because it is too good at one or more elements of the triplet.[6] The critical point is that being too good is often as bad as being not good enough. This is not to say that firms do not have to improve on all three dimensions at once but rather that different rates of improvement are required. When a firm's products fall outside the survival zone, it is imperative to get them back in as soon as possible.

The most important dimension frequently changes over time. For example, when the "bubble" burst and the yen strengthened against the dollar, many Japanese firms changed their most important dimension from functionality to cost.[7] These firms have developed integrated systems flexible enough not to have to change when the most important dimension changes.

SURVIVING THE TRANSITION TO CONFRONTATIONAL COMPETITION

It is not clear that the number of competitors that can survive in a market dominated by mass producers is the same as the number

---

[6] See "The Five Deadly Sins of Japan's Expanding 'High Tech Syndrome'," *Tokyo Business Today*, May 1992, pp. 34–36, for a discussion on "baroque engineering" and excessive functionality.

[7] Robert Neff et al., "How Badly Will Yen Shock Hurt?" *Business Week*, August 30, 1993, pp. 52–53.

that can survive in a market dominated by lean producers, nor is it clear that all firms can survive the transition. Each firm should evaluate its strengths and weaknesses and then decide whether its probability of success is high enough to make attempting the transition worthwhile. For weaker firms, it may be better to withdraw from the market than to die a slow, extended death trying to compete with insufficient resources. Firms that believe they are strong enough to survive need to develop the systems, organizational context, and culture required for the aggressive management of the survival triplet. All three are required and must be in harmony for the successful adoption of confrontation strategy.

To succeed, these firms must create an organizational context and culture that will support the integrated systems required to manage the survival triplet aggressively. Total quality management, product development, and cost management systems must be given a common theme.

The key point is that firms must learn to view the process of managing the survival triplet as a total systems solution, not a collection of independent techniques. For many firms undergoing the transition to confrontation, TQM and product development (time to market) systems function well, but the cost management systems fail to focus on the product design stage and are not adequately integrated into the firm's customer analysis program. Thus, of the three systems, it is the cost management system that requires the most attention.

Once a firm is ready to adopt a confrontation strategy, it must carefully analyze competitive conditions to determine when its avoidance strategies are no longer appropriate. For many firms, delaying the adoption of confrontation strategy is appropriate because they can use the transition period to prepare themselves for the harsh realities of a confrontational environment. This decision involves a thorough analysis of the competitive environment, product life cycle, and technological maturity to determine the cost management techniques most likely to be beneficial. Each technique is applicable during a different stage of the product life cycle, and, depending on several factors, some techniques may be more or less beneficial for a given firm.

The nature of competition does not change immediately as firms in an industry begin to adopt lean enterprise practices.

Instead, it changes gradually from competition avoidance to confrontation. This gradual change makes sense. Just as the cost leader generates extra profits by allowing the differentiators to create a price umbrella, the lean leader generates extra profits, in the early days, by allowing the mass producers to determine the positions of survival zones. As more companies become lean, however, the nature of competition changes, and the lean players begin to define the position of the survival zones. In time, confrontation becomes the dominant strategy, and the remaining mass producers see their profits disappear as the ability to create and maintain sustainable competitive advantages based on the survival triplet becomes extremely rare.

Firms that have successfully developed sustainable competitive advantages in the old competitive environment may be tempted to make two mistakes. They may expend too many resources, first, trying to protect their existing (but no longer sustainable) competitive advantages and, second, trying to develop new ones. Unfortunately, all too often these firms will discover that all the resources committed to the extension or creation of sustainable competitive advantages were wasted: management has risked draining the firm of the very reserves it requires to adapt to confrontation.

The first step to surviving the transition is to accept that eventually the firm will have to adopt a confrontation strategy. This step is very difficult for many firms to accept because adoption of such strategies implies that profits eventually will fall below their historical levels. Firms that are used to being "profit maximizers" and are now adopting confrontation need to determine the time frame over which they are trying to maximize profits. If the firm uses too short a horizon, it risks adopting strategies that in the end will lead either to bankruptcy or, at least, to some very difficult years ahead. It may, for example, chase profits associated with niches that are no longer growing and therefore are attracting lower levels of competition than the main market. While the lower level of competition allows profits to be higher, the niche may not be attractive for the future.

If a mass producer stays in the main market, the only way it can maintain profit is either by increasing prices or by expending fewer resources on quality and functionality. For a while, this strategy can "succeed," but in the long run the underlying fallacies of such a strategy cannot be avoided. First, the firm is earning its high profit levels at the expense of customer loyalty. It is taking advantage of the loyal customers' willingness to accept products that are at the edge (the negative one) of the survival zone or even slightly outside it. Once this loyalty evaporates, the firm discovers that it has to catch up to survive. The other risk is that the extra resources the firm's competitors are expending on quality and functionality might give those firms the ability to shift the minimum acceptable values of quality and functionality at a speed that the profit maximizer cannot match. The profit maximizer's products rapidly fall out of their survival zones, and the firm is forced to catch up or exit the market.

SURVIVING IN A CONFRONTATION MODE

Even when a firm makes a successful transition to confrontation strategy, it still faces the daunting task of surviving. Survival is achieved by creating an endless stream of temporary competitive advantages through aggressive management of the survival triplet. Every product must be inside its survival zone. Three factors drive alterations in the position of a survival zone: changing customer preferences, the way in which competitors manage the survival triplet, and the firm's distinctive competencies. Changing customer preferences are important because they help determine which characteristics of the survival zone dominate. If the customer is demanding increased functionality, for example, and is not overly concerned with price, low-functionality and low-cost products are in trouble.

While customer preferences may change survival zones, a firm can influence customer preferences and thus survival zones by launching products with different trade-offs among the characteristics of the survival triplet. If a firm chooses to expend more resources on functionality than other firms in the industry do, for example, it may gradually become the high-functionality (and presumably high-price) player. If the functionality of its products can be increased enough to make customers change their preferences, then the firm can change the position of the survival zones for the products it sells, forcing other firms in the industry to catch up.

The challenge for firms in a confrontational market is to determine when they can influence the customer preferences that drive their products. If a firm can identify one or more distinctive competencies, it should try to differentiate its products, even though the differentiation will be only temporary. Olympus, for example, launched the Stylus line of compact cameras because it believed it had a temporary advantage in its ability to develop very small cameras. While its competitors can now match the Stylus, Olympus still dominates the super-small compact camera market, demonstrating that, while first-mover advantages are reduced in confrontational environments, they are still real.

Becoming a Lean Leader

Firms become lean leaders by being better at managing the survival triplet than their competitors. There are two ways to become a lean leader. The first is to find a way to quantum jump the competition. When a firm achieves a quantum jump, it dramatically reshapes the survival zones of products. Topcon's development of near-infrared technology is an example of such a jump. Competitors are then forced either to catch up or go out of business. Unfortunately, it is extremely difficult for a firm to quantum jump its competitors because doing so requires identifying a new way to deliver enhanced product functionality. Like sustainable competitive advantages, a firm should always take advantage of such opportunities but accept that it is risky to rely solely on them to maintain profitability.

The second way in which a firm can become a lean leader is by achieving superior management of the survival triplet through the continuous improvement of its products. Achieving a leadership position in this way is difficult because all the firm's competitors are trying to improve at the same time. Usually each firm develops the leadership position in some of its products but not enough of them for customers to identify that firm as the leader.

A firm that is a lean leader and can maintain this position comes as close to developing a sustainable advantage as is possible in a confrontational market. The firm earns above-average profits or gains market share by sustaining the ability to generate a continuous series of temporary, not sustainable, advantages. This difference in the nature of the competitive advantage is real. Sustainable competitive advantages suggest static equilibrium, whereas temporary advantages suggest a dynamic status. Firms that try to avoid competition are forced to protect the status quo. They rarely take actions that will lead to head-on competition.

In contrast, when advantages are temporary, there is no status quo. Firms must seek continuously to find ways to develop advantages over their competitors so that they can confront them successfully. A market dominated by confrontation contains firms that are actively seeking to destroy the advantages of their competitors while creating new ones for themselves. Because the advantages are temporary, these firms frequently destroy their own current advantages to create new ones. After all, there is no point in trying to defend an advantage if it will disappear in the near future.

Lean Leader Strategies

A lean leader can use two strategies to take advantage of its position and superior profits. It can use its leadership position to accelerate the rate at which survival zones shift. In doing so, the firm attempts to leave its competitors behind so that their products fall outside their survival zones. This strategy increases the leader's market share and, hence, profitability. It forces every other firm into a catch-up mode. In the second strategy, the lean leader can allow the other firms in the industry to dictate the rate at which the acceptable values of each characteristic of the survival triplet shift. This strategy allows the firm to make superior profits because it can deliver products at lower cost through better management of the survival triplet than its competitors. Under this strategy profits increase, but market share remains the same.

While many factors determine which of the two strategies the lean leader adopts, the primary one is the relative technological capability of the firm in comparison to its competitors. If a leader has the most advanced products (i.e., has first-mover advantages), then it should adopt the first strategy. However, there is a risk in selecting this strategy. Continuously launching products at the limit of the firm's ability allows competitors to learn from the products and thus may accelerate the rate at which competitors can catch up. Firms that follow this strategy adopt a role equivalent to the differentiator's without achieving that status in the eyes of their customers. It is the first-mover advantages that generate the superior profits.

If the lean leader's first-mover advantages are small, it should think about adopting the second strategy. The extra profits generated by the firm's superior ability to manage the survival triplet reflect the firm's superior efficiency relative to its competitors. Firms using this strategy adopt a role equivalent to the cost leader's that allows differentiators to create a pricing umbrella from which to generate superior profits. However, as in the case of the first strategy, the firm does not achieve cost leadership status in the eyes of its customers.

If the lean leader's objective is to maximize profits (the traditional American objective), then the relative profits generated by the two strategies will determine which one is chosen. A profit-maximizing objective usually favors adoption of the second strategy. If the objective is to maximize market share (the traditional Japanese objective), then relative sales will determine which strategy is chosen. A growth objective usually favors the first strategy by launching products with higher quality and functionality than its competitors' products but not charging more for them.

Firms that are not leaders are jockeying to find ways to become leaders and could easily become leaders in the future. This ability reflects the dynamic nature of confrontational competition. No firms are "stuck in the middle" in Porter's sense. However, firms that do not aspire to leadership can carry out confrontation strategy in a third way. They can follow the leader. In doing this, the firm does little of the fundamental research and development required to introduce new products but instead uses value engineering and other techniques to quickly match its competitors' new products.

This follow-the-leader strategy works well if there are essentially two types of customers—trendsetters and copycats. Trendsetters buy new products as soon as they are available; copycats buy the products the trendsetters have already bought. If the delay between the trendsetter buying and the copycat buying is less than the time it takes the follow-the-leader firm to introduce its products, then first-mover advantages are small and the follow-the-leader strategy can be successful. If first-mover advantages are strong, which happens when trendsetters are more numerous than copycats are, the follow-the-leader strategy will not succeed.

If the firms undertaking research and development into new products can find ways to develop expertise in the application of technology that cannot be learned through value engineering techniques, the follow-the-leader firms will fall behind. Alternatively, the firms undertaking research and development can license their new technologies to the other firms, and thus they can earn above-average returns.

SUMMARY

As more Western firms convert themselves to lean enterprises, the way they have to compete will change in critical aspects.

- Sustainable competitive advantages will become harder to achieve.
- The generic strategies of cost leadership and differentiation will begin to lose their effectiveness.
- Profit margins will shrink as competition becomes more confrontational.

Western managers must be sensitive to these changes because for many of the organizations the changes will be unavoidable. Managers who do not adjust their mode of competition accordingly will risk their firms. For example, managers who cling to the concepts of sustainable competitive advantage and who invest resources only in lines of business that they believe have such an advantage will discover that the number of investment opportunities they can identify is decreasing over time. Similarly, firms that cling to the traditional generic strategies of cost leadership and differentiation will discover that their ability to maintain those strategies is gradually eroding over time. They increasingly will be forced to retreat from their markets as lean competitors outmaneuver them.

A similar fate awaits firms that try to cling to their historical profit margins. The competition between lean enterprises is fiercer than between mass producers, and the overall profit margins are smaller. Retreating from products that have lower than usual profit margins will be successful only if other, higher-margin products can be identified. Often such products will not be available. If they are, there is the risk that chasing these high-profit products will lead to niches that, while initially highly profitable, eventually turn into technological dead ends.

Consequently, as the number of lean firms in an industry increases, managers should accept that they will have to change the way they compete. They will have to accept:

- The concept of transitory competitive advantages as opposed to sustainable ones,
- Strategies based on confrontation instead of cost leadership and differentiation,
- The fact that niche strategies may no longer be successful,
- Lower profit margins.

Firms that adopt a confrontation strategy will have to learn to manage the survival triplet in an integrated manner. In particular, once the firm achieves near parity with its competitors and its products are within their survival zones, it must choose how much energy to invest in improving each of the dimensions. Unfortunately, many Western managers have failed to understand the role of the survival triplet. They have adopted a rallying call of being the firm with the highest quality, lowest cost, and first-to-market products.[8] Such rallying calls are empty and simply distract the firm from choosing an appropriate strategy. These firms are not using the survival triplet properly. No firm can reasonably expect to be number one in all three elements of the survival triplet. Any firm that actually achieved this distinction would rapidly dominate its competitors. Furthermore, if it could sustain this advantage, it would become a monopoly because all its competitors would be bankrupt.

Many Western firms have adopted this best-in-all-three approach because they encountered Japanese competitors superior to them on all three counts, and to survive they had to improve on all three elements of the survival triplet simultaneously. The resulting struggle for survival caused many Western managers to lose sight of the critical fact that in most markets one element of the triplet is considerably more important than the others. What the managers failed to realize was that, once they were inside the survival zone, they no longer had to improve their performance along all three elements at the same rate. Instead, they had to learn to compete intelligently and select the rate at which they improved their performance on each element of the survival triplet.

To be successful, the cost management, quality, and time-to-market systems will have to be blended so that the survival triplet is

---

[8] Michael Hammer and James Champy, *Reengineering the Corporation: A Manifesto for Business Revolution,* New York: Harper Business, 1993.

managed as efficiently as possible. Managers will have to be sensitive to the changing importance of the three dimensions. The failure to be aware of this shifting can easily lead a firm to launch a new generation of products that fall outside their survival zones.

Another challenge will center on managing innovation and technology diffusion. First, the shift to multifunctional design teams will improve the firm's ability to integrate the three dimensions of the survival triplet but also risks a "sameness" in design. Managers will have to be creative in finding ways to take advantage of multifunctional groups without paying a price in terms of innovation. Management will also have to learn to control the way technology diffuses through supply chains. The technology sharing that occurs so freely in Japanese supply chains has the advantage of allowing firms to make innovations more rapidly, but at the same time it tends to lead to technological equivalence and hence confrontation.

The confrontation strategy is here to stay. It is a direct outcome of the emergence of the lean enterprise. It means more intense competition and lower profits. Adopting a confrontation strategy is not an excuse for senseless head-on competition. Instead, it is a deliberate strategy that acknowledges that lean enterprises do not compete in the same way as mass producers. Western managers must accept that in industries in which lean enterprises are becoming dominant, only those firms that adopt confrontation strategy and aggressively manage the survival triplet will survive.

CHAPTER 2

The Role of Cost Management in Confrontation Strategy

Introduction

Firms that adopt a confrontation strategy must learn to manage costs as aggressively as possible. It is only if firms understand the importance of cost management that they can manage the survival triplet correctly and succeed in using a confrontation strategy.

Cost management plays an important role in the success of many Japanese firms. Japanese firms that have extended experience with the confrontation strategy form of competition have developed sophisticated cost management systems to help them manage costs aggressively. Eight cost management techniques are used to reduce costs aggressively. The first three of these techniques focus on managing the cost of future products. The next three manage the costs of existing products. The final two harness the entrepreneurial spirit of the workers.

MANAGING THE COST OF FUTURE PRODUCTS

Managing the cost of future products is important because it is the only way to ensure that future products will be profitable when launched. Firms have developed three feed-forward cost management techniques to help them manage the costs of future products: target costing, value engineering, and interorganizational cost management systems (see Figure 2–1). These systems are particularly important because evidence shows that most of a product's costs are designed in. Once the product enters production it is too late to make significant cost reductions without essentially redesigning it. The three feed-forward techniques are designed to ensure that, if possible, costs are not designed into products in the first place.

Target Costing

Target costing is the discipline that ensures that new products are profitable when they are launched. It has three major steps. The first is to determine a product's target selling price and target profit margin so its allowable cost can be established. The second is to set an achievable product-level target cost. The third is to decompose the product-level target cost down to the component level so the purchase price of the components can be determined.

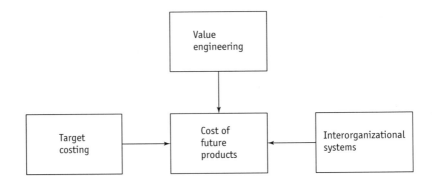

FIGURE 2–1. MANAGING THE COST OF FUTURE PRODUCTS

A product's target cost is arrived at by subtracting its target profit margin from its target selling price and adjusting for the cost-reduction capabilities of the firm and its suppliers. The target selling price of a new product is decided primarily from market analysis. The target profit margin is based on corporate profit expectations, historical results, and competitive analysis.

The critical factor that distinguishes target costing (as opposed to other approaches to managing the costs of new products) is the intensity with which the cardinal rule is applied: the target cost can never be exceeded. Without the application of such a rule, target costing systems typically lose their effectiveness. In practice, the cardinal rule may be broken at times, but the conditions must justify it and specified procedures must be followed to authorize it. Design engineers are definitely not allowed to make decisions of the type, "If we just add this feature, the product will be so much better (and only cost a little more)."

Once the product's target cost has been established, the next step is to decompose that cost to the component level. The chief engineer usually is responsible for allocating the target cost among the major functions of the product. He defines the main themes of the new model. For example, for an automobile it might be a quieter but sportier ride. Once the target costs of the major functions are set, the next step is to identify the target costs of the components they contain. These component-level target costs become the purchase prices of the externally acquired components. That is, they are the suppliers' selling prices as set by their customers.

Value Engineering

Value engineering (VE) is a systematic, interdisciplinary examination of factors affecting the cost of a product so as to devise a means of achieving the specified purpose at the required standard of quality and reliability at the target cost. VE, like target costing, is applied during product development. VE is a multidisciplinary, team-based approach. Teams typically are drawn from multiple functional areas, including design engineering, applications engineering, manufacturing, purchasing, and sometimes even the firm's suppliers and subcontractors.

VE is an organized effort to analyze the functions of goods and services so a firm can find ways to achieve those necessary functions and essential characteristics while meeting its target costs. VE plays a critical role in the cost management of future products because it helps the firm manage the trade-off between functionality and cost. As this trade-off is critical in many competitive environments, it is not surprising that many Japanese firms have strongly embraced VE practices.

VE requires identification of each product's basic and secondary functions and analysis of the functions' value. A basic function is the principal reason for the existence of the product. For example, an automobile's basic function is to provide transportation. The secondary functions are outcomes of the way the designers chose to achieve the basic function, for example, the heat and pollution generated by the auto engine.

An important aspect of Japanese VE programs is that their objective is not to minimize the cost of products but to achieve a specified level of cost reduction (the product's target cost). This difference between the Japanese and Western approaches is significant because designing to a specified low cost appears to create more intense pressure to reduce costs than designing to an unspecified minimum cost.

Interorganizational Cost Management Systems

The intense pressure to become more efficient causes many firms to try to increase the efficiency of their suppliers of raw materials and components by developing interorganizational cost management systems. These systems emerge because it is no longer sufficient to be the most efficient firm; it is also necessary to be part of the most efficient supply chain.

To achieve this objective, many Japanese firms are opting to blur their organizational boundaries in numerous ways. Organizational blurring typically occurs when another firm further up or down the supply chain possesses information critical to one firm. The two or more firms then create relationships that share organizational resources, including information that helps improve the efficiency of the interfirm activities. Mechanisms for information sharing include joint research and development projects, which place employees of one firm in others.

Firms can undertake interorganizational cost management in three major ways. The first is to work jointly with buyers and suppliers to make the interfaces between the firms more efficient. The second is to create conditions in which the design teams of the buyer and supplier can interact jointly to find ways to design the product and the components it contains at a lower cost. Finally, the buyers and suppliers can jointly find ways to reduce manufacturing costs.

The two aspects of interorganizational cost management during product design deal with disciplining the process and with enabling the savings to be achieved through design team interactions. The discipline is achieved through target costing and, in particular, through chained target costing. Target costing systems are said to be chained when the component-level target costing system of the buyer's target costing systems feeds directly into the market-driven costing section of the supplier's system.

The primary mechanisms of interorganizational cost management enable the design teams of the buyer and supplier to interact and apply value engineering techniques across the interorganizational boundary between the buyer and supplier. These mechanisms include FPQ trade-offs, interorganizational cost investigations, and concurrent cost management. These three approaches differ in the extent and timing of the interactions among the design teams. The extent of the interactions is smallest for FPQ trade-offs and greatest for concurrent cost management. In concurrent cost management the involvement occurs very early in the conceptualization and design process, while it occurs much later for the other two mechanisms.

MANAGING THE COST OF EXISTING PRODUCTS

Managing the cost of existing products is the second way costs are reduced. It includes three feedback techniques: kaizen costing, product costing systems, and operational control (see Figure 2–2). Their primary purpose is to create cost-reduction pressures on the production processes. The need for both feed-forward and feedback cost-management techniques reflects the different objectives of the two types. Feed-forward techniques focus on reducing costs through more efficient product design, and feedback techniques focus on reducing costs through more efficient production. Together, the six

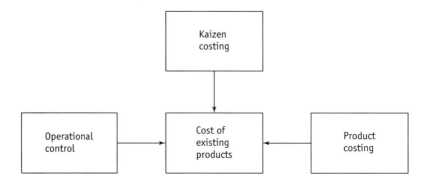

FIGURE 2-2. MANAGING THE COST OF EXISTING PRODUCTS

techniques are used to create a continuous downward pressure on costs across the entire life cycle of the firm's products.

Product Costing

Given the importance Japanese firms attach to cost management, their cost systems might be expected to be technically advanced and capable of reporting extremely accurate product costs. In particular, activity-based costing (ABC) systems might be expected to be either emerging or already in place. Despite this expectation, many of the systems we encountered were relatively traditional, and equivalent systems can easily be found in Western firms. Not all the systems we encountered, however, were conventional in their design. Several contained very innovative designs that reflected the economic realities of the competitive environments the firms faced, the nature of their production processes, and the types of decisions that management considered most important. For example, some systems reported product-line as opposed to product costs.

The dominance of product-line as opposed to product-level decisions reflected the fact that some of the firms studied sold carefully designed families of products. The underlying marketing rationale of such a strategy is to break the market into a number of distinct segments, each containing a large number of customers. Each of these segments demands a different primary function or set of functions for the product. In the case of compact cameras, it might be the focal length of the lens or its zoom capabilities. For a car it might be the type of engine, the comfort of the ride, and the appearance. Using these primary functions, the firm designs a set of products that will satisfy virtually every customer. Customers then choose the product that best satisfies their requirements. By designing a complete product line, the firm gives the consumer no reason to look at competitive offerings. In contrast, if the customer is not satisfied with the product offering, then he or she will go elsewhere. Only if that firm fails to keep the customer satisfied will the original firm have an opportunity to win the customer back.

Leaving a "hole" in the line by choosing not to fill one of the segments because the product is unprofitable is unacceptable because everyone trading up or wishing to buy the missing product will simply switch to another firm. Consequently, any estimate of the profitability of a product must include the future profits from subsequent sales to customers who buy "unprofitable" products. Most firms believe that all high-volume segments are profitable in the long term, so the firms provide products accordingly. Given this strategy, many firms did not consider product-mix management particularly important at the individual-product level. All significant product decisions were made at the product-line level, for example, whether to manufacture all black-and-white televisions off-shore or, as was the case with Topcon, whether to cease manufacturing all cameras. Only rarely did these firms make discontinuance decisions about individual products. As a reflection of the diminished importance of product-level decisions, some of the firms studied implemented cost systems that could report only product-line costs.

Operational Control

Operational control requires holding people responsible for the costs they control and determining how well they manage them. The two primary techniques of operational control are the establishment of responsibility centers and variance analysis. For an individual to be held responsible for a cost, that cost must be assigned directly to the center over which that person has control. If indirect cost assignments are used, then it is impossible to hold the person responsible for any apparent changes in the level of resource consumption. No individual can be held responsible because there is no way to know if apparent changes in resource consumption are due to distortions in the indirect assignment process or to an actual change in the level of consumption. At the firms studied, Japanese managers were well aware of the problems of trying to hold individuals responsible for indirect costs. For example at Mitsubishi Kasei (an industrial chemical manufacturer), the existing cost system suffered from a very high level of allocations. These allocations made it almost impossible to assign responsibility for costs. This inability was considered critical and was the primary motivation to design a new system that would provide increased cost control.

The traditional use of variance analysis is to monitor how well the responsible manager is keeping control over costs. The aim is to ensure that the budget is achieved. Some of the Japanese firms studied used variance analysis in this way. For example, the variance analysis performed at Komatsu is taken straight from the textbooks with only minor variations. Typically, variance analysis is used to determine if task performance is adequate.

Other firms used variance analysis to monitor how well they were achieving their kaizen objectives. In environments with kaizen costing programs, the standards used to generate variances usually reflect the expected improvements due to continuous improvement activities.

At several of the firms, the standard cost system and the kaizen program were integrated so that the two supported each other. The simplest approach used to achieve this objective was to embed the anticipated kaizen improvements into the standards.

Kaizen Costing

Kaizen costing stands for continuous improvement. It is the application of kaizen techniques to reduce the costs of components and products by a prespecified amount. The difference between target and kaizen costing focuses on the point in the life cycle at which the techniques are applied and their primary cost-reduction objective. Target costing is applied during the design stage of the product life cycle. It achieves its cost-reduction objective primarily through improvements in product design. In contrast, kaizen costing is applied during the manufacturing stage of the product life cycle. It achieves its cost-reduction objectives chiefly through increased efficiency of the production process.

There are two types of kaizen costing: product-specific and general. Product-specific kaizen costing is applied under two conditions: when a product is launched above its target cost and when an existing product's profitability is threatened by price reductions. In both cases, engineering teams are created to find ways to reduce costs without altering product functionality, for example, by replacing metal components with plastic ones or reducing parts count by shifting to more integrated components. The second type of kaizen costing does not focus on individual products but on making the firm's production processes more efficient. In environments in which products have short lives, production processes are often extended across several generations of products, which reduces the cost of the production process and can lead to long-term savings.

HARNESSING THE ENTREPRENEURIAL SPIRIT

Another way to create pressure to reduce costs is to implement cost management techniques that harness the entrepreneurial spirit of the work force. These techniques are fundamentally different from those described above because they do not focus on either the product or the production process but on motivating the work force. There are at least two cost management techniques for accomplishing this objective. The first technique creates pseudo micro profit centers from cost centers, and the second technique converts the firm into a large number of real micro profit centers (see Figure 2–3).

Pseudo Micro Profit Centers

Firms that use the first technique convert cost centers into profit centers and change work group leaders from cost center managers to business managers. The development of this technique is motivated by the belief that the way in which people view their responsibilities sometimes can be as important as the responsibilities themselves. The technique is useful for four primary reasons:

- By using profit as the performance metric, work groups can get a better feel for the impact of their contributions on company performance.
- The creation of profit centers provides management with a

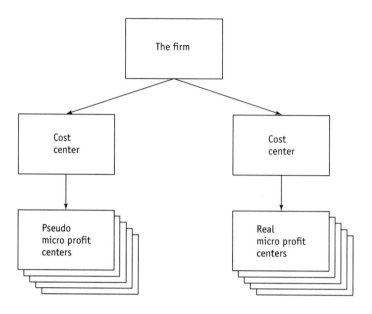

FIGURE 2-3. HARNESSING THE ENTREPRENEURIAL SPIRIT

mechanism to reward individuals publicly and thus reinforces behaviors that lead to increased profits.

- Because profits are a universal metric, each work group can
  evaluate its own performance and compare it to that of
  other groups.
- The creation of profit centers can revitalize the firm's cost
  management systems.

Real Micro Profit Centers

The second technique consists of breaking the firm into a collection
of autonomous small enterprises that must be profitable to survive.
Under the approach used by Kyocera, a large number of profit centers, called amoebae, are created. They are not independent firms but
highly independent pseudo firms responsible for selling products
both internally and externally. In contrast, the approach used by the
Taiyo Group creates separate legal entities, each responsible for several products. At the heart of both approaches is the fundamental
assumption that small firms are inherently more efficient and effec-

tive than large firms—they do not require an expensive and ineffective bureaucracy, and they can react quickly to changes in competitive conditions. Both firms believe the ability to reduce or control the growth of bureaucracy is a major mechanism to control costs.

SUMMARY

When firms adopt a confrontation strategy, aggressive management of the survival triplet becomes critical. For such firms, a highly effective cost management program is a necessity, not a luxury. Reflecting the importance of cost management to their strategy, many Japanese firms have developed integrated cost management programs that create a discipline throughout the firm to reduce costs across the entire life cycle of the firm's products.

These programs consist of six product- and production process-related techniques and two that harness the entrepreneurial spirit. Of the six product- and process-related techniques, three are feed-forward techniques designed to help manage the costs of future products. They are target costing, value engineering, and interorganizational cost management systems. The next three techniques are feedback techniques designed to help manage the costs of existing products. They are kaizen costing, product costing, and operational control. The last two techniques, pseudo micro profit centers and real micro profit centers, focus on harnessing the entrepreneurial spirit of the work force.

Japanese cost management programs are designed to affect all aspects of the economics of manufacture. They influence the supply of purchased parts, the design of the products, and the manufacture of the products. At each stage of the production and delivery process, Japanese firms have developed techniques to reduce costs.

For a given firm, the effectiveness of the various cost management techniques appears to depend on several factors, including the competitive environment, the maturity of the technologies used in the products, and the length of the product life cycle. The role of these three factors in determining the effectiveness of the six cost management techniques is shaped primarily by how the firm is using the survival triplet.

Feed-forward techniques are particularly effective when firms are competing primarily on the functionality of their products. Such firms must continuously introduce new products with enhanced functionality to survive. Typically they rely on the latest technologies and reduce product life cycles to a minimum. The feedback techniques are particularly effective when firms are competing primarily on price. Such firms usually are dealing with more mature technologies and longer life cycles and to reduce costs to a minimum have to make their production processes as efficient as possible.

Firms that are competing primarily on quality probably will rely on a mixture of the techniques depending on whether they are using technology to enhance quality or improve production processes. Firms relying on new technologies will benefit from target costing, while those relying on production process improvements will benefit from kaizen costing.

CHAPTER 3

THE RESEARCH PROJECT

INTRODUCTION

In the summer of 1994, the Institute of Management Accountants and the authors launched a joint research project to document and analyze the cost management practices at Japanese firms. This project was a continuation of one initiated by Robin Cooper that had culminated in the publication of 23 Harvard Business School cases on the cost management practices at 19 Japanese firms and the book *When Lean Enterprises Collide: Competing Under Competition.*

The primary objectives of the continuation project were to: (1) complete the study of the cost management techniques identified in the original study, (2) develop additional case studies on Japanese cost management practices, (3) present the cases in a more accessible form to managers, and (4) create an in-depth analysis of the practices at the firms so that the following questions could be answered:

- What is the technical nature of each cost management technique?

- How is it applied in practice?
- What are the implications for Western managers?

THE RESEARCH APPROACH

The researchers visited 25 firms to collect information about the issues that led management to implement advanced cost management systems, the insights obtained from the information reported by those systems, and the actions taken based on those insights. After the research team had reviewed the findings from all the research sites, the team analyzed and synthesized the information. They developed a framework for understanding the practice of each cost management technique encountered and did an in-depth analysis of that practice.

The research process consisted of five major steps:

- Forming the project committee and research team,
- Selecting the research sites,
- Visiting the firms and collecting information about the cost management techniques used and how they were applied,
- Writing the cases,
- Analyzing and synthesizing the findings.

FORMING THE PROJECT COMMITTEE AND RESEARCH TEAM

At the outset of the project, the IMA established a project committee to oversee the entire project. Its members were Robert C. Miller, Boeing Corporation, and Hank Davis, Dodge Rockwell Automation. The research team, consisting of Robin Cooper and Regine Slagmulder (plus coauthors), selected the research sites, visited the sites, researched the individual cases, prepared and cleared the cases, analyzed the research findings, and prepared a synthesis of those findings. Robin Cooper provided overall management of the project, including the liaison with the IMA and the project committee.

SITE SELECTION—THE SERIES

All the research sites documented in this series are located in Japan. Japanese firms were chosen because they have extensive experience with competition among lean enterprises. This experience has given them time to develop mature cost management systems required to compete in a confrontational mode. The 31 cases document the cost management practices at 25 manufacturing organizations (listed in the Appendix). These firms are drawn from a number of different industries and vary in size from very large to quite small.

To ensure that the sample for the entire project included a broad range of cost management techniques in different industries, the research team established four site selection criteria.

- All the sites had to have been lean enterprises for some time. This criterion reflected the objective of the research project, to study the cost management systems of lean enterprises.
- The firms had to have well-developed and frequently updated cost management systems. The objective of this criterion was to ensure that the cost management systems documented were not out of date but reflected best practices.
- The firms were to be chosen from a cross section of manufacturing industries (heavy manufacturing, light manufacturing, and process). This criterion was established to explore both the range of cost management practices in Japanese lean enterprises and the range of application of those techniques.
- When possible the firm had to have a reputation for being well managed and having innovative cost management systems. This objective helped ensure that the best Japanese cost management practices would be documented.

Approximately 50 firms were contacted in a variety of ways. Japanese academics and professional contacts of the researchers identified some of the firms. Others were chosen because articles and cases had been written about them. Managers at firms in the sample pointed out a third group of firms as having highly innovative systems. Finally, some were contacted directly based on their general reputation for being well managed and having innovative products and management systems.

The final selection was based on whether each company satisfied the site selection criteria, agreed to become a research site, and was willing to allow the field research teams to complete the site visits within a reasonable time frame. Because of the selection method, the company sample is neither random nor necessarily representative of the population of lean enterprises in Japan.

SITE SELECTION—THIS MONOGRAPH

The firms selected for this particular monograph were identified in several ways. Michiharu Sakurai of Senshu University identified Komatsu as having an excellent target costing system. Takeo Yoshikawa of Yokohama National University identified the Tokyo-Yokohama-Kamakura supplier chain. It was selected because the chain contains three firms that are essentially independent as opposed to being part of a keiretsu. Independence was considered critical because it allows interorganizational cost management systems to exist in their purest form. If the firms are part of a keiretsu, "invisible" offsetting transactions such as low-interest loans might cause one of the firms to agree to "subeconomic" selling prices.

Olympus and Citizen were contacted directly based on their reputations for innovative and competitive products. In both cases, a letter was sent to the firm's president requesting involvement in the research project. Both companies agreed to participate and selected their target and kaizen costing systems, respectively, as the most noteworthy part of their cost management systems.

The firms with well-established target and kaizen costing systems were asked to contact one of their most highly regarded suppliers and invite them to participate in the research. Komatsu identified Toyo Radiator, an independent supplier, as an excellent example of a first-tier supplier. The other two firms, Omachi Olympus and Miyota, are 100% subsidiaries of Olympus Optical and Citizen Watch, respectively. These firms were included to discover whether interorganizational cost systems can be used effectively when the supplier is a wholly owned subsidiary. Since any losses of the subsidiary are borne by the parent, a risk is that the discipline of interorganizational cost management will be lost when the supplier is also a subsidiary.

The nine firms included in the interorganizational cost management sample are described below:

Citizen Watch Company, Ltd.

This company was the manufacturing arm of the world's largest watch producer, Citizen, founded in 1930. It was responsible not only for manufacturing watches but also was diversified strategically into products that required expertise in watch technology: numerically controlled production equipment, flexible disk drives, liquid crystal displays for television and computers, dot matrix printers, and jewelry. The non-watch products accounted for almost half its revenues in 1990.

Kamakura Iron Works Company, Ltd.

Kamakura, founded in 1910 as a blacksmith shop, was a family-run firm located in a distant suburb of Tokyo. The firm remained relatively small with 1993 sales of nearly ¥6 billion and profits of ¥35 million. The firm was a supplier of automotive parts and had 21 major customers, including Yokohama Corporation (40% of sales), Isuzu Motors (20%), Hino Motors (15%), Jidosha Kiki Company (10%), and Yamaha Motors (5%). Most of its customers were either automobile manufacturers or suppliers to that industry. Other customers included Iseki, Kayaba Industries, and Shinryo Heavy Equipment. Although large portions of the revenues were from vertically integrated companies, Kamakura was an independent company and did not belong to a keiretsu.

Komatsu, Ltd.

Founded in 1917 as part of the Takeuchi Mining Company, this firm was one of the largest heavy industrial manufacturers in Japan. It was organized in three major lines of business—construction equipment, industrial machinery, and electronic-applied products—which accounted for 80% of total revenues. The remaining 20% consisted of construction, unit housing, chemicals and plastics, and software development. These products together generated revenues of ¥989 billion and net income of ¥31 billion in 1991, making Komatsu a large international firm. Since 1989, the company has been aggressively diversifying and expanding globally.

Miyota Company Ltd.

Miyota Company Ltd. (Miyota), founded in 1959, was a 100%-owned subsidiary of Citizen Watch Company, Ltd. In 1995, its sales were just over ¥36 billion. The firm was originally dedicated to the assembly of watches for its parent but over the years, it diversified along technology lines by specializing in miniature mechatronic (the fusion of mechanical and electronic technologies) products. By 1995, Miyota produced four major product lines: completed watches, watch movements and parts, quartz oscillators, and viewfinders for camcorders.

Olympus Optical Company, Ltd.

As part of Olympus, Olympus Optical Company manufactured and sold opto-electronic equipment and other related products. Originally called Takachiho Seisakusho, Olympus was founded in 1919 as a producer of microscopes. Major product lines were cameras, video camcorders, microscopes, endoscopes, and clinical analyzers. By 1995, Olympus was the world's fourth-largest camera manufacturer with consolidated revenues of ¥252 billion and ¥3 billion in net income.

Omachi Olympus Ltd.

Omachi Olympus Company, Ltd. (Omachi) was a 100%-owned subsidiary of Olympus Optical Company, Ltd. (Olympus). It specialized in producing complex, curved, plastic moldings primarily for incorporation into the camera products made by its parent's Consumer Products Division. The firm was located in Omachi City, in the Nagano Prefecture some 150 miles from Tokyo.

Tokyo Motors Ltd.

Tokyo Motor Works, Ltd. (TMW), when measured in terms of worldwide production, was by 1990 one of the world's top 10 automobile manufacturers. In 1990, TMW produced just over 2 million vehicles, supplying approximately 4% of the world's demand for cars and trucks. Of these vehicles, slightly more than 1.2 million were passenger cars. TMW, founded in 1945, produced vehicles at 20 plants in 15 countries and marketed them in 110 countries through 200 distributorships and more than 6,000 dealerships.

Toyo Radiator Company Ltd.

Toyo Radiator Company Ltd. (Toyo) was founded in 1936 as a radiator supplier to the fledgling Japanese automobile industry. Toyo was not associated with any of the major keiretsu. Over the years it had diversified into all areas of heat-exchange applications. By 1995, it sold heat-exchange products for use in automobiles, heavy construction and agricultural vehicles, air conditioners for home and office, and freezers. Its product lines included radiators, oil coolers, inter-coolers, evaporators, and condensers. In 1995, it was one of the world's largest independent heat-exchange equipment manufacturers for construction equipment.

Yokohama Corporation, Ltd.

Yokohama was founded in July 1939 as a joint venture between a Japanese automobile manufacturer and the Japanese government. The objective of the firm was to manufacture hydraulic systems for automobiles and trucks and associated equipment under license from a German firm. Firm ownership changed over the years, and in 1993 only three major shareholders remained: Isuzu Motors, Nissan Motors, and The Industrial Bank of Japan. By 1992, the firm had 13 overseas affiliates, seven liaison offices, and a worldwide service network of more than 100 distributors and 2,000 service representatives with sales of ¥257 billion and 6,800 employees. Yokohama was split into three corporate divisions: injection pump, air conditioning, and hydraulics and pneumatics.

VISITING THE SITES AND WRITING THE CASE STUDIES

Interviews were conducted with managers, design and manufacturing engineers, and blue-collar workers at the seven firms who were actively involved in the application of interorganizational cost management. In-depth interviews in English, with translator support as appropriate, typically were held with three to five persons in each firm. These persons were responsible for one or more target costing projects. Job titles included general manager of product planning, manager of corporate planning, chief engineer, and senior manager of group accounting. Site visits lasted a total of 25 days. The typical time spent at each firm was between two and three days. Initially, the researchers visited a firm for two days and from the collected information prepared a draft of the case. Follow-up visits took place to clear up any major outstanding issues and to obtain agreement to sign the final draft.

Copious notes and tape recordings of the interviews were used to prepare research cases of approximately 5,000 words each. These cases were sent to the contact manager in each firm for review. The first draft of the cases contained numerous questions that the authors could not answer from their tape recordings and notes.

The cases typically went through two to three revisions before being cleared, and it took from 12 to 18 months to clear each case. When necessary, the questions and appropriate textual portions of the case were translated into Japanese so those managers with inadequate English skills could answer the questions and review the text for accuracy. In a typical clearance procedure approximately 60 questions were answered and about one-third of the case was rewritten or amended in some way. While most of these changes related to the author-initiated questions, others were corrections made to the drafts by the reviewing managers. If necessary, competitive or sensitive information was disguised at the request of the participating company. After these questions were answered and the reviewing managers at the firms were satisfied that the cases were factually correct, the cases were used as a basis for writing this monograph. Ultimately, each company signed a representation letter authorizing release of the final document.

ANALYZING AND SYNTHESIZING THE FINDINGS

Once the cases were completed, the authors analyzed them to identify the techniques and processes that underlie interorganizational cost management. To begin with, the role of cooperative lean supply was analyzed. Lean supply has two aspects: the nature of lean buyer-supplier relations and the blurring of organizational boundaries, explored in Chapter 4, and the role of lean supplier networks, examined in Chapter 5.

The next nine chapters document the techniques of interorganizational cost management. The first provides an overview of interorganizational cost management (Chapter 6). The following five chapters document the techniques associated with interorganizational cost management in the product design process: target costing (Chapters 7 and 8), chained target costing (Chapter 9), interorganizational cost investigations (Chapter 10), and concurrent cost management (Chapter 11).

Chapters 12 and 13 discuss kaizen costing and interorganizational kaizen costing. Chapter 14 describes how firms can increase the efficiency of their buyer-supplier interfaces. Chapter 15 uses a case study of a hypothetical company to show how interorganizational cost management is applied. Finally, Chapter 16 provides a checklist of the steps that potential adopters of interorganizational cost management systems should take to adopt the approach successfully.

PART 2

THE PRINCIPLES OF
LEAN SUPPLY

CHAPTER 4

LEAN BUYER-SUPPLIER RELATIONS

INTRODUCTION

At the heart of lean supply lies the concept of single-piece flow, with the supplier acting as an extended just-in-time factory for the buyer. The tight connections between each production step that are characteristic of lean production, with failure at one step bringing the entire production process to a stop, are replicated in the supply chain. If one supplier delivers defective parts, the buyer's production process will be forced to stop until new, nondefective parts are delivered.

In contrast, mass producers rely on inventories at their factories and at suppliers to buffer them from disruptions. If the supplier delivers defective parts, the solution is to pull replacement parts from inventory so that production can continue unabated. The defective parts are either thrown away or returned to the supplier. The cause of the problem is not immediately addressed. When both the buyer and the supplier have adopted lean thinking, however, the safety net of inventory is removed. The resulting heavy reliance on supplied parts that meet specifications explains why most lean suppliers have resident engineers at their buyers. These engineers identify problems as they emerge, discover their source, and instigate solutions at the supplier's factory. The endless search for perfection is thus extended into the supply chain.

The heavy reliance on suppliers forces the lean producer to develop rich relationships with its suppliers because the firms are tightly connected through their production processes. There are four major characteristics of lean buyer-supplier relations. The first characteristic deals with the reduced supplier base compared to mass producers. The second deals with the level of the relationship, which depends on the extent to which the buyer is relying on the supplier for innovation in product design. The third characteristic captures the nature of the lean buyer-supplier relationship, in particular, they are stable over time, highly cooperative, and mutually beneficial. The final characteristic looks at the way organizational boundaries are blurred as the buyer and supplier firms begin to share resources dynamically. Once the right types of relationships have been developed, the two firms can begin to take advantage of the relationship and, in particular, they can begin to undertake interorganizational cost management.

REDUCING THE NUMBER OF SUPPLIERS

The level of coordination required between lean buyers and suppliers is much greater than in the world of mass production. In lean supply, for example, volume fluctuations have to be kept as low as possible and production schedules have to be highly synchronized. This tight interaction makes it difficult, if not impossible, for lean producers to rely on a large number of suppliers because the transaction costs would be too high. Consequently, lean enterprises rely on a smaller supplier base than their mass production counterparts.

There are three ways to contract the number of suppliers: reduce the number of suppliers for each part; reduce the number of suppliers for each family of parts; and outsource fewer parts. The advantage of having multiple suppliers for a given part (typically one primary and one secondary supplier) lies in reduced reliance on a single source. The disadvantage lies in loss of economies of scale and minor differences in the parts supplied by the two firms that may cause problems on the production floor. Most lean producers, however, rely on a single lean supplier for each part, trusting that particular supplier to deliver near-perfect products on time.

Lean producers adopt a different solution at the parts-family level. A parts family is a group of different parts with similar functionality. Here the lean producers opt to select several competing suppliers. Thus, while each individual part is single-sourced, the parts family is typically multi-sourced.[1] The advantage of this approach lies in the creativity induced by the competition and the sharing of improvements among the suppliers involved. An exception is made, however, when major functions are outsourced. The multiple suppliers approach usually is not adopted for major functions. Instead, a single supplier is identified and a near-equal partnership is created.

The number of outsourced parts can be decreased by manufacturing more in-house and by outsourcing group components (such as starter motors) and major functions (such as engine cooling systems) as opposed to individual components (such as fan blades). The problem with the first approach is that it leads to increased vertical integration. Lean enterprises do not heavily integrate vertically because experience has shown that heavy vertical integration leads to reduced responsiveness and flexibility. Instead, they adopt the second approach to reduce the number of suppliers.

For outsourced group components and major functions, mass producers order individual components from numerous subcontractors (see Figure 4–1). In contrast, lean producers order the group component or major function from a single supplier (see Figure 4–2). Consequently, the number of suppliers from which the buyer directly purchases parts is reduced. For example, one immediate outcome of Komatsu's decision to adopt simultaneous engineering was a reduction in the number of Komatsu suppliers. Under the old approach, Toyo would supply the radiator, other companies would

---

[1] If the volume of business is too small to support multiple suppliers, then an alternative approach can be adopted. First, a single supplier is chosen, and then every few years the competitiveness of the chosen supplier is explored by having other suppliers bid for the business. If the chosen supplier is as or more efficient than the other suppliers, then the status quo is maintained. If one or more of the other suppliers turn out to be more efficient, then a new supplier is chosen.

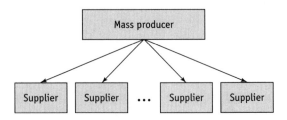

FIGURE 4–1. MASS PRODUCER SUPPLIER BASE FOR MAJOR FUNCTION

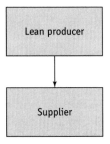

FIGURE 4–2. LEAN PRODUCER SUPPLIER BASE FOR MAJOR FUNCTION

produce the other components for the engine-cooling system (such as the condenser, fan, and electric motor), and Komatsu would assemble the final system. Under the new approach, however, Toyo was responsible for the entire engine-cooling system.

The decision to outsource group components and major functions leads to a tiered supplier structure (Figure 4–3). The direct or first-tier suppliers are responsible for the design and manufacture of the group components and major functions that are being outsourced by the end buyer. In turn, they identify second-tier suppliers for the components that they outsource. If the second-tier firms outsource to external suppliers, a third tier is created, and so on. The result of this approach is that each firm deals with a relatively small number of suppliers and that, overall, there are fewer suppliers. For example, the end buyer might identify 200 first-tier suppliers, and on average each first-tier supplier might recognize 30 second-tier suppliers, who in turn recognize five to 10 third-tier suppliers (see Figure 4–4). Typically, the size of the firm drops at

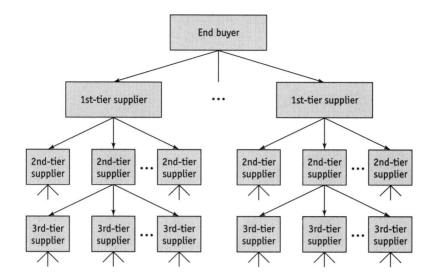

FIGURE 4-3. TIERED SUPPLIER STRUCTURE

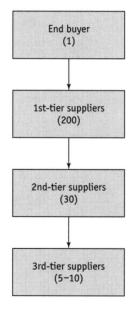

FIGURE 4-4. TYPICAL NUMBER OF RELATIONSHIPS IN A SUPPLY CHAIN

each tier. The firm at the top of the supply chain might employ thousands of people, while the average first-tier firm might have about 500 employees, the average second-tier firm about 100, and the average third-tier firm fewer than 10 employees.

One of the critical outcomes of outsourcing group components and major functions is that their research and development is also outsourced. Most mass producers design the major functions themselves and thus keep the design skills in-house, irrespective of where the components are produced. This method makes suppliers essentially interchangeable; their skills are in manufacturing, not design. In contrast, in a world of lean supply the suppliers have to develop their own design skills. While many of these design skills are common to all customers, some are idiosyncratic to individual buyers. To develop these skills and successfully design the group components and major functions requires that the buyer and supplier share considerable information about the underlying technologies that support the functionality of the outsourced items. Ultimately, the buyer ceases to have any expertise in the design of the parts and becomes totally dependent on its suppliers.

The suppliers, in turn, are highly dependent on their buyers. This dependency has two primary sources. First, the suppliers are themselves lean producers and therefore very sensitive to swings in production volume. Even a buyer that generates only a relatively small percentage of the supplier's total sales is important to the supplier, and so losing any customer is a serious event. This reality motivates the suppliers to try very hard to maintain their buyers' business. Second, it takes time to develop the necessarily rich relationship that exists between lean buyers and suppliers. Consequently, it is rarely possible to make up the loss of one customer immediately by replacing that customer with a new one. In Japan, the fact that many buyers take an equity position in their suppliers reinforces the dependency of the suppliers on the buyers.

The outcome of all these forces is interdependent buyer-supplier relations. Interdependence is critical because it ensures that neither party has an incentive to renege at any time. Interdependence motivates the buyers and suppliers to develop long-term relationships characterized by stability, cooperation, and mutual benefit. Mutual benefit occurs when each party depends on resources controlled by the other party, and both firms can gain by pooling their resources.

It is within the context of such relationships that interorganizational cost management can be applied successfully. However, not all suppliers are equally important and therefore a hierarchy of buyer-supplier relationships has evolved.

FOUR LEVELS OF BUYER-SUPPLIER RELATIONS

The level of a buyer-supplier relation is determined primarily by the degree of interaction between the design teams of the two firms. As that interaction becomes more sophisticated, closer relationships are required. The different levels of buyer-supplier relations represent the outcome of a cost/benefit trade-off. The greater the value that can be derived from the relationship, the more effort both sides are willing to invest in the relationship.

Four distinct levels of buyer-supplier relations can be identified: common suppliers, subcontractors, major suppliers, and family members (see Figure 4–5). This four-level categorization to a certain extent oversimplifies the complex relationships between buyers and suppliers that are observed in practice. Suppliers can interact with a given buyer in more than one way. For example, a supplier can act as a subcontractor for components for which only minor design

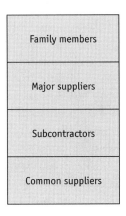

FIGURE 4–5. THE FOUR LEVELS OF BUYER-SUPPLIER RELATIONS

skills are required and as a major supplier for products that require considerable design skills. Such multi-category supplier behavior is especially common when the buyer is evolving its supplier relations toward the more sophisticated forms.

Common Suppliers

Common suppliers supply components that are commonly available and are purchased by many buyers. Examples include nuts and bolts and valve stems for automobile tires. Most of these standard components have established market prices, and other than negotiations to do with volume and delivery, the supplier's selling price is a given. If no market price exists, then the buyer will try to set the supplier's selling price.

The buyer's relationship with its common suppliers is the least sophisticated of all the supplier categories. Typically, common suppliers are viewed as interchangeable, and cost is often the deciding factor in the choice of supplier. Little or no interorganizational cost management involving product design is possible with such suppliers, though costs can be reduced by using techniques such as electronic data interchange (EDI) and auto-stocking.

The lack of sophisticated interorganizational cost management is an outcome of the fact that essentially no buyer-specific research and development skills are required on the part of this class of supplier. Therefore, the two firms can do little to reduce costs other than through negotiating minor changes in component specifications. None of the firms in the sample acted as common suppliers, though all the firms purchased goods from them.

Subcontractors

Subcontractors are brought into the process after the product has been designed. The buyer designs the components of the new product and then instructs the subcontractor to manufacture them. For example, for an engine cooling system the major components will be the radiator, the fan, the electric motor, the tubing, and the overflow bottle. The subcontractors' task is to manufacture these components to buyer specifications. Their design responsibility is limited to suggestions for minor improvements to the component design. As such, subcontractors have relatively little need to develop extensive research and development expertise. Often the components for a given major function are manufactured by different subcontracting firms and then assembled by the buyer.

The buyer's relationship with subcontractors is richer than that with common suppliers but still fairly unsophisticated. The buyer often will help the subcontractor to become more efficient by providing engineering and sometimes managerial support. Olympus Omachi and Kamakura acted primarily as subcontractors to Olympus Optical and Yokohama, respectively.

Major Suppliers

For major suppliers, the buyer provides high-level specifications and then requests the supplier to design the major function or subassembly. Major suppliers get involved in the design process after the product has been conceptualized but before its detailed design is established. For example, for an engine cooling system the buyer might specify the required cooling capacity of the system, the physical envelope in which it must fit, and the airflow through the engine compartment. It is then up to the supplier to design and manufacture the engine cooling system so that it provides the desired level of cooling while fitting inside the envelope.

The buyer's relationship with its major suppliers is much richer than with its common suppliers and subcontractors. Here, both the buyer and supplier have technological expertise in the design of the major function or subassembly. The engineers of the two firms interact on a regular basis and try to help each other become more efficient. They often work together to find ways to relax the specifications so that the major functions and subassemblies can be produced at an acceptable cost. Miyota and Yokohama acted as major suppliers to Citizen Watch and Tokyo Motors, respectively.

Family Members

Family members are responsible for completely designing and delivering a major function of the final product. They have the highest degree of autonomy and act almost as an integral part of the buyer's design team. Family members are full-service providers that have extensive research and development capabilities in their own right. They often develop new technological solutions independent of their customers in an attempt to gain a strategic advantage over their competitors. Family members typically are involved in the product development process from the very early stages—they can provide valuable assistance in designing the end product so that it takes full advantage of their technological expertise.

The buyer's relationships with its family members are the richest of all the supplier categories. It is with these suppliers that the greatest level of organizational blurring occurs. The two firms' engineers are in continuous contact and reinforce each others' design skills. Typically, the buyer and supplier jointly develop the specifications for the end product and, in particular, the major functions it contains. The supplier's superior knowledge of the design of the major functions allows it to find low-cost solutions that the buyer would otherwise miss. Komatsu considered Toyo Radiator a family member.

The interactions between the firms is somewhat richer than suggested by the above categorization of relationships. For example, major suppliers might also be subcontractors, and family members might also act as major suppliers. For example, Komatsu might order radiators from Toyo Radiator as well as entire engine cooling systems. In addition, first-tier suppliers can act as second- or third-tier suppliers to the same buyer. For example, Kamakura is both a first- and second-tier supplier to Tokyo Motors.

Once the appropriate level of buyer-supplier relations has been determined, the next step is to create the stable, cooperative, and mutually beneficial relationships necessary to support lean supply. The more important the supplier, the more attention needs to be paid to the nature of the buyer-supplier relation. For example, while common suppliers are viewed as somewhat interchangeable, family members are viewed as unique resources that have to be protected and nurtured.

THE NATURE OF
BUYER-SUPPLIER RELATIONS

The nature of buyer-supplier relations deals primarily with the creation of trust between buyers and suppliers. While interdependence is the glue that holds the relationship together, it is trust that enables the buyer and supplier to interact in sophisticated and mutually beneficial ways. Trust is the basis of interorganizational cost management, which reduces costs effectively while simultaneously increasing product functionality and quality (see Figure 4–6). Trust is created primarily through the stability of the buyer-supplier relationship and the high level of cooperation between the two firms.

Stability of the Relationship

All firms in the sample maintain stable relationships with their suppliers for four major reasons (see Figure 4–7). First, both sides believe that it takes time to develop a mature, trusting relationship. Second, stable relationships help ensure that goal congruence is achieved. Third, stability increases the willingness of both sides to make mutually beneficial investments. Finally, the knowledge that each firm has about the other makes it possible to coordinate interorganizational activities more efficiently.

Trust can be developed and maintained only when both parties support the relationship over an extended period of time. In particular, the relationship will be tested when economic conditions change and, to avoid economic distress, one party must act in ways that are detrimental to the other. For example, if demand drops, does the buyer take the supplier's work in-house or does it maintain the relationship? Only by interacting over an extended period of time so that a range of economic conditions has been experienced

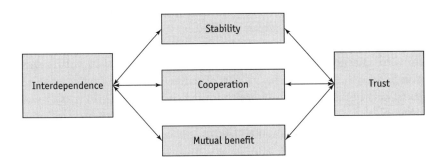

FIGURE 4–6. NATURE OF BUYER-SUPPLIER RELATIONS

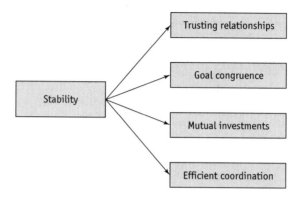

FIGURE 4-7. ROLE OF STABILITY IN BUYER-SUPPLIER RELATIONS

and by developing a history of positive interactions will the two firms know that they can trust each other. In addition, each party must demonstrate that they will not take advantage of the information shared by the other. In an interorganizational cost investigation all the firms involved know one another's costs. If the most powerful of the firms used this information to its sole advantage, then the willingness of the other firms to initiate a cost investigation would disappear, and the ability of the supply chain to remain competitive would be compromised.

A second benefit of stable relationships is that the firms' goals become congruent. When the buyer-supplier relationship is expected to be unstable, with sales volumes between the two firms changing dramatically from year to year, the best strategy for both firms usually is to maximize their own well-being, even if this objective is achieved at the expense of the other. However, when the relationship is expected to be stable, then both parties are better off acting in ways that are mutually beneficial. For example, the supplier might accept a loss now to enable the buyer to achieve its target cost, in return for anticipated future profits. Such a sacrifice does not make sense in short-term relationships where there is no guarantee of future business. Hence, it is more natural to develop goal congruence in long-term relationships than in short-term ones.

A third benefit from establishing stable buyer-supplier relations lies in the willingness of both parties to invest in specific assets for each other. One way Toyota supports its suppliers is to help them adopt the Toyota Production System, which contains four key elements: just-in-time production, kanban, total quality management, and multifunctional work teams. It takes considerable resources on Toyota's part to educate suppliers in this manner. The benefit to the suppliers is an increase in efficiency. The benefits to Toyota include lower overall costs and greater coordination inside the supply chain. Similarly, lean suppliers invest in their relationship with buyers by developing technical skills and production processes that are idiosyncratic to a given buyer. For example, if a particular customer requires very high surface tolerances, then the supplier will develop that expertise if the customer is considered sufficiently important.

A fourth benefit of stable buyer-supplier relations lies in the increased efficiency that results from the prior experience the two firms have in dealing with each other. They do not have to keep going down the initial portion of the interaction learning curve. For example, the chief engineer at the buyer knows which engineers to contact in the supplier to discuss problems; there is no need to call around until the right person is found. In addition, the buyer has considerable knowledge of the supplier's product development process, as does the supplier about the buyer's. This knowledge helps the two firms efficiently coordinate their development processes. This efficient coordination is especially valuable for major suppliers and family members. These long-standing personal relationships have another benefit; they are the backbone of intercompany trust.

There is a potential drawback to maintaining long-term buyer-supplier relationships, which centers on a lack of stimulation between the two firms as the relationship matures. Once the two firms have been interacting for an extended period of time, the product engineers at each firm might cease to suggest ideas that are new to the engineers from the other firm as each side already knows the other's perspective. Changing suppliers would introduce new engineers and, potentially, new ideas. Thus, a delicate balance has to be maintained in buyer-supplier relations. On one hand, there are great advantages to maintaining stability, but on the other hand, there are benefits from creating cooperative relationships with new suppliers who can become a source of innovative technologies and ideas.

Within the constraint of stability, some of the firms have developed mechanisms to ensure that stability does not lead to stagnation. For example, the Parts Design Department at Tokyo Motors is highly supportive of Yokohama. The engineers in that department want to maintain good relations with Yokohama and are more accommodating about price and functionality than other Tokyo departments such as Purchasing. Occasionally, Purchasing will intervene in the negotiations between Yokohama and the Parts Design Department and cause the contract to go to a competitor with a lower bid. Thus, the Parts Design Department from time to time disciplines the buyer-supplier relationships by destabilizing them. This destabilization reduces the supplier's confidence of always winning the bid.

Great care has to be taken with these disciplining actions to ensure that they do not shatter the trust between the buyer and supplier. If the relationship between the buyer and supplier becomes too unstable, excess resources will be consumed as each side tries to monitor the other's behavior. For example, the buyer might be forced to expend considerable effort to ensure that the supplier's products meet specifications because the supplier is taking a short-term view on maintaining the relationship. Similarly, the supplier might be forced to expend additional resources trying to ensure that its business with the buyer continues.

Cooperative Relationships

Unlike the conventional Western model of buyer-supplier relations, which is essentially adversarial in nature, the Japanese firms in the sample maintain highly cooperative relations with their suppliers, particularly their major suppliers and family members. Cooperative relationships are at the heart of Japanese buyer-supplier relations because they enable the two sides to work together to reduce costs and solve design problems (see Figure 4–8). All the interorganizational cost management techniques described in this volume rely heavily on cooperative relationships between the buyer and supplier. For example, target costing could be used to create excessive cost-reduction pressures on suppliers, risking to transfer all the supplier's profits to the buyer. However, in a world of lean supply the buyers moderate the cost-reduction pressures placed on the suppliers so that they make adequate returns over the long haul. If the target costs are too onerous, the buyers will relax them, even if only temporarily. For example, most of Yokohama's customers will not agree

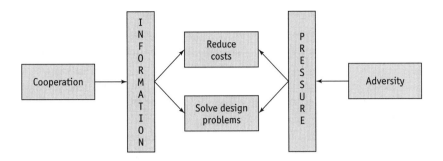

FIGURE 4–8. ROLE OF COOPERATION AND ADVERSITY IN BUYER-
SUPPLIER RELATIONS

to long-term changes to target prices. However, they will sometimes allow the price to rise above the target for the first few years after introduction to allow Yokohama time to find ways to reduce costs sufficiently to make an acceptable return at the target cost. This relaxation is necessary for the suppliers to be able to survive in the long run and be willing to accept the intense cost-reduction pressures placed on them by the buyers.

Achieving Mutual Benefits

The third cornerstone of a lean buyer-supplier relationship lies in the mutual benefits for both parties. The relationship can be characterized as operating in a win-win mode. Suppliers' benefits include increased market share, the ability to sell higher-value-added products and hence make higher profits, and increased access to the buyer's technology. For example, the decision to introduce finished products at Kamakura was driven by three factors. Kamakura's customers wanted to reduce their logistics costs by decreasing the number of layers in their supply chains. Shifting to firms that both forged and finished parts was considered advantageous because it meant that only one firm was responsible for processing finished parts. In addition, the decision allowed Kamakura to gain a better understanding of post-forging processing, so it could design forgings that were easier and more efficient for the buyer to finish. Finally, it gave Kamakura better access to new finishing technologies that would allow it to increase its value-added ratio.

A lean buyer-supplier relationship gives the buyer several advantages. It allows the buyer to outsource the design and manufacture of significant value-added portions of its products that do not rely on core competencies. Second, the external suppliers often can achieve greater economies of scale than the firm by selling its products to other customers. These economies of scale are reflected in the lower selling prices of the supplier. Third, the external suppliers are often better at designing and producing the outsourced item than the buyer. Finally, the level of innovation and cost savings that can be achieved is increased because of the greater number of people dedicated to finding new solutions.

There is a potential dark side to the adoption of lean supply. As the buyer-supplier relationship becomes stronger, a risk emerges that one of the firms will become too powerful and will extract an unfair proportion of the profits. To avoid this outcome both buyers and suppliers take actions to reduce the power of the other. The buyer reduces the power of suppliers by multi-sourcing, and the supplier reduces the power of buyers by ensuring that no single buyer represents an excessive share of the business.

Reducing the Power of Suppliers

Buyers can significantly reduce the power of suppliers by adopting a single-sourcing/multi-sourcing strategy. Under this strategy, several suppliers are invited to bid on each component (see Figure 4–9). Unless the component is to be produced in very large volumes, only a single supplier will be awarded the contract for each component. However, any family of parts will have several suppliers, each producing multiple components but being the sole source for those components. This approach to multi-sourcing takes advantage of both the reduced power of the supplier and of the benefits of single sourcing. For each component, economies of scale are achieved, but no single supplier gains excessive power. For example, at Isuzu for some components three suppliers are contacted and asked to develop prototypes. The suppliers are told the target quality, functionality, and price of the component and are expected to produce prototypes that satisfy all three requirements. Once the three prototypes are submitted, Isuzu engineers analyze them to determine which one provides the best value. The product with the highest

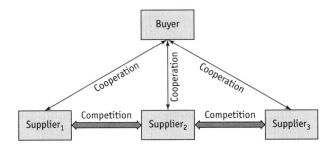

FIGURE 4–9. REDUCING THE POWER OF SUPPLIERS BY MULTI-
SOURCING COMPONENT FAMILIES

perceived value is selected, and the component's supplier usually is awarded the total contract. The primary benefit of this "maximize value" approach is that it brings out the strengths of each supplier.

An additional advantage of this approach to multi-sourcing is that it creates supplier-based competition. All the suppliers are aware that they have to compete against a number of competitors and that the highest-value supplier usually will win the bid. This supplier-versus-supplier competition creates intense pressure on the suppliers to innovate and reduce costs. For example, Yokohama competes by finding new ways to add value to its products, thus making them superior to those of its competitors. The multi-sourcing makes this competition more intense.

The award of a contract for 50% or 100% of the volume to a particular supplier for a multi-year period might be seen as reducing the level of competition between suppliers because that one supplier is now isolated from competitive pressures at least temporarily by the size of the award. A lessening of competition does not occur, however, as the buyer is continuously developing new products and is therefore continuously placing orders for parts. The single-sourcing/multi-sourcing strategy coupled with continuous new-product development means that suppliers are always bidding on new contracts and therefore are always under pressure to become more efficient through innovation.

The supplier-versus-supplier competition has to be kept at appropriate levels so that the long-term viability of all the suppliers is maintained. The buyer achieves this objective by ensuring that every supplier wins at least some of the business for its component family. This buffering strategy ensures that all the suppliers are able to compete for future business. Only if a supplier really fails to remain competitive over an extended period of time will it fail to win any bids. For example, at Isuzu, although the supplier rated as having the highest value generally wins the order, firms that have a reputation for being good suppliers often are awarded at least some part orders, even if their products do not have the highest value. Examples of such companies include Yuasa for batteries, Toyo Valve for valves, and Nihon Seiko for bearings. These firms are awarded contracts for at least some of the components for the new product to maintain their relationship with Isuzu. The disadvantage of sourcing parts families from multiple suppliers is a reduced ability to take advantage of any economies of scope across the family. These lost economies of scope are offset by the enhanced creativity of highly competitive suppliers.

Reducing the Power of Buyers

Suppliers can use two mechanisms to decrease the power of their buyers. The first is to diversify their customer base so that no single buyer represents an excessive portion of their business (see Figure 4–10). Early in its history, Taiyo Kogyo purposely set out to gain the ability to sell to multiple firms in the electronics industry. The motivation behind this strategy was to "escape from the endless cycle of reward and punishment that the Japanese subcontractor was forced to endure."

The second mechanism to reduce buyer power is to introduce a rule against selling unprofitable products. For example, one of Yokohama management's objectives is to create a corporate culture that enables them to say "no" when they cannot find a way to make a product profitably. They are trying to instill the same culture at Kamakura to help protect that firm from excessive buyer pressure. Yokohama's management believes that developing such a culture is critical to their (Yokohama's and Kamakura's) survival, as it ensures that they do not become a slave to their customers. Yokohama is able to say no because it deals with a sufficiently large number of customers that losing a single order from any one of them does not place the firm at significant risk.

The ability to say no is critical for the survival of most suppliers as the buyers place intense pressure on them to reduce costs.

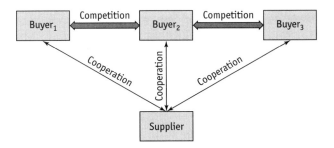

FIGURE 4-10. REDUCING THE POWER OF BUYERS BY EXTENDING THE
CUSTOMER BASE

This pressure is necessary because neither side benefits if the pressure on suppliers to reduce costs becomes less than that demanded by the end market. The buyer must push the suppliers as hard as possible to reduce selling prices. The suppliers' task is to find ways to reduce costs and also to push back if placed under too much pressure. Consequently, the negotiations between buyers and suppliers are aggressive and should not be viewed as amicable discussions on how the overall profits are to be shared.

Furthermore, mutual benefit does not imply equitable sharing of profits. The more powerful firms, be they buyers or suppliers, will extract most of the profits. However, these firms have to be careful to ensure that the weaker firms still perceive that they benefit from the overall interactions. When the dominant firms are under considerable pressure to achieve profitability, they have to balance the principle of mutual benefit and predatory behavior. The dominant firms can, within limits, abuse their power in bad times and extract all or nearly all profits from the supply chain. However, they do so at the risk of destroying the fundamental trust that underlies lean buyer-supplier relationships.

TAKING ADVANTAGE OF
LEAN BUYER-SUPPLIER RELATIONSHIPS

Once a stable, cooperative, mutually beneficial relationship has been established, the next step for the buyer and supplier is to take advantage of that relationship. The firms can benefit from the relationship because organizational boundaries are blurred, information sharing increases, and the level of innovation rises (see Figure 4–11).

Blurring of Organizational Boundaries

As stable, cooperative buyer-supplier relationships are being developed, the boundaries between the buyer and supplier begin to blur. In particular, three practices make it difficult to define where one firm's responsibilities begin and the other's end (see Figure 4–12). These practices are employee sharing, research and development sharing, and making dedicated investments specifically designed to benefit the other firm.

Employee Sharing[2]

Employee sharing can be used in several ways to strengthen the effectiveness of buyer-supplier relations (see Figure 4-13). One way is for middle managers at the buyer to be transferred either temporarily or permanently into senior management positions at the supplier. Temporary assignments of this kind are motivated by the desire to increase the managerial skills of the supplier. Permanent assignments are motivated in addition by the desire to remove older managers from the buyer's promotion path. These transfers are more common when the buyer has an equity position in the supplier.

The next type of employee sharing occurs when engineers from the supplier are seconded temporarily to the buyer. These engineers are known as resident or guest engineers. For example, at Toyo guest engineers are design engineers who work at Komatsu for two days every two weeks. Typically, during these visits joint technical design meetings are held. Guest engineers are assigned for three years at a time. This period is dictated by Komatsu's three-year design cycle. The engineers become members of a multifunctional design team and stay on that team from the start of the project until the product is released for manufacturing. A similar program often involves manufacturing engineers, but here the secondment is usually shorter, often

---

2 See P. Hines, *Creating World Class Suppliers,* London: Pitman Publishing, 1994, pp. 154–156.

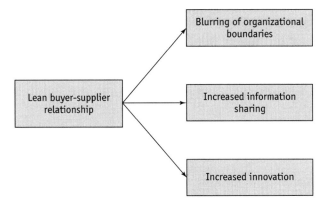

FIGURE 4–11. MAJOR CHARACTERISTICS OF LEAN BUYER-SUPPLIER
RELATIONSHIPS

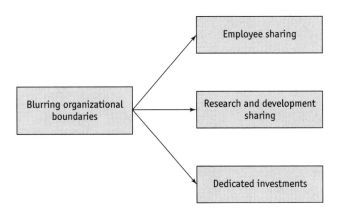

FIGURE 4–12. BLURRING ORGANIZATIONAL BOUNDARIES IN LEAN
BUYER-SUPPLIER RELATIONSHIPS

about a year. This shorter assignment period reflects the nature of the tasks these engineers undertake, which include rapidly communicating any problems in the assembly process that the buyer encounters with the supplier's products. These engineers also help identify kaizen improvements or better designs for manufacturability. These design improvements typically are incorporated into the next generation of the supplier's products, not the current one because there is often insufficient time before the new model is introduced.

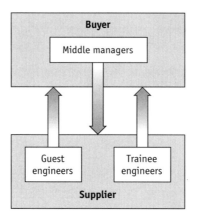

FIGURE 4-13. EMPLOYEE SHARING IN LEAN BUYER-SUPPLIER RELATIONSHIPS

A third type of employee sharing occurs when the buyer is help-ing to train a supplier's engineers. If the training program is expected to take several months or even years, young engineers from the sup-plier are often transferred to the buyer. The primary benefit to the supplier lies in the increased experience and managerial skills of the engineers when they return. The buyer also benefits because such engineers develop rich networks of contacts within the buyer orga-nization and better understand the buyer's products and processes. These contacts help cement the buyer-supplier relationship.

These various employee-sharing schemes are all designed to strengthen the buyer-supplier relationship and make it more effec-tive. Such sharing has important implications for interorganiza-tional cost management systems because it increases the knowledge that the engineers at each firm have about the manufacturing eco-nomics and policies of the other. This increased knowledge allows the establishment of better cost-reduction objectives and more meaningful price negotiations between buyers and suppliers.

Research and Development Sharing

A second type of organizational blurring occurs when the buyer and the supplier share research and development activities. Such sharing underlies two powerful interorganizational cost management techniques—parallel and simultaneous engineering. Under simultaneous engineering considerable interaction between the buyer and supplier design groups is necessary. For example, when the supplier's design team wants to make alterations to the design of their major function that have significant implications for the end product, the two teams must jointly analyze the implications of the suggested change.

Outsourcing research and development for a major function again requires considerable interaction between the two design groups. Initially, the supplier has relatively little knowledge about the buyer-specific research and development requirements while the buyer has considerable skill. The buyer must transfer those skills to the supplier. For example, Komatsu test engineers are often asked to visit Toyo to explain how Komatsu's test procedures and evaluation criteria operate. No Komatsu personnel are specifically assigned to Toyo, so they are not viewed as guest engineers. Instead, Komatsu engineers visit Toyo when there are specific design issues to discuss. The purpose of their visits is to reduce the probability that Komatsu will not approve a solution that Toyo feels is acceptable. In the process of these meetings considerable engine cooling system proto-typing skills are transferred to Toyo. These transferred skills play an important role in reducing costs and creating competitive advantages for both buyer and supplier. For example, Toyo can test the cooling capacity of its prototypes before submitting them to Komatsu. This earlier testing enables problems to be resolved in a more timely fashion at lower cost, thus giving Komatsu both a time-to-market and cost advantage.

Dedicated Investments

Within the context of their stable relationships, both the buyer and supplier frequently make significant dedicated investments for the other's benefit. These investments often have implications for the application of interorganizational cost management techniques. For example, target costing assumes the ability to set arm's-length selling prices. However, if either party has made significant dedicated investments, an arm's-length approach may be inappropriate. To maintain the relationship it may be necessary for the buyer to sus-pend the target costing system until the supplier has learned to manufacture the product at an acceptably low cost. For example, when Yokohama is heavily involved (i.e., has made significant investments) in the design process and in the scheduling of the product, the customer is often forced to accept a higher price that provides Yokohama with an adequate return. However, even under these conditions, only a temporary reprieve is given. In the long run, Yokohama is expected to sell the product to the customer at the target price. Similarly, Isuzu often makes investments in its suppliers to enable them to produce the advanced components required for the next generation of products. Again, such investments limit the applicability of arm's-length target costing, although again, any reprieve is temporary in nature.

Increased Levels of Information Sharing

Despite being separate firms, the amount of cost and other information shared between the firms is significant (see Figure 4-14). This information sharing is critical to the success of interorganizational cost management techniques, especially interorganizational cost investigations and concurrent cost management. Many of the buyers and suppliers have "open-book" or partial open-book policies. For example, Yokohama and Kamakura have a full open-book policy. Kamakura provides Yokohama with a complete breakdown of its costs including the profit it expects to make on the part. In contrast, Komatsu and Toyo Radiator have a partial open-book policy. Komatsu has access to all of Toyo's cost information regarding purchases for Komatsu-related products, even to the level of knowing the price that Toyo paid for a single bolt used in a part that went into a Komatsu product. However, it does not have access to Toyo's production costs. The objective of this sharing of purchasing cost information is to allow Komatsu to find new ways to reduce costs through sourcing of Toyo's inputs. For example, it might increase cost savings by purchasing the bolt centrally and have the bolt's manufacturer deliver shipments directly to all users of that bolt in the Komatsu group and its family of major suppliers.

Not all firms believe that open-book policies are beneficial under all circumstances. For example, Miyota, despite being a wholly owned subsidiary, retains a high degree of autonomy from Citizen and acts more like an independent supplier. Unlike many of

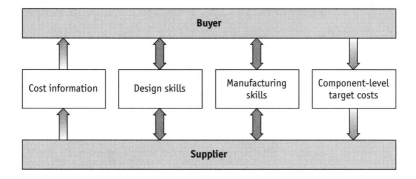

FIGURE 4-14. INFORMATION SHARING IN LEAN BUYER-SUPPLIER
         RELATIONSHIPS

the subsidiaries of other companies in Japan, it does not share detailed cost information with its parent. All prices and other contractual relations with Citizen are negotiated at arm's length. The negotiations between Miyota and Citizen are perceived by both sides as tough but cooperative. Given Miyota's high level of autonomy, Miyota management views the negotiations between the two firms as critical to the success of their firm. As Kazuo Tanaka, the president of Miyota, describes it:

> Citizen derives great advantage from treating each subsidiary as an independent company even though they are wholly owned. Treating them as independent companies puts teeth into the negotiations. If Miyota was totally controlled by Citizen, I would be very disappointed and would have little incentive to work hard. As president of Miyota I want to set my own target costs and profits as well as contributing to Citizen. I call the relationship between Citizen and Miyota supportive autonomy. I can call on Citizen for help but if I do a good job, they leave me alone. This freedom creates a stimulating environment for Miyota. We have to find our own ways to achieve our objectives.

Thus, like cooperation and adversariness, cost information sharing has both its pros and cons. The main risk with the open-book policy appears to be that the supplier will abrogate responsibility for continuous improvement to the buyer: "They know our costs and can therefore make the right decisions." Yokohama believes that a total open-book policy with Kamakura is beneficial. In contrast, Komatsu believes that an open-book policy for input costs (but not its supplier's process costs) is the right approach. Citizen on the other hand believes that creating as much arm's-length pressure as possible is beneficial. The degree to which cost information is shared reflects both the beliefs of the buyer and supplier about the benefits of open-book policies and their relative strength in the relationship. Kamakura and Miyota have no choice but to adopt the information-sharing policies of their customers.

It is not only cost information that is shared between the firms, it is also know-how. The buyer's engineers will often visit suppliers and make suggestions on how they can improve their production processes. For example, the cost-reduction program for watch movements at Citizen encompasses the entire production chain, including subsidiaries and outside suppliers. Corporate technical staff provides engineering support to help the subsidiaries and outside suppliers find ways to become more efficient. The technical staff visits the subsidiaries and outside suppliers to observe their production processes and make suggestions on how they might be improved.

Information sharing occurs in both directions. The supplier also provides the buyer with specialty know-how when appropriate. Because Yokohama has identified Kamakura as a superior supplier, Kamakura employees are invited to give a presentation on their value engineering techniques. Kamakura holds technical exchange meetings with its customers four or five times a month. Most of its customers, including Yokohama, are not knowledgeable about forging technology. Kamakura often gets involved in the design process by requesting functional specifications from customers and then working with their engineers to design the appropriate part.

This rich sharing of information can occur only in an environment of cooperation and trust. It is critical to the success of interorganizational cost management. Without the shared information the firms would have less ability to reduce costs by taking actions such as rationalizing input supply across the supplier family and designing end products so that they take full advantage of the manufacturing and design skills of the firms in the supplier network.

Increased Level of Innovation

For the buyer-supplier relationship to be truly successful, the level of innovation it engenders has to be as high as possible. Many buyers help foster supplier innovation by rewarding their most innovative suppliers with significant orders. Isuzu's treatment of its suppliers illustrates this process. Once it receives the prototypes from the three suppliers previously identified, Isuzu engineers analyze the prototypes to determine which one provides the best value. The product with the highest perceived value is selected, and the component's supplier typically is awarded the total contract. This award both rewards innovation and signals to the suppliers (both successful and rejected) the importance that Isuzu attaches to innovation. Nissan has a similar program; the most innovative supplier will be awarded a significant percentage of the contract for a specified time period, say 50% for 12 months.

It is within lean relationships that buyers and suppliers can successfully undertake interorganizational cost management. The level and nature of the buyer-supplier relationship and the ways that the two firms have taken advantage of that relationship shape the process of interorganizational cost management.

IMPLICATIONS FOR INTERORGANIZATIONAL COST MANAGEMENT

The way that costs are managed across the buyer-supplier interface is highly dependent on the level of supplier (see Figure 4–15). For common suppliers, only minimal cost management is undertaken. The buyer simply has to choose the lowest total cost provider for the component from among the available suppliers. Total cost is more than just purchasing price; it includes quality, timeliness, and other factors that can increase the buyer's costs. The way the buyer and this category of suppliers interact is based primarily on target costing, with the buyer's target costing system identifying the price the firm is willing to pay for the supplied part (for a more detailed description, see Chapters 7 and 8).

For subcontractors, the focus of cost management is on finding ways to relax the buyer's specifications so that the product can be manufactured at a lower cost. Frequently, both the buyer and supplier have target costing systems and they operate together to reduce costs. The way the buyer and this category of suppliers develop innovative, low-cost product designs is described in Chapter 9 on chained target costing and functionality-price-quality trade-offs.

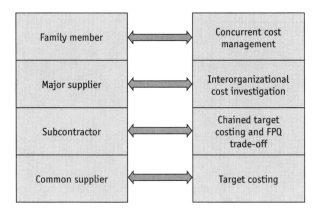

FIGURE 4-15. MOST SOPHISTICATED INTERORGANIZATIONAL COST
MANAGEMENT TECHNIQUE OBSERVED AT EACH TYPE
OF SUPPLIER

For major suppliers, the interactions enable costs to be reduced by redesigning the major function and, when necessary, the end product. Such redesigns require more sophisticated interactions between the buyer's and supplier's design teams than can be achieved through the functionality-price-quality trade-offs that support chained target costing. The way the buyer and this category of suppliers develop low-cost product designs is described in Chapter 10 on interorganizational cost investigations.

Finally, the interactions with family members start at the earliest stages of the product development process. The buyer's and supplier's engineers work together to design the product and the major functions it contains. Only a limited number of firms are viewed by any buyer as being in this category. For example, Komatsu sees Toyo as part of a cooperative group that consists of Komatsu and a few dozen specially chosen suppliers. It is only within this tight group that cost information sharing is high. Suppliers outside the group are treated more conventionally. The process of cost management between buyers and family members is captured in Chapter 11 on concurrent cost management.

The way costs are managed across the buyer-supplier interface also depends on the nature of the relationship. The most sophisticated of the interorganizational cost management techniques, such as interorganizational cost investigations and concurrent cost management, can be undertaken effectively only when buyer-supplier relations are based on mutual trust and goal congruence. The other interorganizational cost management techniques, target costing and chained target costing, are less demanding but also benefit from cooperative buyer-supplier relations when some modifications to the part specifications are required.

All the interorganizational cost management techniques are more effective when the buyer-supplier relationship is predominantly cooperative in nature, with the two design teams working together to achieve the cost-reduction objectives established by the buyer's target costing system. However, sufficient pressure must always be exerted on suppliers to keep them innovative and focused on cost reduction.

As buyers and suppliers begin to blur their organizational boundaries, interorganizational cost management becomes more feasible. First, the sharing of employees enhances both the richness of the relationship and the joint knowledge of production economics. It provides an adequate background against which constructive buyer-supplier negotiations can be undertaken. These negotiations play a critical role in the process of setting target costs. For target costing to be effective, the component-level target costs must be achievable if the suppliers expend considerable effort to achieve them. If the target costing process at the buyer results in component-level target costs that are always considered unachievable by the suppliers, they will be ignored and target costing will lose its interorganizational effectiveness.

Lean enterprises derive much of their efficiency from integrating horizontally, not vertically. As firms become leaner, they must transfer research and development responsibilities to their suppliers. This sharing of research and development makes two powerful interorganizational cost management techniques possible: parallel and simultaneous engineering. The use of these techniques requires the design teams of the two firms to work together to find innovative solutions that improve the functionality of the end product and at the same time reduce costs.

Finally, dedicated investments render at least one interorganizational cost management technique, target costing, less effective because the buyer is less willing (at least temporarily) to discipline the supplier by using arm's-length prices. Cost-reduction pressures must be applied intelligently, and at times it is better to relax them for the sake of future benefits. Target costing adopts a relatively narrow this-product-this-generation view that sometimes has to be adapted to fit circumstances.

All the interorganizational cost management techniques, and in particular interorganizational cost investigations and concurrent cost management, require extensive information sharing between the buyer and supplier. Such information sharing requires high levels of trust between the firms. The buyer must reveal its product strategy to the supplier, and the supplier must share proprietary technology with the buyer. Only stable relationships, in which both parties' behavior is governed by norms of acceptable behavior, will induce the desired level of information sharing. Interorganizational cost management is most effective when the two firms choose to work for each other's benefit.

CONCLUSION

At the heart of interorganizational cost management are sophisticated buyer-supplier relationships designed to enable both firms to be as efficient as possible. Buyers can choose from a range of supplier relations that depend primarily on the degree of design autonomy of the supplier. For a few select firms, the so-called family members, the design process is concurrent, with both the buyer's and supplier's design teams having significant input into the design of the end product and its major functions. At the other end of the range are common suppliers from whom standard parts are purchased. These suppliers are asked to bid competitively for the order.

The buyer and supplier are expected to work for each other's mutual benefit. Neither is expected to take excessive advantage of the other and extract all the profits. Typically, the buyer-supplier relationships studied were mature and expected to be stable. Extended buyer-supplier relations are necessary if the two firms are to develop the necessary level of trust and goal congruence so that they work for each other's benefit.

A steady increase in the sophistication of the buyer-supplier relations leads naturally to a reduction in the number of suppliers. As the supplier base decreases, the individual buyer-supplier relations become more important to both firms. This increased importance makes maintaining an adequate power balance critical to the success of the relationship. Both sides have developed strategies to keep the balance of power at reasonable levels. The buyers achieve this objective by single-sourcing/multi-sourcing components. The suppliers reduce buyer power by diversifying their customer base and developing the ability to reject unprofitable orders.

Once a stable, cooperative, and mutually beneficial environment has been created, the two firms can take advantage of the relationship. The boundaries between the firms begin to blur. The buyer and supplier are willing to share proprietary information with each other about their products and production processes. Finally, as part of the process to develop effective buyer-supplier relations and stimulate supplier creativity, some buyers develop incentive plans that reward supplier innovation.

All these aspects of the buyer-supplier relationship are designed to increase the effectiveness and efficiency of the relationship. It is within the context of these rich, stable, and highly cooperative relationships that interorganizational cost management systems thrive. However, simply taking a narrow buyer-supplier perspective is not sufficient. Competitive markets based on lean supplier relationships can be described as undertaking network sourcing. In network sourcing, the interactions between multiple buyers and multiple suppliers, not just a single buyer and supplier, create a broader perspective that shapes the interorganizational cost management process.

CHAPTER 5

LEAN SUPPLIER NETWORKS[1]

INTRODUCTION

The emergence of lean supply is the first step in the larger process of creating a lean supplier network. The high degree of outsourcing that characterizes lean enterprises means that each firm in a supply chain is responsible for only a small percentage of the total value-added of a product. To achieve the full advantages of lean design and production, all the firms in the supply chain have to adopt lean buyer-supplier relations. However, when they do, the whole turns out to be larger than the sum of the parts because the individual lean supply chains form a network of suppliers. These lean supplier networks function in many respects as a single entity dedicated to producing low-cost products that have the high functionality and quality the end customers demand. The primary advantages of these networks are their flexibility and responsiveness compared to vertically integrated mass producers.

---

[1] The author of Chapter 5 is Kathleen Gumbleton.

At the heart of lean supply lies cooperation. This cooperation extends throughout the supplier network with all of the firms operating for the good of the network. Frequently, tight linkage of buyers and suppliers creates a geographic concentration of regional producers, where firms are dependent on cooperative relations to achieve collective efficiencies. Cooperation within this context does not lead to price cartels or other forms of monopolistic practice, which attempt to limit competition. Rather, cooperation is carried out within a context of increased competition where firms find it advantageous to pool resources and share risks in the development of collective competitive advantages. If firms within a network wish to become more efficient through a decentralized production strategy, they must find ways to lower transaction costs in the pursuit of common strategic objectives.

Sourcing from a lean supplier network provides three major advantages (see Figure 5–1). The first, *product linkages,* deals with the enhanced ability of the core firms to access new technologies and other innovations and incorporate them rapidly into their products. The second, *knowledge linkages,* deals with the enhanced access to embedded knowledge within the network. Embedded knowledge is difficult to transfer outside of learning by doing; therefore finding ways to access it efficiently creates an important competitive advantage. Finally, *process linkages* deal with the way the network can become more efficient by cooperatively focusing on

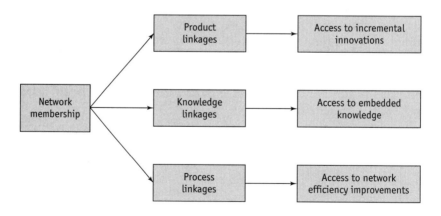

FIGURE 5–1. ADVANTAGES OF NETWORK MEMBERSHIP

ways to reduce costs. While some of this efficiency comes naturally through the adoption of lean thinking, much of it is achieved by applying interorganizational cost management.

Networks that shape the environment for interorganizational cost management have two major aspects: the type of network and the existence of network protocols. The type of network is important because it shapes the power balance between buyers and suppliers. Network protocols are critical because they moderate the behavior of all the firms in the network to ensure that buyer-supplier relationships retain the characteristics of lean supply. Once such a network has been created, the firms must learn to take advantage of it so that they can become more efficient. It is the existence of a disciplined, lean supplier network that enables costs to be managed in a coordinated manner across the entire network.

Types of Networks

The primary determinant of the type of supplier network is the number of core firms that dominate the network (see Figure 5–2). The first type of network, a "kingdom," emerges when a single firm adopts the core position. Typically, this is the firm that sells the end product to the ultimate customer. These networks operate to support the central firm that dominates the entire network. The second type of network, a "barony," emerges when several firms adopt the core position. Here the barons dominate the other firms, but their power is significantly reduced compared to the core firm in a kingdom. Finally, the third type of network, a "republic," emerges when there is no core firm. Here, none of the firms has any significant power over the others. Thus, one of the primary differentiators of network type is the level of power that the core firm or firms have over the other members of the network (see Figure 5–3).

Type of network	Kingdom	Barony	Republic
Number of core firms	One	Several	None

FIGURE 5–2. TYPE OF NETWORK AND THE NUMBER OF CORE FIRMS

Type of network	Kingdom	Barony	Republic
Number of core firms	One	Several	None
Contracting power	High	Medium	Low

FIGURE 5-3. TYPE OF NETWORK AND CONTRACTING POWER

These three arrangements for the coordination of production represent the complete spectrum of networking arrangements. While hybrid forms can exist, they typically occur during transitional times, for example, when a kingdom is transforming into a barony. The type of network that evolves is driven primarily by the economics of the industry and, in particular, whether competitive advantage can be gained through economies of scale (kingdoms), scope (republics), or a mixture of the two (baronies) (see Figure 5–4).

To enable the network to maximize its advantages, protocols that govern individual firm behavior must be created and enforced. Network protocols or rules of conduct extend the behavior patterns developed between individual buyers and suppliers to the level of the network as a whole. They represent common values and shared behaviors. These protocols are designed to mitigate negative repercussions from excessive competition and to encourage the necessary cooperation where coordination of activities across the boundaries of firms is required. This coordination can be horizontal or vertical in nature. For example, the adoption of standards such as IS9000 provides horizontal coordination, while target costing systems provide vertical coordination. Network protocols are operative throughout any lean supplier network. However, the way in which

Type of network	Kingdom	Barony	Republic
Number of core firms	One	Several	None
Contracting power	High	Medium	Low
Network objective	Economies of scale	Economies of scale and scope	Economies of scope

FIGURE 5-4. TYPE OF NETWORK AND NETWORK OBJECTIVE

these protocols are established and enforced differs across the three network types (see Figure 5–5). In a kingdom the protocols are developed top-down and enforced by the core firm. In a barony they are negotiated, with the barons dominating the process. Finally, in a republic the protocols are developed by mutual agreement. Network protocols play an important role in ensuring that stable patterns of inter-firm collaboration are maintained, without sacrificing the benefits from competition between firms in the network.

Kingdom Networks: A Single Core Firm

In a kingdom a single firm, the king, dominates the network because it generates a disproportionately high share of the total demand for the goods and services produced by the other firms in the network. Kingdoms are typically capital intensive and rely heavily on economies of scale to be efficient. Firms that control the strategic assets required to produce the final product, such as capital-intensive manufacturing equipment, technology-intensive components, and system-integration capabilities, will act as dominant volume producers within the industry. When such a firm either stimulates the development of or grows up in a regional cluster of highly specialized suppliers, it is in a dominant position to take advantage of external economies of scale.

External economies of scale are achieved through the purchase of inputs that are available at a higher quality and/or lower cost from specialized niche producers compared to those that can be produced by an internal division. In a highly competitive environ-

Type of network	Kingdom	Barony	Republic
Number of core firms	One	Several	None
Contracting power	High	Medium	Low
Network objective	Economies of scale	Economies of scale and scope	Economies of scope
Network protocols	Top-down enforced	Enforced by suppliers	Mutual agreement

FIGURE 5–5. TYPE OF NETWORK AND NETWORK PROTOCOLS

ment with a limited number of final producers, external economies of scale provide the king with efficiency advantages that are critical in the development of products that meet customer requirements at an acceptable price. Achieving economies of scale through a network of suppliers leads to efficiency advantages at the core firm that exceed those attainable when acting independently.

As the external competitive environment faced by the king becomes more intense, the firm is forced to outsource as much of the value-added of its products as possible to take advantage of the greater efficiencies of its external suppliers compared to its internal ones. As the dominant firm in the network, the king is primarily responsible for determining the division of labor in the network, that is, who is responsible for designing and manufacturing each item. Outsourcing becomes critical when the internal suppliers cease to remain competitive with the external suppliers because they are not exposed to competitive and cooperative forces to the same extent. However, if the king is to sustain its dominant position in the network, it must be careful to retain control over strategic functions to ensure that suppliers do not become too powerful. Therefore, it must continually determine what functions need to remain internal to the firm in order to maintain its lead as the dominant customer in the network. The limit to outsourcing is defined by the firm's core competencies, i.e., the technologies and hence components that must be kept in-house to protect the king's competitive position, and the relative capabilities of affiliate firms.

As the final producer of products, the core firm within a king-dom network maintains control over strategic functions in the manufacture of the final product, such as product design, the capital- or technology-intensive phases of production, and final assembly. As the dominant customer for the majority of firms supplying it, the king takes on the role of a centralized strategic planning unit or strategic core for the network as a whole. The strategic core communicates the terms of interdependence among firms in the network from its most valued suppliers to its least valued suppliers, or from top to bottom in a hierarchical pyramid structure (see Figure 5–6).

The king does not have competitors inside the network. Typically, a kingdom will compete with other kingdoms (see Figure 5–7). It is unlikely that a kingdom could compete effectively against a barony unless it was by far the largest firm in the industry. Over

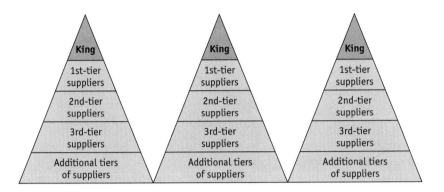

FIGURE 5-6. STRUCTURE OF KINGDOMS

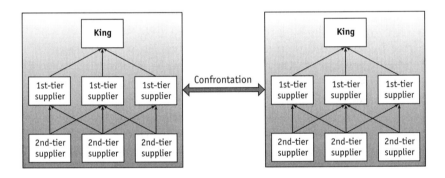

FIGURE 5-7. KINGDOMS IN CONFRONTATION

time, the barony is likely to dominate as it can take advantage of the creativity of all the barons, not just the king. A single firm is unlikely to survive against a kingdom as it lacks the shared creativity of all the firms in the kingdom. However, in industries in which barriers to competition exist or where the transition to lean competition is still occurring, mixed competition is observed.

The Toyota Motor Company and its suppliers provide an example of a well-managed kingdom. Toyota is the largest industrial company in Japan, when measured by sales, and the third largest automobile manufacturer in the world. However, in terms of employment, Toyota remains a relatively small firm compared to

General Motors.[2] The smaller size reflects Toyota's strategy of sourcing from a dense supply of parts manufacturers and sub-assemblies. The network of suppliers that participate in the Toyota Production System is characterized by a highly specialized division of labor, whereby thousands of different companies produce components and subsystems, allowing Toyota to concentrate on its core competencies of design and final assembly.

Increasing Network Efficiency

The king can stimulate efficiency in the network in three ways. First, it can ensure rich information sharing among competing firms in the network. Second, it can create high levels of competition and cooperation among noncompeting suppliers. Finally, it can develop network infrastructures that ensure the suppliers are efficient. The rich information sharing among competitors is facilitated through a reward system—the king rewards the innovative suppliers with part of the business and then shares the innovation with the supplier's competitors within the network. For example, information on cost-reduction solutions obtained by Toyota from one supplier is sometimes shared with other suppliers. This sharing of information makes it difficult for evenly matched suppliers to gain anything more than a temporary advantage over other firms. Thus, one of the outcomes of the information sharing is to maintain a confrontational environment within the kingdom.

When firms in the network compete with each other in confrontation, they rapidly increase the quality and functionality of their products while reducing costs. The king can encourage this process by multi-sourcing families of parts and awarding marginal business to the most aggressive competitor. This approach is effective because the more intense the competition, the more rapidly the products are improved by the suppliers. In contrast, the king encourages firms in the network that are not competitors to cooperate by sharing their innovative ideas. This idea sharing leads the cooperating firms to become more efficient and deliver products

---

[2] W. M. Fruin, *The Japanese Enterprise System: Competitive Strategies and Cooperative Structures*, Oxford: Clarendon Press, 1994, p. 256.

with higher quality and functionality. The outcome is thus a network consisting of two types of suppliers. The first type are the competing suppliers, which do not help each other directly but only indirectly through their customer's information sharing processes. The second type, noncompeting suppliers, act through supplier associations to help each other directly by sharing innovations. These suppliers may still assist each other at the general level but are in confrontation at the product level (see Figure 5–8).

Finally, the king can increase network efficiency by developing network infrastructures that ensure that the suppliers are able to evolve their core competencies in a direction that supports the competitive requirements of the king. These support structures consist of any arrangement that improves collective capabilities and can range from technical seminars and training programs to on-site consulting and interorganizational problem-solving mechanisms. The core firm can afford to invest in improving the capabilities of its suppliers because of the long-term market returns to all firms involved. For example, to ensure that production is carried out and coordinated in the most cost-efficient way, Toyota created the Toyota Supplier Association as an organizational mechanism for

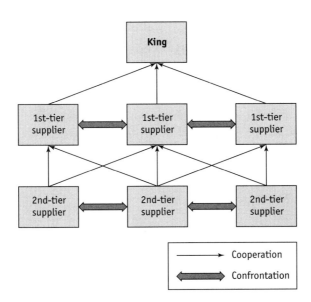

FIGURE 5–8. LAYERED CONFRONTATION IN A KINGDOM

giving supplier firms access to technological and managerial information developed by Toyota in the operation of its Toyota Production System (TPS). Toyota has achieved great success at diffusing the TPS to each level of the supplier hierarchy by building system-wide incentives for mutual problem solving and profit sharing.[3] To help network firms achieve the cost, quality, and functionality demands Toyota places on them, Toyota willingly diffuses know-how on methods of production management to its first-tier suppliers, who then pass on the expertise to second-tier firms and so on. In this way, uniform standards are achieved and coordination across the network firms is maximized with minimal centralized control.

The Role of Network Protocols

The core firm in a kingdom must legislate network protocols to ensure that the network continues to function effectively. The primary purposes of network protocols are to ensure that the more powerful firms in the network do not appropriate all the profits of the weaker firms, and to mitigate the negative consequences of intense competition.

As the most powerful firm in the network, the king is in a perfect position to appropriate a disproportionate share of profit from the value created through joint collaboration. However, the king needs to ensure that target profits are made for both itself and its suppliers if the suppliers are to remain viable partners over the long term. This sharing of profits is particularly important because valued supplier relationships are not built overnight and are not easily replaceable. Furthermore, the king must ensure that the same profit-sharing philosophy is adopted by all the firms in the network. If it does not police profit sharing, then firms further down the supply chain may be placed at excessive risk.

The control the king has in communicating and enforcing accepted practice provides it with the ability to manipulate the level of cooperation and competition in the network. Due to the sharing of information across firm boundaries within the network, relations

---

[3] W. M. Fruin and T. Nishiguchi, "Supplying the Toyota Production System" in B. Kogut, ed., *Country Competitiveness: Technology and the Organizing of Work*, New York: Oxford University Press, 1993.

among suppliers internal to the network can become highly competitive. If the level of competition between firms within a kingdom is not tempered, however, by a set of cooperative norms of behavior, networking arrangements may fail to bring about desired outcomes. Therefore, the core firm must find ways to encourage a competitive environment to spur innovation yet be careful not to let the level of competitive intensity interfere with the suppliers' willingness to cooperate when required. This balance between cooperation and competition is particularly critical to the effective functioning of interorganizational cost management systems, which require firms to share sensitive information to achieve mutual cost-reduction goals.

Thus, to ensure that the level of competition within the network does not exceed the point at which firms become unable to collaborate in joint production processes that require interorganizational coordination, the king legislates expectations on accepted norms of conduct. It uses financial or nonmonetary incentives to reinforce desired behavior or to punish undesirable behavior between firms. For example, if a particular supplier is having difficulty attaining cost-reduction targets established by the king, the king may send engineers from another supplier to help the firm find ways to reduce costs. If the firms do not cooperate, they may risk losing future contracts with the core firm.

The king uses the network protocols to impose behavioral constraints on its suppliers. One of the key constraints that it tries to enforce is the suppliers' ability to convert the kingdom into a barony. The suppliers are motivated to undertake such a conversion as it increases their power vis-à-vis the core firm.

Barony Networks: Multiple Core Firms

When a network is dominated by multiple firms that are essentially equally matched in their ability to dominate the other members of the network, a barony emerges (see Figure 5-9). Like kings, barons make products that are sold in the final market. These products require capital-intensive input and/or capital-intensive production equipment that gives it superior cost and/or quality advantages. Because barons must manufacture and sell products in large volumes to justify the high fixed costs of production, they also operate under the principle of external economies of scale. However, unlike kings, barons must contend with the other strategic core firms

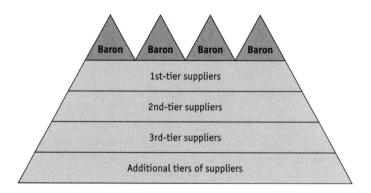

FIGURE 5-9. STRUCTURE OF A BARONY

within the network. Because all barons within a given network have access to a shared supplier base, supplier-driven technological innovations diffuse rapidly to all barons as embedded knowledge is transferred from one firm to the next.

Thus, the disadvantage of being a member of a barony is a significant loss in the ability to achieve product differentiation via outsourced items. When the barons are in the same industry, the result is confrontation and intense competition. The firms can differentiate their products only through the core competencies that they have retained in-house or managed to contractually isolate externally. The benefits of membership lie in the access to the high rate of innovation and cost reduction that the network delivers and the economies of scale that the barons together provide to their suppliers. The primary side-effect of the increased production volumes in a barony, compared to a number of independent kingdoms, is the increased scope of products that can be supported. A barony thus provides the core firms with the ability to support more complicated product mixes at lower cost than kingdoms. The barony can take advantage of the external economies of scale of its suppliers and their economies of scope. The external economies of scope are driven by the suppliers providing products for multiple barons.

Increasing Network Efficiency

The existence of multiple barons reduces the ability of any one firm to dominate the network and influence its structure and operations. This reduction in power has two sources. First, the requirements of other barons have to be considered when the sourcing decisions are made. Whereas in a kingdom the core firm is free to determine the division of labor in the network, in a barony the core firms have to allow a division that reflects all of their demands. Second, the first-tier suppliers can reduce their dependency on any single firm by selling their outputs to multiple barons.

The process of increasing the efficiency of the network in baronies is much the same as in kingdoms. The primary difference is that while vertical relations dominate kingdoms, in a barony the horizontal relations become considerably more important. The need to operate within a context of vertical and horizontal relations requires that networking in baronies be carried out with the support of two types of infrastructure arrangements. In transactions where vertical relations dominate, network infrastructure is created by the barons, such as channels of communication for conveying information between the core firms and their suppliers. Interorganizational cost management operates primarily through these vertical channels between buyers and suppliers by increasing the richness of the interactions between the firms' design and manufacturing teams.

In transactions where horizontal relations dominate, network infrastructure is established by groups of suppliers who share facilities and have shared access to information and know-how. These interactions lead to the development of enhanced production capability within the network. The horizontal interactions consist primarily of information sharing between noncompetitors. Thus, like kingdoms, baronies contain both suppliers that are cooperating and suppliers that are in confrontation. The cooperating suppliers are noncompetitors; they act together, often through supplier associations, to become more efficient. In contrast, suppliers of the same families of components are in confrontation and are trying to outperform each other (see Figure 5–10). However, unlike a kingdom, the barons themselves are also in confrontation. The result is that at each level of the network, firms are confronting each other and survive by becoming as efficient as possible. The network thus acts as a meta-firm. The entire network becomes more efficient at essentially the same rate; consequently, while no individual firm in the network gains advantage over any other firm, the entire network gains advantage over its competitors (see Figure 5–11).

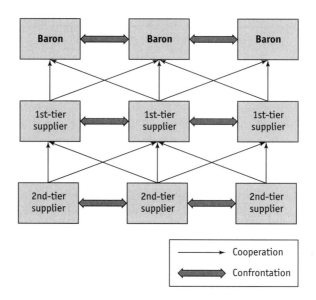

FIGURE 5-10. LAYERED CONFRONTATION IN A BARONY

The heavy earth-moving equipment firms in Japan—Komatsu, Hitachi, Kobelco, Caterpillar Mitsubishi, and Sumitomo—constitute a barony. Most of these firms use a common set of suppliers for many of their outsourced items. For example, they all use Toyo Radiator for engine cooling systems.

The Role of Network Protocols

In baronies, the core firms lack the power to legislate the network protocols individually. Furthermore, if the barons tried to establish the protocols, the result could easily be several sets of potentially conflicting rules that would be almost impossible for the suppliers to follow. Consequently, in baronies it is not the core firms that develop the network protocols but the suppliers. The suppliers achieve this objective by holding regular meetings in which they discuss network issues. In some baronies, these meetings are under the umbrella of a supplier association, and in other baronies they are held for the sole purpose of managing the network. At the meetings, the suppliers discuss issues that are of mutual benefit, including the development of protocols. Once a mutually accept-

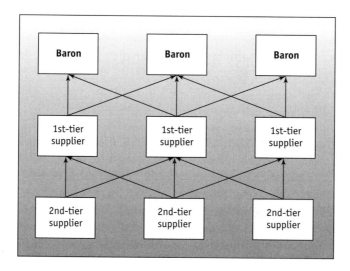

FIGURE 5-11. A BARONY AS A META-FIRM

able set of protocols has been established, they are communicated to the core firms.

The protocols are designed to protect the long-term survival of the network. They typically include rules against selling at a loss and against predatory behavior. Thus, like the protocols of a kingdom, they focus on avoiding the detrimental effects of excessive competition among firms inside the network. Obviously, the protocols have to be acceptable to the core firms; they must not excessively favor the suppliers. They should lead to the overall benefit of all the firms in the network. The core firms react to the protocols independently and individually. If one or more protocols are considered excessive by several barons, the suppliers usually will relax them until they are considered acceptable.

It is in the best interest of the suppliers to discipline firms that attempt to violate the protocols. Two factors motivate the disciplining of firms. First, suppliers do not want one of their members to set a precedent—that violating protocols to win business is acceptable. Therefore, if a baron tries to put excessive pressure on suppliers, it is punished by losing its preferred status with the first-tier suppliers. The suppliers still provide the errant baron with products, but if they run out of capacity, it is that baron that first encounters shortages. Second, if a supplier violates the protocols, then the other suppliers remove their support from that firm. For example, they might stop sharing innovations and cost-reduction ideas with the errant supplier. In addition, if one of the suppliers has excess business that it has to farm out to other suppliers in the network, the errant supplier will not be invited to bid for the work. The removal of support is usually detrimental to the supplier's long-term competitiveness.

In many respects, the suppliers in a barony form a quasi-republic. They act cooperatively by forming loose horizontal relationships (associations and meetings) to enable them to offset the superior power of the core firms. However, most of the time they act as independent firms that are competing aggressively for business. As such, they operate similarly to suppliers in a kingdom. For example, the first-tier suppliers individually negotiate with the barons and the second-tier suppliers. They use interorganizational cost management and other techniques to govern their vertical relationships. The ability of suppliers in a barony to operate cooperatively in this manner helps balance the power of the barons and enables the suppliers to ensure that excessive competition does not cause them to become unprofitable.

Republic Networks: No Core Firm

When there are no dominant firms in a network, a republic emerges. Firms within republic networks are organized collectively as an organic system of specialized niche producers. Working on a highly flexible basis, they provide a wide range of interrelated inputs to meet the rapidly evolving needs of customers that compete in the final market (see Figure 5–12). Thus, one of the primary differences between a republic and the other two networks is the nature of the customer. For kingdoms and baronies, the customers are the end users; for republics the customers are firms that sell to the end user.

Due to the nature of the products they produce, i.e., specialized, intermediate outputs produced in small batch quantities for purchase by volume producers, firms within republics compete based on their collective ability to attain external economies of scope. The sharing of machinery, technological know-how, and production facilities across boundaries of firms in republics creates positive synergies between firms. These synergies result in collective cost effi-

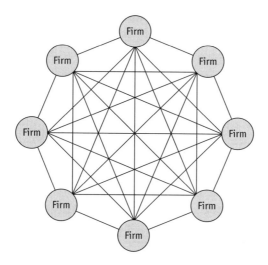

FIGURE 5-12. STRUCTURE OF A REPUBLIC

ciencies that enable firms to develop capabilities to match the evolving need for specialized outputs purchased by final producers.

The majority of business transactions within a republic network consist of horizontal subcontracting between firms internal to the network. As highly specialized, flexible producers, these firms compete in an environment where it is advantageous to remain small—an environment that is conducive to the development of external economies of scope. Because scale economies are not a requirement to the survival of firms within the network, dominant core firms do not emerge, and as a result, relations between firms in the network are symmetrical. While republican networks lack a dominant core firm or group of core firms that provides strategic coherence to the network, the totality of firms within a republic function together as an eco-system, with each firm playing an important role in the survival and prosperity of the group as a whole. In this fashion, the entire network is capable of acting as a single power nexus, garnishing enough power to stand up to large customers when it is deemed necessary to protect their collective interests.

Under these conditions, firms organize themselves on a cooperative basis to manage their terms of interdependence between themselves and customers external to the network. Because firms are not linked together by a common strategy articulated by one or more core firms, they establish informal collaboration mechanisms on an ad-hoc basis. The transitory and informal nature of these relationships reduces the need for formal interorganizational cost management systems in republic networks. More typically, it is the internal market of bids and acceptances and rejections that disciplines the republic and creates a steady pressure to reduce costs.

Because buyers and suppliers within republic networks are evenly matched in terms of their degree of power over one another, they voluntarily agree on accepted norms of behavior without the influence or discipline of a dominant customer. Mutual recognition of the interdependent nature of interfirm relations establishes a context of economic solidarity that facilitates the willingness of firms to forgo a degree of independence in exchange for collaborative gains. Norms of behavior are developed consensually over time and become accepted by all as critical for ensuring mutual cooperation and co-existence in hard times. The threat of sanctions by the collective produces a powerful incentive to self-regulate behavior. Adherence to established norms of behavior is rewarded with future acts of cooperation. A history of successful repeated interactions between firms based on accepted norms of behavior establishes strong foundations of social trust or the expectation that relations among firms will be based in the future on reciprocal rather than self-help principles.

The appropriate social context must exist before collaboration can emerge in republic networks. Because these networks lack a strategic core to discipline and structure relations between firms within the network, firms develop protocols for structuring relations that reach beyond individual self-interest to forge collective identities. Without this foundation, firms will find it difficult to develop and carry out, on a collective basis, strategies that facilitate resource sharing and collective capacity building, without the discipline of a dominant customer.

Contrary to kingdoms and baronies, formal interorganizational cost management does not occur in republics. The mechanisms of interorganizational cost management require cooperative, stable, and balanced buyer-supplier relationships that can support vertical interactions. In the transitory horizontal relationships of a republic, they are not effective. Instead, firms in republics discipline each other primarily through their voluntary willingness to enter into contractual agreements, not through formal interorganizational cost management processes.

Taking Advantage of the Network

Once a network has been established, the next step is to take advantage of the opportunities it offers. From a cost management perspective, being part of a supplier network provides three major benefits (see Figure 5–13). The first benefit derives from the ability to structure the interfirm linkages. The second lies in the increased level of horizontal and vertical technology sharing that is possible, and the third derives from managing the terms of interdependence. These benefits cannot be achieved at the individual buyer-supplier level.

Structuring Interfirm Linkages

Lean enterprises outsource the majority of required inputs, which makes them highly dependent on their supplier networks. The availability of suppliers that can produce specialized inputs at the cost and quality desired by the customer is critical. When market conditions are volatile, outsourcing can enhance manufacturing efficiencies if suppliers are able to adjust their capabilities continuously to

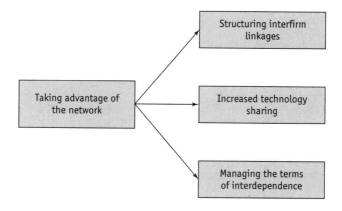

FIGURE 5–13. TAKING ADVANTAGE OF THE NETWORK

satisfy the changing needs of customers. The division of labor within the network (i.e., what inputs the customer decides to produce internally and purchase externally) depends on the relative capabilities of affiliate firms. This division of labor largely determines the structure of interfirm linkages (see Figure 5–14).

The core firm within a kingdom network, which specializes in the capital-intensive or technology-intensive phases of production and final assembly, is in a position to structure the division of labor among firms because of its control over the strategic assets required to produce the final product. It relies on a large number of suppliers with various capabilities. A hierarchical structure for communications and interorganizational collaboration gives the king an efficient structure for managing relations between firms. The core firm is at the apex, suppliers with advanced capabilities directly beneath the king form the first tier of suppliers, and the second and subsequent tiers of firms, which provide the lowest value-added components relative to other firms within the network, are at the bottom. This structure facilitates predominantly vertical or top-down linkages within the network. These vertical relationships make economies of scale possible across the network. Within this top-down hierarchical structure, target costing can act as the disciplining mechanism for interorganizational cost management. The core firm's target costing system communicates the competitive pressure it faces to its direct suppliers, and their target costing systems in turn transmit that pressure to their suppliers. The only predominant horizontal interactions in the kingdom are those between

Type of network	Kingdom	Barony	Republic
Number of core firms	One	Several	None
Contracting power	High	Medium	Low
Network objective	Economies of scale	Economies of scale and scope	Economies of scope
Network protocols	Top-down enforced	Enforced by suppliers	Mutual agreement
Interfirm linkages	Vertical	Horizontal and vertical	Horizontal

FIGURE 5–14. TYPE OF NETWORK AND INTERFIRM LINKAGES

suppliers that are in the associations. These interactions are relatively informal.

Core firms within barony networks, as the owners of strategic assets for the production of final products, are also in a position to structure supplier relations within the network. However, because supplier firms are not dependent on any one particular baron for most of their output, they can negotiate the terms of interdependence with the network core firms. Under these conditions, relations are structured both vertically and horizontally. The vertical relationships allow economics of scale, and the horizontal relationships support the development of economies of scope across the network. As in kingdoms, the vertical relationships enable target costing to discipline the cost management process in the network. In addition, the horizontal relationships, by sharing innovative cost-cutting ideas, help the firms identify ways to achieve the cost-reduction objectives set by their buyers' target costing systems.

Firms within republic networks serve predominantly as subcontractors to one another, engaging in horizontal production arrangements not influenced by the outside control of a dominant customer. Because of the constantly changing nature of relations among firms that share contracts on an ad-hoc, flexible basis, firms within republic networks are largely self-organized into constantly evolving arrangements. These horizontal arrangements permit economies of scope across the network, with each firm free to develop its own expertise and hence products. However, such arrangements are not conducive to formal interorganizational cost management programs. The discipline of target costing is replaced by the discipline of the network's internal market of bids, acceptances, and rejections.

Increased Technology Sharing

Technology sharing within a network plays a critical role in creating new sources of competitive advantage, which support the network's strategic objectives (see Figure 5–15). In kingdom networks new sources of competitive advantage are generated from both the core firm and supplier firms through the development of production processes that provide superior manufacturing efficiencies. The king, as a volume producer of capital-intensive goods, establishes a dominant position in the final market based on cost and quality

Type of network	Kingdom	Barony	Republic
Number of core firms	One	Several	None
Contracting power	High	Medium	Low
Network objective	Economies of scale	Economies of scale and scope	Economies of scope
Network protocols	Top-down enforced	Enforced by suppliers	Mutual agreement
Interfirm linkages	Vertical	Horizontal and vertical	Horizontal
Technology sharing	Core firm-supplier	Core firm-core firm Core firm-supplier	Firm-firm

FIGURE 5-15. TYPE OF NETWORK AND TECHNOLOGY SHARING

advantages. These advantages derive from efficiency gains due to revolutionary process innovations. Toyota, for example, introduced the Toyota Production System, which was widely diffused throughout the supplier base, providing Toyota with a cost and quality advantage in the development of automobiles. The internal development of superior production processes has a radical impact on the development of the final product, thereby positioning the king as a market leader within its respective industry. The pressure the core firm places on suppliers constantly to improve efficiency also stimulates the development of new sources of competitive advantage, for example, as a result of experimentation with manufacturing processes that is based on the need either to reduce costs or improve the functionality or quality of a part over its entire life cycle.

Barons gain sources of competitive advantage based on production process efficiencies developed through access to pathways of technology. In particular, barons can benefit from investments in new-product development made by other barons through their commonly shared supplier network. They can attempt to compete by restricting the flow of information and thus the diffusion of innovations by maintaining proprietary control over a few key components. However, it is very difficult for a baron to develop core competencies that can successfully differentiate it for a lengthy period of time due to the extensive sharing of suppliers and hence supplier-generated innovations.

In republic networks, firms are typically small, highly innovative, and flexible producers that need to continually develop, refine, and evolve unique market niches as a strategy for diversifying risks. The continual branching off of satellite firms by older firms to nurture the growth of new market niches supports the creation of a wide breadth of highly specialized areas of expertise within the network. It is this continuous evolution that provides the network with a collective competitive advantage. Firms within the network remain competitive by continuously evolving incremental improvements to production processes or products and act as an incubator for nurturing the development of new applications of their expertise.

Managing the Terms of Interdependence

When market demand conditions are subject to rapid or constant change, firms that are integrated into a decentralized production network require a network-wide system of governance. A governance structure that operates at the level of the network as a whole maximizes individual firms' ability to take advantage of new market opportunities, while minimizing the risks to varying degrees. Depending on the distribution of power between firms within the network, the terms of interdependence are top-down enforced, negotiated, or based on mutual agreement (see Figure 5–16).

Type of network	Kingdom	Barony	Republic
Number of core firms	One	Several	None
Contracting power	High	Medium	Low
Network objective	Economies of scale	Economies of scale and scope	Economies of scope
Network protocols	Top-down enforced	Enforced by suppliers	Mutual agreement
Interfirm linkages	Vertical	Horizontal and vertical	Horizontal
Technology sharing	Core-supplier	Core-core Core-supplier	Firm-firm
Terms of interdependence	Top-down enforced	Negotiated by barons	Mutual agreement

FIGURE 5–16. TYPE OF NETWORK AND TERMS OF INTERDEPENDENCE

Furthermore, the collaborative mechanisms that lead to network advantages can be either formal or informal or a mixture thereof (see Figure 5–17).

The core firm in a kingdom, which competes in the market as a volume producer with a large market share, requires formal arrangements for achieving interorganizational collaboration to ensure that the overall group strategy is being met. Within a collaborative context, the dominant customer uses its influence over suppliers to foster the sharing of knowledge across boundaries of firms so as to ensure that its suppliers continue to provide it with value-added inputs that support its competitive strategy. This process stimulates the development of the network's ability to innovate rapidly as it reduces costs. This ability leads to collective network advantages, i.e., the core firm continues to capture a dominant market share and suppliers continue to receive large orders from the dominant customer.

The coordination of production across firms within barony networks is achieved through a combination of formal and informal collaboration mechanisms. Dominant customers, as the producers for the final market, will take the lead in organizing the production of inputs that are developed by suppliers. These lead firms communicate their expectations on standards for the quality and function-

Type of network	Kingdom	Barony	Republic
Number of core firms	One	Several	None
Contracting power	High	Medium	Low
Network objective	Economies of scale	Economies of scale and scope	Economies of scope
Network protocols	Top-down enforced	Enforced by suppliers	Mutual agreement
Interfirm linkages	Vertical	Horizontal and vertical	Horizontal
Technology sharing	Core-supplier	Core -core Core-supplier	Firm-firm
Terms of interdependence	Top-down enforced	Negotiated by barons	Mutual agreement
Collaboration mechanisms	Formal	Formal and informal	Informal

FIGURE 5–17. TYPE OF NETWORK AND COLLABORATION MECHANISMS

ality of inputs and develop formal mechanisms for working with suppliers to ensure that they are able to attain these required standards. Suppliers, on the other hand, will develop informal collaboration mechanisms to coordinate subcontracting arrangements or the sharing of production orders to support their ability to meet the requirements of the dominant firms.

Small firms that operate in republics are not strategically integrated by a core firm and thus do not find it necessary or beneficial to establish a formalized system of collaboration. Rather, these firms establish informal collaboration mechanisms on a project-by-project basis to meet the particular needs of a given situation. Firms in a republic will collectively find ways to share resources to take advantage of the opportunity at hand. This method of informal collaboration supports the firms' ability to diversify their capabilities and thus the range of customers they can serve. It gives them a high degree of flexibility to maximize opportunities and minimize risks collectively.

IMPLICATIONS FOR INTERORGANIZATIONAL COST MANAGEMENT

Lean kingdom and barony networks enable interorganizational cost management to spread beyond the single buyer-supplier interface to all the buyer-supplier interfaces in the supply chain of each outsourced item. Thus, interorganizational cost management is practiced effectively at the network level with dominant buyers initiating the process, which then cascades down to the lowest levels of the supply chains. Such a process does not occur in a republic. In that type of network, the short-term nature of the relationships and the specialization of the firms' productive capabilities make formal interorganizational cost management almost impossible to practice. Instead, firms in a republic network rely on competitive bids to discipline their efficiency and effectiveness.

Network protocols enable interorganizational cost management to be practiced at the network level by creating a consistent set of buyer-supplier relationships throughout the network. Without these protocols, individual buyer-supplier relations would vary too much to enable cost management systems to extend across multiple buyer-supplier interfaces. For example, some buyers might abuse their power and extract all the profits from their suppliers. While such buyers would be highly profitable (at least in the short run), they would not enable the entire network to become efficient. Their adversarial and selfish behavior would place at risk the development of long-term, stable relationships that are conducive to the efficient sharing of information among buyers and suppliers.

In a kingdom network, the single core firm uses its power over its suppliers to create horizontal confrontation and vertical cooperation. Each supply chain consists of a series of firms acting together to find the most efficient way to produce the outsourced item. By carefully managing the sourcing of components, the king either has a family relationship with a single supplier for a major function or has relationships with several suppliers for each component family. It is these multiple suppliers for the same component family that are in confrontation. The king nurtures this confrontation through the sharing of nonproprietary innovations. Each innovation is rewarded by a special contract and then shared with the innovator's competitors so as to ensure that the next round of negotiations with suppliers will reflect the innovation.

The process is similar for barony networks. Each baron uses its power over its suppliers to create horizontal confrontation and vertical cooperation. The primary difference between the kingdom and the barony lies in the reduced power of the barons and the role of the competition among barons in shaping the network relations. One of the primary challenges a barony network faces is how to control the diffusion of technology. In a kingdom, all innovations can be shared among the suppliers for the king's benefit. In a barony, the individual barons often benefit by declaring some innovations proprietary. These proprietary innovations give the individual barons at least a temporary competitive advantage.

Conclusion

To be fully effective, interorganizational cost management techniques must operate across multiple buyer-supplier interfaces. To achieve this objective (and to develop other competitive advantages) the entire supplier base must begin to operate as a network. There are three types of networks: kingdoms, which have a single strate-

gic core; baronies, which have multiple strategic cores; and republics, which have no strategic core firm. The stable, cooperative
relationships that characterize kingdoms and baronies coupled with
the dominance of the core firm(s) provide the basis for interorganizational cost management. In contrast, the transitory, informal, and
essentially equal relationships that characterize republics do not
provide such a basis.

Target and kaizen costing lie at the heart of interorganizational
cost management in kingdoms and baronies. They are the central
disciplining mechanism, with the other interorganizational cost management techniques acting as enabling mechanisms. The process
begins with the king's and barons' target and kaizen costing systems
setting their first-tier suppliers' selling prices. The target and kaizen
costing systems of the first-tier suppliers then transmit the cost-
reduction pressure to the second-tier suppliers. The process continues in this manner throughout the network to the lowest levels of
suppliers that can be influenced in this way by the network. In contrast, interorganizational cost management in republics is achieved
through an informal internal market process, where the bids and
their acceptances and rejections act as the primary disciplining mechanism. Other disciplining mechanisms include the central resources
that emerge to support republics and that diffuse technology and
information across the network. The enabling mechanisms used in
republics are the internal ones: value engineering and value analysis.

PART 3

Interorganizational
Cost Management

CHAPTER 6

AN OVERVIEW OF INTERORGANIZATIONAL COST MANAGEMENT

INTRODUCTION

Interorganizational cost management is a disciplined approach to managing costs through the cooperative actions of firms in a supplier network. The objective is to find ways to reduce costs through joint efforts. This objective is achieved by having all the firms involved adopt the view that "we are all in this together" and encouraging them to act in ways that increase the efficiency of the entire supplier network in which they operate, not just themselves. If the entire network can be made more efficient, there will be more profits for the firms to share. Thus, interorganizational cost management is a way for supplier networks (and the firms in them) to increase their overall profitability.

INTERORGANIZATIONAL COST MANAGEMENT

Interorganizational cost management is a *structured approach to coordinating the activities of firms in a supplier network so that total costs in the network are reduced.* The objective of interorganizational cost management programs is for firms to find lower-cost solutions, through coordinated actions with their buyers and suppliers, than would be possible if the firms attempted to reduce costs independently. Given its heavy reliance on cooperation, interorganizational cost management can be undertaken only in lean supplier networks, in which the buyer-supplier relations are characterized by interdependence, trust, and extensive information sharing. The alternative approach, in which buyers and suppliers believe in "every firm for itself," are not conducive to interorganizational cost management. Unfortunately, such adversarial relationships currently dominate the way many Western firms deal with their buyers and suppliers.

Since lower overall costs mean higher profits for the entire network, all the firms are potentially better off if they adopt interorganizational cost management. In contrast, if the firms operate in isolation, they will make decisions that minimize their own costs but not necessarily those of the network as a whole. For interorganizational cost management to work, the additional profits from any improvements have to be shared among all the firms involved.[1] This sharing creates an incentive for everyone to cooperate irrespective of how powerful they are. The weaker firms will not cooperate unless some of the benefits are shared with them. The powerful firms will be willing to adopt such an "altruistic" position (i.e., sharing additional profits) only if they believe that sustaining the network's ability to undertake interorganizational cost management is to their benefit.

Interorganizational cost management is a powerful way to motivate independent, external buyers and suppliers to become more efficient in ways that benefit the entire supplier network. It can also be used to motivate internal divisions and subsidiaries acting as suppliers. The central problem with such internal suppliers lies in the potential lack of freedom to refuse to transact business with their parent. Experience shows, however, that interorganizational cost management can also be applied, with some modification, to internal suppliers. In that case, it centers on establishing transfer prices that create realistic pressure on the division or subsidiary to reduce costs at about the same rate as external suppliers.

---

[1] All that is required is that some profits be shared. However, if the sharing is perceived as equitable, then the motivation to improve is maximized.

THE DOMAIN OF INTERORGANIZATIONAL COST MANAGEMENT

Using interorganizational cost management to coordinate the cost-reduction programs at the firms in a supplier network can help reduce costs in three different ways. First, it can help the firm and its buyers and suppliers find new ways to design products so that they can be manufactured at lower cost. Second, it can help the firm and its suppliers find ways to further reduce the cost of products during manufacturing. Finally, it can help identify ways to make the interface between the firms more efficient.

Cost Management During Product Development

The first way to apply interorganizational cost management is during product development. Here, interorganizational cost management is a structured approach to coordinating the product development activities of firms in supplier networks so that the products and components those firms produce can be manufactured at their target costs. It is of particular importance to lean enterprises because these firms typically outsource as much as 70% of the value-added of their products. With such a high degree of outsourced value, coordinating product development throughout the supplier network is critical to the firms' success. In contrast, mass producers outsource considerably less of both value and design and therefore derive less benefit from interorganizational cost management. Consequently, as firms become lean and undergo vertical disaggregation, they discover that it is no longer adequate for each firm in the supplier network to undertake cost management independently. Instead, they find that product development programs have to become coordinated across the buyer-supplier interfaces.

Interorganizational cost management achieves its objective in the product design phase by both disciplining and coordinating the product development processes of firms throughout the supplier network. The primary disciplining mechanism of interorganizational cost management is the application of target costing. The primary source of coordination lies in the application of three enabling mechanisms of cost management: functionality-price-quality (FPQ) trade-offs, interorganizational cost investigations, and concurrent cost management.

Target costing is at the heart of interorganizational cost management. It is a structured approach to determining the cost at which a proposed product with specified functionality and quality must be produced to generate the desired level of profitability over its life cycle when sold at its anticipated selling price. Target costing disciplines the interorganizational cost management process by establishing the cost-reduction objectives for the products and the components they contain. By chaining target costing systems, that is, connecting the target costing system of the buyer to that of its suppliers, the discipline of target costing can be extended from a single firm to the supplier network.

When a supplier finds that it cannot achieve the target costs set by the buyer's component-level target costing process, it can initiate an FPQ trade-off. Under such a trade-off, the buyer and supplier negotiate to lower the level of quality and functionality required so the supplier can generate an adequate profit at the buyer's component-level target cost. In an interorganizational cost investigation, the design teams of the two firms get together to determine whether the specifications set by the buyer can be altered in ways that enable the component's costs to be reduced significantly. The changes to the component's specifications usually are greater than those considered under an FPQ trade-off. In concurrent cost management the entire design of the major function is outsourced to the supplier. If little synergy between the buyer's and supplier's design teams is expected, then high-level specifications of the major function are set by the buyer, and the supplier is expected to design a solution that meets them. In contrast, if a high level of synergy is expected, then the two design teams work together to design both the product and the major function simultaneously.

Cost Management During Manufacturing

Additional opportunities for cost reduction occur during the manufacturing phase. Interorganizational cost management during product manufacture is a structured approach to coordinating the production activities of firms in supplier networks so that the products and components those firms produce can be manufactured at their kaizen costs. The buyer uses kaizen costing to set cost-reduction objectives for its suppliers. Like their target costing counterparts, these objectives should reflect the competitive pressure that the buyer is facing in the marketplace. The objectives can either apply across the board for all outsourced items (for example, 3% per year) or set a specific cost-reduction target for each item (for example, 6% for radiators and 3% for starter motors).

The real benefit of interorganizational kaizen costing is realized when the firms in the supplier network cooperate to find new, low-cost solutions that they cannot identify in isolation. When the supplier finds it impossible to meet the price reductions required by the buyer and still make an adequate profit, it can ask the buyer to provide engineering support. The joint engineering teams can explore solutions that require both firms to modify their manufacturing processes. When the net result is lower costs, then the changes are implemented. The buyer can also help its suppliers reduce costs in other ways. For example, the buyer can use the combined buying power of itself and its suppliers to negotiate better discounts than the firms can achieve on their own. The buyer will benefit from these negotiations by reduced prices from its suppliers.

Improving the Efficiency of the Buyer-Supplier Interface

The final application of interorganizational cost management occurs when buyers and suppliers cooperate to find ways to make the interfaces between their firms more efficient. One way is to reduce the costs of transaction processing by using electronic data interchange (EDI) and bar coding. A second way is to reduce uncertainty by increasing information sharing and shortening cycle times. Reducing uncertainty is important because then both the buyer and the supplier can keep lower levels of buffer inventory.

THE PROCESS OF INTERORGANIZATIONAL COST MANAGEMENT

Interorganizational cost management, to be effective, must be a highly disciplined process that operates on two dimensions—network and product (see Figure 6–1). The relationship dimension starts at the network level with the establishment of the appropriate network protocols. These protocols ensure that excessive competi-

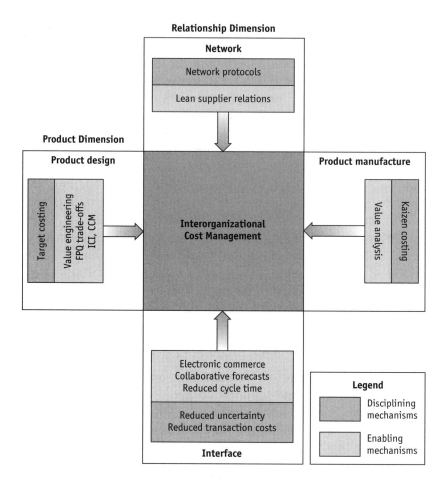

FIGURE 6–1. THE INTERORGANIZATIONAL COST MANAGEMENT
PROCESS

tion does not render the interorganizational cost management process ineffective. Once the protocols are established, the firms can take advantage of the primary enabling mechanism of the network level, which is the lean buyer-supplier relationship. These relationships are shaped primarily by high levels of cooperation, stability, and mutual benefit. Cooperation is required for all three areas of interorganizational cost management—product development, manufacturing, and buyer-supplier interface—because they all require the firm and its buyers and suppliers to change their behavior. While unilateral behavior changes may be beneficial, it is only when numerous firms change their behavior that the real savings of interorganizational cost management are achieved. Stability is required both to motivate and to justify these behavioral changes. Finally, mutual benefit is required so that all the firms involved share in the increased profitability resulting from the behavioral changes.

The network level provides the environment in which the product dimension can operate. The product dimension operates at two levels, product design and manufacture. Target costing is the primary disciplining mechanism of product design. It is the process by which the competitive pressure faced by the end firm is transmitted to the firm's product designers and suppliers. The enabling mechanisms that allow the target costs to be achieved include value engineering (VE) and the three cooperative mechanisms of interorganizational cost management during product design. These mechanisms are FPQ trade-offs, interorganizational cost investigations (ICI), and concurrent cost management (CCM). Kaizen costing is the primary disciplining mechanism of interorganizational cost management during product manufacture. It, like target costing, helps communicate the competitive pressure faced by the firm to the firm's manufacturing engineers and suppliers. Kaizen cost reduction objectives are primarily achieved though the application of value analysis (VA).

The relationship dimension also operates at the interface level. This level deals with the way goods and services are transferred between the buyer and supplier. The primary discipline mechanisms are reduced uncertainty and decreased transaction costs. Uncertainty is reduced by shortening order-to-fulfillment cycle times and by collaborative forecasts. Both ways lessen the need for the buyer and supplier to maintain safety inventories. Transaction costs are reduced in four ways: by eliminating redundant ones, simplifying others, standardizing them across firms, and automating them. Electronic commerce is the primary approach to transaction automation.

The Key Questions of Interorganizational Cost Management

The essence of interorganizational cost management can be captured in the following three questions:

- Can we reduce the cost of products by taking advantage of interorganizational synergies in product development?
- Can we reduce the cost of products by taking advantage of interorganizational synergies in manufacturing?
- Can we make the interfaces with our buyers and suppliers more efficient?

These three key questions are designed to identify the greatest opportunities for cost management. If the firm believes that its buyer-supplier interfaces are inefficient and that significant opportunities for cost reduction exist, then this is probably the place to start. If the interfaces are relatively efficient, then instigating synergies in production will give the most immediate benefits. However, the greatest benefits of all will be derived from undertaking interorganizational cost management during the product development process.

Taking Advantage of Interorganizational Synergies in Product Development

For interorganizational cost management during the product development process the four key questions are:

- What is the product-level target cost?
- How can we achieve this product-level target cost?
- How can we distribute the cost-reduction objective among components?
- Are any suppliers unable to achieve the component-level target costs?

The first question requires the application of target costing. The setting of a product-level target cost reflects the integration of the subtraction and addition approaches. The subtraction approach takes the expected selling price and subtracts from it the target profit margin to give the allowable cost. The addition process takes the current cost of the product, i.e., the cost at which it could be made today (this cost is determined by summing up the current cost of all the components it contains). A cost-reduction objective is established by using the information provided by suppliers and internal manufacturing units. Subtracting the cost-reduction objective from the current cost gives the product-level target cost. The comparison of the current cost and the allowable cost leads to an iterative process by which the final product-level target cost is set.

The second question requires the application of value engineering (VE). VE is an organized, multidisciplinary effort to analyze the functions of goods and services so a firm can find ways to achieve those functions while meeting its target costs. VE helps to manage the trade-off between functionality and cost, the two dominant characteristics of the survival triplet. The objective of most Japanese VE programs is not to minimize the cost of products in general, but to achieve a specified level of cost reduction established by the firm's target costing system. Setting out to achieve a concrete cost-reduction target has been shown to be more effective than setting a fuzzy objective such as "design to minimal cost."

The third question deals with decomposing the cost-reduction objective to the component level. Once the target cost of a new product is established, multifunctional product design teams decompose it to determine component and subassembly target costs. The cost-reduction objective is not spread evenly across all the components and subassemblies. Historical trends, competitive designs, and other data are used to estimate how much cost can be removed from each component or subassembly. An iterative process is used to ensure that once the component and subassembly target costs are set, they add up to the product-level target cost. At many firms, the chief engineer is responsible for establishing the main themes of the new product. These themes are chosen to give the new product a distinctive character that the firm hopes will make it successful when launched. For example, for an automobile one of the themes might be a quieter but sportier ride. The design team can then allocate more costs to those features, but under the cardinal rule of target costing every extra dollar allocated to improving a feature of the vehicle must be taken out somewhere else.

If the answer to the last question, "Are any suppliers unable to achieve the component-level target costs?" is no, then the product-level target cost will be achieved. However, if the answer is yes, then further cost-reduction efforts are required. The questions that capture the essence of these efforts depend on the particular cost management technique that is being used to address the cost overrun problem. Therefore, a branching in the questions occurs in the process at this stage (see Figure 6–2). The two questions relating specifically to FPQ trade-offs are:

- What relaxations of the quality and functionality specifications of components are acceptable?
- Are there any extenuating circumstances that allow component-level target costs to be relaxed?

The first question deals with the willingness of the buyer to relax the quality and functionality specifications established for the component. If the supplier can negotiate such relaxations, then it will be easier to achieve the component's target cost. For example, if the component is allowed to have lower functionality, its design might be simplified so that the number of parts it contains can be reduced. Such a parts reduction can lead to lower cost. The willingness of the buyer to allow such relaxations is constrained by the need to maintain the specifications of the product itself. The supplier has to understand the role of the component in achieving the end product's functionality so that it can make intelligent recommendations. The buyer often overspecifies at the component level because it does not take into account the economics of the supplier's production processes. The buyer is driven by the pressures placed on it by the marketplace and tends to demand improvements on all three characteristics of the survival triplet.

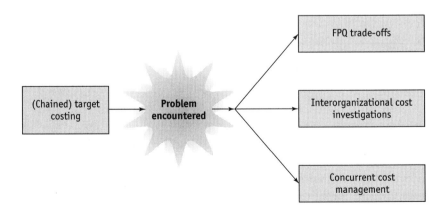

FIGURE 6–2. THE BRANCHING PROCESS

The second FPQ-related question covers conditions when holding the supplier to the component-level target cost is inappropriate. Component-level target costing assumes an arm's-length relationship between the buyer and the supplier. Under such conditions, the component-level target cost captures the entire economic transaction between the two firms. However, if, for example, the buyer requires that the supplier make a significant up-front investment and subsequently it is discovered that the target cost is not achievable, then the buyer will usually relax the target cost temporarily. In that case, the buyer decides that the supplier will be placed under excessive economic stress if it is held to the component-level target cost or if the contract for the part is sourced elsewhere and the investment has to be written off.

The three questions relating to interorganizational cost investigations are:

- What design changes to the specifications of the end product and its components are acceptable?
- What changes can be made to the production process to reduce costs, especially by moving production steps to other firms in the supplier network?
- How are the cost-reduction objectives redistributed among the firms?

The objective of interorganizational cost investigations is to find ways to redesign the products and the components they contain so that they can be manufactured at their target costs. Consequently, the first question has to do with what changes can be made to the design of the end product and the components it contains. These design changes may affect the specifications of the end product. Therefore, the supplier cannot initiate them unilaterally. Instead, the buyer and supplier design teams must get together to identify which design changes are acceptable to the buyer and reduce costs across the supply chain. If there are more than two firms in the supply chain, often multiple design teams must interact to find ways to reduce costs.

The second question deals with changes in the production process that require moving activities across organizational boundaries. The first two reasons to change the production process deal with shifting activities and the third, with avoiding them. If certain activities can be performed more efficiently at another firm in the supply chain, then costs will be reduced if these activities are moved. Second, if collocating two activities allows costs to be reduced, then shifting one of the activities so it is performed in the same location as the other will allow costs to be reduced. Finally, if changing the production process can eliminate certain activities, then costs will be also reduced. For example, if there is a way to start with raw material that has a smooth surface as opposed to a rough one, then the production step that prepares the surface of the rough component can be eliminated.

As the product design and production processes are modified, the costs incurred in each firm change. These changes often require that the target costs of the components be modified. For example, if costs are increased at one firm and decreased at another (but reduced overall), then the target cost of the component at the firm with increased costs may have to be raised and at the firm with the lower costs, reduced. The third question points out that these changes redistribute the cost-reduction objectives and hence profit levels among the firms in the supply chain. Typically, it is the firm at the top of the chain that sets the new target costs.

The two questions relating to concurrent cost management are:

- Should the research and development for a given major function be outsourced?
- Can the design of that major function be undertaken by the supplier in isolation from the buyer?

For concurrent cost management to be practiced, the research and development associated with group components and major functions must be outsourced to the firm's major suppliers and family members. The suppliers will have to develop the necessary expertise so that the buyer can relinquish design responsibility to them. For design responsibility to be outsourced, it must not represent a core competency for the buyer. Outsourcing core competencies weakens the buyer's strategic position in several ways. It reduces the firm's ability to differentiate its products, and it can enable new competitors to emerge. The only time that core competencies should be acquired from external sources is when those sources have a significant technological advantage over the buyer. The buyer's best strategy under such conditions is to try to control its suppliers' access to that competency by entering into agreements that limit its spread.

The second question determines whether parallel or simultaneous engineering will be used in the design process. If the two design teams can operate essentially in isolation, then parallel engineering is appropriate. The buyer's team provides the supplier's team with high-level specifications such as size, capacity, and effectiveness. The two teams are then free to operate independently as long as they do not make any design changes that violate the high-level specifications of the product or the component. While the two design teams operate in isolation, they keep in contact with each other to ensure that they achieve their joint objectives.

If the buyer and supplier design teams cannot effectively operate in isolation, simultaneous engineering is used to design the product and component concurrently. In simultaneous engineering, the two design teams work closely together to identify ways to increase the quality and functionality of the end product and its major function, while at the same time reducing overall costs. The two design teams make suggestions to alter the design of both the end product and the major function, which could not be made if the two teams acted in isolation. For example, redesigning the component to reduce its costs may require some major changes in the design of the end product. Identifying the scope of such changes and whether, overall, they reduce costs without sacrificing quality and functionality requires frequent interactions between the design teams.

Taking Advantage of Interorganizational Synergies in Production

For interorganizational cost management during manufacturing the four key questions are:

- What is the product-level kaizen cost?
- How can we achieve this product-level kaizen cost?
- How can we distribute the cost-reduction objective among suppliers?
- Are any suppliers unable to achieve the cost-reduction objective?

The first question requires the application of kaizen costing. The starting point for setting a kaizen cost-reduction objective is the price pressure that the firm is exposed to in the marketplace. Unlike target costing, where the pressure used to establish cost-reduction objectives is specific to the product, in kaizen costing it is typically the general cost-reduction pressure that the firm encounters for all similar products. The primary exception to this difference is when a product-specific kaizen intervention is initiated.[2]

The second question requires the application of value analysis (VA). VA is an organized effort to find ways to reduce costs while maintaining product functionality. It is applied during the manufacturing phase of a product's life. Like value engineering, the objective of most Japanese VA programs is not to minimize the cost of products in general, but to achieve a specified level of cost reduction.

The third question deals with decomposing the kaizen cost-reduction objective to the supplier level. In kaizen programs, suppliers usually are subjected to a flat cost-reduction rate, for example, 3% per year. This approach differs significantly from the one used for target costing, where specific targets are set at the individual product level. In kaizen costing, only for very expensive components will most firms set specific cost-reduction objectives. The aggressiveness of the flat rate objective is determined primarily by the cost pressures the buyer encounters in its marketplace.

If the answer to the last question is no, then the suppliers will achieve their kaizen objectives and make a reasonable profit. In contrast, if the answer is yes, then additional cost-reduction efforts are required. The buyer and supplier can cooperate in three ways to further reduce costs. First, the buyer can use its engineering expertise to help the supplier find lower-cost ways to manufacture the components it sells to the buyer. Second, if such solutions cannot be identified, the buyer can change the design, but not functionality, of its product to enable the supplier to develop new, lower-cost components. For example, several integrated circuits might be combined into a single chip. This solution lowers the cost for the supplier, but requires that the buyer change its circuit design. Finally, the buyer can agree to change its production processes, but not product designs, to accommodate changes in the supplied component. For example, the buyer might agree to take a machining operation in-house because it can be integrated with an existing one at a lower cost than the supplier can undertake it. When activities are transferred in this way, the buyer's costs are increased and the supplier's

---

[2] See Robin Cooper and Regine Slagmulder, *Kaizen Costing and Value Engineering,* Volume 3 in this series.

costs decreased. However, the increase is less than the decrease; therefore, overall costs are reduced. To compensate for the shift in costs, the buyer adjusts the component-level target cost downward, but typically by more than the avoided costs at the supplier. This adjustment makes it easier for the supplier to achieve its target costs for the component. The buyer is better off because the extra amount in the adjustment is less than the savings from the activity transfer. Thus, both firms have higher profitability as they share the increased profits.

If, in contrast, the buyer transfers an activity to the supplier, then the buyer's costs are reduced and the suppliers' costs increased, but by a lesser amount. Now, the buyer adjusts the component-level target cost upward by a lesser amount than the costs transferred. The buyer is thus better off as its profits have been increased. As long as the adjustment is greater than the additional costs of the supplier, then the supplier is better off. Once again both firms are sharing in the increased profits.

Improving the Efficiency of Buyer-Supplier Interface

Three questions capture the process of making the buyer-supplier interface more efficient:

- Are there any actions that the firm as a buyer can take to reduce the overall costs of its buyer-supplier interface?
- Are there any actions that the firm as a supplier can take to reduce the overall costs of its buyer-supplier interface?
- Are there any actions that the firm can take jointly with its buyers and/or suppliers to reduce the overall costs of the associated interfaces?

The first question captures how the firm can change its behavior as a buyer in ways that help reduce customer service costs for its suppliers. For example, if the firm is a lean enterprise, it will typically be placing a large number of small orders with its suppliers. If the suppliers have high sales order processing costs, their customer service costs will be high. The firm should use its insights into the economics of customer service to identify new ways to order products. For example, the firm might agree to undertake data entry that feeds directly into the suppliers' sales order systems. Other potential improvements for the firm as a buyer include reducing its reliance on custom as opposed to standard products, ordering as many different products at a time as possible, increasing sales order lead times, and reducing the number of changes to sales orders.

The second question captures how the firm as a supplier can change its behavior in ways that reduce procurement costs for its customers. For example, if its customers are lean enterprises, then late deliveries will be very expensive (because the buyers might have to interrupt production). To reduce these costs, the firm might initiate a program to become lean itself and significantly increase on-time deliveries. Other potential improvements for the firm as a supplier include improved quality, smaller batch deliveries, and shorter lead times.

The third question deals with the need of the buyers and suppliers to cooperate to reduce the cost of their interfaces in the supplier network. The interfaces between the firm and its buyers and suppliers will become truly efficient only when the firm asks its buyers and suppliers to modify their behavior to reduce its costs and they reciprocate by asking the firm to change its behavior.

For each interface, the firm has to identify both the savings it will obtain from the changes it has recommended and any costs associated with the changes requested by the other firm. The critical point is that win-win scenarios can be identified by extending cost management beyond the walls of the factory and realized by extending it beyond the boundaries of the firm. Clearly, only if both firms are better off will changes be approved (unless one of the firms can legislate changes in the other). Such improvements will enable the supply chain to become more efficient. Consequently, the ultimate customer will benefit from this interorganizational cost management process.

Summary

Interorganizational cost management is an approach to cost and profit management that takes advantages of synergies existing across multiple firms in a supplier network. These synergies are realized by coordinating activities at the firms in the network, with the aim of reducing the overall costs of the network. Interorganizational cost management has three major areas of coordination.

The first area requires coordinating the product development process of the firms in the network. Experience has shown that it is easier to design costs out of products than to find ways to eliminate them after the products enter production. When a firm outsources a large percentage of the value-added of its products, it is not sufficient for just that firm to develop low-cost products. Rather, it is necessary for all the firms involved in the development process to develop low-cost designs. Often, the choices made by one firm about how to design its part of the product have cost implications for the other firms involved in the process. Only if all these firms cooperate will the end product be low cost.

Target costing acts as the disciplining technique that identifies where individual firms are having problems achieving sufficiently low-cost designs. By chaining the target costing systems of several firms in the supplier network, the competitive cost pressures that the end firm(s) encounter(s) in the market can be communicated throughout the network. Failure to achieve a target cost indicates that interorganizational cooperation is required. Three enabling mechanisms foster such cooperation: functionality-price-quality (FPQ) trade-offs, interorganizational cost investigations, and concurrent cost management programs. Each of these mechanisms causes the product design teams of two or more firms to interact, with the specific objective of reducing costs through improved design. In these meetings, value engineering is the primary technique used to reduce costs.

The second area of coordination in interorganizational cost management requires coordinating the manufacturing processes at the firms in the network. The kaizen costing systems in the firms create pressure on their suppliers to continuously reduce the costs of the products they manufacture. When a supplier finds that it cannot achieve the required level of cost reduction, it can ask the buyer to help it lower its costs. The two firms can reduce costs together in various ways. They can jointly find ways for the supplier to manufacture the component at a lower cost. Alternatively, they can redesign the buyer's product so that the supplier can develop a new, lower-cost component. Finally, activities can be moved between the buyer and supplier so that they can be performed more efficiently at lower cost. Value analysis is the primary technique to reduce costs of existing products. In value analysis, the functionality of the product and its components are held constant while costs are removed.

The third area focuses on increasing the efficiency of the interface between buyers and suppliers. As these interfaces become more efficient, the cost of transferring goods between the firms decreases.

The key questions capture the logic behind interorganizational cost management. However, they do not capture the details of practice, which is complex and requires considerable expertise. These details are documented in the next eight chapters. Target costing and its interorganizational implications are documented in Chapters 7 and 8. The process of chaining target costing systems and the use of FQP trade-offs are documented in Chapter 9. The other two enabling techniques, interorganizational cost investigations and concurrent cost management, are documented in Chapters 10 and 11, respectively. Kaizen costing and its interorganizational implications are documented in Chapters 12 and 13. Finally, the ways that firms can increase the efficiency of their buyer-supplier interfaces is documented in Chapter 14.

CHAPTER 7

TARGET COSTING

INTRODUCTION

Target costing[1] is a feed-forward cost management technique that focuses on the design stage of a product's life. Its objective is to determine the cost at which a proposed product with specified functionality and quality must be produced to generate the desired level of profitability over its life cycle when sold at its anticipated selling price. Target costing lies at the heart of interorganizational cost management for product design: it acts as the primary disciplining mechanism. The buyer's target costing system establishes the supplier's selling prices and signals to the supplier where it should focus its cost management efforts. When the supplier takes advantage of these signals, it automatically coordinates its cost management activities with those of the buyer.

---

[1] For a more detailed description of target costing see Robin Cooper and Regine Slagmulder, *Target Costing and Value Engineering*, the first volume in this series.

Target costing is primarily a technique for profit management (see Figure 7–1). Its objective is to ensure that future products generate the profits identified in the firm's long-term profit plan. This objective can be achieved only if products satisfy the demands of the firm's customers and can be manufactured at their target costs. Transmitting the competitive pressure that the firm faces in the marketplace to its product designers and suppliers via *market-driven costing* promotes the necessary level of aggressive cost management. Subtracting the desired profit margin from the target selling price set by the market identifies the target cost at which the product must be manufactured. *Life-cycle costing* ensures that the target profit margins take into account the up-front investment in product development and any cost savings that can be anticipated over the product's life.

To create intense pressure on the product designers to reduce costs, *product-level target costing* focuses designer creativity on reducing the costs of future products to their target levels. These target costs are set so that they can be achieved only if the product designers expend considerable effort on designing future products. *Value engineering* is the primary technique used to find ways to decrease product costs while maintaining the functionality and

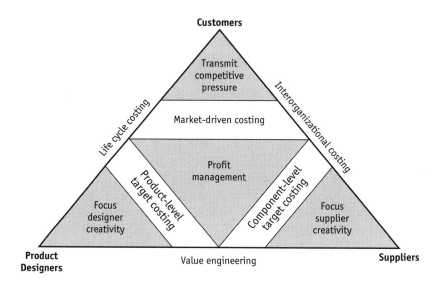

FIGURE 7–1. THE TARGET COSTING TRIANGLE

quality customers demand. It is key to achieving the target cost. As such, it is an integral part of target costing.

To create an equivalent cost-reduction pressure on the firm's suppliers, *component-level target costing* is used to focus supplier creativity on reducing the costs of the components they supply. *Interorganizational costing* creates relationships that link customers and suppliers with the firm's design engineers, helping them find ways to design lower-cost products.

Target costing transmits the competitive pressure to the suppliers by setting the selling prices of components. If target costing is appropriately practiced, these selling prices will force suppliers to reduce costs aggressively in order to remain adequately profitable. Suppliers are thus encouraged to be innovative in the way they design the components so that these parts can be manufactured at lower cost. It is this ability to pressure suppliers through setting their selling prices that enables target costing to act as an interorganizational cost management technique.

The Target Costing Process

The target costing process consists of three major sections (see Figure 7–2). In the first section, market-driven costing is used to establish the allowable cost of the product. This is the cost at which the product must be manufactured if it is to generate the desired level of profitability when sold at its target selling price. The allowable cost is determined by subtracting the target profit margin from the target selling price.

The market-driven costing section does not take into account the capabilities of the firm's product designers and suppliers. Consequently, the allowable cost is often unachievable. Since continuously setting unachievable target costs will make it impossible to maintain the discipline of target costing, effective target costing systems contain procedures that enable the allowable cost to be reduced to attainable levels. Therefore, the second section of the target costing process consists of establishing achievable product-level target costs. These product-level target costs, if properly set, require that the firm's designers and suppliers expend considerable but realistic levels of effort and creativity to achieve them.

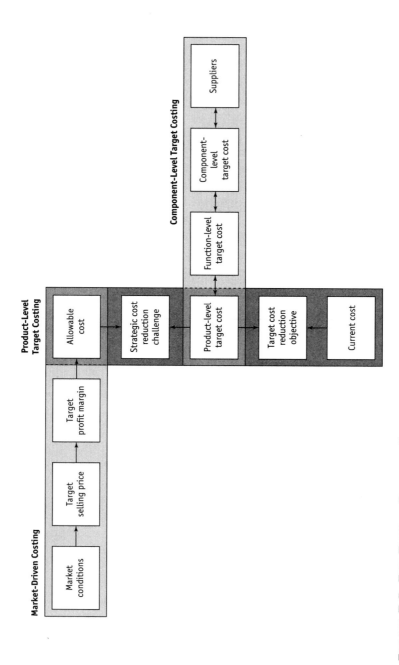

FIGURE 7-2. THE TARGET COSTING PROCESS

For most lean enterprises, a significant portion of a product's cost is represented by externally acquired components. Therefore, it is necessary to exert pressure on the suppliers to reduce costs so that the target costs of new products can be achieved. Consequently, the third section of the target costing process consists of setting the target costs of every component the product contains.[2]

Market-Driven Costing

The primary purpose of the market-driven costing section of the target costing process is to transmit the pressure faced by the firm in the marketplace to its product designers and suppliers. The process can be viewed as consisting of three major steps. The first step is identifying the target selling price of the product, the second step involves determining the target profit margin, and the final step consists of subtracting the target profit margin from the target selling price to give the allowable cost (see Figure 7–3).

Three major factors must be taken into account in setting the target selling price: customer requirements, competitive offerings, and the firm's strategic objectives for the product (see Figure 7–4). Customer requirements identify the perceived value that customers place on a product with a given level of functionality and quality. The perceived value sets the highest acceptable price for the product. Customer loyalty helps determine the degree to which the survival zone of the product can be relaxed. Highly loyal customers are often willing to purchase products that theoretically fall outside their survival zones, either because their selling price is too high or their functionality and/or quality are too low. However, in the intensely competitive environments in which the firms in the sample compete, customer loyalty is typically very low and cannot be relied on to save products that fall outside their survival zones.

The primary aspects of competitive offerings that have to be considered in setting the target selling price are their relative functionality and selling price. The relative functionality helps determine the relationship between the selling prices of competitive offerings and the firm's products. If the relative functionality of the competi-

---

[2] The term *component* is used to cover all externally acquired parts including major functions.

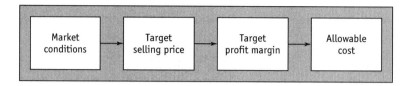

FIGURE 7-3. MARKET-DRIVEN COSTING

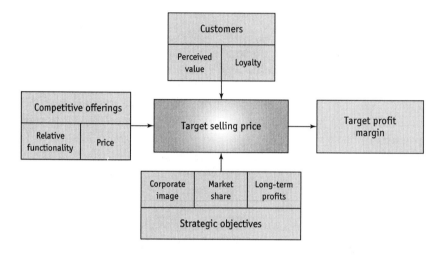

FIGURE 7-4. SETTING THE TARGET SELLING PRICE

tor's product is higher, then the firm's selling price typically will be lower to maintain perceived equivalent value. The selling prices of competitive offerings thus create a starting point for setting the firm's target selling prices.

Three aspects of the firm's strategy for the product play a significant role in the process of setting the target selling price. These aspects are whether the product can help improve or reinforce the firm's corporate image, the market share objective that the firm has for the product, and its long-term profit objectives. The ability of a product to strengthen the firm's corporate image influences the target selling price because the firm is often willing to sell such products at relatively low prices compared to their cost.

There is always a trade-off between the market share of a product and its overall profitability. If the firm's objective is to increase market share for this and future generations of the product, it might choose to set the target selling price lower than if it wants to maximize profits for this generation only. The lower selling price will enable more units to be sold and thus increase market share. However, each unit will generate lower profits, and if the increase in volume is too small to offset the reduced unit profitability, overall profits will fall. The motivation for such a strategy is the belief that the lost profit for this generation will be made up through increased sales and hence profits for future generations of the product.

The factors that influence the process of setting the target profit margin are the product's historical profit margin, its life-cycle cost profile, and the long-term profit objectives of the firm (see Figure 7–5). The historical profit margin for earlier generations of the product is usually the starting point from which the new product's target profit margin is established. If there is reason to suspect that the new product can support a relatively higher selling price than its predecessors could, then the target profit margin might be set higher. Alternatively, if the product's relative selling price is expected to be lower, so might its target profit margin.

Life-cycle costs have to be taken into account in setting the target profit margin because they influence how profitable the product must be on launching if it is to achieve its long-term profit objectives. life-cycle costing considerations include the magnitude of the up-front investments, the anticipated level of kaizen costing savings during the

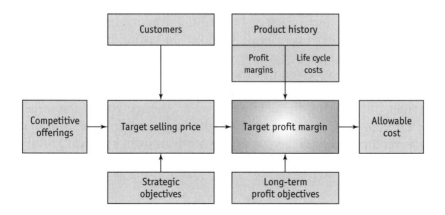

FIGURE 7–5. SETTING THE TARGET PROFIT MARGIN

manufacturing stage of the product's life, and any disposal costs. The higher the up-front investment, the greater the target profit margin must be to generate the same total life-cycle profitability.

The long-term profit objectives of the firm also influence the target profit margin of the new product. The more aggressive the long-term profit objectives, the higher the target profit margins of individual products must be to achieve them and, hence, the lower the resulting allowable costs. However, for the target costing process to be effective, the target profit margins must be realistic. Otherwise, the allowable costs will be too low and not credible.

Product-Level Target Costing

Since the allowable cost does not take into account the internal design and manufacturing capabilities of the firm, there is a risk that the allowable cost will be unachievable. To maintain the discipline of target costing, however, it is important to ensure that only achievable targets are set. Consequently, many firms differentiate between the allowable cost and the product-level target cost.

The product-level target cost is established by determining the current cost of the product, which assumes that no cost-reduction activities are undertaken, and identifying how much it can be reduced through aggressive design improvements and value engineering. The difference between the current cost and the product-level target cost is called the target cost-reduction objective (see Figure 7–6). This objective is determined by taking into account the design and production capabilities of the firm and its suppliers (see Figure 7–7). Great care must be taken in setting the target cost-reduction objective. If it is consistently set too high, not only will the workforce be subjected to excessive cost-reduction pressures, risking burn-out, but also the discipline of target costing will be lost as target costs are too frequently exceeded. Alternatively, if the target cost-reduction objective is systematically set too low, the firm will lose competitiveness because new products will have excessively high costs.

The gap between the allowable cost and the product-level target cost is called the strategic cost-reduction challenge (see Figure 7–8). It represents the inability of the firm to earn the target profit

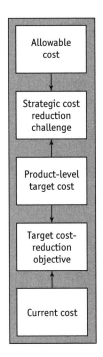

Figure 7-6. Product-Level Target Costing

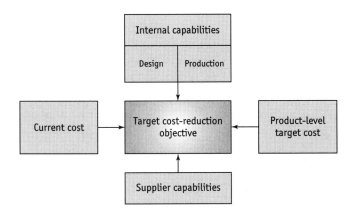

Figure 7-7. Setting the Target Cost-Reduction Objective

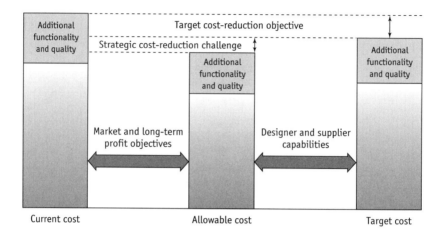

FIGURE 7-8. THE STRATEGIC COST-REDUCTION CHALLENGE

margin for the new product. For the discipline of target costing to be maintained, the magnitude of the strategic cost-reduction challenge must be carefully managed. It should reflect the true inability of the firm to match the efficiency of its competitors. To ensure that the strategic cost-reduction challenge meets this requirement, the target cost-reduction objective must be set so that it is achievable, but only if the entire organization commits significant effort toward its attainment.

Once the product-level target cost has been established, it is broken into three elements: the component-level target cost, the assembly target cost, and the indirect manufacturing target cost. Next, the target costing process switches to finding ways to achieve the product-level target cost. Most firms use a mixture of techniques, such as value engineering and quality function deployment (QFD), to help achieve the component-level target cost. They use design for manufacture and assembly (DFMA) to help achieve the assembly and indirect manufacturing target costs.

To help ensure that the target cost is achieved, several disciplining mechanisms are used, including continuous monitoring of the progress made toward achieving the target cost-reduction objective and the application of the cardinal rule of target costing. Continuous monitoring serves to ensure that the target cost-reduction objective will be achieved and that all identified savings will be realized when the product enters manufacturing. This monitoring is designed so that real savings, not wishful thinking, are driving the cost-reduction process. The latest estimate of what the product is expected to cost is known as the drifting cost (see Figure 7–9). The cardinal rule, namely that the target cost must never be exceeded, ensures that only profitable products are released for production. Consequently, if a product is expected to exceed its target cost, it is usually not released to manufacturing and the project is canceled.

Sometimes there may be extenuating circumstances, where products that appear unprofitable or that cannot meet their target costs must still be launched. These exceptions are not necessarily violations of the cardinal rule but rather are instances of an occasion when a narrow individual product perspective is deemed inadequate. Typically, the products in question have future revenues associated with them that are not captured in their individual selling prices. Common examples are flagship products, products that use the next generation of technology, and products that protect market share. If these additional revenues are included in the target cost derivation, the products will be found to meet the requirements

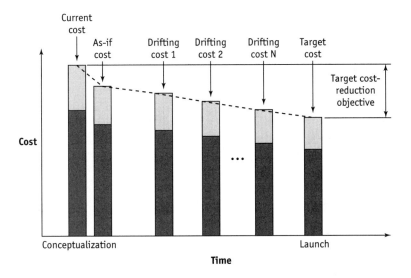

FIGURE 7–9. ACHIEVING THE TARGET COST

of the cardinal rule.[3] Occasionally, a product whose cost exceeds its target cost may still be launched when the losses from not launching the product are expected to exceed the losses from violating the cardinal rule. However, such events represent only temporary violations of the cardinal rule.

Component-Level Target Costing

The objective of the component-level target costing section is to set the target cost of every component in the new product, thereby establishing the selling prices of externally acquired components and the transfer prices for internally acquired ones (see Figure 7–10). Component-level target costs play a critical role in the target costing process because they distribute profits among the buyer and its suppliers. If the target cost of a component is increased by $1, then—if everything else remains equal—the supplier's profits on that component will increase by $1 per unit and the buyer's will fall by the same amount. Consequently, the buyer is motivated to set the component-level target costs as low as possible, and the suppliers are motivated to try to negotiate them as high as possible. For this reason, the negotiations that surround the establishment of component-level target costs usually are intense.

The intensity of negotiations between buyers and suppliers depends on a number of factors (see Figure 7–11). If the component

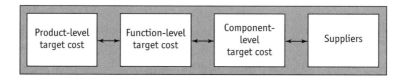

FIGURE 7–10. COMPONENT-LEVEL TARGET COSTING

---

[3] The well-known razor-razor blade marketing strategy developed by Gillette illustrates a situation in which an individual product perspective is inadequate. Target costing—if applied naively—will show that the razor is unprofitable and should not be introduced, while the blades are profitable and should be introduced. Clearly, there is no point in introducing the blades but not the razor. Only by treating the razor and blades as a single product will target costing be effective and suggest whether both or neither should be introduced.

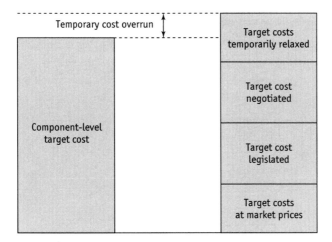

FIGURE 7-11. FOUR WAYS TO SET COMPONENT-LEVEL TARGET COSTS

has an established market price, typically that price will be the basis of the component-level target cost set by the buyer. If no market prices are available, then the component-level target costs will be negotiated. In those instances when the buyer has considerable power over the supplier, the negotiations will be one-sided, and the component-level target costs essentially will be dictated by the buyer. Alternatively, if the buyer has little power over the supplier, the target costs will be truly negotiated. The starting point for these negotiations will be the supplier's bid. If extenuating circumstances come into play, then the target costs may be relaxed, at least temporarily, and the product-level target cost will be exceeded.

For most products the component-level target costing process can be broken into two steps. In the first step, the target costs of the product's major functions are established (see Figure 7–12). Major functions are the subassemblies that provide the functionality that enables the product to achieve its primary purpose; for example, for an automobile they include the engine and the audio system and for a camera the flash unit.

In the second step, the target costs of outsourced items are established. In the first level of outsourcing (see Figure 7–13), the buyer designs the major function and subcontracts for many or all of the components (these components are outsourced to common

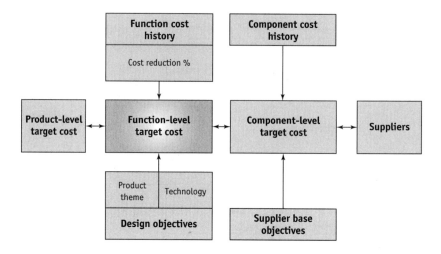

Figure 7-12. Setting the Target Costs of Major Functions

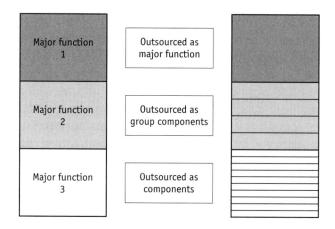

Figure 7-13. The Three Ways to Outsource Major Functions

suppliers and subcontractors). In the second level, the buyer also designs the major function, but the group components it contains are outsourced (these group components are outsourced to major suppliers). The supplier is thus responsible for designing and manufacturing the group components to the specifications provided by the buyer. In the final level, the design and manufacture of the major function are completely outsourced (these are the major functions outsourced to family members). The buyer develops a high-level specification for the major function and lets the family member design and manufacture the part. For some major functions, a mixed outsourcing strategy is adopted, with some of the group components outsourced while others are designed in-house and subcontracted. The component-level target cost setting process reflects these three levels of outsourcing.

The chief engineer, who has total responsibility for the product, sets the target costs of the major functions. He distributes the product-level target cost for the major functions based on the historical cost-reduction rates that have been achieved for each major function and the design objectives set for that function. For example, if the chief engineer wants a given major function to be superior to the one used in the current model, the target cost of that function might be increased. However, under the cardinal rule of target costing, any such increases must be offset elsewhere in the design.

Each major function is the responsibility of a dedicated design team. Every team has the objective of finding ways to achieve the target cost for their major function. At the heart of this process is the establishment of target costs for each component of the major function (see Figure 7–14). If the major function is outsourced, then the component-level target costing process will take place at the suppliers; otherwise it will be at the buyers. Just as for the major functions, the starting point for the component-level target costs is the cost-reduction rate that has historically been achieved for each component. This cost-reduction rate is modified based on the supplier-base objectives of the firm and the capabilities of the suppliers (see Figure 7–15).

The supplier-base objectives include maintaining supplier relations, extending the supplier base, and inducing supplier creativity. When a long-term supplier fails to make the lowest bid or develop the most innovative solution, the buyer may still award part of the contract to that firm in order to create a stable buyer-supplier relationship. To increase the rate of innovation and, in particular, to enable new technologies and production processes to be adopted, the firm must continually look for new suppliers. The objective is to identify suppliers that are highly creative and innovative or have developed considerable expertise in technologies that the firm is

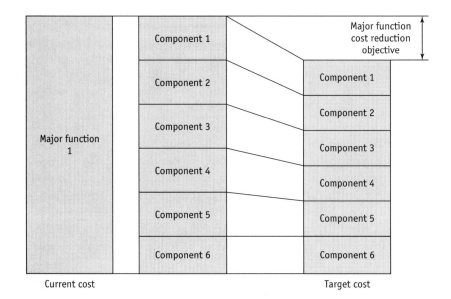

Current cost   Target cost

FIGURE 7-14. DECOMPOSING THE TARGET COST OF A MAJOR
FUNCTION TO THE COMPONENT LEVEL

now incorporating into its products. Finally, the contracts can be used to reward suppliers for being innovative.

Suppliers are selected based on the competitiveness of their bids, their reputation, and the degree of innovation they have brought to the particular component. The bids from suppliers are collected as early as possible in the target costing process and incorporated via an iterative process into the component-level target cost setting process. This process is designed to ensure that the component-level target costs of the individual components are achievable and sum in total to the target cost of the product. Supplier reputation for innovation plays an important role in determining the willingness of the firm to accept slightly higher prices or occasional lower levels of innovation from some suppliers and still grant them part of the business. The objective is to ensure that innovative suppliers are retained in the supplier base. For a given component, the degree of innovation that the supplier introduces influences the value that the firm associates with the component. The higher the degree of innovation, the greater the value, all else being equal. Since the firm wants to reward innovation, it will usually select the most innovative design.

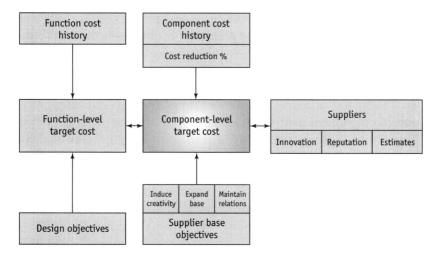

FIGURE 7-15. SETTING THE TARGET COST OF COMPONENTS

SUMMARY

The target costing process is considerably more complex than simply taking a target selling price and subtracting a target profit margin. Instead, it consists of three major sections: market-driven costing, product-level target costing, and component-level target costing. In the market-driven costing section, customer requirements and competitive offerings are incorporated into the target costing process. The resulting allowable cost is the cost at which the proposed product must be manufactured to generate its target profit margin when sold at its target selling price. The limitation of the market-driven costing section is that it does not take into account the cost-reduction capabilities of the firm or its suppliers.

In the product-level target costing section, the cost-reduction capabilities of the firm's product design and production engineers are incorporated into the target costing process. The objective is to set an aggressive but achievable product-level target cost. It is only by setting achievable target costs that the discipline of target costing can be maintained. The difference between the allowable cost and the product-level target cost determines the strategic cost-reduction challenge. This challenge indicates the firm's inability to generate the target profit margin for the proposed product. If the strategic cost-reduction challenge is too great, the cardinal rule of target costing, namely "do not launch products that cannot be manufactured at their target cost," is invoked and the new product project is scrapped.

One of the primary objectives of target costing is to manage the cost of components, in particular those that are externally acquired. The output of the last section of the target costing process, component-level target costing, is the target cost of every component that the product contains. The costs of the components are then added to the assembly and indirect manufacturing costs to give the target cost of the product. The component-level target costs establish the purchase price of each component and hence the suppliers' selling prices. Thus, the suppliers' design and manufacturing capabilities are incorporated into the target costing process through the component-level target costing section. It is this setting of supplier selling prices that makes target costing an interorganizational cost management technique.

CHAPTER 8

INTERORGANIZATIONAL IMPLICATIONS OF TARGET COSTING

INTRODUCTION

Target costing is a technique for proactive cost management during product design (see Chapter 7). It acts as an interorganizational cost management technique through the establishment of target costs for the components and other outsourced items that the product contains. The buyer's component-level target costs essentially establish the supplier's selling prices and thereby transmit the competitive pressure faced by the buyer to its suppliers. Since this pressure is transmitted component by component, it helps the supplier identify where to focus its cost-reduction efforts. The result is a coordination of the buyer's and supplier's cost management programs. It is this coordination that is so critical to the effectiveness of target costing as an interorganizational cost management technique.

Target costing and its multifirm extension, chained target costing (see Chapter 9), are the primary disciplining mechanisms of interorganizational cost management during product design. By setting component-level target costs, target costing establishes how much and where cost reduction will occur at the component level.[1] The other techniques of interorganizational cost management for product design are enabling mechanisms that help the firms achieve the target cost. They cause value engineering to be practiced across the interorganizational boundary by giving the buyer's and supplier's design teams the opportunity to work together on specific cost-related design problems.

The interorganizational implications of target costing have four major aspects. First, the buyer has to set achievable component-level target costs. If the suppliers do not perceive the component-level target costs as attainable, their motivation to achieve them will be reduced. Second, the buyer has to choose the appropriate way to apply target costing to its suppliers. At the heart of this decision is the degree of freedom given to the supplier to identify the cost-reduction objectives built into the component-level target costs and the way to achieve them. Third, the buyer can develop reward systems that create incentives for the supplier to increase its level of innovation and rate of cost reduction. Finally, when internal suppliers are involved, the application of component-level target costing has to be modified to accommodate the status of the supplier as a subsidiary.

Setting Achievable Component-Level Target Costs

The discipline of target costing can be maintained only when the established cost-reduction objectives are considered achievable by the individuals involved. If the achievement level is very low, violations of the target cost become too common and the stigma attached to failure begins to dissipate. Consequently, the pressure to achieve the objectives drops, and the target costing process loses its effectiveness. However, if the target costs are always achieved, they are

---

[1] Theoretically, the supplier could ignore the signals being transmitted by the buyer's target costing system and reduce costs as and where it believes appropriate. The problem with this approach is that some components would become highly profitable and others unprofitable. As we shall see later, most firms avoid this scenario.

probably being set too low and cost-reduction opportunities are being missed. Thus, achievable does not mean that the objectives are easy to achieve; on the contrary, for target costing to be effective the targets must place considerable pressure on the product designers to reduce costs. However, the pressure must be realistic, and the designers must believe that with considerable effort they stand a good chance of meeting their objectives. Experience suggests that if the cost-reduction objectives can be achieved about 80% of the time, the target costing process will be effective.

Theoretically, target costing should lead automatically to achievable target costs if the firms in a supply chain are as efficient as their competitors. Minor inefficiencies can be accommodated in the product-level target costing process by establishing strategic cost-reduction challenges at each firm in the supply chain. However, if the inefficiencies are too large to be accommodated in this manner, then either the project has to be abandoned (under the cardinal rule of target costing) or more aggressive cost management processes have to be initiated while redesigning the product.

There is no guarantee, however, that the component-level costs established from a subtraction process (target selling price – target profit margin) will indeed be achievable. To ensure that the component-level target costs are attainable, an addition process (summing the component and manufacturing costs) is initiated that incorporates information about the suppliers' and the firm's design and manufacturing capabilities into the target costing process.

Achievability is thus introduced into the component-level target costing process by ascertaining the suppliers' capabilities and then incorporating this information into the component-level target costs. A firm can learn about the design and production economics of suppliers (see Figure 8–1) by:

- Obtaining price estimates from the suppliers early in the component-level target costing process;
- Obtaining cost information directly from the supplier;
- Obtaining cost information indirectly;
- Using historical trends to predict supplier costs.

The first three approaches depend on current information about supplier capability, whereas the last one depends on historical trends in cost reduction.

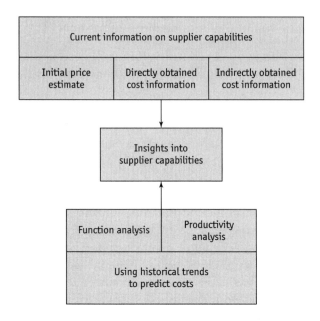

FIGURE 8-1. GAINING INSIGHTS INTO SUPPLIER CAPABILITIES

Incorporating Current Information on Supplier Capabilities

Current information on suppliers can be incorporated in three ways to help ensure that only achievable component-level target costs are set. First, when supplier price estimates are obtained as early as possible in the target costing process, they can be used to estimate the component-level cost of the product. If the sum of the supplier prices equals the total component-level target cost of the major function in which they are used, they are simply accepted. If not, they are pro-rated to the appropriate extent, and informal discussions with the suppliers are held to help establish appropriate component-level target costs. If the resulting component-level target costs are considered unachievable, then the supplier price estimates are compared with the equivalent target costs of each major function and an iterative process is used to align the target costs of each major function with supplier capability. The target costs of the questionable major functions are increased, while others are decreased accordingly to adhere to the cardinal rule of target costing. In either scenario, when the supplier price estimates are too high, some form of negotiation must occur to bring them into line with the buyer's component-level target costs. If there is no way to achieve the target costs without changing the specifications of the end product or the components it contains, one of the enabling mechanisms of interorganizational cost management is initiated. For example, if Yokohama cannot achieve Tokyo Motor's target cost, it will initiate either a functionality-price-quality trade-off or an interorganizational cost investigation.

The second way to ensure achievement of component-level target costs is through direct sharing of cost information. Despite being separate firms, the amount of cost information being shared between the buyers and suppliers under target costing is often significant (see Chapter 4). The purpose of this information sharing is to help both the buyer and the supplier achieve adequate returns on their products. Direct sharing of cost information enables the buyer to establish target costs that provide the supplier with an adequate return. This form of information sharing typically occurs when it is difficult for the buyer to establish arm's-length selling prices. There are many reasons why such selling prices cannot be identified—the component being outsourced is unique (hence there are no direct competitors); the item requires significant investment on the part of the supplier (which cannot be used for other products that the supplier manufactures); and the acceptance of the order places considerable risk of failure on the supplier (for example, because the item relies on unproven technologies).

The third way to ensure achievability is by indirect sharing of cost information. In theory, under target costing customers are unaware of the profits that their suppliers earn on the products they sell. The buyer's component-level target costs create an appropriate level of pressure on suppliers to become more efficient, but if the suppliers can exceed the rate of cost reduction their customers demand, their profits will increase. For example, at Citizen Watch all external suppliers are expected to deliver at least a 5% annual cost-reduction rate. If a supplier is able to exceed the 5% target, it retains the surplus.

In practice, however, the sharing of design and manufacturing information and the exchange of engineering personnel allows buyers to estimate their suppliers' costs fairly accurately. For example, if a supplier is unable to achieve the target set by Citizen's target cost-ing system, there is no punishment, but Citizen's engineers will assist them in achieving it the following year. This assistance is beneficial to the supplier but does mean that the buyer's engineers often have detailed knowledge of the suppliers' product designs and production processes. The buyer's engineers can take this knowledge into account when setting component-level target costs. In addition, when a prod-uct appears to be generating excessive profits according to the buyer's engineers, the target cost of the next generation is typically revised downward so that the profit it is thought to generate is considered more reasonable. Thus, even if cost information is not shared explic-itly, the rich interactions between the buyer and supplier design teams act as a mechanism to ensure both that target costs are achievable and that profit margins are within acceptable bounds.

Incorporating Historical Information on Supplier Cost-Reduction Performance

Another way to build achievability into the component-level target costs is through the use of historical cost-reduction trends. When current information about supplier capabilities is not available, the process of setting component-level target costs relies heavily on his-torical information that the buyer has about its suppliers' cost-reduc-tion achievements. The amount of information about the compo-nent's design and manufacturing processes that is available to the buyer depends on whether the supplier or the buyer designs the com-ponent. When the component is sourced from a major supplier, then the buyer has limited control over the component design and knows relatively little about the underlying production process. In contrast, when the component is subcontracted, the buyer controls the design process and is familiar with the details of the production process.

Given the differences in the level of control over the design process and in the degree of knowledge of the production process, it is not surprising that the way the target costs are established using historical trends is often different for the two types of sourced com-ponents. For example, Komatsu uses either functional analysis or productivity analysis to help set component-level target costs depending on how the product is sourced. Functional analysis, a procedure for identifying the target cost of a subassembly based on its functional characteristics, is used for parts designed and produced outside of Komatsu. Such parts include engine cooling systems, hydraulic devices, and electrical subassemblies. Functional analysis is used for externally designed parts because it does not rely on the buyer's detailed knowledge of the design or production processes at the supplier. In contrast, productivity analysis, a procedure for identifying the target cost of a subcomponent based on its manufacturing process, is used for subassemblies designed by Komatsu and manufactured either by Komatsu or one of its subcontractors. Such parts include vehicle main frames, buckets, and gears. Productivity analysis requires more in-depth knowledge of the production process and is therefore used for internally designed parts. The value of the two techniques is that they generate component-level target costs that incorporate reasonable estimates of the future capabilities of the firm's suppliers.

Functional Analysis

Functional analysis begins with an analysis of the primary and secondary functions of each subassembly and how they are achieved. The primary or basic functions are the principal reasons for the existence of the product. For example, the primary function of an engine cooling system is to keep the engine within operating temperatures. The secondary functions are outcomes of the ways the designers choose to achieve the basic functions. For example, the secondary functions of an engine cooling system include heating the passenger compartment.

The next step in the process is to identify how each subassembly achieves its primary function, for example, cooling capacity for the engine's cooling system. Often several determinants of primary functionality are identified and ranked in order of importance. These determinants typically relate to physical characteristics of the major components that make up the subassembly. In the case of the cooling system these major components include the radiator, fan, and electric motor. The most important determinant of cooling capacity is the surface area of the radiator. The second most important determinant is the size of the fan, followed by its rotation speed, the volume of water in the system, and the ambient air temperature.

The third step in functional analysis is to use information about the functionality of the major component and its physical characteristics, such as size, to identify the target physical characteristic (e.g., minimum size) of the component. The information for undertaking this analysis is contained in the firm's *function tables*. The target physical characteristic is determined by plotting the capability of each major component in the subassembly with respect to its primary functionality (for the radiator, its cooling capacity) versus the most important determinant (for the radiator, its surface area) for all similar components used by the firm. From this plot, the average and minimum lines for existing components are constructed. The average line is determined using linear regression or other statistical estimation procedures, and the minimum line is drawn so that it passes through the most efficient of existing components. The minimum line and the required functionality for the new component are used to identify the target physical characteristics of the most important determinant of the functionality of the component (see Figure 8–2).

The target cost for each major component is determined by a similar process. This process compares the magnitude of the physical characteristic of the most important determinant of the functionality of existing components (e.g., radiator surface area) to their

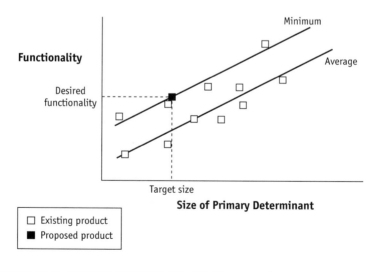

FIGURE 8–2. TARGET COSTING VIA FUNCTIONAL ANALYSIS AT
KOMATSU LTD.: IDENTIFYING THE TARGET SIZE

cost. The appropriate cost and physical characteristic information is maintained in the firm's *cost tables*. The target cost of the components is determined by plotting the cost against their physical characteristics for all similar components used by the firm. The average line is again determined using linear regression or other statistical estimation procedures, and the minimum line is drawn so that it passes through the most efficient of existing components. The minimum line and the target physical characteristic for the new component are used to identify its target cost (see Figure 8–3).

The same techniques are used to generate target costs for the other major components of the subassembly. For example, the target cost of the fan in the cooling system is determined by plotting the size of the fan against the cooling capacity of the engine cooling system and identifying the average and minimum lines for the relation between fan size and cooling capacity. The minimum fan size-to-cooling capacity line is used to identify the minimum fan size. A plot of the cost of fans versus fan size is used to determine the minimum cost/size line and hence the target cost of the fan.

This process is repeated for all major components of the subassembly. Once all component target costs have been identified,

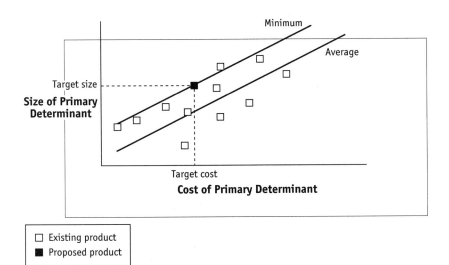

FIGURE 8–3. TARGET COSTING VIA FUNCTIONAL ANALYSIS AT
KOMATSU LTD.: IDENTIFYING THE TARGET COST

their sum can be compared to the target cost of the subassembly. As long as the cost of the components is less than or equal to the target cost of the subassembly, the components' target costs can be approved. Otherwise, additional analysis is required.

Productivity Analysis

Productivity analysis consists of decomposing the production process of the components of new products into detailed steps such as "drill a 10-mm diameter hole of 5-cm depth into stainless steel." Cost tables are used to estimate the cost of each step in the production process. At Toyota cost estimators use cost tables to calculate unit prices for manufacturing. Cost tables are developed for five major production steps: machining, coating, body assembly, forging, and general assembly, and they detail the machine rates for each step. These rates include labor, electricity, supplies, and depreciation costs.

The exact form of the cost table rate depends on the type of production step being analyzed; for stamping, for example, the cost table contains the cost per stroke while for machining it contains the cost per machine-hour. Cost tables are highly detailed, and each production line has its own cost table identifying, for example, the cost per stroke of each press. Rather than the basic costs used for budgeting, a cost table used for cost planning shows costs per production line, with its manufacturing costs broken down into direct labor costs and indirect line costs.

In productivity analysis, the major steps in the production process of the new subassembly are analyzed, and the sum of their costs is compared to the target cost of the subassemblies. If the expected cost is too high, the section leaders responsible for each step in the production process are asked to identify a cost-reduction objective for each step.

At Komatsu, ultimate responsibility for these cost-reduction objectives lies with the product manager, who is responsible for ensuring that the new product enters production successfully. If the initial aggregated cost reductions are insufficient to allow the subassembly to be manufactured for its target cost, then the product manager and the production staff negotiate to increase the expected productivity savings. The final aggregation of the negotiated cost-reduction objectives, when subtracted from the current cost, provides the latest estimate of the subassembly's target cost.

The process of productivity analysis at Komatsu is illustrated by the redesign of a mounting socket in the main frames of the firm's bulldozers. In the old design, the mounting socket consisted of a hole drilled through the body of the frame. This design was simple to manufacture but had the drawback of creating a stress zone around the hole. To ensure that the mounting socket was strong enough, that section of the main frame had to be manufactured from expensive, high-grade materials. Productivity analysis identified lowering the amount of high-grade material in the main frame as one way to reduce costs. The new design involved welding a mounting bracket containing the mounting socket hole to the vehicle main frame. The new mounting unit was designed to reduce the strain imposed on the frame so that normal-grade steel could be used.

Once component-level target costs have been established, they have to be applied. The way they are applied depends quite significantly on whether the supplier is external or internal. External suppliers can develop a high degree of independence by ensuring that no customer represents a major portion of their business (more formally, they create a barony as opposed to a kingdom). In contrast, subsidiaries have less autonomy and often must obey their parent's directives even when they do not want to.

APPLYING TARGET COSTING TO SUPPLIERS

Three central issues surround the application of component-level target costs to suppliers (see Figure 8–4). The first deals with whether the target costs are legislated or negotiated. When the target costs are legislated, the suppliers have no freedom. They have to accept the price, quality, and functionality specifications set by the buyer. In contrast, when they can negotiate, the quality and functionality specifications can sometimes be relaxed to enable the supplier to achieve the target cost. The second issue deals with the degree of independence that the supplier is granted by the buyer. This independence centers on the ability of the supplier to find ways to achieve the component-level target costs without the buyer's assistance. The third issue deals with bundling target costs. When a

Target costing decision	Factor to consider
Legislate or negotiate target cost	Degree of power over supplier
Degree of supplier independence	Faith in supplier's cost management skills
Individual versus bundled target costs	Freedom granted to suppliers to identify locus of cost reduction

Figure 8-4. Target Costing and External Suppliers

single supplier is responsible for multiple components of the same product, the buyer can either establish component-level target costs for each individual component or a single target cost for the entire set. The advantage of bundled target costing lies in the increased freedom it gives the supplier in finding ways to reduce costs, achieve the buyer's component-level target costs, and generate an adequate return.

Legislation Versus Negotiation

At one extreme of applying component-level target costing, the buyer legislates the selling price, quality, and functionality of the component to the supplier. No negotiations are allowed, and the supplier has simply to deliver the product on a timely basis. At the other extreme, the two firms conduct considerable negotiations and make significant adjustments to the specifications of the component, including its selling price (these negotiations are discussed in the next chapter). For most components the process falls somewhere between those two extremes.

Legislation is used primarily for common suppliers and subcontractors. The buyer's knowledge of the supplier's past capabilities and the buyer's production economics provide insights into the level of cost savings that can be anticipated. The buyer either incorporates this historical information into a component-specific cost-reduction objective (as is the case with functional analysis) or simply demands the same cost-reduction rate each year. Sometimes the same rate is demanded for all components; alternatively, the same rate is used for each component within a component family, but different rates are used for different families.

Negotiations are also limited for components that have an active market or for which the supplier is the sole source. When an active market exists, the market price typically will be used as the component-level target cost. The existence of a competitive market makes it impossible for the buyer to legislate selling prices to the supplier. When the supplier is the sole source, that firm will set the selling price (although the long-term relationship may discipline how high that price is set). In both cases, the buyer lacks the power to legislate the selling price to the supplier.

Negotiation typically occurs when an intermediate condition exists. When the buyer and supplier are not working at arm's length, but have made specific investments on each other's behalf, then a relaxation of target costing sometimes occurs. For example, Isuzu provides capital and design support to some suppliers to enable them to produce the advanced components required for the next generation of products. For such bids, the target costs are often relaxed in the early days to give the supplier time to learn how to manufacture the new component at its target cost and to ensure an adequate overall return on the project.

The component-level target costs for a product thus consist of three types: those dictated by the buyer's component-level target costing process, those set by the market, and those relaxed because of special considerations. Even in the latter case, the cardinal rule of target costing—that the product-level target cost can never be exceeded—still applies. The buyer's target costing ensures that, taken collectively, the components have sufficiently large cost-reduction objectives to achieve the product-level target cost after the relaxed target costs return to their original levels.

Subordination Versus Independence

Once the buyer has decided whether to legislate or negotiate the component-level target costs, the next step is to decide is whether the supplier is capable of achieving the desired level of cost reduction on its own. If the buyer decides that the supplier needs considerable help, it will treat the supplier as a subordinate, grant it low autonomy, and subject it to a high degree of monitoring. In contrast, if the buyer believes that the supplier can achieve the cost savings required to meet the component-level target costs, it will treat the supplier as independent, grant it high autonomy, and subject it to a low degree of monitoring.

In most cases, suppliers are allowed to have a high degree of autonomy and are subjected to low levels of monitoring. The degree of autonomy is typically high because the buyer wants to give the supplier maximum freedom to identify cost-saving opportunities. Typically, if the supplier is successful, it will not be subjected to any special attention as the normal levels of buyer-supplier interactions are deemed sufficient. Only if the supplier fails to remain competitive is the level of autonomy reduced. Typically, the buyer will send in its engineers to help the supplier improve its cost-reduction programs. The objective of this support is to maintain the supplier's competitiveness at an adequate level. This granting of conditional autonomy is especially important when the supplier competes directly with other suppliers for a given family of parts.

The level of monitoring captures how closely the buyer keeps track of its suppliers. For most suppliers, the level of monitoring is low as the buyer has sufficient trust in its suppliers to leave them alone. This trust is based on the supplier's history of reducing costs and its willingness to participate in interorganizational cost management if it encounters problems. The degree of monitoring is highest for unsophisticated suppliers that lack the managerial and cost-reduction skills of their more sophisticated counterparts. For these less sophisticated suppliers, the buyer will typically hold regular meetings and provide ongoing engineering support.

Individual Versus Bundled Target Costs

When the supplier has been granted a high level of independence and is responsible for multiple items for a product, the buyer can decide to bundle the target costs. In bundled target costs, all the component-level target costs for each product are added together, and the supplier is held to the total, not the individual target costs (see Figure 8–5). The advantage of bundling is that it gives the supplier more freedom to identify where to reduce costs. In contrast,

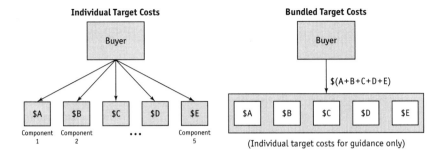

FIGURE 8-5. INDIVIDUAL VERSUS BUNDLED TARGET COSTS

under normal target costing, the buyer dictates where the supplier should reduce costs.

For example, from Komatsu's perspective the important issue is to design cooling systems that can be purchased for their target cost. If a number of firms are involved in delivering a given cooling system, Komatsu has to split the cooling system's target cost among those suppliers based on the parts they are producing. If a supplier produces more than one component for the cooling system, Komatsu will develop target costs for each of these components. However, once the individual component target costs are accepted, the supplier is held to the overall sum of all the components it supplies that go into the new model, not the target costs for individual parts. Thus, in effect Komatsu holds such suppliers to a single target cost for each cooling system, leaving the suppliers' engineers free to decide how much each individual component will cost and hence where to expend their cost-reduction efforts. Both Citizen and Olympus adopt similar bundling approaches.

Even though the component-level target costs are bundled, the supplier typically is given the individual targets. The benefit of being given both total and individual targets lies in the additional guidance that the individual target costs provide the supplier about where the buyer believes cost reduction is feasible. This guidance is valuable because the buyer often gains insights from the cost-reduction programs of many of its suppliers. These insights can give the buyer ideas about cost reduction that are not immediately obvious to an individual supplier. The advantage of bundling target costs is that it allows the supplier to decide where it actually will achieve the cost reduction. Thus, bundling target costs and providing the individual target costs give the supplier both maximum freedom and access to the buyer's insights on cost reduction.

As firms increase their reliance on a smaller number of suppliers, the nature of the component-level target costing process changes as bundling becomes feasible. Component-level target costs, rather than acting as immutable targets, become guidelines to help the supplier identify where its costs are too high. The core advantage of bundling the individual target costs of all the components for a single product is that it gives the supplier greater freedom to find ways to achieve the total target cost.

Rewarding Suppliers for Innovation

Many firms use incentive schemes that reward the supplier with all or part of the order for a given component. The purpose of these incentive schemes is both to reward innovation and to signal where additional cost reduction should occur. For example, Nissan uses such an incentive plan to motivate its suppliers. If a cost-reduction idea for a component is accepted, the supplier that suggested the idea is awarded a significant percentage of the contract for that component for a specified time period, say 50% for 12 months. If the supplier's innovation leads to higher functionality of the buyer's product, then in some circumstances, the component-level target costs will be increased to reflect the higher value that the buyer places on the new component. Such increases are more common if the increased functionality leads to either reduced costs at the buyer or an increase in the final selling price.

Even with the discipline of target costing, it is not always the lowest-cost or highest-value supplier that wins the bid. Firms actively manage their supplier base to ensure that the suppliers remain both efficient and innovative. At Isuzu, although the supplier rated as having the highest value generally wins the order, firms that have a reputation for being good suppliers are often awarded at least part of the order even if their products do not have the highest value. Examples of such companies include Yuasa for batteries, Toyo Valve for engine valves, and Nihon Seiko for bearings. These firms are awarded partial contracts to maintain their relations with Isuzu as Isuzu's objective is to achieve stability in its supplier base.

When a component-level target cost is increased either because its value is higher or because a supplier is being protected, then the increase (net of any savings or end-product price increases) has to be offset elsewhere. Thus, as one target cost is relaxed, others are tightened up to compensate, helping ensure that the buyer achieves its target cost.

TARGET COSTING AND INTERNAL SUPPLIERS

When the supplier is completely owned by the buyer, the two firms are not economically independent of each other and the ability to use target costing in an arm's-length manner is compromised.[2] Establishing a component-level target cost is equivalent to setting a transfer price between the two firms. At some firms, transfer pricing is a political process with the more powerful parent negotiating the most favorable transfer prices at the expense of the weaker subsidiary. Under such circumstances, transfer pricing achieves little more than to move profits from the right-hand pocket to the left-hand one.

The problem with allowing the transfer price-setting process to become political is that it reduces any motivational effects associated with generating profits or achieving targets. For this reason, many Japanese firms continue to use target costing to set the selling prices of internally sourced components. The economic validity of the transfer prices established via target costing ensures that achieving component-level target costs and maintaining or improving the profitability of the subsidiary is viewed as a meaningful objective. Thus, under target costing, setting transfer prices is far more than just moving reported profits between pockets; instead, it becomes a way to effectively transmit cost-reduction pressures to subsidiaries. In addition, the resulting reported profits make it possible to monitor the subsidiary's ability to reduce costs at the rate demanded by the marketplace. Reflecting their importance to both the parent and

---

[2] While partially owned suppliers were not studied, there does not appear to be any reason to suspect that they would be treated in a unique way.

the subsidiary, the negotiations surrounding setting component-level target costs are often as intense as those conducted with external suppliers.

The target costing processes for external and internal suppliers, therefore, often look very similar on the surface, with both parties expending energy to negotiate component-level target costs. This similarity can be misleading because the process can differ in other, more subtle ways, particularly in the negotiations that occur when the supplier believes that the component-level target costs are unachievable. Internal suppliers cannot reduce the power of the buyer, their parent, while an external firm can protect itself from the buyer's power by ensuring that no single customer represents too high a percentage of business. In the extreme, the external supplier can refuse to supply the component at the price set by the buyer's target costing system. The same is not true for internal suppliers. In most cases they will be beholden to their parent. Therefore, it is the parent that has to decide on the nature of the relationship between the two firms. The buyer can either treat the subsidiary as if it were an independent supplier (this is the approach Citizen adopts toward its suppliers), or it can treat it as a dependent supplier (as is the case with Olympus and its suppliers, such as Olympus Omachi).[3]

When the subsidiary is not given full autonomy, there is a risk that the discipline of target costing will be compromised. Two practices observed at Olympus raise this concern. First, to avoid reducing Omachi's profits "unfairly," the target costing process is suspended when a product is introduced too quickly to be subjected to it. When products are introduced in the middle of the planning cycle, there is not always enough time to subject them to the discipline of target costing. Omachi often puts such parts into production before agreeing to a target cost. If it turns out that these parts cannot be manufactured at or below their target cost, then Tatsuno agrees to pay Omachi for their full production costs. In addition, the next six-month plan will reflect a negotiated selling price for such parts that is often greater than their target costs. This process can easily create a loophole in the discipline of target costing.

---

[3] For a more detailed discussion of the relationship between Citizen and Olympus and their subsidiaries see Chapter 13.

Second, if a target cost is considered extremely out of line, Omachi can go back to Olympus to negotiate a higher cost. The most frequent cause for such negotiations is when a new product requires more technical work or is more complex than expected. The usual outcome of the negotiations is a temporary relaxation of the target cost. The objective of the relaxation is to give Omachi time to find ways to reduce the cost of the components for the new products so they will be profitable at their target cost when it is finally invoked.

Neither of these practices is in itself problematic; however, they create avenues for relaxing the discipline of target costing. While such relaxations are also observed for external suppliers, they, too, represent a potential weakening of the discipline of target costing when there is an incentive for the buyer to ensure that the supplier achieves its profit objectives.

Summary

Target costing acts as an interorganizational cost management technique by setting the suppliers' selling prices through the process of component-level target costing. The component-level target costs are allowed to be stretch targets, but for the discipline of target costing to be transmitted effectively to the suppliers, the suppliers must perceive the targets as achievable. In addition, the suppliers must be able to make an adequate profit on most of the components they sell; otherwise, they will be forced to reject the component-level target costs in order to survive. To ensure that reasonable component-level target costs are set, the buyer typically incorporates any available information about its suppliers' design and manufacturing capabilities into the component-level target cost-setting process. The type of information incorporated includes price estimates, any cost information provided either directly or indirectly by suppliers, and historical trends in cost reduction.

The way historical cost-reduction trends are used to establish component-level target costs can be quite different for externally designed components versus those designed internally. For internally designed components the buyer obviously can influence the design of the component significantly. For example, the buyer can change the number of unique materials required as well as the number of components and other design issues that lead to high costs. In addition, the buyer has access to cost tables that identify in detail the costs of each production step. In contrast, for externally designed components, the firm's product designers usually have little control over the design process and relatively little knowledge of the underlying production economics. Therefore, only externally measurable variables such as the selling price and physical capabilities and dimensions can be used in the cost estimation process.

Once component-level target costs are established, they have to be applied. For externally sourced parts three issues have to be addressed. The buyer has to decide, first, whether to legislate or negotiate component-level target costs. Second, it has to decide how much independence to grant the supplier in achieving the cost-reduction objectives incorporated into the component-level target costs. Finally, it must decide whether or not to bundle the target costs. In essence, the three issues all surround the degree of faith that the buyer has in the supplier's ability to reduce costs. When faith is high, the buyer will negotiate the target costs, grant the supplier high independence, and bundle the target costs. In contrast, when faith is low, the target costs will be legislated, the supplier will be treated like a subordinate, and the target costs will not be bundled.

Thus, these decisions leave the central process of target costing unchanged but influence the degree of freedom that the supplier has in identifying where to reduce costs. The aim of interorganizational cost management is to induce high levels of innovation and cost reduction in the supplier base. The whole process of interorganizational cost management has incentives built in because as overall profits increase, they are shared across the supply chain. However, many firms have developed reward systems to increase the incentives for their suppliers both to be innovative and to reduce costs. These reward systems are imbedded in the target costing process.

For externally manufactured components, setting component-level target costs determines the distribution of profits between the buyer and the supplier. Alternatively, when the parts are internally manufactured, the component-level target costs act as transfer prices, and the result could be viewed as nothing more than a simple redistribution of profits between the parent and its subsidiaries. However, when applied properly, target costing can be used to set transfer prices that transmit the competitive pressure faced by the parent to its subsidiaries. The critical decisions the parent has to make about the target costing process revolve around the degree of autonomy granted to the subsidiary and the level of monitoring to which it is subjected.

On the surface, target costing leaves the supplier little freedom. However, when the buyer-supplier relationship is cooperative, stable, and balanced, much can be done to lighten the pressure on the supplier by relaxing the functionality and quality specifications of the component. Such relaxations are usually undertaken when the target costing system of the buyer is chained with the supplier's.

CHAPTER 9

CHAINED TARGET COSTING AND FUNCTIONALITY-PRICE-QUALITY TRADE-OFFS[1]

INTRODUCTION

Target costing systems become especially effective when they are linked to form a target costing chain. Chained target costing systems are created when the output of a buyer's target costing system becomes input to a supplier's target costing system. Component-level target costing at the buyer establishes the target selling prices used by the market-driven costing section of the supplier's target costing system to set the allowable costs of the components (see Figure 9–1). These allowable costs become the basis for setting the product-level target costs and hence the component-level target costs for the supplier. The component-level target costs in turn establish the selling prices of the next firm in the supply chain.

---

[1] Some of the material in the chapter is drawn from "Interorganizational Cost Management Systems: The Case of the Tokyo-Yokohama-Kamakura Supply Chain," by Robin Cooper and Takeo Yoshikawa, *International Journal of Production Economics* 37, No. 1, 1994.

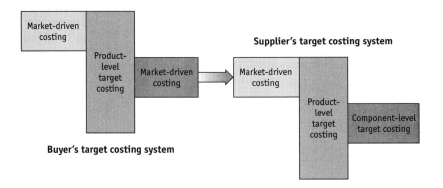

FIGURE 9–1. CHAINED TARGET COSTING—TWO FIRMS

The primary benefit of chained target costing systems lies in their ability to transmit the competitive pressure faced by the firm at the top of the chain to the other firms in the chain (see Figure 9–2). The pressure is created by the quality and functionality specifications of the components that the buyers demand and the component-level target costs they set. It is this transmitted pressure that makes chained target costing systems so valuable, by creating a powerful incentive for the entire supply chain to become more efficient. In particular, the rate at which the firms are expected to become more efficient matches that demanded by the marketplace. Chained target costing systems force each firm in the chain to reduce costs at a rate that will enable all the firms involved to maintain adequate levels of profitability.

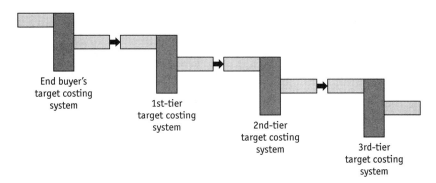

FIGURE 9–2. CHAINED TARGET COSTING—MULTIPLE FIRMS

A target costing chain can consist of all or part of a supply chain. It is the ability of the buyer to dictate selling prices to its suppliers that identifies both the beginning and end of a target costing chain (see Figure 9–3). A firm is at the top of the chain when its customers lack the power to dictate its selling prices and the firm has the power to use its target costing system to dictate selling prices to its suppliers. Firms in the middle of a chain are characterized by having their selling prices set by the target costing systems of their customers and by their ability to use their own target costing system to dictate selling prices to their suppliers. Finally, a firm is at the end of the chain when its selling prices are set by the target costing systems of its customers and it purchases its inputs from suppliers that are more powerful than itself. Since its suppliers are more powerful, the firm at the end of the chain cannot use target costing to set the prices of the components and raw materials it purchases.

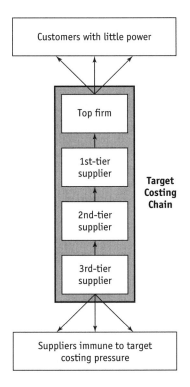

FIGURE 9–3. A TARGET COSTING CHAIN

Because target costing operates at the product and component level, the supply chain path each component of a product takes defines a potential target costing chain. Therefore, for a given product there can be as many target costing chains as there are outsourced components. As the defining condition for the start and end of a target costing chain is the ability to dictate selling prices to suppliers, the target costing chain can start and end anywhere in the supply chain, though of course the firms in the chain have to be juxtaposed. In addition, nothing (other than the length of the supply chain) stops there being more than one target costing chain in a given supply chain (see Figure 9–4).

While a target costing chain can have only one firm to start and one firm to end it, theoretically, it can have any number of firms in

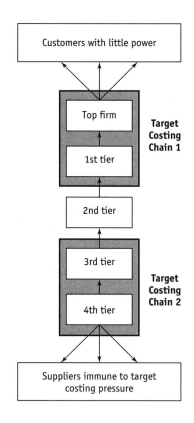

FIGURE 9–4. MULTIPLE TARGET COSTING CHAINS IN A SINGLE SUPPLY CHAIN

the middle. However, since in practice the number of firms in a supply chain is typically quite small (two to six firms), most target costing chains contain between two and four firms. For example, the Tokyo-Yokohama-Kamakura (TYK) target costing chain contains three firms (see Figure 9–5). Tokyo Motors is at the top of the TYK chain because it sells its products primarily to consumers. While market prices clearly exist, individual customers lack the ability to dictate selling prices to Tokyo. Tokyo Motors buys from Yokohama, the firm in the middle of the chain. Tokyo uses its target costing system to set Yokohama's selling prices. Yokohama, in turn, buys from Kamakura and uses its target costing system to set Kamakura's selling prices. Kamakura is at the end of the chain because it buys from major steel producers, such as Nippon Steel, and lacks the ability to dictate selling prices to them.

When all the target costing and supply chains for a given product are drawn, the product's network of suppliers will be identified (see Figure 9–6). Drawing the equivalent for all the end buyer's products gives the end buyer's supplier network (see Figure 9–7). This network contains a single firm at the top of the chain and many firms at the middle and end positions. When the target costing and

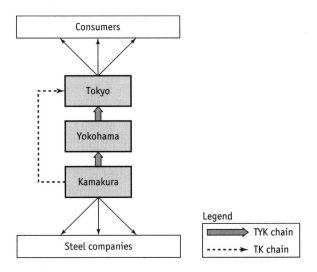

FIGURE 9–5. THE TOKYO-YOKOHAMA-KAMAKURA TARGET COSTING CHAIN

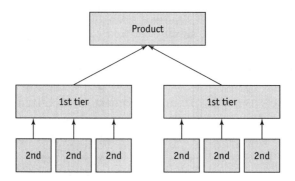

</br>

FIGURE 9-6. SUPPLIER NETWORK FOR A SINGLE PRODUCT
(SIMPLIFIED TO TWO TIERS AND FEW FIRMS)

supply chains for all of the buyers' and suppliers' products are drawn, then the entire supplier network will be identified. If the network is a kingdom, i.e., it has only one end buyer, the king, then the end buyer's network and the total supplier network are identical.[2] If the network is a barony containing several end buyers (i.e., the barons), then one end buyer's supplier network will form only part of the overall supplier network. Finally, if the network is a republic, then any given end buyer's network will form all or part of the overall network.[3]

Interorganizational cost management occurs primarily at the interface between the buyer and supplier. The nature of the interface and the chained target costing process at the interface are shaped predominantly by the relative power of the two firms that constitute the interface. Chained target costing becomes particularly effective when the design teams of the buyer and supplier can interact to change the specifications for the component in ways that make it easier to manufacture the component at its target cost but that do not alter the specifications of the final product. Such functionality-price-quality (FPQ) trade-offs play an important role in ensuring that all firms in the chain remain profitable.

---

[2] This assumes a perfect kingdom where all of the suppliers have only one customer.

[3] Even in a pure republic a single end buyer's supplier network may not encompass all of the firms in the republic. It may require mapping the relationships over time or for several firms to encompass the entire network.

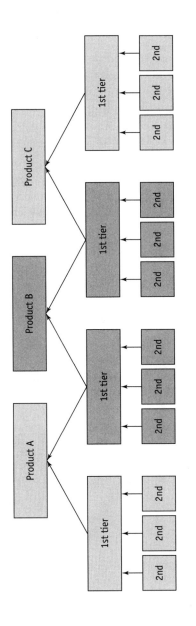

FIGURE 9–7. END BUYER'S SUPPLIER NETWORK

THE BUYER-SUPPLIER INTERFACE

The nature of the interface between the buyer and supplier and the associated target costing process depends on the position of the firms in the target costing chain (see Figure 9–8). For firms at the top of the chain, there is a unique interface between the top firm and the individuals or firms that buy its products (interface A in Figure 9-8). Here, the buyer has little or no individual power over the supplier, although of course via "the market" the buyers have considerable collective power. In the middle of the chain, the firm's buyers exercise considerable power over it, and the firm, in turn, exercises considerable power over its suppliers. Firms in the middle have two interfaces, one where they are the supplier and one where they are the buyer (interfaces B1 and B2 in Figure 9-8). The former interface is between the component-

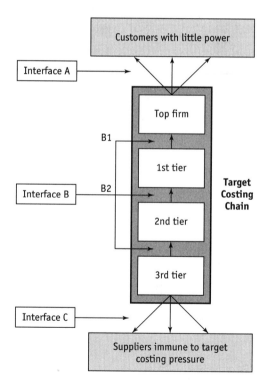

FIGURE 9–8. THE THREE TYPES OF INTERFACES IN A TARGET COSTING CHAIN

level target costing portion of the buyer's target costing system and the market-driven costing portion of the firm's. In contrast, the latter interface is between the component-level target costing portion of the firm's target costing system and the market-driven costing portion of the next supplier in the chain. At the end of the chain, the buyers exercise considerable power over the firm, but the firm exercises virtually no power over its suppliers (interface C in Figure 9–8). This lack of power means that the firm at the end of the chain is subject to intense cost-reduction pressure that it cannot transmit to its suppliers. The interface between the firm at the end of the chain and its suppliers is not considered part of the target costing chain.

The different nature of the various buyer-supplier interfaces influences how firms structure their target costing processes. In particular, it shapes the nature of the market-driven costing and component-level target costing sections. The product-level target costing section is essentially identical for all firms in the chain. Product-level target costing is primarily an internally driven process and thus is relatively unaffected by the firm's position in the chain. The only significant difference occurs when the product engineers look for cost-reduction opportunities. For firms at the top or in the middle of the chain, heavy interaction with suppliers provides a major way to reduce costs. In contrast, the ability of the firm at the end of the chain to influence supplier costs is almost zero. The market-driven costing section is most sophisticated at the top of the target costing chain and less sophisticated in the middle and at the end. This lower degree of sophistication reflects the reduced need to identify target selling prices through market analysis. Most of the time, the target selling price is set by the buyer's target costing system. The component-level target costing process is least sophisticated at the end of the chain because that firm has little ability to influence the selling prices of its suppliers. Thus, firms tailor certain aspects of their target costing systems to the type of interface they have with their buyers and suppliers.

THE CUSTOMER INTERFACE AT THE TOP OF THE CHAIN

Firms at the top of the target costing chain are dealing with customers who lack the power to dictate selling prices individually but collectively determine the success of a new product. The critical challenge these firms face is to develop new products that satisfy their customers even though the customers do not always communicate clearly what they want or do not share the same expectations. To achieve this objective, firms at the top of the target costing chain typically undertake extensive market analysis. The intensity of the analysis required in confrontational markets is illustrated by the way Olympus Optical Co. develops its product plans for its new cameras. At Olympus, new products are introduced through the firm's extensive product planning process. At the heart of this process is the product plan, which identifies the mix of cameras the firm expects to sell over the next five years. The information required to develop this plan comes from six sources: Olympus' corporate plan, a technology review, an analysis of the general business environment, quantitative information about camera sales, qualitative information about consumer trends, and an analysis of the competitive environment (see Olympus' Product Plan).

Similarly, at Tokyo Motors, consumer analysis is used to obtain a better idea of the price range of a given model and the level of functionality that consumers expect. The financial analysis consists of a rough profitability study in which the profitability of the highest-volume variant of the new model is estimated, using historical cost estimates and the latest estimate of that variant's target selling price. This target selling price is determined by taking into account a number of internal and external factors (see Figure 9–9). The internal factors include the position of the model in the firm's product matrix and the strategic and profitability objectives of top management for that model. The external factors include the corporation's image and level of customer loyalty in the model's niche, the expected quality level and functionality of the model compared to competitive offerings, the model's expected market share, and, finally, the expected price of competitive models.

The primary outcome of the market analysis is the target selling price, functionality, and quality of the proposed product. Subtracting the target profit margin from the target selling price gives the allowable cost. Adjusting the allowable cost for the strategic cost-reduction challenge identifies the product-level target cost, i.e., the manufacturing cost to which the product must be designed. This product-level target cost is then decomposed to the component level to give the

OLYMPUS' PRODUCT PLAN

The *corporate plan,* which was developed by Olympus' senior management, identified the future mix of business by major product line, the desired profitability of the corporation and each division, and the role of each major product line in establishing the overall image of the firm.

The *technology review* comprised two sections. The first was a survey of how current and future technological developments, such as digital image processing, were likely to affect the camera business. The second part of the review sought to determine whether Olympus had developed any proprietary technology that could be used for competitive advantage. For instance, Olympus had developed an advanced electronic shutter unit that combined auto-focus control and the lens system, so the camera could be smaller. This shutter unit allowed the firm to develop "small in size" as a distinctive feature of its cameras.

The *analysis of the general business environment* consisted of estimates of how changes in the environment would affect camera sales and the profitability of the business. Factors included foreign exchange rates, how cameras were sold, and the role of other consumer products.

Quantitative information about the world's 35mm camera market was collected from three primary sources. The first was export and domestic market statistics for cameras published by Japan's Ministry of International Trade and Industry. The second was statistics on camera industry shipments, published by the Japan Camera Industry Association. The third source was third-party surveys, commissioned by Olympus, of retail sales by type of camera in each major market.

Qualitative information came from numerous sources. Olympus collected questionnaires from recent purchasers of Olympus cameras. Survey firms conducted group interviews two to three times a year in each of the major markets to spot changes in consumer preferences for cameras. Surveys were conducted in Roppongi, the trendy fashion center of Tokyo; historically, these interviews had proved to be good predictors of future changes in the lifestyle of the Japanese population as a whole.

The *competitive analysis* was based on any information Olympus could gather about its competitors' current and future product plans. Sources of competitive information included press and competitor announcements, patent filings, and articles in patent publications. This information was used to predict what types of products competitors would introduce in the short and long term and what their marketing plans were.

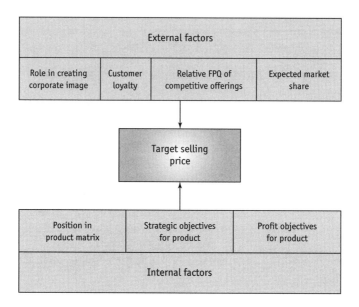

FIGURE 9-9. SETTING THE TARGET SELLING PRICE AT TOKYO MOTORS CORPORATION

component-level target costs. It is these component-level target costs that establish the target selling prices of the suppliers' products.

Applying the Cardinal Rule

If during the design process the firm discovers that the product-level target cost cannot be achieved, then under the cardinal rule it must cancel the project. It is this disciplined application of the cardinal rule that gives target costing its ultimate authority. For example, at Citizen Watch the final step in the product review is to estimate the profitability of the new watch by subtracting the expected costs from the selling price and multiplying the result by the anticipated sales volume. If the watch is profitable, it is introduced and orders are accepted from Citizen Trading Company and other customers. However, if the watch turns out to be unprofitable, then the selling price, production cost, and product design are reviewed. If there is no way for the product to be manufactured profitably, it is never introduced. The primary motivation for the rigorous application of the cardinal rule is to maintain the profitability of the firm.

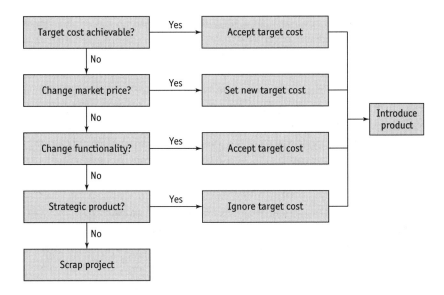

FIGURE 9-10. DECISION PROCESS FOR INTRODUCING THE PRODUCT
AT OLYMPUS OPTICAL INC.

Similar rules are observed at the other companies studied. At Olympus, a structured analysis is undertaken to ensure that only profitable products are launched (see Figure 9–10). This analysis begins with an evaluation of the firm's ability to manufacture the new product at its target cost. If the target cost is considered unachievable, the possibility of raising the price, and hence the target cost, is explored. If it is not possible to increase the price sufficiently, then the possibility of reducing the product's functionality, and thus its cost, is explored. If the functionality cannot be reduced sufficiently without causing the product's price point to fall, any anticipated cost reductions during the manufacturing stage of the product's life are incorporated into the economic analysis. If the product is still insufficiently profitable, even with these savings, it is withdrawn unless a strategic reason to keep it can be demonstrated.

Relaxing the Target Cost at the Top of the Chain

Occasionally, for strategic reasons, it may be necessary for the firm at the top of the target costing chain to relax the cardinal rule and introduce products above their target costs. Usually, the products in question have future revenues associated with them that are not captured in their individual selling prices. Common examples are flagship products, products that use the next generation of technology, and products that protect the firm's market share (see Figure 9–11). Flagship products create general market awareness of the firm's name and presumably lead to increased sales of other products. For example, at Citizen the perpetual calendar watch is considered a flagship product. Given its role, it is not necessary for the flagship product itself to be profitable, but rather that it helps increase the overall profitability of the firm.

Products that use the next generation of technology are also protected because potentially they hold the key to the future of the firm. For example, Olympus manufactures electronic still cameras, which currently sell at a loss. However, these products are not abandoned because it may well be that in 10 years electronic as opposed to chemical film cameras will dominate the photography market. If that scenario becomes reality and Olympus has not developed pro-

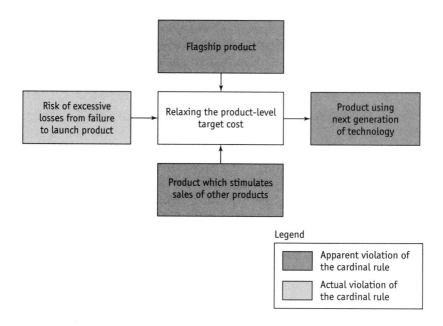

FIGURE 9–11. RELAXING THE TARGET COST AT THE TOP OF THE CHAIN

prietary technologies for electronic still cameras, it will be at risk of having to leave the camera market. The potential future revenues and profits from electronic still cameras thus offset the need to be profitable today.

Finally, some products may be protected because they play a strategic role in the product line. For example, the least expensive cameras Olympus sells typically are entry-level ones. They are the first cameras a person buys or is given as a present. Once someone has bought an Olympus camera, they typically will buy a new camera every few years. Thus, as long as Olympus can keep these customers satisfied, the likelihood is that the cameras they buy in the future will also be from Olympus. Therefore, the starter cameras generate future revenues associated with the replacement cameras. Even if a starter camera cannot be produced at its target cost, it will still be launched if failure to do so would cause a large number of customers to be lost in the long run.

When it is beneficial to the firm, even products that do violate the cardinal rule may be launched. Typically, the rationale supporting the release of these products centers on lost sales. The highly competitive markets in which lean enterprises compete often do not allow product release to be delayed for more than a few weeks. For example, Sony believes that it is imperative to release new products on a timely basis. The Walkman market is so competitive that failure to release a new model on a timely basis usually will result in considerable lost sales. Consequently, the firm does not allow product redesign to extend the launch date. Because the physical production facilities exist, it will launch a product even if its profitability is below the minimum level in order to meet deadlines.

When a product is unprofitable but is still launched for strategic reasons, two additional analyses are undertaken. First, a thorough review of the design process is initiated, to find out why the target cost was not achieved. Second, the product is subjected to an intense, product-specific, kaizen cost-reduction effort immediately after it is launched so that any violation of the cardinal rule is as short-lived as possible. The purpose of these two analyses is to maintain the discipline of target costing, even though a temporary violation has occurred.

When such relaxations occur, great care must be taken to ensure that excessive cost-reduction pressures are not placed on the firm's suppliers. The decision to launch the product is driven by the strategic imperatives of the firm, and its suppliers should not be penalized. To reduce the pressure on suppliers to acceptable levels, the buyer might increase the strategic cost-reduction challenge until the product-level target cost is considered attainable. Depending on the reason why the product is considered strategic, the strategic cost-reduction challenge will either be kept relatively constant (for example, for a flagship product) or reduced over time until it is zero (for example, for a new technology product).

If the introduction of the new product can be postponed, the suppliers can be given time to find ways to reduce costs to the desired level so that the product can be manufactured at its target cost. For example, the original concept for a new Nissan car model included a five-door variant. However, during the conceptual design stage it was determined that developing such a variant would be too costly. Consequently, plans for a five-door variant were postponed until the next version of that automobile. However, the suppliers knew that when the next generation of the product was designed, a five-door version would be included, and they would have to deliver the associated components at their target costs. Thus, the cost-reduction pressure placed on the suppliers was only temporarily postponed not permanently relaxed.

THE SUPPLIER INTERFACE AT THE TOP OF THE CHAIN

Once the firm has established the target cost of a product, it develops target costs for the product's components. This process enables the firm to transmit the competitive cost pressure it faces to its suppliers. When products are complex, the process of setting target costs for externally acquired components is often carried out by first establishing the target costs of the major functions and then, in a subsequent step, of the group components and individual parts they contain.

Major functions are the subassemblies that provide the functionality that enables the product to achieve its purpose. For example, at Isuzu the designers identify approximately 30 major functions per vehicle, including the engine, transmission, cooling system, air conditioning system, and audio system. Group components are the major subassemblies purchased from the firm's suppliers and subcontractors. Group components for an automobile include the carburetor and starter. There are only about 100 such components, yet they amount to as much as 70% to 80% of the manufacturing cost of the entire product. Identifying major functions allows the design process to be broken into multiple, somewhat independent tasks. Typically, the design of each major function is the responsibility of a dedicated team.

Setting the Target Costs of Major Functions

The chief engineer is responsible for setting the target cost of each major function, usually through an extended negotiation process with the design teams. The target costs typically are based on historical cost-reduction rates. If the cost of a major function historically has been decreasing by 5% a year, then probably the same rate will be used. The chief engineer can modify the target costs derived either from historical rates or market analysis for three major reasons. First, if the sum of all the historical rates does not give the desired cost-reduction objective, the chief engineer will negotiate with the head of the design teams of the major functions for more aggressive cost reduction. These negotiations continue until the sum of the target costs of the major components equals the target cost of the product.

Second, if the relative importance of the major function changes from one product generation to the next, the chief engineer will modify the target costs accordingly. The chief engineer typically has objectives for the new product that affect where costs can be reduced. For example, he might want a quieter car or a higher-performance engine. To achieve these objectives, he may decrease the cost reductions expected from the design divisions responsible for those aspects of the product to make it easier for them to achieve both their functionality objective and target cost (see Figure 9–12). At the same time, however, he will increase the expected reductions from other divisions because under the cardinal rule of target costing, the cost increases have to be offset elsewhere in the design.

Third, when the technology on which the major function relies changes, the historical cost-reduction rate of the old technology ceases to be meaningful. Instead, the historical rate for the new technology, if it is available, should be used. When entirely new

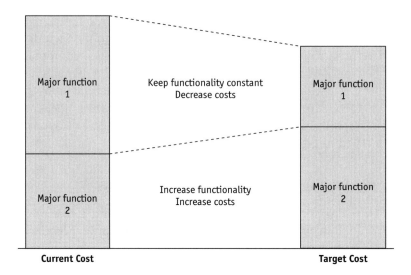

FIGURE 9-12. DISTRIBUTING THE TARGET COST ACROSS MAJOR FUNCTIONS

technologies are used, the cost estimation problem becomes more difficult because no historical data on cost-reduction trends have been developed.

Once the target costs of the major functions have been established, they are decomposed to the group component and parts level as appropriate. The objective is to set a purchase price for every externally acquired group component or part.

Setting the Target Costs of Components

Target costs for components can be set only when the product design has reached the stage at which specific components can be identified. For example, at Nissan value engineering is used after the engineering drawings for trial production have been completed to determine allowable costs for each of the components in every major function of the automobile. Component-level target costs are determined by establishing a cost-reduction objective for each component.

Typically, it is up to the major function design teams to decompose the target cost of the major function to the component level. However, sometimes the chief engineer gets involved in the process to ensure that his objectives for the product are met. At Toyota, the cost-reduction targets are assigned first to the design divisions and then, for certain major parts, to the part level. For example, if one of the design changes is to increase the power of the engine by 10 hp, the engine division might estimate that the improvement will increase the cost of the engine by ¥X. The chief engineer will use the precedents for upgrading engines by 10 hp to estimate a more aggressive cost and then will ask the division to compromise on a cost increase of ¥Y (where Y is lower than X). In contrast, another division might be asked to reduce costs because the new part will be smaller or lighter than the old one. A third division might be asked to maintain the same cost, despite a change in materials, because no change in performance is anticipated.

Once the target costs of the major functions have been accepted, the design teams can take over. They face two major challenges: to design the major functions so that they can be manufactured at their target costs and to develop component-level target costs. Several special techniques have been developed to set component-level target costs. For example, Komatsu uses functional and productivity analysis to set the target costs of the components it acquires externally. Which technique is used depends on the way the product is sourced (see Chapter 8).

The Buyer-Supplier Interfaces in the Middle of the Chain

For firms in the middle of the target costing chain, the market-driven costing process is simplified because their selling prices are set primarily by their buyers' target costing systems. Therefore, these firms typically do not have extensive market analysis subsystems designed to identify the target selling prices of their products. However, while the selling prices are set by the buyers' target costing systems, the functionality and quality of the products can often be modified. For firms in the middle of the target costing chain, survival often depends on their ability to manage the survival triplet of their products by negotiating reductions in functionality and quality with their customers. However, such negotiations will be successful only if the reductions do not lead to a significant decrease in the functionality or quality of the final product.

For example, Yokohama views its negotiations with Tokyo Motors and other major customers as being defined by a functionality-price-quality (FPQ) trade-off. Under such a trade-off, Yokohama explores ways to provide its customers with products that are acceptable even though their functionality and quality are below the levels originally requested by the customer. Successfully achieving this trade-off allows Yokohama to find solutions to a customer's product requirements that generate adequate returns. Lowering the functionality and quality of a component without decreasing the functionality or quality of the end product allows Yokohama's manufacturing costs to be reduced. Since the selling price remains unchanged, the firm increases its profits. Thus, for many firms in the middle or at the end of the chain, the ability to remain profitable is determined in part by their ability to manage the survival triplet of their products.

Negotiations between buyer and supplier firms about reductions in functionality and quality can be successful only when the buyer has overspecified some aspect of the component. Overspecification occurs when the buyer is "pushing too hard" on the survival triplet, lacks knowledge of or ignores the cost-benefit trade-offs within the supplier's survival triplet, or is using component specifications to create negotiating space for the supplier.

The intense competitive pressure that the buyer faces often requires the firm to improve all three characteristics of the survival triplet at once (see Figure 9–13). Overreacting to this pressure, the buyer might demand improvements from its suppliers along all three characteristics. However, often such improvements in the compo-

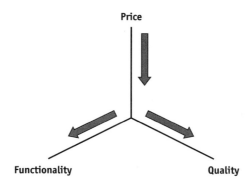

FIGURE 9–13. HOW TOKYO MOTORS PRESSURES YOKOHAMA ON ALL THREE DIMENSIONS OF THE SURVIVAL TRIPLET

nents provide no benefits to users of the end product. If the supplier can identify such overspecifications and get the buyer to relax them, then its costs will be lowered (see Figure 9–14). For example, Yokohama might find a way to produce a part by pressing as opposed to machining it. The pressed product is inherently lower in quality but is less expensive to produce.

Alternatively, the improvements specified by the buyer may provide benefits to users of the end product, but the value users place on these improvements is insufficient to justify the higher costs imposed on the supplier. In such cases, the buyer's target cost for the component will be set too low, and the supplier will be unable to make an adequate return. This condition may emerge because the buyer has insufficient knowledge of the cost functions of its suppliers.

Finally, the buyer might overspecify the component to create some negotiating space for the supplier. The core relationships between the buyer and supplier firms are cooperative; therefore some degree of "successful" negotiations on the part of the supplier might be necessary to maintain the relationship. By gaining some concessions, the supplier might view the contract as more acceptable than if the firm is forced to accept the buyer's specifications outright.

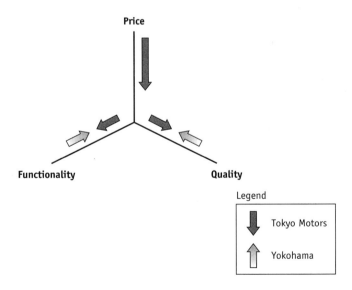

FIGURE 9–14. HOW YOKOHAMA RESPONDS TO TOKYO MOTORS' PRESSURE

Occasionally, FPQ trade-offs can be used to get the buyer to increase component-level target costs by adding value to the components. Value can be added in two ways. First, the increased functionality or quality translates into higher selling prices for the buyer. These higher prices lead to increased product-level target costs and hence higher component-level target costs. Alternatively, value can be added by decreasing the buyer's costs, for example, by rendering a subsequent production step unnecessary. In such a case, the buyer's manufacturing costs will fall so the component-level target costs can increase without violating the overall product-level target cost.

Degree of Information Sharing

In theory, under target costing customers are unaware of the profits that their suppliers earn on the products they sell. The continuous reduction in target costs creates an appropriate level of pressure on suppliers to become more efficient, but if the suppliers can exceed the rate of cost reduction demanded by their customers, then their profits will increase. In practice, however, the sharing of information and the exchange of engineering personnel allows buyers to estimate their suppliers' costs fairly accurately. When a supplier's product appears to be generating excessive profits, its target selling price, and hence its target cost, usually are revised downward by the buyer. For example, it is up to Yokohama engineers to innovate continuously and find ways to manufacture its products so that they can be sold at their target selling price and make adequate returns. If Yokohama finds a way to reduce the cost of one of its products significantly, it can make a high return on that product. However, since there is considerable sharing of production information between Yokohama and its customers, it does not take long for the target selling price to reflect the new production cost.

Applying the Cardinal Rule

The continuous pressure placed on suppliers to reduce costs can create a significant risk of insolvency. To reduce this risk, suppliers must be willing to refuse unprofitable contracts. To support such refusals, many firms establish a "no unprofitable products" rule. For example, one of Yokohama management's objectives is to maintain a corporate culture that enables the firm to say no when it cannot find a way to make a product profitably. The "no unprofitable products" rule can be effective only if the firm is not overly dependent on one or more customers. To reduce the degree of dependency, suppliers try to maintain a broad customer base, with no single customer representing a major portion of their business.

The level of communication between buyers and suppliers is high; therefore selling prices are often considered "public information." This condition strengthens the importance of maintaining selling prices for products that are sold to multiple buyers because these products have an effective market price. If a supplier sells such a product to a given customer below its effective market price, there is substantial risk that, once the new price leaks out, it will rapidly become the market price for that product. Therefore, when accepting a new, lower target selling price, the firm has to consider the entire sales volume of the product, not just the volume of the contract currently being negotiated. In addition, if the product is a member of a product family, the selling prices of other family members might also be adversely affected.

Relaxing the Target Cost in the Middle of the Chain

While target costing could be applied blindly, buyers typically use it intelligently by creating significant but realistic cost-reduction pressures on their suppliers. Therefore, if it is not possible to reduce quality and functionality to an extent that will permit suppliers to manufacture the part profitably, buyers are sometimes willing to relax their target costs temporarily. This relaxation is necessary if the suppliers are to survive. The objective is to allow the suppliers to make a reasonable return while still creating sufficient pressure on them to find ways to reduce costs to the target levels. To maintain the discipline of target costing, however, target costs of components can be relaxed only under very special conditions and usually only for a short time (see Figure 9–15).

The first condition in which the target cost may be temporarily relaxed is when the supplier needs additional time to find ways to achieve the target cost. For example, most major customers of Yokohama typically will not accept long-term changes to their component-level target costs. However, they sometimes will allow the selling

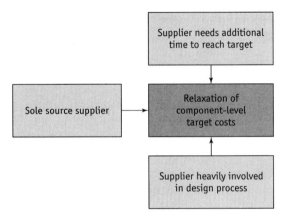

FIGURE 9-15. RELAXING COMPONENT-LEVEL TARGET COSTS IN
THE MIDDLE OF THE CHAIN

price to rise above the target for the first few years after introduction
of a new component to allow Yokohama time to find ways to reduce
its costs sufficiently to make an acceptable return at the target cost.

The target cost may be relaxed under other conditions, in particular when erosion of the arm's-length relationship between the
buyer and supplier changes the respective power levels. In the case of
Yokohama, for example, an opportunity to negotiate a higher selling
price occurs when Yokohama is heavily involved in the design
process of a component and hence in the scheduling of the end product. Under these conditions, it is difficult for competitors to intervene
as Yokohama is acting in many ways like a captive supplier. If
Yokohama is unable to meet the target cost, customers such as
Tokyo Motors are often forced to accept a higher price that provides
Yokohama with an adequate return. Tokyo is forced to make this
concession because it cannot turn to another supplier and expect to
get delivery in a reasonable time period. However, even under these
conditions, only a temporary reprieve is given. In the long run,
Yokohama is expected to sell the product to Tokyo at its target price.

Another opportunity for relaxation of the target cost presents
itself when Yokohama is the sole source of a product. When a product is sold to only one customer such as Tokyo, Yokohama gives
them a preliminary breakdown of the cost structure of the product.
This cost breakdown allows Tokyo to determine the profit margin

that Yokohama expects to earn on this product. If this margin is too low, it provides Yokohama with a rationale for using FPQ trade-offs to try and negotiate some concession in either the target selling price or other specifications of the product.

Firms in the middle of the target costing chain are thus subject to intense cost-reduction pressures created by their customers' target costing systems. As part of their strategy for maintaining an adequate level of profitability, they transmit that pressure to their suppliers via their own target costing system. The power of chained target costing derives from the fact that the pressure applied down the target costing chain reflects the market pressure placed on the chain by the customers of the firm at the top.

THE BUYER-SUPPLIER INTERFACE AT THE END OF THE CHAIN

A company is at the end of the target costing chain if it purchases its inputs from firms that are much more powerful than itself, and therefore it is unable to use target costing to set the prices of the components and raw materials supplied. This inability to dictate selling prices to suppliers implies that the target costing chain ends with this firm. In the TYK chain, this position is held by Kamakura, a small family-owned concern that purchases the majority of its inputs from much larger steel producers.

Life at the end of the target costing chain is not easy because the end firm faces continuous pressure from its customers to reduce costs but cannot transmit that pressure to its suppliers. The firm at the end of the chain is thus squeezed more severely than the firms in the middle or at the top. To survive, the end firm has to become expert at low-cost production and develop a reputation for high quality and functionality. However, its inability to transfer the cost-reduction pressure further down the supply chain places the firm at risk of bankruptcy. Therefore, its buyers take special actions to ensure its survival.

Degree of Information Sharing

The customers of the firm at the end of the target costing chain have to be careful that they do not cause the end firm to go bankrupt. If they exert too much cost-reduction pressure, then the profitability of the firm at the end of the chain will fall below the survival level. For this reason, the firm's customers typically moderate the use of their target costing systems. Instead of simply dictating component-level target costs, they enter into a more complex negotiation process requiring an open-book policy on the part of the firm at the end of the chain. Under this policy, the customers know both the expected costs and the profits of each product that the firm at the end of the chain sells them. This additional knowledge allows the component-level target costs set for the end firm to reflect that firm's production costs.

For example, Kamakura is expected to share most of its cost information with its customers. Yokohama uses a formal cost estimation document that has to be returned with each bid. This document requires Kamakura's bid to be divided into eight categories: material cost, mold cost, facility fees, labor costs, heat treatment costs, shot blast costs, management fees, and profit. Kamakura's customers use this detailed cost information to help them set realistic selling prices for Kamakura's products.

Applying the Cardinal Rule

Kamakura, like Yokohama, has a rule against selling products that do not make an adequate return. Applying this rule is particularly important for Kamakura because of the relatively low returns it achieves. Yokohama management actively supports Kamakura in its efforts to create its own "no unprofitable products" culture to help protect the firm from excessive cost-reduction pressures from its suppliers. This behavior illustrates Yokohama's willingness to take actions to protect its suppliers even if, on the surface, these actions are against its own interests.

Relaxing the Target Cost at the End of the Chain

The customers of the firm at the end of the chain are sometimes willing to relax the target costs, at least temporarily, when the circumstances warrant it (see Figure 9–16). It is not unusual for customers to be willing to pay as much as two or three times the target cost in the early years of production. This situation typically occurs when production volumes are less than anticipated or when production

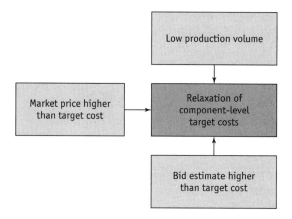

FIGURE 9-16. RELAXING COMPONENT-LEVEL TARGET COSTS AT THE
       END OF THE CHAIN

techniques turn out to be more complicated than expected. For example, when Kamakura's management considers a product's production volume too low to be economical (i.e., under 60% of full production volume), Kamakura presses for a higher price to cover the costs associated with low production volumes. Customers such as Yokohama are usually willing to pay the additional amount because they expect prices to fall in the future as production volumes increase and as costs decrease through application of kaizen costing techniques.

Selling prices for most of Kamakura's products are established either by the market or by the customers' target costing systems. For new products, the customer either identifies the target selling price using its target costing system or asks Kamakura to bid for the work. The approach used depends on the nature of the new product. When the new product is similar to existing products, the target selling price is based on the price of the existing parts. If a part is different from existing products, then a bid is requested. When asked to bid on a new product, Kamakura determines the expected cost of the new product using its price estimation system. The firm's bid is based on the expected cost of the part, the customer in question, and general market conditions. Even for these products, the customer usually compares Kamakura's bid price with the price generated by its own target costing system.

The purpose of requesting bids from Kamakura is to ensure that the customer's target costing system does not create excessive cost-reduction pressures on the firm. Consequently, Kamakura's objective in presenting a bid is to increase the selling price of the product. To obtain higher prices while maintaining the discipline of target costing, it is to Kamakura's advantage to demonstrate that its products have inherently lower costs to use than anticipated by the customer. Often, the customer does not take into account factors such as the quality or functionality of the product. If Kamakura can demonstrate that by increasing the product's quality it can reduce the customer's overall costs (by reducing defects and rework), then the customer is usually willing to increase the selling price accordingly.

If even with such adjustments, Kamakura's required selling price is still considered too high by its customer, then an adjustment process is initiated, with the two firms entering into price negotiations. The objective of this process is to allow Kamakura to demonstrate that the cost-reduction pressure derived from the customer's target costing system is excessive and to get the customer to make some price concessions. The primary purpose of the negotiations is to allow Kamakura to explain why it cannot produce the product at the specified target price. Major customers such as Yokohama (and even minor customers) usually dominate these negotiations and, after listening to Kamakura's arguments, set the desired selling price. However, Kamakura has considerable leverage in these negotiations because of its three areas of relative strength compared to other suppliers: high technological capacity, high quality standards, and reputation for delivering products on time.

The outcome of this price-setting approach is that Kamakura's production costs are reflected in the customers' target costs. In theory, if every customer agreed to pay the selling price determined by this estimation procedure, the approach should allow Kamakura to earn its planned pretax profit margins of 7%. However, in practice, the cost-reduction pressures are such that actual profits are only 2%. The 5% difference is attributed mainly to overly optimistic estimates for products that experience a decrease in production volume or that are subject to price cutting, decreased efficiency, a shortening of product life cycles, or a longer-than-expected machining time.

The low return makes it difficult for Kamakura to expand or acquire more advanced manufacturing equipment. Therefore, the firm relies on a "no loss" rule to maintain its overall profitability.

Only rarely does Kamakura agree to sell a new product at a loss. It is more likely to refuse to manufacture a part than to accept an unprofitable contract. Most of Kamakura's customers recognize that the firm cannot afford to accept unprofitable business and therefore accept this constraint. Because they understand Kamakura's cost structure, they rarely press for an unprofitable price so as to ensure Kamakura's continued existence.

In summary, firms at the end of the target costing chain are subject to even more intense cost-reduction pressures than the firms in the middle because they lack the power to use target costing to transmit the pressure to their suppliers. To ensure the survival of firms at the end of the chain, the buyers have to be careful not to exert excessive cost-reduction pressures on their suppliers. Therefore, instead of simply dictating component-level target costs, the two firms enter into a more complex negotiation process in which the buyers set the selling prices based on detailed information provided by the suppliers about the expected costs and profits of each component they manufacture.

SUMMARY

Target costing systems gain considerable effectiveness when they are chained across one or more buyer-supplier interfaces. Chaining is achieved by linking the component-level target costing section of the buyer's target costing system with the market-driven costing section of the supplier's system. A typical target costing chain contains two to four firms. The firms at the top and bottom of the chain are characterized by the inability of the buyer to dictate selling prices to its suppliers. The firms in the middle are characterized by their buyers' ability to impose selling prices and by their own ability to dictate prices to their suppliers.

Chaining of target costing systems enables the firm at the top of the chain to transmit the competitive pressure it faces to all the firms in the chain. Another advantage is that the resulting cost-reduction pressures across the chain reflect the pressure created by the end market. If the supply chain is as efficient as its competitors, then component-level target costs should be realistic and achievable most of the time. This achievability is important as it maintains the discipline of target costing. If unachievable target costs are set most of the time, violations of the cardinal rule become common, and target costing loses much of its effectiveness.

Target costing chains deal with three types of buyer-supplier interfaces. The first type of interface, between the firm at the top of the chain and its customers, is characterized by detailed analyses of the product and future customer requirements. Consequently, at the top of the chain the market-driven costing section of the firm's target costing system is highly developed. The second type of interface is between a buyer that has a target costing system and its suppliers. For such buyers, the component-level target costing sections of their target costing systems are highly developed. This is especially true for the firm at the top of the chain where the products are usually the most complex. Further down the chain, the products become less complex, and the component-level target costing sections are correspondingly simpler. The final type of interface is between the firm at the bottom of the chain and its suppliers. This interface is characterized by a relatively simple component-level target costing section used only to sum the prices of the outsourced items. The component-level target costing section here is simple because the firm at the end of the chain cannot dictate prices to its suppliers and therefore is primarily a price-taker.

All the firms in the chain must be able to find ways to remain profitable. They can achieve this objective by trying to become as efficient as possible, by undertaking FPQ analyses, by refusing to accept unattainable component-level target costs, and by initiating interorganizational cost investigations, the subject of the next chapter.

CHAPTER 10

INTERORGANIZATIONAL COST INVESTIGATIONS

INTRODUCTION

Chained target costing systems are a powerful way to create significant cost-reduction pressures within the segments of a supply chain connected by target costing systems. The firms at the top and in the middle of the target costing chain transmit the competitive pressures they face to their suppliers. The outcome is a supply chain focused on serving the ultimate customer in a cost-efficient manner.

Chained target costing inherently limits the degree to which suppliers can modify the design of components because it is the buyers who establish the functionality, quality, and selling price of the components they purchase. The supplier's product engineers are expected to find a cost-effective way to manufacture these components as designed; they are not allowed to make fundamental design modifications to the components. The advantage of this approach is that the engineering teams at the buyer and supplier firms can act independently of each other. This independence limits the coordination and information processing loads placed on the design teams at the two firms (see Figure 10–1). While FPQ trade-offs create some interaction between the two design teams, they are sometimes inadequate to resolve the problems (see Figure 10–2).

A limitation of chained target costing emerges when the buyer designs a component that leads to unnecessarily high manufacturing costs for the supplier. The poor design usually is caused by the buyer's limited knowledge of the production economics of the firms in the supply chain. Since the buyer is unable to design components that take full advantage of the supplier's manufacturing skills, the supplier is forced to manufacture components that are not optimized for its production processes. This limitation becomes a problem when the component specifications set by the buyer make it impossible for the supplier to generate an adequate return on the component. Under chained target costing, the supplier has only two choices, either to say no, thus obeying the "no unprofitable products" rule, or try to negotiate a higher selling price, a difficult objective under target costing. However, there is a third option that lies outside the domain of chained target costing—to initiate an interorganizational cost investigation. Under an interorganizational cost investigation, more fundamental changes can be made to the speci-

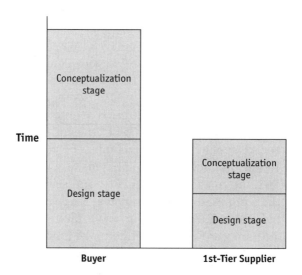

FIGURE 10–1. CHAINED TARGET COSTING WITH NO FORMAL
INTERACTION BETWEEN THE DESIGN TEAMS

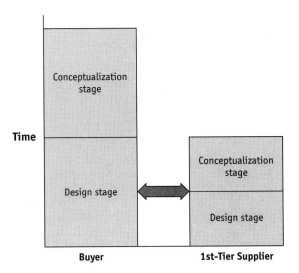

FIGURE 10–2. CHAINED TARGET COSTING WITH FPQ TRADE-OFF

fications of the product and components than can be achieved by using a FPQ trade-off.

The more radical design changes possible under interorganizational cost investigations require more intense interactions among the design teams (see Figure 10–3). These interactions involve the joint application of value engineering techniques.[1] For such investments of time to be worthwhile requires that the part being redesigned be both significant in value and amenable to redesign. Interorganizational cost investigations can be extended to multiple design teams (see Figure 10–4).

THE SCOPE OF INTERORGANIZATIONAL COST INVESTIGATIONS

Interorganizational cost investigations derive their power from the increased scope of the design changes that can be made to both the

---

[1] For a detailed description of value engineering, see Chapter 7 of *Target Costing and Value Engineering* in this series.

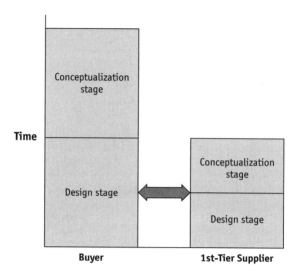

Figure 10–3. Chained Target Costing with Interorganizational Cost Investigation

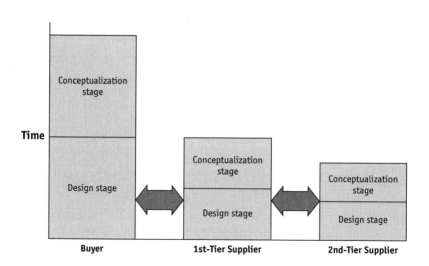

Figure 10–4. Chained Target Costing with Multifirm Interorganizational Cost Investigation

end product and the components it contains. Under chained target costing, the specifications of the end product are essentially fixed. While FPQ trade-offs allow some relaxation of the quality and functionality specifications of components, the buyer basically must be indifferent to these changes. In particular, the functionality and quality of the buyer's product must remain unchanged in the eyes of its customers. However, more fundamental changes, such as redesigning a component in a way that requires the buyer to modify other aspects of the end product, call for an interorganizational cost investigation.

The increased scope of the design changes and the interaction among product designers from both buyers and suppliers allow parts to be designed so that all the steps from raw material to finished product are more cost efficient. Put more formally, products and components can be designed so that they reflect global, not local, production economics. Costs can be reduced in two ways through interorganizational cost investigations. First, the location where activities are performed can be changed so that they can be performed more efficiently (see Figure 10–5). Second, the need to perform activities can be reduced or avoided by redesigning the product and the components it contains to take full advantage of the manufacturing skills available throughout the target costing chain (see Figure 10–6).

The decision to shift the location of an activity requires knowledge about the production processes and economics of the entire chain. Several questions have to be answered before deciding to move an activity (see Figure 10–7):

- Are there other firms in the chain that are able to perform the activity?
- Can any of those firms perform that activity more efficiently? Obviously, costs will be reduced only if the new location can perform the activity more efficiently.
- Are there any synergies between that activity and those already performed at any of those firms that allow overall costs to be reduced by collocating the activities? For example, when machining operations are performed at the same location, they can sometimes be combined and performed in a single step. The ability to combine operations means that even if the activity that is moved is performed less efficiently

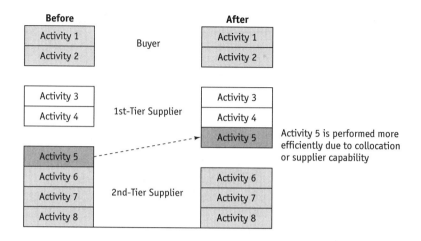

FIGURE 10-5. MOVING ACTIVITIES AMONG FIRMS

at the new location, overall costs will be lower if the savings due to collocation dominate.

• Can the design process be accelerated by moving activities at a reasonable cost?

Toyo Radiator demonstrated the effective movement of activities when it requested that early prototyping of the engine cooling

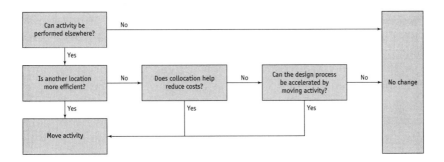

FIGURE 10-7. THE DECISION TO MOVE ACTIVITIES AMONG FIRMS IN
THE TARGET COSTING CHAIN

system occur at its facilities as opposed to Komatsu's. While Komatsu was probably more efficient at prototyping (at least in the early days of the transfer), the advantage of testing at Toyo's facility was that any flaws in the design could be corrected more rapidly, thus avoiding expensive redesigns late in the product development process.

The other way to reduce costs by undertaking an interorganizational cost investigation is to redesign the product or the components it contains to take better advantage of the production capabilities of the entire supply chain. For example, by relaxing the surface specifications for a Yokohama-supplied component, Tokyo Motors enabled Kamakura to use a casting as opposed to a more expensive forging. The use of the casting required extra machining steps at both Kamakura and Yokohama, but overall costs were lower because castings are much cheaper than forgings.

INITIATING AN INTERORGANIZATIONAL COST INVESTIGATION

The interorganizational cost investigations observed at the sample firms all occurred within the context of a chained target costing system. The trigger for the cost investigation usually is the inability of at least one firm in the chain to achieve the target costs set by its buyer. Under the "no unprofitable products" rule, this firm should reject the order. However, interorganizational cost investigations are designed to avoid such occurrences. If the firms are not using chained target costing, then presumably the trigger for an interorganizational cost investigation will be the inability to negotiate a price that enables the supplier to make a adequate profit on the component.

If chained target costing systems are capturing the competitive pressures faced by the top firm in the chain, then the inability to meet the target cost identifies one of two conditions.[2] Either it is caused by the failure of the chain (or one of its members) to maintain a competitive level of efficiency, or it identifies a poorly designed product and/or component. Failure to achieve the target cost indicates that competitors may have found a way to design and manufacture the product or component more efficiently than the top firm and its suppliers. Chained target costing is thus a powerful way to identify opportunities for the firms in the chain to reduce costs. Performing interorganizational cost investigations in those instances where target costs are not met allows firms to achieve the pre-specified targets. This is not to suggest that interorganizational cost investigations would not yield benefits in other places but rather that the firms in the sample do not actively search for such places to reduce costs unless the cardinal rule has been violated.

The ability to initiate an interorganizational cost investigation can be likened to the ability of any worker in a just-in-time production setting to stop the line whenever a defect is encountered. The inability of one of the firms in a supply chain to achieve its target costs demonstrates that a defect has occurred in the target costing process. The usual source of the problem is in the design of the component. As in the production setting, once the defect is identified, all surrounding workers (here the design teams at the other firms) get together to try to resolve the problem.

CONDITIONS FAVORING INTERORGANIZATIONAL COST INVESTIGATIONS

Four factors support the success of interorganizational cost investigations (see Figure 10–8). First, the component must be suf-

---

[2] Target costing systems recognize and accept small failures to achieve competitive levels by creating a strategic cost-reduction challenge. See Chapter 6 of *Target Costing and Value Engineering* in this series.

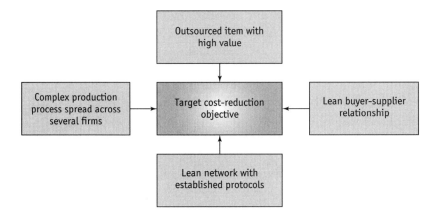

FIGURE 10-8. FACTORS SUPPORTING THE SUCCESS OF AN
INTERORGANIZATIONAL COST INVESTIGATION

ficiently high in value and amenable to redesign to warrant the effort expended by the design teams. Second, the component's manufacturing process must be spread across at least two firms in the supply chain. Third, the buyer-supplier relationships must be lean, that is, stable, cooperative, and mutually beneficial. Finally, network protocols must be in place to ensure adequate sharing of the additional profits among all the firms involved.

Bringing the buyer's and supplier's product designers together to perform an interorganizational cost investigation makes it possible to identify cost savings beyond those achievable through chained target costing. However, interorganizational cost investigations consume considerable resources, namely the time of the product designers. For example, the redesign of power shovels required both Komatsu and Toyo Radiator to make significant changes in their product designs. For an interorganizational cost investigation to be beneficial, the relationship between the buyer and supplier for that component or set of components must be deemed sufficiently important to warrant the effort and the risk to the suppliers of increasing the power of their buyers. Suppliers of components that make up only a small portion of the buyer's total costs are unlikely to warrant an investigation. In contrast, when the part concerned is a group component or major function such as an engine cooling system, then an interorganizational cost investigation is justified. Consequently, interorganizational cost investigations usually are carried out between the buyer and its major suppliers and family members.

Interorganizational cost investigations thus become especially effective when the outsourced items are group components and major functions because their value is high, as is their scope for redesign. In addition, they nearly always have complex production processes spread across several firms. These characteristics lead to interorganizational cost investigations that have a high probability of being successful.

Furthermore, interorganizational cost investigations require highly cooperative and trusting relationships in the supply chain. The suppliers must be willing to allow the buyer's product designers to have extensive knowledge of both their production techniques and economics. In return, the buyer must be willing to allow the suppliers' product designers to gain insights into the designs of future products and suggest changes before the new products are launched. This increased technology sharing requires both sides to trust each other. The suppliers must trust the buyer not to share innovations considered proprietary with other suppliers that are their direct competitors. The buyer, in turn, must trust the suppliers not to share its proprietary innovations with other customers that are in direct competition with the buyer. Consequently, while considerable sharing of innovations occurs in the supply chain, there must be some limits to enable the innovating firms in the chain to reap the benefits of their creativity. If this trust is violated, then the willingness of the harmed firm to continue to be involved in interorganizational cost investigations will be significantly reduced.

Finally, the firms in the supply chain involved in an interorganizational cost investigation learn about each others' costs and hence profits. If the most powerful firm in the chain used this information to extract all the profits, the other firms would rapidly become unwilling to initiate or get involved in such investigations. For example, at Komatsu, sometimes the sharing of cost information and Komatsu's knowledge of Toyo's profits leads to a conflict of interest, with pressure building within Komatsu to reduce target costs where Toyo's profits are known to be high. However, the two firms share a common goal—getting costs as low as possible—that ensures that these conflicts rarely become serious. To reduce the incidence of such conflicts, Komatsu is not meant to set its target costs for parts manufactured by Toyo based on its knowledge of Toyo's costs. Instead it is meant to set its target costs independently of Toyo and let Toyo make as much profit as possible. Maintaining this separation is important if the level of trust in the relationship is to be kept high.

Network protocols play an important role in ensuring the success of interorganizational cost investigations. The protocols ensure that the firms in the network are operating for the good of the entire network and not just their own. While there is no guarantee that profits will be shared equitably, the protocols at least ensure that all the firms involved are more profitable at the end of a successful interorganizational cost investigation.

INTERORGANIZATIONAL COST INVESTIGATIONS IN PRACTICE

In interorganizational cost investigations, the interactions between the buyer's and suppliers' design teams are more extensive than in chained target costing. The objective is to identify product and component designs that reduce the total of the buyer's and suppliers' costs. Such investigations were observed between Komatsu and Toyo Radiator and among Tokyo Motors, Yokohama, and Kamakura. At Komatsu, they were called cost balance verifications (CBVs) and, in the TYK chain, minimum cost investigations (MCIs).

Cost Balance Verifications

A cost balance verification is undertaken when the buyer's target costing system sets a cost-reduction objective for a particular component that the supplier is unable to achieve by a significant margin. To help the supplier achieve the target cost, a joint team of product designers from the two firms looks for innovative ways to reduce the cost of the component. The critical difference between an FPQ trade-off and a CBV lies in the joint design team's ability to suggest design changes to the component that may also require the end product to be modified in some way.

The application of CBV techniques is illustrated by Toyo Radiator's design of the engine cooling systems for Komatsu's A20 and A21 power shovels. Komatsu wanted to increase the functionality of their power shovels by using higher horsepower engines. These larger engines required greater capacity for their cooling systems. In particular, the fan's airflow volume was expected to increase by 36%. In addition, Komatsu wanted simultaneously to reduce noise levels by 5%. These improvements represented a particularly severe design challenge for Toyo Radiator.

The problem was that Komatsu's customers were not willing to pay for the full amount of the performance improvement to the power shovels. Reflecting their customers' unwillingness to pay the full price premium, Komatsu set Toyo's target selling price of the cooling system at 118% of the old price. Therefore, if Toyo wanted to retain its historical profit margin, it would have to find a way to manufacture the new radiator at only 18% more than the existing cooling system. Even with this 18% increase and a highly innovative fan design identified by using concurrent cost management (see Chapter 11), it was not possible for Toyo Radiator to manufacture the new cooling system at an adequate profit. Consequently, a CBV was initiated.

The objective of the CBV undertaken by a joint Komatsu-Toyo design team was to find ways to reduce the costs of the new engine cooling system even more to bring it down to target levels. This CBV merged seamlessly with the simultaneous engineering approach that Komatsu and Toyo were using for these new power shovels. Given the perfect blending of the two programs, they are discussed together in the next chapter on concurrent cost management.

Minimum Cost Investigations

When multiple firms are involved in the production of a component, it is sometimes necessary to get the design engineers from all the firms together to find ways to reduce costs across the entire target costing chain. A minimum cost investigation is a formalized approach to such multifirm meetings. MCIs allow all the players to get together and design a part as if they were employees of a single company. The technique consists of five major steps:

1. Gathering cost information about each function of a product;
2. Searching for ways to minimize costs;

3. Proposing alternative ways to reduce costs and establishing guidelines for developing inexpensive products;
4. Performing feasibility studies for the proposals in step 3;
5. Developing an implementation plan for the cost-reduction proposals approved in step 4.

An MCI is initiated whenever a firm in the chain is unable to manufacture a product for its target cost. An MCI meeting may be called to find innovative ways to reduce costs across the organizational boundaries or, if adequate savings cannot be identified, to negotiate an increase in the target cost of the component at one firm without changing the target cost of the component to the ultimate buyer. An MCI makes cost reduction more likely because the components can be designed so that all the steps in the manufacturing process become more efficient, from raw material to finished product.

One example is when engineers at Kamakura find a way to shift from a forged part to a much cheaper casting (see Figure 10–9). They can design such parts only with the help of Yokohama and Tokyo Motors engineers because often the quality and functionality of the part have to be changed to reduce costs by the required amount. While Kamakura engineers are experts at finding ways to reduce the cost of their parts, without an MCI meeting they would not know about Yokohama's and Tokyo Motors' subsequent processing steps and the way the component is used in the final product.

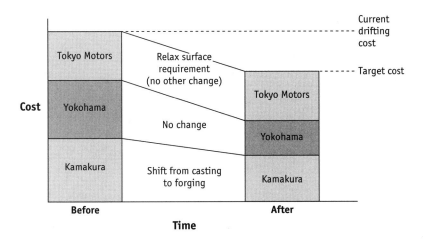

FIGURE 10–9. MOVING ACTIVITIES BETWEEN KAMAKURA AND YOKAHAMA

The second incentive to call an MCI meeting is created by the possibility of increasing the target cost of the component because of reduced costs downstream (see Figure 10–10). When the product designers of the three firms interact, they are able to look at the entire value chain for the product and the components it contains. If changes to the component at Kamakura lead to reduced costs at Yokohama or Tokyo Motors, then Kamakura's target cost can be increased without violating Tokyo's target cost. That is, when the total costs incurred by the buyer are decreased through an interorganizational cost investigation, the buyer's target costing system can increase the component-level target costs without exceeding the product-level target cost and avoid a violation of the cardinal rule. Such interorganizational cost trade-offs make it possible for the supplier to achieve its target costs, which was the objective of the interorganizational cost investigation. For example, when Kamakura designs a forging that reduces Yokohama's machining costs, Yokohama is willing to pay more for such a component. When such savings are identified, it is up to the buyer and supplier to negotiate how much of the savings is used to increase component-level target costs for the supplier and how much is retained by the buyer as increased profits.

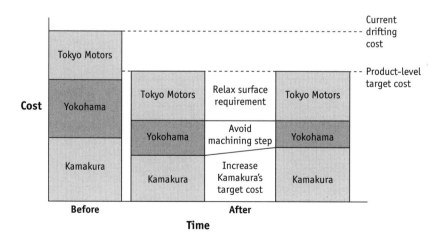

FIGURE 10–10. INCREASING KAMAKURA'S TARGET COST TO REFLECT AN INTERORGANIZATIONAL COST INVESTIGATION

THE IMPLICATIONS OF INTERORGANIZATIONAL COST INVESTIGATIONS

The primary implications of interorganizational cost investigations are the intensive sharing of cost information and the possibility of a shift in the balance of power between the buyers and suppliers (see Figure 10–11). The increased sharing of cost information is a necessary requirement of interorganizational cost investigations because of the greater scope of potential design changes. The risk associated with sharing cost information is that the more powerful members of the chain will use that information to their own advantage.

Intensive Sharing of Cost Information

One of the major differences between (chained) target costing and interorganizational cost investigations is that under an interorganizational cost investigation, the firm at the top of the chain is aware of the selling prices and manufacturing costs and hence profit margins of the suppliers in the target costing chain. In contrast, under chained target costing, cost information is not formally shared between the suppliers and their buyers. Theoretically, the buyers are indifferent to the level of profitability of their suppliers. All that matters is that the component-level target costs be achieved. For

	Chained target costing	FPQ trade-off	Interorganizational cost investigation
Buyer's knowledge of supplier's processes	None required	Some	Considerable
Buyer's knowledge of supplier's costs	None required	None required	Considerable
Buyer's power over supplier	Unaffected	Minor increase possible	Significant increase possible

FIGURE 10–11. KNOWLEDGE AND POWER IMPLICATIONS OF CHAINED TARGET COSTING, FPQ TRADE-OFFS, AND INTERORGANIZATIONAL COST INVESTIGATIONS

example, Tokyo Motors is not interested in the level of Yokohama's profit margins, only in its ability to provide products at their target costs. Thus, if Yokohama finds a way to reduce the cost of one of its products significantly, it can make a high return on that product. However, since there is considerable sharing of production information between Yokohama and its customers, it does not take long for the target price to reflect the new production cost.

Interorganizational cost investigations generally are perceived as beneficial by all the firms in the supply chain. Most believe that such cost investigations increase the overall efficiency of the supply chain and therefore lead to higher overall profits. However, the problem from the suppliers' perspective lies in the increased amount of cost and other information that they must share with their customers and the potential associated loss of power. For this reason, once an interorganizational cost investigation is completed and the target costs have been achieved, the intensive information sharing ceases. From that moment on, chained target costing again is used to establish the component-level target costs. As the suppliers use kaizen costing to become more efficient, the buyer ceases to know the exact profitability of that component as it moves down the supply chain. This reversion to target costing is one of the mechanisms suppliers use to maintain an adequate balance of power in the supply chain.

Maintaining the Balance of Power

Typically, under an interorganizational cost investigation the top firm is responsible for setting the transfer prices, i.e., target selling prices, among the firms in the chain. Thus, it is in fact responsible for managing the profits earned by these firms. As a result, despite the advantages, interorganizational cost investigations are not always popular with suppliers because these firms often feel that they give the firm at the top of the chain too much say in the negotiations.

Interorganizational cost investigations can increase the disparity of power in the supply chain because the more powerful players have the opportunity to use the shared information for their own benefit at the expense of the weaker chain members. Consequently, underlying the intensive sharing of confidential cost information during interorganizational cost investigations is substantial mutual trust. The suppliers must trust the buyer not to use its knowledge of the suppliers' production economics to set component-level target costs that leave them inadequate profits. To maintain this trust, the buyer must try to discipline its target costing process so that it does not incorporate the additional knowledge gained from the interorganizational cost investigations. If after every interorganizational cost investigation the component-level target costs reflected knowledge of the suppliers' underlying economics and squeezed their profits harder than usual, then suppliers would begin to avoid calling for an interorganizational cost investigation.

It is obviously very difficult for the buyer to ignore the information it has collected about the supplier. Fortunately, there are two built-in protections. The first is that both firms are working together to reduce costs aggressively, and the second is the rapid aging of the shared cost information. The first level of protection is illustrated by the way Komatsu interacts with Toyo Radiator. Sometimes Komatsu's knowledge of Toyo's profits led to pressure building within Komatsu to reduce target costs when Toyo's profits were known to be high. However, because the two firms shared a common goal—getting costs as low as possible—these conflicts rarely became serious.

The second level of protection occurs automatically. Once the interorganizational cost investigation is over, the two firms return to the normal level of information sharing. Therefore, as the supplier's cost-reduction program further reduces its costs, the information the buyer has about the supplier's costs becomes obsolete. Fairly rapidly the two firms are back where they started, with the buyer trying to estimate its supplier's costs.

The power structure of target costing chains usually is carefully controlled by all the members of the chain through network protocols. The buyers attempt to maximize their power by purchasing components from a limited number of suppliers. This reliance on a few suppliers increases the size of the orders placed and hence the importance of the buyer to the supplier. The suppliers try to limit the power of their buyers by selling their output to as many firms as possible. In many ways the optimum supply chain is one in which both buyers and suppliers see the two firms as interdependent. The equal reliance on each other means that both firms are willing to work together to find ways to reduce costs. Any factor that threatens to alter the balance of power is therefore treated very seriously by all concerned.

Summary

Interorganizational cost investigations play an important role in supporting and extending the chained target costing process. Typically they are triggered when one of the firms in a target costing chain finds itself unable to achieve the target cost for one of its products. Rather than simply rejecting the order, the firm may initiate an interorganizational cost investigation to enable it to achieve the target cost. Interorganizational cost investigations thus enable suppliers to push back on component-level target costs without having to say no to the buyer and without weakening the discipline of the target costing process.

Interorganizational cost investigations are a powerful extension of chained target costing. They overcome an inherent limitation of that approach by increasing the scope of the changes that can be made to the design of products and components. Increasing the scope of design changes enables greater cost savings across the supply chain to be identified and implemented. Interorganizational cost investigations achieve this objective by having the product designers of all the firms involved share information about both product design and production economics.

While interorganizational cost investigations overcome one limitation of chained target costing, namely the scope of the design changes allowed, they fail to address another limitation, the late involvement of the suppliers in the product development process. The techniques used to address the timing limitation of chained target costing are parallel and simultaneous engineering. These concurrent cost management techniques allow the scope of design changes to be increased even more by giving suppliers more time to identify additional opportunities for cost reduction.

CHAPTER 11

CONCURRENT COST MANAGEMENT

INTRODUCTION

The addition of interorganizational cost investigations to chained target costing increases the scope of the design changes that can be made to the end product and its components. However, these two techniques still limit the extent to which the suppliers can influence the design of the buyer's product. This limitation is caused by the relatively late involvement of the suppliers in the buyer's product development process (see Figure 11–1). This late involvement often makes it impossible for suppliers to get approval for cost-reduction ideas that require fundamental modifications to the end product. This limitation can be removed by involving suppliers much earlier in the design process, so they can suggest design changes while there is still time to incorporate those changes into the end product's design.

When the buyer outsources research and development for a major function or group component, concurrent cost management becomes a powerful approach to cost management. The two major approaches to concurrent cost management are parallel and simul-

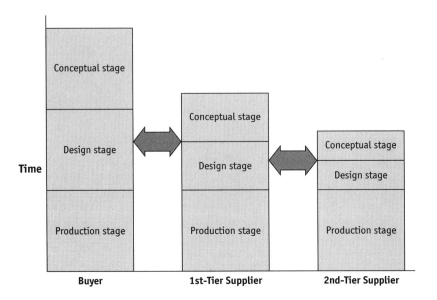

FIGURE 11–1. CONVENTIONAL APPROACH TO SUPPLIER INVOLVEMENT
IN THE PRODUCT DEVELOPMENT PROCESS

taneous engineering. The basic difference between the two techniques revolves around the degree of independence of the design teams at the buyer and supplier (see Figure 11–2). In parallel engineering the buyer provides the supplier with high-level specifications for the major function. These specifications allow the supplier to design the major function in isolation. The buyer's design team can make any alterations to the product as long as they do not lead to changes in the high-level specifications of the outsourced major functions. Similarly, the supplier's design teams can make changes in the design of the major function as long as they do not lead to changes in the high-level specifications. Parallel engineering's primary advantage to the supplier is that the supplier can uncouple its product development cycle from that of the buyer. The buyer keeps the supplier informed about its new product plans, and the supplier uses this information to guide its product development process. For example, Komatsu ensures that Toyo Radiator knows how rapidly engine size will be increased in the next generation of products. This advance notice gives Toyo Radiator more time to find ways to increase the cooling

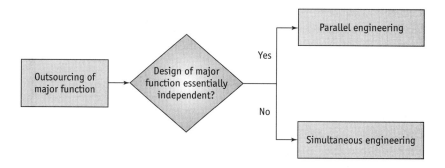

FIGURE 11-2. CHOOSING BETWEEN THE TWO CONCURRENT COST
MANAGEMENT TECHNIQUES

capacity of its products without a commensurate increase in cost. Furthermore, it allows Toyo Radiator to develop new technologies effectively, independent of Komatsu's product development plans.

The second approach to concurrent cost management is simultaneous engineering. Here, the buyer's and supplier's design teams work together to identify mutually beneficial designs for both the end product and the outsourced major function. The choice between the two approaches is driven by the perceived benefits from close interactions between the buyer's and supplier's design teams. If the value of such interactions is considered low, then firms use parallel engineering where the design teams work independently. If the benefit is thought to be high, then simultaneous engineering is used.

Under both approaches a fundamental shift in supplier relations occurs because the buyer now asks its suppliers to design a major function or group component as opposed to individual components. For example, instead of ordering a radiator, fan, and electric motor (components) separately, the buyer now orders a complete engine cooling system (a major function) or starter motor (a group component). The suppliers thus take responsibility for some, if not all, of the research and development for the major function or group component.

The outsourcing of research and development increases the degree of interdependence between the buyer and supplier. The buyer now depends on the supplier for its technical expertise, and the buyer represents a significant portion of the supplier's business. Under such conditions, stable, cooperative, and mutually beneficial buyer-supplier relations are critical. The higher level of interdependence means that the component-level target cost setting process depends more heavily on negotiations and less on legislation. To reflect the important position of the suppliers in the relationship, they are called partners or family members.

One route to becoming a family member is to start as a major supplier and over time evolve into a family member. This is the route that Toyo Radiator has taken. Another way is to deliver expertise in a technology that has become critical to the buyer. For example, modern automobiles contain a significant amount of electronics, and many of the Japanese automobile firms have developed very close relationships with suppliers of electronic components.

Parallel and simultaneous engineering provide the same benefits and suffer from the same drawbacks. One of the benefits is that they give the suppliers more time to design their products and hence greater opportunities to reduce costs. In addition, they enable the suppliers to develop new generations of their products independently of the product development processes of their customers. They also allow faster introduction of products because the product development processes of the buyer and supplier are occurring at the same time. Finally, they reduce overall costs by allowing the supplier to spread development costs over the products of all their customers. The longer lead time allows the firms to develop new technologies that can be used in all their products as opposed to short-term solutions that are customer specific.

The primary drawback to concurrent cost management is that buyers lose much of their ability to differentiate products based on any proprietary technology used in their major functions. This loss of proprietary technology is especially problematic in baronies because the suppliers also sell their products to the other barons, which are direct competitors. In a kingdom, the problem is less serious, as the suppliers are essentially captive. However, unless the technology is considered a core competence, this drawback of concurrent cost management should be minimal.

Parallel Engineering

In parallel engineering, the buyer's and supplier's design teams essentially work independently. The main interaction occurs at the very beginning of the product development process (see Figure 11–3). However, if additional interactions are required, one of the firms involved can initiate an interorganizational cost investigation later in the process (see Figure 11–4).

The transfer of research and development to suppliers to reduce costs for the buyer increases cost pressure on the suppliers. While the suppliers' new products typically have higher value-added and hence higher operating margins, any increase in profitability is at risk of being offset by the increased research and development expenses. For example, the decreased prices that Yokohama faces are aggravated by two other factors: the contraction in product life expectancies from about four years in 1970 to approximately two years in the 1990s, and the transfer of considerable design activities from the customers to Yokohama. The shortened life cycles make it even more difficult for Yokohama to recoup the cost of its R&D efforts because lifetime production levels are necessarily smaller. The transfer of design activities also proves difficult because it increases the firm's up-front development costs. Previously, the customer designed the product and provided

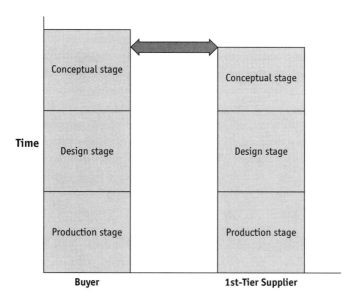

FIGURE 11–3. CONCURRENT APPROACH TO SUPPLIER RELATIONSHIPS: PARALLEL ENGINEERING

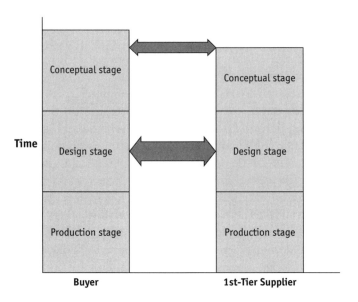

FIGURE 11-4. CONCURRENT APPROACH TO SUPPLIER RELATIONSHIPS:
PARALLEL ENGINEERING AND INTERORGANIZATIONAL
COST INVESTIGATION

Yokohama with the product's specifications; now, Yokohama engineers have to design products as well as manufacture them. Taken together, these two changes mean that higher development costs have to be recovered on sales of fewer units: a challenging objective in a confrontational environment dominated by the target costing systems of the firm's customers.

The transfer of research and development from the buyer to the supplier sometimes occurs in more subtle ways. By rewarding suppliers for their degree of innovation, buyers may create incentives for their suppliers to undertake more research. For example, if one of Isuzu's suppliers identifies a way to add extra functionality to a component, thereby increasing its value, Isuzu engineers incorporate this functionality into the part's specifications. Typically, the creative supplier will achieve a higher value than will the other two suppliers because its design already contains the extra functionality. In this way, suppliers are encouraged to act as ancillary research and development laboratories for Isuzu.

SIMULTANEOUS ENGINEERING

The adoption of a richer relationship with the suppliers by involving them earlier and more intensively in the product development process makes simultaneous engineering possible (see Figure 11–5). Simultaneous engineering, also known as concurrent engineering, is a well-established engineering method that has been shown to reduce costs. In simultaneous engineering, the buyer's and supplier's product designers work together over an extended period of time to find ways to reduce costs by making fundamental changes in the design of the end product. These designer interactions start right at the beginning of the buyer's product development process, typically when the product's specifications are first being established.

The primary benefit of simultaneous engineering over parallel engineering lies in the ability of the two design teams to work closely together during the product conceptualization phase of product development. This situation allows the two teams to find ways to reduce costs and increase functionality that could not be

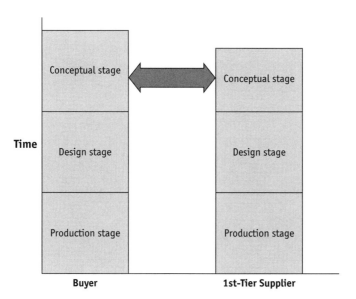

FIGURE 11–5. CONCURRENT APPROACH TO SUPPLIER RELATIONSHIPS:
SIMULTANEOUS ENGINEERING

identified if they were operating in isolation. For example, changes in the design of a particular major function may be possible only if the design of the end product is also modified. If costs must be reduced even more during the product design stage, then the two firms can initiate an interorganizational cost investigation (see Figure 11–6).

Komatsu, for example, has been heavily involved in developing a simultaneous engineering approach in recent years. Players in the highly competitive market for excavators and bulldozers have begun to compete on the basis of the time it takes to get new products to market. Unfortunately, the existing Komatsu-supplier relations were not well structured to allow Komatsu to decrease significantly the time-to-market of new products. To achieve this objective, Komatsu has implemented a new simultaneous engineering program that is used to develop major components and subassemblies manufactured by its chief suppliers. To allow the suppliers greater input in the design process, Komatsu initiates periodic meetings between the suppliers' research and development staffs

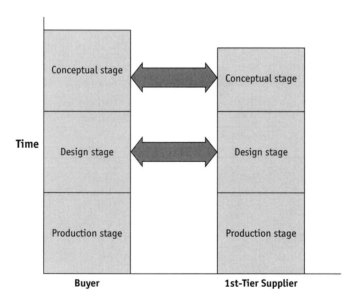

Figure 11–6. Concurrent Approach to Supplier Relationships: Simultaneous Engineering and Interorganizational Cost Investigation

and its own. Three benefits can be derived from these simultaneous engineering meetings. First, they integrate the research and development efforts of the two groups, thereby avoiding wasted efforts due to miscommunication. Second, they allow suppliers to provide input much earlier in the product development process, thus enabling them to have a greater influence on the design. Finally, they help ensure that target cost negotiations are more substantive, with suppliers having a greater say in the component-level target cost setting process. Under the old approach, Komatsu engineers felt that the negotiations were too one-sided and did not allow the full creativity of the firm's suppliers to be harnessed.

The fundamental difference between the traditional sequential and the new simultaneous approach is illustrated by the product development process adopted for the engine cooling systems for the A20 and A21 power shovels designed by Toyo Radiator. The engine cooling systems for these power shovels created a significant cost-reduction challenge for Toyo Radiator because Komatsu had significantly increased the horsepower of the engines. Under the old approach, Toyo Radiator would design the parts for Komatsu and submit a blueprint for approval. The objective was to design parts that met Komatsu's specifications. Once the specifications were met, Toyo Radiator's sales department and Komatsu's purchasing department would study Toyo Radiator's expected costs and negotiate each part's selling price. These negotiations were undertaken fairly late in the design process.

The problem with this approach was that it did not leave Toyo Radiator enough time to improve its designs significantly. Toyo Radiator would have to wait until Komatsu presented it with the concept of the new model before commencing design. This delay was unavoidable, as Toyo Radiator did not know the performance specifications for the new heat-exchanger unit until Komatsu gave it the work order. Therefore, if the new model required increased heat-exchange capacity and improved performance in terms of noise level, then often the only feasible solution, given the time left, was simply to increase the size of the unit. Unfortunately, increasing the size meant increasing the cost.

Under the traditional engineering approach, the cost of the cooling systems would have increased and exceeded Komatsu's target cost for that subassembly by a large amount. Komatsu was unable to pass such a cost increase on to its customers, and Toyo Radiator was not in a position to reduce costs sufficiently. It required a joint effort on the part of engineers at both firms to find ways to reduce costs to an acceptable level. Therefore, a simultaneous engineering approach has been adopted to give Toyo Radiator engineers as much time as possible to find ways to radically redesign the engine cooling system.

Under the new simultaneous engineering approach, design work at Toyo Radiator on the cooling systems for the A20 and A21 models began 24 months before the prototype was developed, instead of 12 months as in the old Komatsu design process (see Figure 11–7). The first two years of the simultaneous engineering project for the A20 and A21 models was the prototype stage. In this period, Komatsu engineers worked on developing the general designs of the new construction vehicles based on customer requirements. Simultaneously, Toyo Radiator engineers were working on the design of a new heat exchanger. At the heart of the new design for the A20 and A21 power shovels was a specially developed fan that both increased effective airflow around the engine and reduced the noise level. The new radiator-fan package was also designed to increase parts commonality across all the firm's construction equipment products.

Having two design teams work on the same product simultaneously as opposed to sequentially introduces the risk that the two teams will produce conflicting designs. To overcome this problem, coordination meetings are held in which the two groups of engineers keep each other up to date on their progress so that they have a commonality of objective. The additional coordination required by the simultaneous engineering approach makes it difficult to support too many suppliers for a given subassembly, so one of the outcomes of adopting simultaneous engineering is a further reduction in the number of suppliers.

The resulting integration makes it easier for new designs to be introduced. For example, at Komatsu, a major benefit from this integration was realized almost immediately. To improve the performance of the A20 and A21 power shovels, the airflow around the radiator had to be increased. The problem was that conventional fans pushed the air horizontally, causing a portion of the airflow to

Old Approach

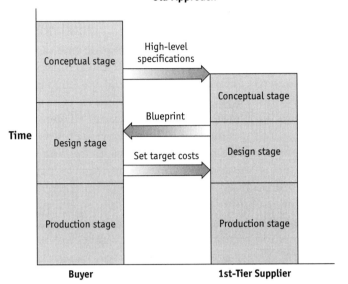

New Approach

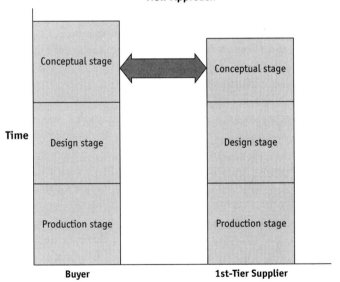

FIGURE 11-7. COMPARISON OF OLD AND NEW APPROACH TO DESIGN
        AT KOMATSU

be directed at the engine where it was deflected back into the air stream, thus reducing the overall flow of air cooling the engine. A "mixed flow" fan was introduced that directed the airflow around the engine so it was more effective in cooling the engine, thus allowing a smaller radiator to be used in the A20 and A21 models. Under the old approach to engineering, there would not have been enough time to design, test, and prepare a new design for manufacture.

The adoption of simultaneous engineering makes it possible to introduce new products more rapidly because it removes the possibility of the buyer testing the supplier's design and finding it unsatisfactory, requiring the supplier to redesign the product late in the process. For example, under the simultaneous engineering approach Komatsu test engineers are often asked to visit Toyo Radiator to explain Komatsu's test procedures and evaluation criteria. From this interaction, Toyo Radiator develops its own simulation program to test prospective designs in order to reduce the chance that when it receives Komatsu's prototype, it will discover that its heat-exchange solution is inadequate. In addition, Toyo Radiator engineers can borrow Komatsu's prototypes for their own testing purposes. In the past, Komatsu would test Toyo Radiator's designs on its prototypes, with the resulting delays and reduced information available to Toyo Radiator engineers causing the development process to take too long. Now, the entire process can be completed in less time.

Integrating Simultaneous Engineering and Cost Balance Verification

When the adoption of simultaneous engineering does not remove the ability (or sometimes the need) for interorganizational cost investigations, the two programs typically merge seamlessly. The only difference between the two is the scope of the design changes contemplated and the point in the product development process at which they occur. This merging is illustrated by the development of the engine cooling system for Komatsu's A20 and A21 power shovels (see Figure 11–8).

Despite the advantages of simultaneous engineering, Toyo's costs for the new engine cooling system were still above target. The problem was that even with the new fan design, Toyo engineers decided

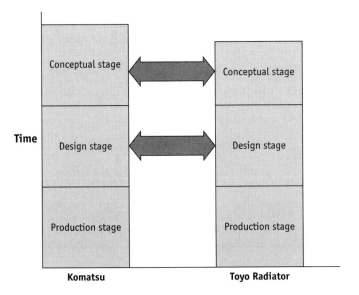

FIGURE 11–8. INTEGRATING SIMULTANEOUS ENGINEERING AND COST
BALANCE VERIFICATION (CBV)

the size of the radiator had to be increased from 830 mm to 880 mm to achieve the required cooling capacity. This increase required real-locating the target costs—or value targets as they were called—for components in the cooling system. The reallocations reflected changes in performance required for the various components in the cooling system once the size of the radiator was increased. The increases in target costs for some components had to be offset by decreases in the target costs for other components so that the over-all target cost of the engine cooling system remained constant. However, the cost of increasing the size of the radiator could not be offset; consequently, more aggressive cost management was required.

To reduce the cost of the new cooling system, a joint Komatsu-Toyo cost balance verification (CBV) was undertaken. The objective of the CBV was to find a way for Toyo to manufacture the new cool-ing system and sell it at the target price set by Komatsu while still making the desired level of profit. The CBV focused on two areas of cost reduction. First, it looked at ways to reduce costs through redesign of the cooling system using value analysis, and second, it looked at individual parts that cost too much (see Figure 11–9).

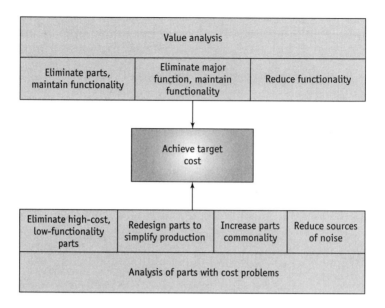

Figure 11-9. The major Cost-Reduction Activities in a CBV at Komatsu

Three different cost-reduction approaches were involved in the value analysis stage. The first approach focused on finding ways to eliminate parts without changing the fundamental design of the cooling system, for example, finding ways to reduce the number of brackets needed to mount the radiator and other components of the cooling system. The objective of the second cost-reduction approach was to find ways to eliminate major components through product redesign, while maintaining the cooling capacity. For example, by placing the condenser in front of the radiator instead of behind it, only one fan and motor were required instead of two. The third approach aimed at reducing the required cooling capacity—if the capacity requirements were reduced sufficiently, the size of the radiator could remain at 830 mm. This reduction in size was considered critical because it would allow Toyo Radiator to manufacture the new radiator on an existing high-volume production line. The reduced size and the resulting application of higher-volume production techniques would enable the firm to manufacture the cooling systems at a much lower cost.

The analysis of the parts with cost problems focused on four major cost-reduction approaches. First, an analysis of the cost and functionality of the parts was undertaken. Parts that cost a lot but added little functionality were targeted for elimination. For example, a water-level gauge was eliminated once it was determined that it really served no useful purpose. Second, ways to change the shape of parts that would reduce their costs were explored. For example, a deep-draw pressing technique was developed that allowed several complex parts to be manufactured at lower cost. While pressing required a high initial up-front cost for the die, it was cheaper per unit than the welding approach it replaced. Third, the wire net used to make the spinning fan safer was analyzed and the way it was mounted was changed, allowing standardized parts to be used across models, thus reducing costs. Finally, parts used for noise insulation were studied. A decision was made to explore whether it was better to reduce noise at the source rather than insulate against the noise. This comparison allowed parts to be eliminated and simplified, again reducing costs. For example, previously some components were protected by building heavy frames around them to contain the noise; by installing cheaper cushions that reduced the noise at its source, the frames could be eliminated.

The CBV was successful and Toyo Radiator was able to reduce the size of the radiator and to manufacture the new cooling systems on the high-volume production line. It was the combined savings of the value analysis and parts redesign programs that enabled the cost of the cooling systems to be reduced to below their target costs. Since the savings were greater than required by Komatsu's component-level target costs, Toyo was able to spend more on overall functionality of the cooling system, thus improving the product, meeting the target cost objectives, and still making an adequate return.

Bundled Target Costing

The adoption of simultaneous engineering often leads to the adoption of bundled target costing (see Chapter 8). Under the simultaneous engineering approach, the buyer tells the suppliers the target costs for each of its major functions and then expects the suppliers to find a way to achieve them. For example, since Toyo Radiator has responsibility for the entire cooling system design, Komatsu no longer expects it to achieve target costs on a component-by-component basis but instead for the entire cooling system. From Komatsu's perspective, the important issue for Toyo Radiator is to design the cooling system so that it can be purchased for its component-level target cost.

Negotiations occur only when Toyo Radiator decides it is impossible to meet the target cost for a new model established by Komatsu's target costing system and still make an adequate profit. The advantage to Toyo Radiator of the new approach is that much earlier in the design process it knows what its selling prices (and hence target costs) have to be to make an adequate profit. If Toyo Radiator sees a potential problem with Komatsu's target costs, it can negotiate with Komatsu to relax them.

The overall outcome of the simultaneous engineering approach is a shorter time period to develop products, faster introduction of new technology, and an improved ability to reduce costs. One outcome of the adoption of simultaneous engineering is that Komatsu transfers greater responsibility for research and development to Toyo Radiator.

Implications of Concurrent Cost Management

Concurrent cost management requires stable, cooperative, and mutually beneficial buyer-supplier relations. For this reason, lean supply is almost a precursor to effective application of concurrent cost management. The design engineers of the buyer and supplier firms must be able to interact almost continuously over an extended period of time, thereby frequently sharing confidential information. These are the same requirements that underlie interorganizational cost investigations; the main difference lies in the degree of integration of the buyer's and supplier's product design processes. Outsourcing of research and development and, in particular, simultaneous engineering require the highest levels of cooperative behavior and trust.

As part of the concurrent cost management process, the supplier accepts responsibility for a major function as opposed to individual components. Since a major function typically represents a significant portion of the product's cost, the greater responsibility that the buyer places on the supplier has some significant implications for the cost management process.

One implication is that the target costing negotiations are more substantive under concurrent cost management than under any other interorganizational cost management program. The design changes can be more fundamental with greater implications for the end product, and multiple components are involved. Simultaneous engineering provides the potential for greater cost-reduction opportunities because the product is still in the formative stages of design and expending more energy on the target cost negotiation process is therefore justified. If the supplier anticipates problems with achieving the target cost of the major function or group component, then it can alert the buyer to the problem early in the process. This early warning gives the two design teams more time to react and allows them to make fundamental design changes that have significant impact on the cost of the major function or group component and, hence, the product itself. Furthermore, the outsourcing of the production and assembly of a major function or group component means that a single supplier is responsible for all the components in the part. This greater responsibility leads to a reduction in the number of suppliers. Consequently, the buyer can focus on a limited number of more important negotiations.

Having a single supplier take sole responsibility for a major function leads to significant cost savings because the supplier can develop greater expertise than the buyer for designing the major function. In addition, when product design is located in a single location, the risk of duplications and delays as the buyer's design team examines the major function is reduced, if not eliminated. However, the primary risk in outsourcing major functions is that they will be incompatible when they are assembled into the final product. Therefore, the buyer has to expend sufficient resources to coordinate the suppliers' design processes.

Under simultaneous engineering, the buyer is still involved in the design process and can develop target costs for each component. These component-level target costs can be used to establish the target cost of the major function or group component. Under conventional target costing practices, the supplier would be held responsible for achieving the individual component-level target costs (see

Figure 11–10), whereas under simultaneous engineering, the target costs for the components are aggregated and the supplier is measured at the total cost level (see Figure 11–11). The advantage of this approach is that the supplier can choose where to reduce costs. It gives the supplier greater freedom to find cost-reduction opportunities through redesign of the components. Alternatively, when the research and development of the major function or group component are outsourced, the buyer loses the ability to develop component-level target costs and can develop only major function or group component-level target costs. The supplier is now totally free to change the design of the major function or group component as well as the individual components it contains and reduce costs even further.

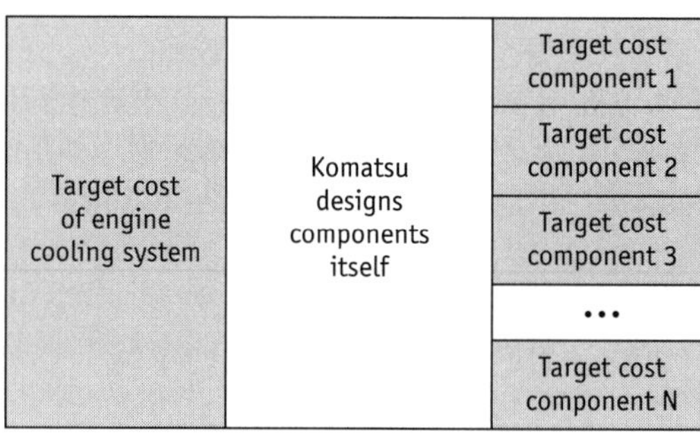

		Target cost component 1
Target cost of engine cooling system	Komatsu designs components itself	Target cost component 2
		Target cost component 3
		•••
		Target cost component N

FIGURE 11–10. THE OLD APPROACH TO ENGINE COOLING SYSTEM
OUTSOURCING AT KOMATSU

				Target cost component 1
Target cost of engine cooling system	Komatsu outsources major function design to Tokyo	Komatsu establishes a single target cost for entire major function	Toyo establishes the component-level target costs	Target cost component 2
				Target cost component 3
				•••
				Target cost component N

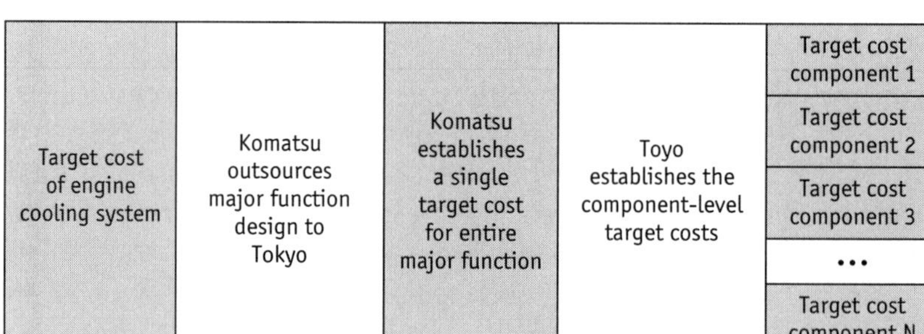

FIGURE 11–11. THE NEW APPROACH TO ENGINE COOLING SYSTEM
OUTSOURCING AT KOMATSU

SUMMARY

Firms face a trade-off in deciding which major functions to outsource. If the supplier has greater design skills and can develop major functions of equal or superior functionality and quality at lower cost, then the buyer will be better off outsourcing the research and development. The offsetting risk of outsourcing is the loss of core competencies and the hollowing out of the factory. Consequently, a careful decision has to be made as to who will undertake the research and development of each major function. If the firm chooses to outsource research and development, it has to decide whether to use parallel or simultaneous engineering.

Outsourcing research and development to the supplier is the ultimate step in interorganizational cost management. It creates the highest levels of interdependence between the buyer and the supplier. Under parallel engineering, the supplier has more time to undertake new designs than in more conventional buyer-supplier relationships. In addition, the supplier can uncouple its new-product development timetable from that of its buyer. Simultaneous engineering requires the most sophisticated cooperation between buyers and suppliers. Its benefits are more substantive target costing negotiations and greater opportunities for cost reduction. Simultaneous engineering creates a middle ground between keeping the research and development in-house and outsourcing it by enabling the buyer's and supplier's design teams to act as through they were a single team during the very early stages of product development. It allows the firm to take advantage of the suppliers' design skills by getting the suppliers involved early in the product development process, without losing control over the total design process. If simultaneous engineering is used appropriately, the suppliers will be able to design the major functions so that they have equivalent or better functionality than the firm's designers but at a lower cost.

CHAPTER 12

KAIZEN COSTING

INTRODUCTION

Kaizen costing is a powerful cost management technique that focuses on the manufacturing stage of a product's life. It operates in feed-forward mode by setting cost-reduction objectives in anticipation of the need to reduce costs rather than reacting to cost overruns after they occur. Kaizen costing is in essence a technique for profit management. Its objective is to help ensure that each product earns an adequate profit across its life. It complements target costing by extending the discipline that target costing creates in the product development process to the manufacturing stage (see Figure 12–1). In well-designed cost management programs, target and kaizen costing operate together seamlessly to ensure that adequate cost-reduction pressures are in place across the entire life cycle of the firm's products.

Kaizen costing as a mechanism to reduce costs during product manufacture should be practiced by all members of the supplier network, not just the most sophisticated ones. For this reason,

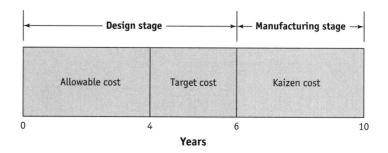

Figure 12–1. The Switch from Allowable Cost to Target
Cost to Kaizen Cost

sophisticated buyers often help some of their less-advanced suppliers to develop their own kaizen costing programs. This transfer of know-how represents one aspect of interorganizational kaizen costing. The other aspect of interorganizational cost management is achieved when the buyer's kaizen costing systems transmit the cost-reduction pressure it faces in the market to its suppliers.

Kaizen costing is the primary disciplining technique of interorganizational cost management during manufacturing. The buyer's kaizen costing system establishes the supplier's selling prices. This process is typically legislated, with the buyer establishing a common kaizen cost-reduction percentage for all outsourced items. This percentage is applied to all established products and to products introduced during the prior period. If the products are established, the factor is applied to their previous kaizen cost and if they are new products to their target costs (see Figure 12–2). The suppliers then use their own kaizen costing system to identify where they are going to reduce costs and also to transmit the pressure to their suppliers. Internally, the buyer and the suppliers use value analysis to find ways to reduce costs. The overall aim of the kaizen costing process is to help achieve the long-term profit objectives of the firm.

The Kaizen Costing Process

There are three different types of kaizen costing programs—period-, item-, and overhead-specific. Each of these interventions has a dif-

New product
Current kaizen cost = $\dfrac{\text{Target}}{\text{cost}}$ * $\dfrac{\text{Kaizen cost}}{\text{reduction factor}}$
Established product
Current kaizen cost = $\dfrac{\text{Previous}}{\text{kaizen cost}}$ * $\dfrac{\text{Kaizen cost}}{\text{reduction factor}}$

FIGURE 12-2. SETTING KAIZEN COSTS

ferent objective and focus (see Figure 12–3). The objective of period-specific kaizen costing is to reduce the cost of production processes by a predetermined amount in the current period. In most firms, the level of this cost reduction is set to maintain the profitability of the firm. The objective of an item-specific kaizen costing intervention is to reduce the cost of a specific product so that it achieves its long-term profit objectives. Such interventions can be applied to either a new product whose costs on launching are too high or to a mature product whose selling price is falling faster than its costs. Finally, overhead-specific kaizen costing has the objective of reducing overhead costs through programs aimed at reducing product-mix complexity.

Kaizen costing program	Objective	Focus
Item-specific	Reduce costs of production processes	Direct costs
Period-specific	Reduce costs of specific products	Direct costs
Overhead-specific	Reduce overhead and support costs	Indirect costs

FIGURE 12-3. TYPES OF KAIZEN COSTING PROGRAMS

The three types of kaizen costing interventions each play a critical, but different, role in helping achieve overall firm profitability. Period- and item-specific kaizen costing focus on the direct costs, and overhead-specific kaizen costing, on the indirect costs. From an interorganizational perspective, the three types of interventions differ primarily in the way they transmit the cost pressure faced by the buyer in the market to its suppliers. Under period-specific kaizen costing, the selling prices of all components are reduced, while under item-specific kaizen costing it is only the specifically targeted components whose costs are reduced. Overhead-specific kaizen costing does not transmit pressure to the suppliers but typically leads to a decrease in their costs through reduced complexity of the orders placed. As the buyer reduces the complexity of its parts mix, it automatically reduces the complexity of the parts sourced from its suppliers. The result is that suppliers have simplified product mixes (fewer different types of parts are ordered) and increased production volumes for the remaining parts (while overall production volumes remain the same). These two changes lead to lower costs through increased economies of scale and decreased diseconomies of scope.

Period-Specific Kaizen Costing

Period-specific kaizen costing achieves its objective by finding ways to perform production and associated support processes more efficiently. For production processes, the aim is to find ways to produce products so that they consume less material and labor and trigger fewer overhead activities. For support processes the objective is to find ways to perform them so that they consume fewer resources. The primary technique used to identify these savings is *value analysis,* the application of value engineering to the manufacturing phase of the product life cycle. Value analysis is an integral part of kaizen costing.

For short-life-cycle products, period-specific kaizen costing typically operates within the discipline of a target costing system. The objective of target costing is to ensure that new products earn an adequate return across their lives. Therefore, if certain cost savings that will manifest themselves during the manufacturing phase of the product's life can already be anticipated during product design, they are included in the life-cycle profit analysis. These imputed cost savings translate into period-specific kaizen objectives that have to be achieved if the product is to meet its profit objectives. For long-life-cycle products, product-specific kaizen costing is typically disciplined by the market. As pressure mounts on selling prices, period-specific kaizen costing acts as the primary cost-reduction mechanism used to maintain the firm's profitability.

In environments in which product lives are short, period-specific kaizen costing might appear to have little potential. Any savings that can be achieved are so short-lived that they cannot justify the costs of identifying them. However, this perspective is often incorrect because many production and support processes are multi-generational with respect to products. That is, while product designs might change every year, the bulk of production and support processes remain unchanged over many years. Consequently, the savings occur over the life of the processes, not the life of the current products. In addition, savings are cumulative. Thus, while individual kaizen savings may at first appear modest, when accumulated over time, they can be significant. For example, if 3% per year can be saved from the cost of the processes used to manufacture products, then even without compounding, after five years the cost of the latest generation of the product will have been reduced 15%. It is this accumulation of savings that makes period-specific kaizen costing so valuable.

The process of period-specific kaizen costing begins with establishing the cost-reduction objectives for each group in the firm's production facilities. There are two ways to establish such objectives. The first way, the subtraction approach, starts with the enterprise-level cost-reduction objective and decomposes it via the facility level to the group level (see Figure 12–4). At the end of this process each group has a distinct cost-reduction objective to achieve. For the kaizen costing process to be effective, these group-level cost-reduction objectives have to be perceived as achievable by the groups. If they are not considered attainable, the groups will have little incentive to commit to them.

The process of setting achievable cost-reduction objectives consists of an informal bottom-up process followed by a more formal top-down process. In the bottom-up process, the groups' inputs as to the appropriate magnitude of their cost-reduction objectives are sought. These inputs are used as the basis for setting the final group-

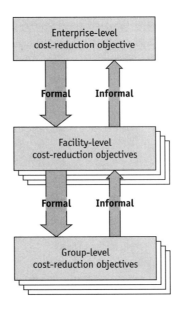

FIGURE 12–4. PERIOD-SPECIFIC KAIZEN SUBTRACTION APPROACH:
TOP-DOWN PROCESS

level cost-reduction objectives. The top-down process ensures that the savings identified in the bottom-up process are sufficient to maintain the firm's planned level of profitability. If the top-down process requires more aggressive cost-reduction objectives, these objectives are negotiated with the groups. The underlying principle is again that group-level objectives should be achievable most of the time. Unrealistic cost-reduction objectives serve no purpose and are avoided in well-managed kaizen costing programs.

The second way, the addition approach, starts with the cost-reduction opportunities identified by the groups (see Figure 12–5). These opportunities are added together to develop the enterprise-level savings. If top management accepts this level of savings, then the cost-reduction objectives are established. Obviously, because of the way they are established, the groups will always view these cost-reduction objectives as achievable. This approach is most effective when the groups are highly motivated and demand more aggressive cost-reduction objectives of themselves than top management does. If the cumulative savings are not sufficient, then the

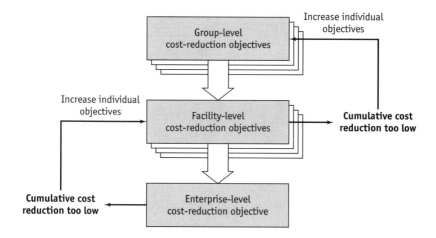

FIGURE 12–5. PERIOD-SPECIFIC KAIZEN ADDITION APPROACH: BOTTOM-UP PROCESS

management at the next higher level sends the plans back and requests that each team reviews its cost-reduction objectives to see if they can be increased so that the firm can achieve its planned levels of profitability.

There is a third approach to setting cost-reduction objectives, but it is not very effective and only rarely used. In this approach, the same objective is established for each group irrespective of the production processes they are using. The advantage of this approach lies in its simplicity. The primary disadvantage is that to ensure that the cost-reduction objectives are achievable by all groups requires setting a relatively low overall objective for each group (the lowest common denominator effect).

Once the group-level cost-reduction objectives have been established, they are decomposed to the material, labor, and purchased-parts level (see Figure 12–6). Period-specific kaizen cost-reduction objectives for direct material are established at the product level because there is a one-to-one relationship between the product and the material it consumes. Consequently, multiple objectives are set for each product line (one per product). Most kaizen costing programs establish cost-reduction objectives at the overall, not individual, material level, leaving it up to each group to find ways to achieve the objective.

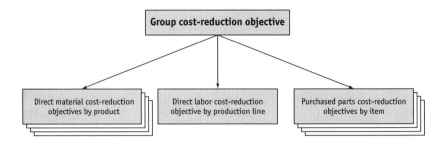

FIGURE 12-6. DECOMPOSING THE GROUP-LEVEL COST-REDUCTION
         OBJECTIVES

Period-specific kaizen cost-reduction objectives for direct labor are established at the production line, not the product level. Therefore, typically only one objective is set for each product line and hence team. Cost-reduction objectives for labor cannot be meaningfully set at the product level because the production line is balanced for multiple products. Therefore, reducing the labor content of a single product will not lead to either a reduction in the number of workers on the line or an increase in the speed of the line. No reduction in the number of workers will occur while at least one of the other products requires that the line be staffed at its current level.

To reduce the number of workers or to increase the speed of the line requires that a new balance be achieved. Such a balance requires that processing times for most, if not all, of the products produced on the line be reduced. Consequently, it is more effective to focus the kaizen intervention on improving the performance of the line as a whole rather than on a single product. In many lean enterprises, each manufacturing cell is used to produce a family of products. In such environments, the labor cost-reduction objectives are therefore set at the product-family level.

For purchased parts, the period-specific kaizen costing program consists of setting lower selling prices for all existing components that have been outsourced. Thus, multiple cost-reduction objectives are set for each product line (one per outsourced component). It is these semi-legislated lower prices that transmit the cost-reduction pressure faced by the buyer to its suppliers. The level of pressure transmitted to suppliers should be determined by the rate at which the buyer's selling prices are falling. The higher the price pressure on the buyer, the higher the kaizen cost-reduction factor required to maintain overall profitability. The kaizen cost-reduction factor established by the buyer places pressure on the suppliers. If the suppliers in turn use kaizen costing to pressure their suppliers, the pressure will be continue down the supply chain. In this way, period-specific kaizen costing programs link to create cost-reduction pressures throughout the supply chain and hence the supplier network.

Item-Specific Kaizen Costing

The focus of item-specific kaizen costing interventions is to maintain the profitability of a given product. These interventions are initiated primarily under two conditions. The first condition is when a new product is launched above its target cost and the second is when the selling price of a long-term, mature product is falling faster than its cost. The first condition should occur relatively infrequently if the firm's target costing system is functioning well. Under the cardinal rule of target costing, all products should either achieve their target costs or never be launched. However, strategic products, that is, those considered too critical to cancel, have to be launched even if they violate the cardinal rule. Strategic products include those that utilize new technologies, create an image for the firm, or help maintain market share. When such overcost products are launched, the pressure to reduce costs is not suspended but continued into the early stages of manufacturing by the immediate initiation of an item-specific kaizen costing intervention. The objective of this intervention is to find ways to redesign the product to lower its costs to the target level. In contrast, for products that are launched at their target costs usually no further product-specific cost reduction is undertaken. For these products, the period-specific kaizen cost reduction is in most cases adequate to maintain their life-cycle profitability.

When the firm has an effective target costing system, most item-specific kaizen costing interventions will involve mature products for which the period-specific kaizen costing reductions have proved insufficient. While these products earned adequate returns when they were launched, changing conditions have reduced those returns to the extent that they are either unacceptable or at risk of becoming so in the foreseeable future. Such interventions are not triggered simply by a gradual decrease in profitability over time but by unexpected and significant decreases in profitability (current or future). For example, the profitability of a product might be expected to fall linearly by 10% per year. Such reductions will not trigger an item-specific kaizen costing intervention. However, if in year three, profitability falls unexpectedly to 50% of the previous year's level, then a kaizen costing intervention will be initiated to bring the profitability back to anticipated levels.

Item-specific kaizen costing is undertaken at two levels, product and component. Product-specific kaizen costing is undertaken when the cost overrun problem is at the product level. Typically, a single product is failing to achieve its profitability objectives. Component-specific kaizen costing is undertaken when the problem is associated with a specific component and not the product as a whole. Two conditions may lead to a component-specific intervention—when most, if not all, of the products that contain the component have inadequate profit levels or when it becomes apparent that the component costs too much.

Product-Specific Kaizen Costing

Product-specific kaizen costing initiatives focus on individual products. They are undertaken when a given product fails to earn its desired level of profits. Typically, a cost-reduction objective for the product is established, and the purpose of the kaizen costing intervention is to find ways to achieve it. Product-specific kaizen costing is a natural extension of target costing. The primary difference between target costing (which is by definition product specific) and product-specific kaizen costing lies in the ability to change product functionality. In target costing, the functionality of the product is, to some extent, a variable in the cost determining process. If the product as specified cannot be manufactured at its target cost, its required functionality can sometimes be modified to reduce its costs. In contrast, in kaizen costing the functionality of the product is essentially fixed. The first unit of the production line must be functionally identical to the last unit produced. This constraint does not require that the material content and the way the product is manufactured cannot change, only that any changes made must be invisible to the customer.

A product-specific kaizen costing intervention is initiated when the profitability of a product that is currently being manufactured is or will become unacceptable unless specific actions are taken to reduce the cost of that product. Three conditions typically trigger product-specific kaizen costing (see Figure 12–7). First, when a new product fails to meet its target cost, actions are required to reduce its costs to target levels. Second, when aggressive kaizen cost savings have been imputed to the product's target cost, actions have to be taken to ensure that these savings are indeed achieved. Finally, when due to changing conditions the relationship between a mature product's selling price and its cost deteriorates rapidly, steps must be taken to bring the costs back into line with its revenues. The first of these three conditions is the only time when kaizen costing operates in feedback mode, the intervention being in response to the failure to achieve the target cost on launch. In all other cases, kaizen costing operates in feed-forward mode.

There is no significant difference between product-specific kaizen costing interventions for new products and mature ones. For both classes of products, the critical issue revolves around there being enough time to undertake a successful intervention and recoup the cost of that intervention. The primary way that costs are reduced using value analysis is by substituting less expensive components for more expensive ones and integrating several components into a single, less expensive one.

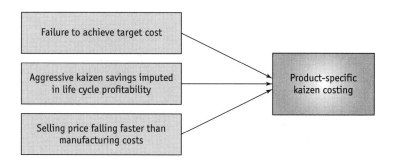

FIGURE 12–7. THE TRIGGERS FOR PRODUCT-SPECIFIC KAIZEN COSTING

Component-Specific Kaizen Costing

Component-specific kaizen costing initiatives focus on individual components that are thought to have excessive costs. In many ways, the process of setting a component-specific kaizen cost-reduction objective is similar to component-level target costing for internally designed components. A cost target is set for the component, and the design engineers have to find ways to achieve that cost. The primary difference is that, in identifying ways that will enable the component to be redesigned so that it can be manufactured at a lower cost, there is considerably less freedom to change the design of the rest of the product.

Component-specific kaizen costing opportunities can be identified in several ways (see Figure 12–8). First, if the item is a group component or major function that represents a significant fraction of the product's total value-added, its high cost might cause all the products that contain it to report relatively low profitability. Second, tear-down of a competitive product might indicate that considerable savings are possible if the item is redesigned. Third, the cost reductions achieved in previous periods might not be sufficient, and the kaizen costing intervention is designed to bring the component's cost in line with expectations. Finally, increases in material or other input costs might cause the item to exceed its original target cost and hence become a candidate for kaizen cost reduction.

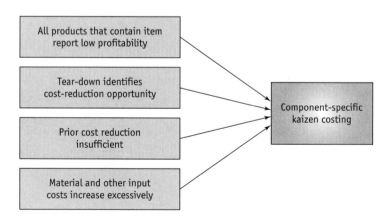

FIGURE 12–8. THE TRIGGERS FOR COMPONENT-SPECIFIC KAIZEN COSTING

From the suppliers' perspective, product- and component-specific kaizen costing have the same implications. The components that they supply are subjected to increased cost-reduction pressures in addition to those created by the period-specific program. This additional pressure causes the suppliers to initiate their own item-specific kaizen costing programs. The item-specific kaizen costing program thus effectively transmits the cost-reduction pressure faced by the buyer to the supplier and hence deeper into the supply chain.

Overhead-Specific Kaizen Costing

Overhead-specific kaizen costing interventions are designed to reduce indirect costs by systematically addressing their underlying causes (see Figure 12–9). Typically, the cause of high overhead is excessive complexity so overhead-related kaizen initiatives aim to reduce any unnecessary complexity in the production support functions. For example, having to produce too many unique parts leads to excessive parts administration costs. Only by reducing the number of distinct parts can parts administration costs be lowered.

To achieve the savings in overhead costs, complexity must be reduced enough to enable resources to be redeployed. Typically, this means that the overhead-specific kaizen costing initiative must be spread over multiple products. For example, while decreasing the

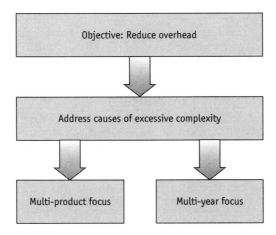

FIGURE 12–9. OVERHEAD-SPECIFIC KAIZEN COSTING

number of unique parts required by a single product will lead to reduced demand for parts administration, the level of reduction will be too small to detect. It is only when the number of parts required by numerous products have been reduced that the reduced consumption of overhead can be converted into real savings.

Overhead-related kaizen costing initiatives often extend over several years. Their objective of reducing complexity can rarely be achieved quickly due to the extended scope of the project. Consequently, these programs often contain several phases, with each subsequent phase taking a more aggressive and fundamental approach to complexity reduction until the objective has been achieved. At that point, a maintenance program is typically initiated to ensure that unnecessary complexity does not return.

The implications for the suppliers of an overhead-specific kaizen costing intervention lie in the reduced diversity of parts that they are asked to manufacture. As the buyer reduces the complexity of its parts lists, a corresponding reduction in the complexity of the suppliers' product lines will typically occur. The result for the suppliers is reduced overhead and higher production volume of the buyer's remaining parts, both leading to lower costs. How the savings are shared between the buyer and supplier depends on the nature of their relationship.

SUMMARY

A full kaizen costing program consists of three types of interventions: period-specific, item-specific, and overhead-specific. The period-specific interventions focus on reducing the costs of the firm's production processes so that planned profit levels are maintained for all products. Such programs are of particular importance in markets where selling prices are declining over time, thereby placing pressure on the firm's profitability. The item-specific interventions are used to compensate either for the inability of the firm's target costing system to reduce the cost of a new product sufficiently in the design stage or for the period-specific kaizen program to reduce costs as fast as selling prices are falling. Finally, the overhead-specific interventions focus on the drivers of overhead and identifying ways to reduce them.

The level of savings that are achieved by kaizen costing programs are generally lower than those achieved through target costing, primarily because product design and functionality are a given. However, period-specific kaizen cost savings are cumulative, and over time even quite modest savings can accumulate to significant levels. For period-specific kaizen costing this is particularly true in environments in which the life cycle of production processes is long compared to product life cycles.

The savings from item-specific interventions are achieved through redesign of the product to reduce its cost. The focus of an item-specific intervention can be either the entire product or only the high-cost components it contains. The scope is determined primarily by the level of cost reduction required. The greater the level of cost reduction, the more likely the intervention is to focus on the entire product. The primary difference between item-specific kaizen costing and target costing lies in the inability to change the functionality of the product. This inability reduces the scope of the design changes that can be accommodated in an item-specific program. The reduced scope of the changes in turn reduces the magnitude of the savings that can be achieved. However, by focusing on expensive aspects of the product's design, costs can often be reduced significantly.

Overhead-specific kaizen costing focuses on the factors that drive indirect costs. These interventions typically deal with the complexity of the product mix produced by the firm. Reducing the complexity of the mix reduces the demand for overhead resources. The primary difference between overhead-specific and the other two types of kaizen costing is that to achieve any real savings, the overhead-specific program has to be applied to a large number of products and over an extended period of time.

The interorganizational aspects of kaizen costing emerge in two ways. First, when sophisticated buyers assist their less-advanced suppliers in developing their own kaizen costing programs and, second, when the buyer transfers the cost-reduction pressures it faces in the marketplace to its suppliers by setting cost-reduction objectives for existing components. For period-specific kaizen costing, the pressure is transmitted by setting cost-reduction objectives for all outsourced components as well as the internally sourced ones. In item-specific kaizen costing, the pressure is transmitted by requesting additional cost reduction for the major components in the product in question. The interorganizational aspects of overhead-specific kaizen costing are created by the reduction in complexity of the supplier's product mix that typically follows a reduction in complexity of the buyer's product mix. The interorganizational implications of kaizen costing are the focus of the next chapter.

CHAPTER 13

INTERORGANIZATIONAL IMPLICATIONS OF KAIZEN COSTING

INTRODUCTION

Limiting kaizen costing to the boundaries of the firm ignores the potential for further cost savings both upstream and downstream in the supply chain. The buyer can achieve some of these cost savings unilaterally, while others require coordination on the part of the buyer and supplier. Actions that require coordination between the two firms, such as the buyer providing specialized engineering support to the supplier to increase its ability to reduce costs, are considered interorganizational kaizen costing. In contrast, unilateral actions, such as eliminating the need for an outsourced item, are simply considered kaizen costing. Thus, under interorganizational kaizen costing, the actions to reduce costs must be taken jointly by the buyer and the supplier.

Like target costing, it is important that all parties involved view the process of setting kaizen cost-reduction objectives as being unbiased and perceive the resulting objectives as achievable most of the time. If the objectives are too aggressive, then the discipline of kaizen costing will be lost. However, if they are too easy, then cost-reduction opportunities will be forgone. One of the great differences between target costing and kaizen costing is that in target costing those opportunities are lost until the next generation of the product is introduced. In contrast, under kaizen costing they can be recaptured the following year by setting more aggressive cost-reduction objectives. This ability to recapture forgone opportunities means that firms typically adjust their kaizen cost-reduction objectives to reflect current market conditions as opposed to anticipated future conditions, as is the case with target costing.

Kaizen costing can also be used to discipline subsidiaries that act as internal suppliers. However, the balance of power between the parent and the subsidiary is typically decided by the parent. There are two possible scenarios—either the parent treats the subsidiary as if it were independent or it treats it as a subordinate. In the first approach, the parent gives the subsidiary a high degree of autonomy and subjects it to a low level of monitoring. This is the approach that Citizen adopts with respect to its subsidiaries. In the second approach, adopted by Olympus, the parent grants the subsidiary a low degree of autonomy and subjects it to a high level of monitoring.

SETTING COST-REDUCTION OBJECTIVES FOR SUPPLIERS

Interorganizational kaizen costing starts when the buyer transmits the cost-reduction pressure it faces in the marketplace to its suppliers by telling them how rapidly it expects their selling prices to fall over time. These kaizen cost-reduction objectives can either be set as a flat rate for all suppliers or as specific kaizen costing objectives, depending on the outsourced item. Citizen uses a flat rate approach for external suppliers. For example, the firm's kaizen costing objective in 1995 was 5% per annum. All external suppliers were expected to deliver at least this level of annual cost reduction. If a supplier was able to exceed the 5% objective, then it retained the surplus. A supplier that was unable to achieve the objective was not punished, but Citizen's engineers would assist it in achieving the 5% the following year. Several years prior to the downturn of the

Japanese economy in the mid-1990s, the cost-reduction rate was only 3%. Citizen uses the rate to establish how aggressive it wants its suppliers to be in reducing costs.

Olympus uses a similar flat rate percentage for its suppliers as a starting point for supplier cost reduction, but it places more aggressive cost-reduction pressures on high-cost components supplied by firms outside the Olympus group. For example, Olympus does not produce any electronic components. Instead it acquires them from independent suppliers such as Matsushita's Panasonic division. When a product's costs are excessive, Olympus often meets with representatives from Panasonic to discuss ways to increase the level of automation while simultaneously reducing the number of separate integrated circuit chips utilized. The difference in treatment between the two types of components demonstrates a cost/benefit trade-off. For relatively low-value components, setting individual cost-reduction objectives is not cost justified, whereas it is for high-value components.

The flat cost-reduction objectives established for suppliers by the buyer's kaizen costing program differ significantly from the component-specific objectives set by the buyer's target costing program. The difference in the two approaches reflects two fundamental differences between the cost-reduction capabilities of target and kaizen costing. First, the savings that can be achieved from target costing are larger than those that can be achieved from kaizen costing. These larger savings reflect the greater ability of the firm to manage costs proactively during the product design phase as opposed to the manufacturing phase. Therefore, it makes sense to expend more energy on setting item-specific target costing objectives than kaizen costing ones.

Second, any cost-reduction opportunities forgone during the design stage are almost impossible to recapture at a later date because once the product is designed, the majority of the costs are fixed. Therefore, unless the cost savings are achieved during the design phase, they are essentially lost until the next generation of the product is designed. In contrast, most cost savings during the manufacturing stage deal with improving production processes. Therefore, if they are not identified this year, they can be captured next year as long as the process is still in use. Reflecting this ability, many firms set their kaizen cost-reduction objectives based on current market conditions. If prices are holding, the cost-reduction objectives are low, and if cost pressure is high, the objectives are more aggressive. For example, the increase in cost-reduction objectives from 3% to 5% by Citizen reflected such a change in competitive conditions. Furthermore, production processes often remain the same across multiple generations of products. So while the savings are smaller on an annual basis, they accumulate over a longer period of time than for target costing and so there is a multi-year opportunity to achieve them. These two properties of kaizen costing—smaller cost savings that can be achieved over multiple periods—make it less critical to achieve the savings in a given year. Therefore, it makes sense to set a single cost-reduction rate at the level demanded by the market and fine-tune that overall rate from year to year rather than to set specific objectives for each outsourced item.

APPLYING KAIZEN COSTING TO SUPPLIERS

Like many interorganizational cost management techniques, kaizen costing interventions can be initiated by either the buyer or the supplier (see Figure 13–1). For buyer-led interventions, the buyer is either augmenting the cost-reduction capabilities of the supplier or giving it access to cost-reduction opportunities that it cannot access on its own. In supplier-led initiatives, the supplier finds new ways to manufacture components that lead to lower overall costs in the supply chain.

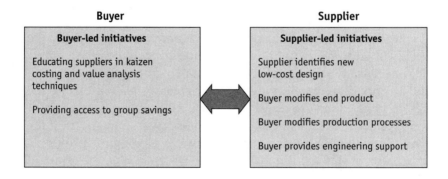

FIGURE 13–1. APPLYING KAIZEN COSTING TO SUPPLIERS

Buyer-Led Initiatives

The buyer often has to take a proactive role in helping the supplier become more efficient. Two fundamental approaches to reducing costs at suppliers are educating them and giving them access to cost savings they cannot achieve in isolation. The education route is most effective when the level of outsourcing is high and the buyer's engineering skills are higher than those of its suppliers. At Olympus, for example, given the high percentage of components that are sourced from outside Tatsuno, one of the major ways to reduce costs is through educating suppliers (both independent and subsidiaries of Olympus) in ways to reduce their costs. For the new Stylus camera project, eight highly skilled product engineers were given the responsibility of visiting suppliers to identify ways to modify their production and assembly processes to reduce costs. Often this type of savings is achieved by redesigning the part so it is easier for the suppliers to manufacture.

Isuzu adopts the same approach—sending engineers to its suppliers. Interorganizational kaizen costing is particularly important to Isuzu because of the high degree of outsourced items in its products. Approximately 70% of the total cost of its products is represented by parts purchased from external vendors. Therefore, many of the firm's cost-reduction activities are focused primarily on supplier-related activities, including value analysis performed by Isuzu engineers jointly with its suppliers, negotiations with and on behalf of suppliers to obtain price reductions for their materials (also called "price-down"), and global sourcing. The total cost savings across all models are in the range of ¥20 billion per year. The portion of the cost reduction that had to be achieved through value analysis during 1991, the first year of the firm's new cost management program, amounted to ¥3 billion. In subsequent years, the annual cost-reduction objective was increased to ¥7 billion.

The other approach to buyer-led kaizen costing centers on the buyer giving the supplier access to cost savings that the supplier cannot achieve in isolation. Firms achieve this objective in two ways. The first way affects only a single supplier, while the other affects many suppliers. In the single-supplier approach, the buyer identifies a less expensive source for items used by the supplier. The savings are then passed on to the buyer via supplier price reductions. This approach is demonstrated by Isuzu identifying a French manufacturer of valve stems on behalf of Yokohama Tires. Yokohama previously sourced valve stems from domestic manufacturers, whereas under the new arrangement, Isuzu bought the stems from the foreign supplier and supplied them to Yokohama. This change in supplier allowed Isuzu to save ¥70 per piece (and thus ¥350 in total per vehicle), a significant level of savings.

The multiple supplier approach takes advantage of the combined buying power of the firm and its suppliers. In this approach, the buyer identifies components used in its products by multiple suppliers and, often, itself. The buyer arranges with a single firm to source all of the supply chain's requirements for these components. The combined volume allows the buyer to negotiate greater discounts than the individual suppliers. The savings again are passed on to the buyer via reduced supplier prices. Komatsu and its suppliers, including Toyo Radiator, use this approach. Komatsu has access to all Toyo's cost information regarding Komatsu-related products, even to the level of knowing the price that Toyo pays for a single bolt used in a part that goes into a Komatsu product. If possible, Komatsu will increase discounts by purchasing the bolt centrally and have the bolt's manufacturer deliver the product directly to all users of that bolt in the Komatsu group and its major suppliers.

Supplier-Led Initiatives

Suppliers can also initiate interorganizational kaizen costing by identifying new ways to design a component so that it has lower costs. The functionality and quality of the component will typically remain constant during the redesign process as the buyer will not want its customers to perceive its product as having changed. If the design change has no implications for the buyer, it is an example of kaizen costing at the supplier. However, if the buyer has to be involved in the process, then it should be viewed as interorganizational kaizen costing.

The buyer's cooperation can take three forms. First, the most significant level of cooperation consists of the buyer's changing its product in some way to accommodate the new low-cost component. This level of cooperation will occur only for major components that have developed serious cost problems or for which the supplier's new design significantly reduces the buyer's costs through price reductions on the supplier's part.

The second level of cooperation consists of the buyer's agreeing to change its production processes to accommodate changes in the design of the component. The buyer will be motivated to agree to such changes if it views them as beneficial. These benefits can be either direct or indirect. Potential direct benefits include elimination or simplification of the buyer's production activities, or supplier price reductions that offset any additional costs for the buyer. Potential indirect benefits include increasing the perceived value of the buyer's relationship with the supplier. The buyer will view such strengthening as valuable if the supplier is an important one that can be expected to reciprocate in the future.

The third level of cooperation is for the buyer to provide the supplier with engineering support to help identify changes in the design of the component or its production processes. By making such requests the supplier demonstrates its willingness to work with the buyer to find new, low-cost solutions. In turn, the buyer demonstrates its willingness to expend resources on behalf of the supplier to help it achieve its cost-reduction objectives.

ROLE OF LEAN BUYER-SUPPLIER RELATIONS

The interactions between buyers and suppliers that lead to effective interorganizational kaizen costing during manufacturing rely heavily on the stable, cooperative, and mutually beneficial nature of lean buyer-supplier relations. The need for cooperation lies at the heart of interorganizational cost management. It is only when buyers and suppliers actively cooperate that real opportunities for interorganizational cost reduction can be identified. Stability is important because of the long-term nature of the savings, as kaizen savings accumulate over time. Each side is more willing to invest in the other if they both perceive that the relationship will exist for an extended period of time. Finally, mutual benefit ensures that any savings are shared among the buyer and its suppliers. Otherwise, the suppliers are unlikely to participate in any cost-reduction processes initiated by the buyer or especially to initiate their own interorganizational kaizen costing programs.

Linked Kaizen Costing Systems

The buyer's and supplier's target costing systems automatically form a chain that coordinates the cost management programs of the two firms. A chain is created because the output of the buyer's target costing system, the component-level target costs, are the inputs to the market-driven costing portion of the supplier's target costing system. The supplier's component-level target costs in turn feed its suppliers' target costing systems, extending the chain across multiple firms in a supply chain. The advantage of chaining target costing systems in this manner is that it pushes the competitive pressures faced by the buyer deep into the supply chain. This chaining is possible because target costing systems focus on reducing the costs of a single product and set specific cost-reduction objectives for the components it contains.

Kaizen costing systems do not chain in the same manner as target costing systems. A given supplier will often sell its products to several buyers, each applying a potentially different overall kaizen cost-reduction rate. These various rates will be averaged by the supplier's kaizen costing system to develop an appropriate kaizen cost-reduction rate for its suppliers (see Figure 13–2). For this reason, kaizen costing systems can be said to be linked but not chained. It is only when the buyer sets a specific cost-reduction objective for a high-value component that real chaining might take place.

Kaizen Costing and Internal Suppliers

When the buyer is the supplier's parent, interorganizational kaizen costing reduces the transfer prices between the subsidiary and its parent. Given the power of the parent, these reduced prices can be legislated even if the subsidiary does not achieve the required cost savings. While an external supplier could refuse to sell the goods, the subsidiary may be forced to comply. The outcome is reduced profitability of the subsidiary but a zero sum for the group because the apparent extra profitability of the parent is offset by the lower profits of the subsidiary. In addition, the discipline at the subsidiary to remove costs from existing products is reduced because the subsidiary perceives the cost-reduction objectives as unachievable. To

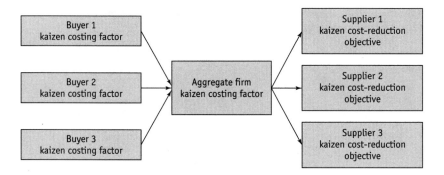

Figure 13-2. Linked Kaizen Costing Systems

offset this risk, the parent has to ensure that the pressure on the subsidiary is perceived as reflecting true market pressures, not some arbitrary cost-reduction objective of the parent. The parent can achieve this objective either by treating the subsidiary as if it were an independent supplier or by systematically managing cost reduction at the subsidiary. The two factors that drive this difference in the ways subsidiaries are treated appear to be corporate policy (how much freedom is considered optimal for subsidiaries) and the degree of skill of the subsidiary's management team (how much reliance the parent can place on the subsidiary to manage itself). These two factors are highly interdependent—corporations that believe in giving their subsidiaries a great deal of freedom make sure that the management teams at those subsidiaries have the requisite skill levels.

If the subsidiary is treated as if it were an independent supplier, the degree of autonomy granted is high and the level of monitoring that it is subjected to is low. Citizen Watch adopts this approach with respect to its internal suppliers. In contrast, if the subsidiary is managed by its parent, it is granted low autonomy and is subjected to a high level of monitoring. This is the approach Olympus adopts for its subsidiaries.

Most firms, irrespective of the way they manage their subsidiaries, use the same flat rate approach to setting kaizen cost-reduction objectives for internal as for external suppliers. For example, Citizen's subsidiary, Miyota, was subjected to the same 5% cost-reduction objectives as the group's independent suppliers. Similarly, at

Olympus the 3% cost-reduction objective was the same for all subsidiary companies that reported to Tatsuno. There was no attempt to set different targets for different subsidiaries or for internally sourced components unless they were of relatively high value.

Degree of Autonomy

Autonomy captures the degree of freedom that the subsidiary is granted in achieving profitability. A highly autonomous subsidiary is free to set its own profit objectives and, hence, cost-reduction objectives. In contrast, when subsidiary autonomy is low, those objectives are set by the parent company.

Citizen grants a high degree of autonomy to its subsidiaries. It treats them exactly as it treats its external suppliers. For example, unlike many of the subsidiaries of other companies in Japan, Miyota does not share detailed cost information with its parent. Instead, all prices and other contractual relations with Citizen are negotiated at arm's length. The negotiations between Miyota and Citizen are viewed by both sides as being tough but cooperative. The motivational implications of a high level of autonomy are captured in the following quote from Kazuo Tanaka, president of Miyota Co. Ltd.:

> I have a very high level of autonomy as the president of Miyota. I set my own targets and try to ensure that Miyota is profitable, thus contributing to the Citizen Group. If our parent Citizen knew every detail of our costs, I would be nothing more than a cost center manager.

While Miyota is treated as if it were an independent company, Tanaka's behavior is modified by the economic reality that the two firms are part of the same group. Each year Citizen's top management reviews competitive conditions and sets the group's long-term cost-reduction objectives. These objectives are transmitted to the Tanashi factory, which in turn informs Tanaka. At these meetings, Tanaka typically will not argue about the aggressiveness of the targets. He believes his responsibility is to deliver the cost-reduction objectives set by Citizen, not to take a narrow perspective and simply try to optimize Miyota's position. Thus, Tanaka views his primary role as president of Miyota as achieving Citizen's cost-reduction objectives while simultaneously maintaining Miyota's profitability. No contracts for long-term cost-reduction objectives are ever established. Both parties know what is expected, and that is considered sufficient.

However, there are limits to the autonomy that Tanaka is granted. If Miyota fails to deliver the long-term cost-reduction objectives, Tanaka will be held responsible. If Miyota continues to fail to deliver the cost-reduction objectives required by the long-term trends set by Citizen, then Tanaka will eventually be fired. In contrast, if Miyota were an external supplier, no such action could be taken. The lack of negotiations coupled with the severe penalty for failure requires that Tanaka perceive the component-level target costs set by Citizen as being achievable with reasonable effort. Consequently, Citizen's engineers take great care to ensure that their kaizen costing process generates cost-reduction objectives that Miyota's engineers consider attainable.

Olympus grants a lower degree of autonomy to subsidiaries, such as Omachi, than Citizen does. Olympus reduces Omachi's autonomy in five major ways (see Figure 13–3): (1) by budgeting Omachi's profits as opposed to letting them be self-determined; (2) by taking responsibility for any of its actions that adversely affect Omachi instead of letting Omachi stand on its own; (3) by managing the mix of products passing through Omachi instead of letting Omachi identify its own new products; (4) by adjusting expectations to reflect any errors in its planning process as opposed to making Omachi find its own solutions; and (5) by actively monitoring Omachi's performance in areas such as quality.

The first way in which Olympus reduces Omachi's autonomy is by budgeting its profits. Unlike Miyota, which has to find ways to be as profitable as possible, Omachi is expected simply to achieve a 3% profit target. In addition, unlike Miyota, which is expected to be at least as profitable as external suppliers, Omachi's budgeted profit is not equivalent to that made by external suppliers. Omachi faces intense competition from outside suppliers and is not expected to generate profits above the 3% target because as a wholly owned Olympus subsidiary it does not have to stand on its own. Therefore, its profitability, although low by industry standards, is considered acceptable.

The second way that Omachi's autonomy is reduced is by Olympus accepting responsibility for any actions it takes that

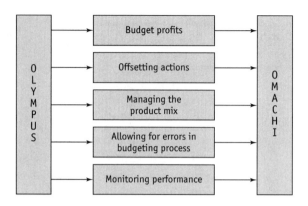

FIGURE 13-3. HOW OLYMPUS LIMITS OMACHI'S AUTONOMY

adversely affect Omachi's performance. For example, when Omachi's production volumes were decreasing as Olympus moved camera and parts production offshore, Tatsuno agreed to cover any losses that resulted. If Omachi became unprofitable, Tatsuno made a total cost allowance that would enable Omachi to break even. In contrast, if the same thing happened at Citizen, Miyota would be expected to find ways to solve the problem or become unprofitable.

The third way to reduce Omachi's autonomy revolves around who determines Omachi's product-line mix. At Olympus, it is Olympus that makes those decisions, while at Citizen it is Miyota. For example, in the late 1990s, Olympus Camera expected to move up to 60% of its domestic production capacity overseas, primarily to China, in a short time period. This restructuring was expected to reduce production volume at Omachi by 30%. To keep the work force gainfully employed, Olympus camera shifted simple mold production from external subcontractors to Omachi. Thus, it was Olympus that drove the move into mold production, not Omachi.

The fourth way centers on Olympus' willingness to accept responsibility for any errors it makes in the budgeting process. If Omachi can identify any such errors, Tatsuno will modify the budget and adjust selling prices accordingly. However, Tatsuno will not make adjustments for any "natural events" such as changes in sales volumes due to market conditions. The final way in which Olympus reduces Omachi's autonomy is by Olympus demanding changes in the way Omachi runs its business. For example, Olympus will subject Omachi to tighter quality control if it feels that Omachi is not doing an adequate job in that regard.

Despite the lower degree of autonomy granted to Omachi, the negotiations between the parent and the subsidiary are considered tough by both sides, with neither side readily conceding. Given the nature of these negotiations, Omachi, like external suppliers, needs protection against Olympus exerting excessive cost-reduction pressures. To maintain its profitability, Omachi retains the ability to turn down business if it will not generate acceptable profit margins. This ability is considered critical to maintaining an adequate balance of power between Tatsuno and Omachi. Otherwise, there is a real risk that Omachi will fail to achieve its 3% profit objective.

There is some indication that the way Olympus has reduced Omachi's autonomy may lead to reduced effectiveness of the target costing process. Olympus causes the problem by setting both the cost-reduction target and the budgeted profit. Consequently, the incentive for Omachi to make higher profits in good years is removed. In contrast, Miyota is motivated to become as profitable as possible. For Omachi the problem is compounded by the relatively easy 3% cost-reduction objective that Olympus has established.

Level of Monitoring

The level of monitoring captures how much information the subsidiary is asked to supply about its progress toward achieving the cost-reduction objectives. In a low-monitoring condition, the subsidiary is not required to supply the parent with any such information. In contrast, in a high-monitoring situation, the subsidiary is required to supply the parent with almost all the cost information it has available.

At Omachi, the low level of autonomy is accompanied by high levels of monitoring of cost information and, in particular, the progress the firm is making in achieving its cost-reduction objectives. The purpose of this monitoring is to help Omachi find ways to achieve its profit objectives. Olympus monitors Omachi in two ways: through variance analysis and by having in-house engineers at Omachi.

Olympus holds production conferences every other month to discuss Omachi's and other firms' production variances. These meetings used to be held monthly, but experience has shown that a longer interval is preferable because it makes trends easier to spot. the meetings are attended by individuals from Olympus, its subsidiaries, and subcontractors. Their aim is to determine how close to plan the firms are and what actions should be taken to improve their performance if it is below expectations. The primary output of the meetings is the Tatsuno Cost Result. This report summarizes the performance over the last two months of the production results of all subsidiaries and subcontractors.

The other way that Olympus monitors Omachi's performance is through the Olympus engineers who reside at Omachi. These engineers are responsible for using value analysis to help Omachi find ways to reduce costs. For example, they might find ways to change the production steps so that either cycle time or material consumption is reduced. Cycle time might be reduced by decreasing the amount of material in the stems that are attached to the finished parts because the reduced material content allows the part to cool more rapidly. The material costs might be reduced by using less expensive polymers or increasing yield rates. The guest engineers have in-depth knowledge of Omachi's production processes, which helps them evaluate the firm's progress toward achieving its cost-reduction objectives.

The high level of monitoring at Olympus can be contrasted with that at Citizen, where the subsidiaries share very little information with their parent. All prices and other contractual relations with Citizen are negotiated at arm's length. Therefore, Citizen is forced to use more indirect mechanisms than variance analysis and in-house engineers to monitor Miyota's and other subsidiaries' performance.

While Citizen does not have direct access to detailed cost information from Miyota, Tanashi engineers believe that they can quite accurately estimate the cost of Miyota's products (see Figure 13–4). These cost estimates enable Tanashi engineers to place considerable short-term pressure on Miyota to reduce costs. The first source of information used for cost estimation comes from Citizen's own cost system. Citizen Watch produces parts and sub-assemblies similar to many of the parts supplied by Miyota. Since the Tanashi engineers know the cost of these parts exactly, they can use them as a basis for accurately estimating the cost of the

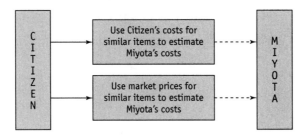

FIGURE 13-4. HOW CITIZEN PASSIVELY MONITORS MIYOTA'S COSTS

similar parts supplied by Miyota. The second source of information for estimating the costs of Tanashi-supplied parts comes from the multiple sourcing of parts. Most of the components that Miyota sells to Tanashi are also produced by other subsidiaries or by external suppliers. These multiple sources create a competitive market, which generates arm's-length prices for these parts. These prices are also used by Citizen's engineers as a basis for developing their own cost estimates.

In addition, the short-term negotiations between Miyota and Citizen act as a signaling mechanism. Miyota engineers will push harder to have the cost-reduction objectives relaxed when they are considered unachievable and not as hard when they are considered achievable. Thus, the intensity of the short-term negotiations acts as a subtle signal of how well Miyota is achieving its cost-reduction objectives. Finally, Miyota's profitability is determined by the relationship between Citizen's cost-reduction objectives and the amount of costs that Miyota actually takes out of the parts and subassemblies it sells to Citizen. If Miyota can take more costs out than required by Citizen, it can increase its profitability. Alternatively, if it cannot take out sufficient costs, its profitability will suffer. Thus, Citizen's top management can monitor how well Miyota is performing overall simply by looking at its profitability.

Citizen's top management uses these two sources of information—the intensity of short-term negotiations and Miyota's profitability—to help them set the long-term cost-reduction objectives for Miyota. Their aim is to create a reasonable degree of pressure on Miyota to maximize its ability to reduce costs.

Summary

Kaizen costing can be used to transmit the cost pressure faced by the buyer to its suppliers. In this way it acts as a disciplining mechanism for interorganizational cost management during manufacturing. The focus of the interorganizational kaizen costing process is the production processes the supplier uses to manufacture the items outsourced by the buyer. Unlike target costing, where the cost-reduction objectives are set for each individual component, kaizen costing uses the same flat rate objectives for all components. One notable exception is very high-priced components, for which specific cost-reduction objectives are set. This simplified approach to setting cost-reduction objectives is adopted because in kaizen costing the annual savings are lower and because missed savings one year can be captured in a later period (though they will be lost for the intervening period). In contrast, in target costing the savings are larger but can be achieved only during the design process. Once the product is designed, it is very difficult to recover any savings that were forgone because of poor design. Furthermore, any design changes that are undertaken to reduce costs further often have a destabilizing effect on the production process. These effects lead to higher costs and often render such changes uneconomic. Consequently, many firms freeze the design of the product once it has been introduced and limit cost savings in the manufacturing phase of the product's life to kaizen costing improvements to the production processes. The decision to freeze product design means that it is imperative to ensure that the savings during the design phase help achieve the target cost.

The kaizen cost-reduction objectives set by the buyer must be considered achievable by the supplier if the discipline of kaizen costing is to be maintained. The aim of interorganizational kaizen costing is to set relentless but attainable cost-reduction pressure on suppliers. For this reason, the buyer takes great care to ensure that the cost-reduction objectives set are realistic and reflect the capabilities of the suppliers. The primary source of information to ensure that realistic objectives are set is the detailed knowledge the buyer has about supplier capabilities. The other source is the end market. While the short-term selling price of a product might not reflect the long-term cost-reduction trends, over time it will. As long as the buyer interprets the cost-reduction signals being sent by its customers correctly, the kaizen costing objectives will be realistic and should be achievable.

In most settings, the kaizen costing process is designed to keep the firms in the supplier network competitive. This objective is achieved in the first place through aggressive application of target costing. It is only when the products have long manufacturing cycles that kaizen costing becomes the primary mechanism to maintain competitiveness.

Internal suppliers create a distinct challenge for interorganizational kaizen costing because of the lack of independence between the buyer (parent) and supplier (subsidiary). This lack of independence can lead to a loss of discipline if the subsidiary ignores the signals sent by the parent's kaizen costing system. Most firms set the kaizen costing objectives for subsidiaries in exactly the same way that they set those of external suppliers, that is, by using a flat rate. Parents can treat subsidiaries in two distinct ways during the kaizen costing process. They can treat them just like external suppliers, giving them a high degree of autonomy and subjecting them to a low level of monitoring, or they can treat them as part of the parent, giving them virtually no autonomy and monitoring them heavily.

Besides managing costs across their organizational boundaries during product design and manufacture, buyers and suppliers should also cooperate to make the transfer of goods and services and associated transactions between their firms more efficient. Increasing the efficiency of the buyer-supplier interface can be achieved by lowering the costs of transaction processing and by reducing uncertainty so that both the buyer and the supplier can maintain lower levels of buffer inventory. These cost management actions are the focus of the next chapter.

CHAPTER 14

INCREASING THE EFFICIENCY OF THE BUYER-SUPPLIER INTERFACE

INTRODUCTION

The third and last aspect of interorganizational cost management focuses on increasing the efficiency of the buyer-supplier interface. This interface includes all activities and processes associated with the transfer of goods or services from one firm to another. Examples include order placement, billing and payment, inventory management of finished goods at the supplier and purchased parts at the buyer, and transportation and external logistics. Increasing the efficiency of the buyer-supplier interface deals with reducing the costs associated with these activities and processes. The primary ways that the interface can be made more efficient are by reducing transaction processing costs and by decreasing uncertainty (see Figure 14–1).

All the firms in this study had adopted lean practices, such as single-piece flow in product design and manufacturing, and they all had well-developed total quality management programs. As a result, the buyer-supplier interfaces were quite efficient and buffer inventories were low, typically measured in terms of hours, not days.

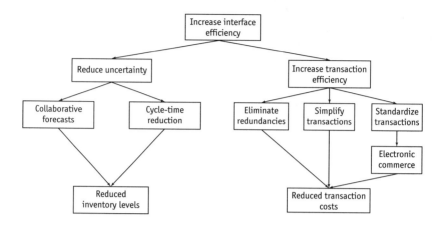

FIGURE 14-1. OVERVIEW OF INCREASING THE EFFICIENCY OF THE
          BUYER-SUPPLIER INTERFACE

However, the progress that they had made in using information technology to make their interfaces more efficient was not as advanced as at some Western firms. Rather than describe non-leading-edge practice, in this chapter we provide an overview of the general steps required to render the buyer-supplier interface efficient.

Four activity-related improvements lead to reduced transaction processing costs. First, eliminating inefficient and redundant activities can reduce interface costs. The primary candidates for elimination are activities that are duplicated at both locations. Second, some processes can be simplified so that they consume fewer resources. Processes that trigger common activities at both firms are prime candidates for simplification. Third, activities and processes can be standardized. Standardization is particularly effective when the activities and processes are high volume, routine, and common to all buyer-supplier interfaces. Finally, activities can be automated. Standardized activities that are repetitive and high volume are most suitable for automation via the adoption of electronic commerce.

The improvements aimed at reducing uncertainty lead to lower inventory levels at both firms. The buyer uses inventory to buffer against the supplier's failure to deliver goods to the line on time, and the supplier uses inventory to buffer against unexpected demands from the buyer. If these two sources of uncertainty can be eliminated, buffer inventories can be reduced, which frees up cash flow and increases both firms' asset turnover ratios. To reduce these uncertainties, the two firms can increase the amount of information they share and reduce the time it takes to process transactions that bridge the interface.

Other benefits can be derived from more efficient buyer-supplier interfaces. Customer and supplier relations may improve—the more accurate transactions are, the fewer disagreements there will be. More efficient processing of invoices can speed up the rate of cash flow between firms. Finally, the cost of administering the procurement function can be decreased significantly as the number of persons involved in the function drops.

To improve the efficiency of the interface, both firms need to make changes in the way they interact. Some of these changes are joint projects that require close cooperation and coordination, while others are initiated predominantly by either the buyer or the supplier.

JOINTLY INITIATED IMPROVEMENTS

Joint improvements are those that require both the buyer and supplier to take cooperative and coordinated actions to increase the efficiency of their interface. One of the major initiatives that is typically undertaken is to use information technology to automate the information transfer between the two firms. The other is to standardize the order-delivery process so as to reduce its cycle time.

Automated Information Transfer

Electronic commerce (EC) systems offer the promise of considerably reducing the cost of buyer-supplier interactions while significantly increasing their effectiveness. Several related developments make EC possible: the rapid development of the commercial Internet over the last few years, the spread of corporate intranets, and the recent introduction of commercially viable electronic commerce software. These three technologies support effective interfirm communication in electronic form. An EC program can increase the efficiency of the buyer-supplier interface in numerous ways. Potential applications include:

- Purchasing,
- Order entry,
- Inventory management,
- Accounts payable,
- Accounts receivable,
- Invoicing,
- Payment,
- Transportation and logistics.

One approach to EC is to use the commercial Internet, while the other is to develop customized solutions (see Figure 14–2). Internet solutions are most appropriate for subcontractors and common suppliers while customized solutions work best for major suppliers and family members. The commercial Internet has the advantage of being widely accessible to virtually everybody. Individuals who want to obtain information about the firm and its products can use the Internet to access the firm's Web pages. Furthermore, there is no need for the user to be known to the firm beforehand. Thus, if the firm wants to make any information readily available to anyone 24 hours a day, seven days a week, such as catalogues, price lists, and product availability, they can publish it on the Web.

A more custom-made application of EC is electronic data interchange (EDI). EDI is the electronic transmission of standard business documents in a predefined format from one company's business computer application to that of another company with which it is doing business. EDI increases efficiency through improved

	Open system	Closed system
Many-to-many	Commercial Internet (e.g., catalogues)	Industry-wide application (e.g., airline reservations)
One-to-many	Intranet	Dedicated application (e.g., electronic order entry)

FIGURE 14–2. TYPES OF ELECTRONIC COMMERCE APPLICATIONS

transaction handling and increased information sharing. EDI can reduce the costs of processing transactions between two firms by reducing the need to create, handle, and store paper documents. Also, it eliminates the need to reenter data supplied by one firm into the IT systems of the other firm, thereby reducing clerical errors introduced by reentering data. Finally, it reduces the cycle time needed for the transaction to be initiated at one firm and acted on by the other.

Another purpose of EDI is to increase the flow of useful information between the firms. When the transmittal medium is paper, typically only a fraction of the total information transmitted is entered into the other firm's computer system. The high cost of data entry causes firms to adopt an "only if definitely needed" policy. The information that is not entered is frequently ignored or accessed only if a problem is encountered. With EDI, all the information is electronically available, usually in a uniform format. These two characteristics enable the data to be used to support better decisions and in some cases to automate the decision process.

The three primary applications of EDI are order processing, billing, and advanced shipment notices. For these high-volume, routine transactions, activities that rely on the same information are carried out at both locations. Furthermore, these transactions are performed by all the firms in the supplier network. To be effective, EDI requires standardization of the order and billing processes of all the participating firms. This standardization allows the firms to communicate electronically with each other. A less common, more sophisticated application of EDI is to automate the release of inventory from the supplier to the buyer. Such applications require both sophisticated computerized inventory management capabilities and translation software and hardware that enable the various computer systems to communicate with each other.

As EC systems mature, they move away from just capturing instructional or action documents (such as orders and bills) and expand to include status information (such as shipment or payment status). These status applications help reduce uncertainty by ensuring that both parties are current about changing business conditions of mutual interest. For example, if price lists are transmitted via EDI, then the risk of using out-of-date prices is reduced to a minimum. One of the great advantages of having automated access to status information is that it is available 24 hours a day, seven days a week. For firms that compete in a global marketplace, this availability can provide a competitive advantage.

Some special applications of EC are designed to link the buyer with specified suppliers. For example, the buyer can identify a list of standard items that can be purchased electronically without formal approval. The supplier has to develop the capability to process such orders and ensure that only authorized items are shipped. Another such application is using the Internet to communicate an open order broadly to a number of pre-specified suppliers. The buyer prepares a standardized e-mail that includes the order form the supplier has to complete and sends it to all the approved suppliers for that item. The suppliers complete the order if they can have the items available by the specified date and e-mail it back to the buyer. The buyer then selects a supplier (or suppliers) to fill the order and sends back confirming e-mails to all suppliers. Thus, the entire process is undertaken electronically. In a similar process, the buyer can initiate e-mail bidding among suppliers.

Another application of information technology is to automate the collection of information about physical transfers, for example, through the use of bar coding. Here the buyer and supplier have to invest in the equipment to prepare and read bar codes. In addition, they have to develop a common set of codes that can be used to identify each of the items exchanged between the two firms.

The justification for adopting any of the techniques to increase the efficiency of a buyer-supplier interface is governed by a cost/benefit trade-off. As the costs of implementing and operating the technique increase, so must the benefits. The larger the supplier and the more business transacted, the more likely that the more sophisticated techniques to increase the efficiency of the buyer-supplier interface will be justified. The interface of a core firm with its first-tier suppliers, who are family members and major suppliers, represents most of the value of outsourced items. Consequently, these firms are prime candidates for electronic commerce based on EDI. The advantage of using customized solutions is that the communications can be undertaken very rapidly compared to the commercial Internet. The disadvantage is their high cost. For the low-value-added suppliers, such as common suppliers and subcontractors, the commercial Internet approach usually is adopted.

The benefits from increasing the efficiency of multiple buyer-supplier interfaces across a supply chain are additive. Consequently, considerable benefit can be derived from increasing the efficiency of the interfaces across the entire supplier network. However, the firms in a typical supply chain decrease in size and increase in number at each tier (see Figure 14–3). The supplier base of any given firm can thus be seen as a triangle with four levels. The family members are at the apex, followed by the major suppliers, then the subcontractors, ending with the common suppliers (see Figure 14–4). Only the larger firms in the chain usually can support the more expensive techniques to increase the efficiency of the interface. The firms at the lower end of the chain are often too small to justify the more sophisticated approaches. However, since these firms produce the

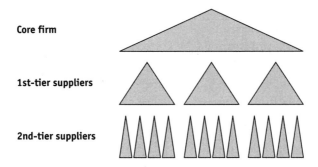

FIGURE 14–3. THE SUPPLIER NETWORK FOR A LEAN ENTERPRISE

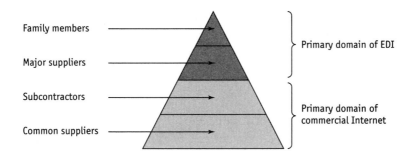

FIGURE 14–4. THE SUPPLIER BASE STRUCTURE OF A LEAN ENTERPRISE AND ELECTRONIC COMMERCE

largest number of items (at each tier, the items manufactured by the tier below are assembled into more complex but fewer items), it is these firms that generate most transactions in the network. Because of the potential high overall savings but small individual savings, the automation of these interfaces represents at the same time a great opportunity to reduce costs and a major challenge.

Order-Delivery Process Improvement

The second major joint initiative to make the buyer-supplier interface more efficient is to improve the order-delivery process between the two firms. Three types of initiatives can be taken to improve the process. The first is to standardize the order-delivery process for all the participating firms. The second is to reduce the cycle time to process and deliver orders at each firm through improved integration of order processing systems. Finally, the firms should develop collaborative forecasts.

The order process used by the major firms in the supplier network should be standardized before it is automated, to simplify the process and make it as common as possible to all the firms. As part of this standardization, the firms should reduce to a minimum the time it takes for orders to be processed. The shorter the overall order-delivery cycle, the lower the buffer inventories that will be required at the buyers.

Collaborative forecasts are developed when all the participating firms share their forecasts with each other and coordinate them across the network. The development of common forecasts across multiple firms in the network has several advantages. Any shortages are identified much earlier in the planning process, so corrective actions can be taken sooner. For example, if a third-tier supplier's factory is heavily damaged for some reason, the firms in the second tier can either find or create new sources for the outsourced item. Also, the tendency to introduce slack into the forecasts at each interface is avoided. For example, if each firm adds 10% to the anticipated volume to "ensure available capacity," by the time the fourth-tier firms are involved, the forecasts will contain 30% excess volume. Finally, the forecasts for each supply chain can be developed faster and more efficiently. The increased speed is a direct outcome of the joint involvement, and the increased efficiency comes from not having to rework the forecasts as new information arrives from the lower-tier firms.

BUYER-INITIATED IMPROVEMENTS

Buyer-initiated improvements require that the buyer change its behavior in ways that are beneficial to the supplier, although they sometimes also require minor changes at the supplier. The buyer can adopt seven major initiatives to improve the efficiency of the buyer-supplier interface. Four of these—managing demand, providing adequate order lead time, reducing special ordering, and sharing forecasts—primarily reduce uncertainty. The other three—the use of purchase contracts, payment-on-receipt, and improved accuracy of communications with the supplier—reduce transaction processing costs.

The reduction of inventories that characterizes lean supply means that the supplier has less buffer to handle unexpected surges in demand. To reduce the uncertainty for the supplier, the buyer must manage demand actively so that it is as level as possible. In addition, the buyer must tell the supplier as soon as possible about any anticipated changes in demand and indicate whether the change is considered temporary or permanent.

Furthermore, the buyer should ensure that its order lead times are reasonable and give the supplier sufficient notice so that it can manufacture the order without having to expedite material or production. The buyer must also minimize changes to orders that have already been placed. Changes that can disrupt the supplier's normal production flow include altering the volume and specifications of items ordered and their delivery dates.

Another initiative that the buyer can undertake is to reduce the number of special orders it places. While lean enterprises can economically produce a broader range of products than their mass producer counterparts, there are limits to the diversity of products that can be supported. Consequently, the supplier's (and hence the buyer's) costs can be reduced if the buyer orders standardized parts whenever possible.

In addition, the buyer can share its forecasts with its suppliers. Sharing forecasts is valuable because it reduces uncertainty. The supplier has a better idea of what will be demanded in the coming period and can identify possible capacity constraints. Thus, the primary advantage of shared forecasts is a reduction in the safety stocks of finished inventory. These forecasts should include sales plans and production schedules because they are of direct interest to the supplier. Sharing forecasts is the first step in developing collaborative forecasts.

The adoption of extended purchase contracts for outsourced items that are considered critical, as opposed to individual purchase orders, is another way in which the buyer can reduce transaction costs. Extended purchase contracts serve two purposes. First, they lock in the supplier to help guarantee availability. Second, they allow individual requests for products to be accumulated and a single payment made each period. In contrast, when individual purchase orders are utilized, each order has to be treated as a separate economic transaction. Typically, purchase contracts are prepared for either a specified quantity of items or for a specified amount of money. Only when the contract is completed are renegotiations required.

For the less critical items, the buyer can shift to spot purchases and adopt payment-on-receipt. Here the receipt of the packing slip automatically triggers payment. The supplier does not have to generate an invoice and wait 30–60 days to get paid. Bar coding plays an important role in payment-on-receipt because of the greater accuracy, ease of data entry into the buyer's system, and standardized format.

Finally, the buyer can work to increase the accuracy of its communications with its suppliers. For example, it can increase the accuracy of its orders and payments. Removing these defects means that both sides have to undertake fewer reconciliation and error-correction activities.

Supplier-Initiated Improvements

Supplier-initiated improvements require that the supplier change its behavior in ways that are beneficial to the buyer, although they sometimes also require minor changes at the buyer. The supplier can adopt eight different initiatives to improve the efficiency of the buyer-supplier interface. Six of them—increasing the ratio of on-schedule deliveries, reducing delivery cycle time, reducing production cycle time, sharing performance metrics, sharing forecasts, and giving the buyer access to order status information—primarily help reduce uncertainty. The other two—extended supplier control over inventories and improved accuracy of its communications with the buyer—help reduce transaction processing costs.

One of the ways the supplier can improve the efficiency of the interface is to increase its ratio of on-schedule deliveries. This improvement allows the buyer to reduce buffer inventories since the supplier is now more reliable.

Reducing delivery cycle times also helps reduce uncertainty at the buyer as it helps contract the overall order-delivery time. This reduction allows the buyer to place orders later in the cycle without increasing the level of uncertainty at the supplier. The primary advantage is that the buyer has more timely information when the order is placed.

Another way the supplier can increase the efficiency of the interface is to reduce its production cycle time. This cycle-time reduction has the advantage of increasing the supplier's ability to produce the items ordered by the buyer in the interval between order receipt and scheduled delivery. The other advantage of decreased cycle times is that any defects in the production process are more rapidly observed and corrected, reducing the risk of not delivering on time. The full supplier cycle includes the time it takes to deliver the order. If that time can be reduced, then the order fulfillment cycle time will be further reduced. The primary advantage of these efforts is a reduction in uncertainty for the buyer.

Suppliers can also reduce the uncertainty for the buyer by sharing their performance metrics. The type of information that can be shared includes defect levels, cycle times, and on-time delivery statistics. This information sharing enables the buyer to identify the suppliers that perform the best and to source accordingly.

The supplier also can share forecasts and information about shipping status, inventory, and order status. This information helps the buyer plan its production schedule because it can avoid launching products into manufacturing that will not have all the outsourced parts available. In addition, the buyer can manage its customers' expectations better as it has earlier notice of when it will fail to deliver on time because of parts shortages.

Another major improvement the supplier can undertake is to adopt total quality management and reduce defects to as near zero as possible. High supplier quality enables the buyer to eliminate inspections when it receives the outsourced items. The elimination of buyer-based inspection allows the supplier to adopt new approaches to the management of the interface inventory. Some of these approaches all but eliminate the concept of separate buyer and supplier inventories. Instead, the supplier has control of the inventory until the buyer is ready to incorporate the items into its products. The three primary techniques for improved inventory handling are automated replenishment, vendor-managed inventory, and JIT delivery to the line.

In automated replenishment the buyer sends the supplier a signal that it is time to replenish inventory. It is up to the supplier to take all further actions, including filling the inventory bins at the buyer. This process can be extended further by having the supplier take all responsibility for inventory, including managing the levels at the buyer and making the replenishment decisions without explicit buyer involvement. Furthermore, the supplier can deliver the order at exactly the point in time that the items are needed by the buyer's production process. The supplier is now fully integrated into the just-in-time production process of the buyer.

Finally, the supplier can work to increase the accuracy of its interactions with the buyer. For example, it can increase the accuracy of its advance shipment notices and of its invoices. Removing these defects means that both sides can reduce the number of reconciliation and error-correction activities.

Not all of these techniques are cost justified from the supplier's perspective. Smaller suppliers, in particular, will find it hard to justify all of them. However, for the buyer, the benefits can be significant, especially if it has already automated its interactions with its larger suppliers. One way the buyer can reward the supplier is by giving it access to its advanced technology. For example, the buyer can let the supplier have access to its enterprise resource planning system. The supplier can use this system to gain access to the EC capabilities of the buyer.

SUMMARY

One way in which interorganizational cost management can reduce costs is through joint product design, where the collaboration of the buyer's and supplier's design teams leads to increased functionality and quality at lower cost. A second way costs can be reduced throughout the supplier network is through joint improvements to the manufacturing processes. Finally, the firms can collaborate to make the interface between them more efficient: they can decrease the cost of transaction processing and reduce uncertainty by sharing information more fully and reducing the time it takes to communicate and respond to events. The primary benefit of reducing uncertainty lies in the lower levels of inventory the firms must maintain, leading to improved cash flow and higher asset turnover ratios.

CHAPTER 15

INTERORGANIZATIONAL COST MANAGEMENT IN ACTION

INTRODUCTION

A hypothetical company, the Acme Pencil Co. Ltd., will be used to illustrate interorganizational cost management in action.[1] Acme, a writing instrument manufacturer, wants to introduce a new pencil sharpener that differs from existing products because of its enhanced appearance. Despite the simplicity of the product, this example captures much of the richness of the interorganizational cost management process. The process begins with target costing at the core firm and its suppliers and continues with a full range of interactive design processes that occur in the supplier network. This supplier network consists primarily of Belgium Electric Motors, Inc. (BEM), China Injection Molding Corporation (CIM), Delta Gears, Inc. (DGI), and a number of common suppliers that supply items such as nuts and bolts and packaging (see Figure 15–1). When the new product enters

---

[1] The cases that make up Chapters 17 to 20 describe actual practice in four supply chains.

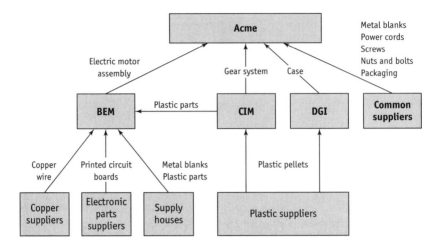

FIGURE 15-1. ACME'S SUPPLIER NETWORK FOR THE NEW ELECTRIC SHARPENER

production, the process continues with interorganizational kaizen costing. At the same time, the firms in the supplier network are exploring ways to make their interfaces more efficient.

THE ACME PENCIL CO. LTD.

Acme produces a wide variety of writing instruments including traditional graphite pencils, ballpoint pens, highlighters, and fountain pens. It also produces a line of pencil sharpeners. The three types of pencil sharpeners are manual powered, battery powered, and electric powered. Acme is a well-established firm with a reputation for innovation. It has four major competitors, all essentially evenly matched. None of these firms can point to a sustainable competitive advantage. Their products are very similar and they compete for the same customers, both commercial and retail.

Feedback from customers indicates an appearance problem with the firm's electric-powered pencil sharpener. The sharpener has straight sides and its appearance is viewed as too boxy and out of date (see Figure 15–2). The product is perfectly functional; it sharp-

FIGURE 15-2. THE EXISTING CASE DESIGN

ens pencils but does not look acceptable in offices with modern decor. To overcome the problem, the firm wants to design a new, contemporary-style product. The firm wants the new product to sell, at discount, for between $13.50 and $16.00. This price range places the new product at a new upper end for standard models on the market but below the price range of the deluxe models.

Customer analysis indicates that there should be significant demand for the product at that price. Acme had first considered a higher price range of $20–$25 but then rejected it. The pencil sharpener market contains two product types—the standard products that sell at discount in the $10–$15 price range and the deluxe products that sell at discount for $20 to $30. Acme historically has sold products only in the standard range and does not feel confident that they can succeed at the higher price point. Firms that manufacture the high-end products also produce other office desktop products such as staplers, hole-punches, and organizers. These products are designed to be part of a coordinated set for executives, though they are sold separately. Since Acme does not manufacture or sell the other products, it is at a competitive disadvantage in the deluxe market.

Focus group interactions with customers identify the relative importance of features that the customers value in electric pencil sharpeners. The most important feature is the sharpener's ability to produce a sharp point. The second most important feature is the ability to sharpen the pencil with minimum waste. The third most important feature is the level of noise the sharpener makes when operating. The final feature is appearance. Customers want an attractive product that blends into their office decor. The standard products have a less attractive appearance than the high-end prod-ucts. Acme's strategy is to develop a new standard product that has the attractive appearance of the deluxe models but sells within the standard selling price range. The feature weightings of the current and proposed products, based on a scale of 10, are shown in Table 15–1. Since the competitors' products are identical to Acme's exist-ing standard product, there is no need to undertake feature analysis on their products.

The product engineers have reacted enthusiastically to the con-cept of the new product and have begun to experiment to see if they can find a simple way to overcome the limitations of existing designs, for example, by using a different shape case but the same components. So far, they have failed to find an easy solution because the components are designed to operate in serial layout (see Figure 15–3). This linear layout automatically leads to a long, boxy design that cannot be camouflaged. A different internal lay-out of the major functions is required to achieve the objective. The engineers have identified a parallel layout (see Figure 15–4) that has the potential of creating a new, more contemporary look (see Figure 15–5).

The new product will become part of the firm's pencil sharp-ener product line. However, the number of products in that line will remain constant since the current electric model will be withdrawn at the time of launch of the new product. The sharpener line repre-sents 28% of the firm's sales and currently contains three sub-lines. Each sub-line consists of a single product that is designed to be the best of class. The manual sharpener sells at $7 in the high-volume,

TABLE 15–1. FEATURE WEIGHTING FOR LONG-LIFE AND EXISTING HIGH-END PRODUCTS

	Product	
	Existing score	Proposed score
Feature		
Sharpens effectively	10	10
Sharpens efficiently	7	7
Sharpens quietly	5	5
Looks attractive	5	8

discount office-supply stores and for about 50% more at stationers. The battery model sells at $10 at discount and $15 otherwise. Finally, the electric sharpener sells at $12.50 in the discount and $20 in the non-discount channels.

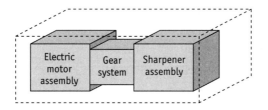

FIGURE 15-3. THE EXISTING SERIAL LAYOUT

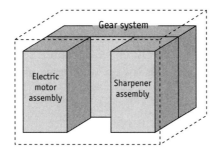

FIGURE 15-4. THE NEW PARALLEL LAYOUT

FIGURE 15-5. THE NEW CASE DESIGN

TARGET COSTING AT ACME[2]

Acme has had a well-developed target costing system in place for just over five years. All new products are subjected to the discipline of target costing. If a product cannot achieve its target cost, it is not introduced unless it is considered strategic. The new pencil sharpener is no exception. If there is no way to design the product so it can be manufactured at its target cost, it will not be introduced. Over the years target costing has developed into an integral part of the firm's approach to product development.

The Process

Acme's target costing process can be broken into three major sections. The first part is market-driven costing, in which the allowable cost of the product is established. The second section, product-level target costing, establishes the target cost of the product. The gap between the allowable cost and the target cost becomes the strategic cost-reduction challenge. In the final part, component-level target costing is used to set the target costs for each component in the product.

Market-Driven Costing

The firm's long-term sales and profit objectives are based on five-year projections of what top management think is realistically achievable if everyone in the firm expends significant efforts to reach their goals. The profit objective for the next five years for the pencil sharpener line is 15%, and the sales volume objective is 200,000 units. To help achieve this objective, the new product is expected to earn above-average profits and have sales levels between 40,000 and 60,000 units in the first year, with subsequent years' sales being at least 50,000 units.

After considerable analysis and discussion, the target retail list price is set at $25, and the discount price is set at $15.50. These target selling prices are selected for three reasons. First, top management believes that customers will feel that they are getting good

---

[2] For a more complete description of Acme's target costing system see the first volume in this series, *Target Costing and Value Engineering*.

value for their money. A high perceived value for money is important because top management views the new product as having a
significant role in reinforcing the firm's reputation as an innovator.
While no firm can claim to be the technological leader, Acme
believes that it currently has a slight technological advantage over
its competitors. Being the first to market with innovative products
plays a critical part in giving the firm what it perceives as a small
competitive advantage over its competitors.

Second, top management believes the target selling price is low
enough to ensure acceptable market penetration. They expect a
large percentage of customers to switch to the new, contemporary
design from their competitors' standard-shaped models. In addition,
they expect to take some market share from the deluxe products.
People who want an attractive sharpener but are not interested in
matched sets are thought likely to become new customers. If Acme
can launch the new product with little or no warning to its competitors, top management believes that they can increase their market share of electric sharpeners from 30% to 50%. Hopefully, this
increase in market share can be maintained when the competitors
introduce equivalent products about six months later. To be conser-
vative, the 50,000 future annual sales volume anticipates a long-
term 35% market penetration.

Finally, management believes that the target selling price is high
enough to enable the firm to make an adequate return on the product. The extra $5 above the full retail selling price and $3 above the
discount price of the existing electric-powered product provide the
firm with the extra proceeds required to support both the product
development costs and the anticipated higher manufacturing costs
of the new model. In addition, the anticipated increase in units sold
will help offset these additional costs.

Since 80% of the product's sales are expected to be at discount
and 20% at full retail, the average selling price is expected to be
$17.40 ($25 × 0.20 + $15.50 × 0.80). If the firm sells the new prod-
uct at the same 70% ratio of full retail list price to wholesale price as
the existing electric-powered product, then Acme's target average
wholesale selling price will be approximately $12.18 (70% × $17.40).
Given this price and the estimated target selling volumes, the firm can
establish the target profit margin. The target profit margin calcula-
tion begins with a projection of historical profit margins against

price. Historically, the firm has earned an average return of 15% on the sharpener line in total and 20% on electric-powered models. The firm has decided that there is no reason for the new product not to maintain the historical margin of electric pencil sharpeners. A life-cycle profitability analysis is undertaken. This analysis includes both revenue and cost projections over the life of the product. The revenue projection includes the estimated sales volumes and the anticipated reduction in selling price over the life of the product. The cost projections include the development and launch costs, the manufacturing costs, and the anticipated savings as the production processes are subjected to kaizen costing. The analysis indicates that the overall profit generated by the new product over its anticipated five-year life is acceptable.

A 20% profit margin for the new sharpener means that the allowable cost to sales ratio is 0.80 of the firm's selling price. This profit margin thus results in an allowable cost of $9.74 ($12.18, the target average wholesale selling price, times 0.80, the cost-to-sales ratio). This is the cost at which the new product must be manufactured if it is to earn its target profit margin at its target selling price. This allowable cost is $1.90 higher than the current cost of the existing product (see Table 15–2).

Product-Level Target Costing

At Acme, the product-level target cost for the new pencil sharpener is set in an iterative process in which the value engineering team integrates supplier cost quotes with the cost estimates provided by

TABLE 15–2. THE SELLING PRICES, PROFIT MARGINS,
            MANUFACTURING COSTS, AND PRODUCTION VOLUMES
            OF THE EXISTING PRODUCTS

	Product	
	Existing	Proposed
Full retail list selling price	$ 20.00	$ 25.00
Discount retail list selling price	12.50	15.50
Average retail selling price	14.00	17.40
Average wholesale selling price	9.80	12.18
Profit margin	20%	20%
Current/allowable cost	7.84	9.74

design and manufacturing. The process begins by determining the current cost of the product, that is, the cost at which it could be produced by buying the components today and using existing production processes. The starting point for this analysis is the current cost of the existing product.

The pencil sharpener has five major functions: sharpener assembly, electric motor assembly, gear system, case, and power cord. The new product is so revolutionary that, with the exception of the power cord, the designs of all the major functions are expected to change considerably. In particular, the electric motor assembly has to change completely if the new contemporary shape is to be achieved. The current design uses a transformer and motor mounted on the same transformer core. This design leads to a large, rectangular cross section (see Figures 15–6 and 15–7), which limits the firm's ability to produce a pencil sharpener with a contemporary shape.

Acme outsources all but the manufacture of the sharpener assembly. It believes that the ability to design and manufacture sharpener assemblies with extra durability is a core technology that must be protected at all cost. The technologies associated with the electric motor assembly, which has a current cost of $2.50, gears, and case are all considered sufficiently mature that they are unable to give the firm any competitive advantage. Consequently, these technologies and their associated major functions are all outsourced.

The electric motor assembly is the most complicated of the outsourced items, and BEM, an Acme family member and the firm's primary source of electric motors, is selected as the supplier. The

FIGURE 15–6. THE EXISTING ELECTRIC MOTOR ASSEMBLY (FRONT VIEW)

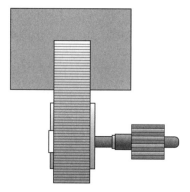

FIGURE 15–7. THE EXISTING ELECTRIC MOTOR ASSEMBLY (SIDE VIEW)

new electric motor is expected to increase the cost of the new product over the existing one. The current cost of the existing sharpener model is $7.84 (Column 1 of Table 15–2). However, this cost is expected to rise considerably when the firm converts to a concentric electric motor design (see Figures 15–8 and 15–9). The advantage of a concentric design is the ability to produce a smaller, rounded sharpener. As anticipated, discussions with the firm's primary supplier of electric motors indicate that a concentric design will indeed cost more. However, the initial estimate of $5, more than double the current design, is much higher than expected.

The gears are designed by Acme and outsourced to one of three subcontractors. These subcontractors have few in-house design skills and rely on Acme and their other customers for design and value engineering support. Typically Acme gets the three subcontractors to bid on the contract and then selects the subcontractor that represents the best value. The one selected for the new gear system is CIM, which indicates that the new gears will cost $1.

The case is outsourced to a new supplier. The previous generation of electric-powered sharpeners used simple, rectangular case designs. These cases were designed by Acme and injection molded by one of the three subcontractors that also produced gears for the firm. For the new product, the case is going to be more complex, both in shape and internal structure. For this reason, Acme turns to DGI, which has considerable design skills.

FIGURE 15-8. THE NEW ELECTRIC MOTOR ASSEMBLY (FRONT VIEW)

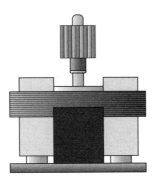

FIGURE 15-9. THE NEW ELECTRIC MOTOR ASSEMBLY (SIDE VIEW)

DGI will be given the dimensions of the case and the location of the connect points and be expected to design the case. DGI's core competency lies in designing complex molds that enable a single piece of plastic to perform several functions. For example, one piece of the new case is expected to position the electric motor, integrate the gears, and position the sharpener. Given the complexity of the interrelationship of the case to the other major functions, the case design will be finalized late in the overall development process. Acme engineers will develop prototypes using wooden cases to support the other components. When they are satisfied with the design, they will call DGI and give its engineers detailed specifications of the various components and their locations. The DGI case designers will then develop detailed drawings and clay models of the final case for Acme to review. Acme will pick the design that it feels provides the greatest value, based on both appearance and cost. To avoid unexpected design problems, the case designers are expected to review the prototypes to see if they can make suggestions in the layout of the major functions that will reduce the cost of the case. DGI's original estimate for the case is $3.

The final component, the power cord, is procured from any of a number of common suppliers for a market price of $0.50. The power cord consists of a two-pin electric plug, five feet of 18-gauge insulated copper wire, and a through-the-case connector. This connector is molded onto the wire. Its purpose is to protect the connections of the wire to the electric motor from strain and to make the place where the wire enters the case look attractive.

The preliminary estimate for the target cost of the new product is the sum of the current costs of the various major functions and the anticipated $1 for assembly and miscellaneous suppliers. This sum is $13 (see Table 15–3), which is more than $3 above the allowable cost of $9.74 (Column 2 of Table 15–2). The chief engineer has to decide whether to establish a strategic cost-reduction challenge or try to find ways to achieve the allowable cost. After some preliminary discussions with several of the suppliers, he decides that the allowable cost is achievable and therefore sets the product-level target cost at $9.74. The primary motivation for this decision is the unwillingness of Acme's senior management to vio-

TABLE 15–3. TARGET COST OF THE PROPOSED PRODUCT

Major Assembly	Product	
	Existing	Proposed
Sharpener assembly	$ 2.50	$ 2.50
Electric motor assembly	2.00	5.00
Gear system	0.50	1.00
Case	1.50	3.00
Electric power cord	0.50	0.50
Assembly and supplies	1.00	1.00
Total	$ 8.00	$ 13.00

late the cardinal rule of target costing: never launch a product above its target cost.

Component-Level Target Costing

Once the product-level target cost is established, it can be decomposed into major function-level target costs. The interactions with BEM have already established a first cut at the target cost of the electric motor assembly. Despite the reduction in the estimated cost of the concentric motor, the current cost of the new product is still too high. Consequently, the chief engineer for the new sharpener project has to develop target costs for all of the major functions so that the product-level target cost can be achieved.

The chief engineer is responsible for setting the target costs of all the major functions through an iterative process in which he discusses estimated costs with the firm's suppliers. He sums up the various estimates and compares the result with the product-level target cost. If the result is too high, he goes back to the various suppliers and the internal design teams and asks them to find ways to further reduce the costs of their major functions.

The sharpener assembly provides the best opportunity for cost reduction, and the chief engineer sets the new target cost at $1.50, which is $1 below the current cost of $2.50. This aggressive target will require complete redesign of that assembly. The next opportunity for cost savings comes from the electric motor assembly. To offset the increased cost, the firm initiates a simultaneous engineering project with BEM, its supplier of new motors. The target cost assigned to the new motor is $4. This figure is the outcome of extended negotiations between Acme and BEM. The resulting target cost is considered aggressive but achievable by all concerned.

The new product will require a more complex gearing system because of the location of the sharpener and electric motor assemblies. Even though the initial target cost was increased to $1, it was subsequently reduced back to the $0.50, the cost of the existing gear system. Consequently, the cost-reduction objective for this assembly is set at $0.50. This target is considered realistic because of recent decreases in the price of the types of polymers used in the product.

The cost-reduction objective for the case is set at $0.50 below DGI's original estimate. The new case will use a more expensive polymer that has a shiny surface, as opposed to the current one, which has a mat surface. However, the new case is about 35% smaller than the existing design, thus reducing material content. The cost-reduction objective for the case will reduce the cost of the new case to the current cost of the existing case. This is considered a very aggressive objective that will probably place great strain on the new supplier.

The cost-reduction objective for the power cord is set at zero because it is a commodity, and Acme has no way to pressure its common suppliers to reduce their costs. The only way that Acme can reduce the cost of common components is to shop actively for the lowest cost among several high-quality suppliers. Finally, the cost-reduction objective for the assembly and miscellaneous supplies is set at $0.26, which reflects improvements in the assembly capabilities of the firm and some price breaks that have been negotiated for the supplies.

The sum of these component-level target costs, when added to the assembly and supplies costs (supplies include packaging and assembly items such as screws), equals the product-level target cost of $10 (see Table 15–4). Consequently, the chief engineer sets the component-level target costs and communicates them to the suppliers. The assembly costs are not expected to decrease because the new product is expected to be slightly more difficult to assemble than the existing one. Therefore, any savings in assembly due to increased efficiency are expected to be offset.

TABLE 15–4. MAJOR FUNCTION-LEVEL TARGET COSTS OF THE PROPOSED PRODUCT

	Target cost	Cost-reduction objective
Sharpener assembly	$ 1.50	$ 1.00
Electric motor assembly	4.00	1.00
Gear system	0.50	0.50
Case	2.50	0.50
Electric power cord	0.50	0.00
Assembly and supplies	0.74	0.26
Total	**$ 9.74**	

An Analysis of the Process

At Acme, the role of the customer in the market-driven costing process is two-fold. First, customers are instrumental in identifying the improved appearance that lies at the heart of the new product. When asked, they are able to identify the improvements they want in the functionality of Acme's products. Given the nature of the product, there is little opportunity to introduce revolutionary new functionality that the customer does not expect. Consequently, Acme's chief engineer plays a relatively small role in setting the "themes" of the new product. For the new sharpener the critical theme is improved appearance.

The second role customers play is in setting the target selling price. The new appearance allows the firm to charge slightly more for the new product than the existing one. However, the price is bounded by the existence of the deluxe line. At the $25/$15.50 target prices, there are still enough savings to make the new product competitive against even the cheapest deluxe products. The target selling prices thus position the price of the new product at a new top end of standard pencil sharpeners but comfortably below the price of deluxe ones.

The role of competitors in the price-driven costing process is defined by the way they influence customer expectations. Acme is not expecting its competitors to launch new products that shift the survival zones of existing products, so the primary role competitors play is in the way their competitive products help define the target selling price. The selling price of deluxe sharpeners influences the upper price limit because the price differential between the standard and deluxe models must be sufficient for the customer to be willing to buy the standard, lower-functionality products. The competitors' products that are equivalent to the firm's standard product help determine the lower price limit because, even though Acme is going to withdraw its standard product, the competitors' equivalent products still help establish the target selling price for the new sharpener.

The target selling prices of $25/$15.50 are set to make a trade-off between the market share Acme wants to achieve, the degree to which they want to strengthen their corporate image as an innovator, and the long-term profitability of the product. This trade-off is a complex one that can be made only in light of Acme's strategy and profit objectives. The market-share objectives have to allow for cannibalization. There is no point in setting an aggressive market-share objective for the new sharpener if the market is predominately from existing electric-powered sharpener customers. Here, customer loyalty may work against the firm. However, since customer loyalty in the industry is known to be low, the bulk of additional sharpener sales is expected to come from new, not existing, customers.

The average target profit margin is based on a number of factors. Acme uses the historical relationship between selling price and profit margin to establish the starting point for setting the target product margin for their new product. The next step is to incorporate life-cycle costs into the target profit margin. The final target profit margin of 20% incorporates the up-front investment, changes in the selling price over time, and changes in the manufacturing cost over time. In addition, it reflects the firm's capability to earn the target profit margin. Such realism is critical if the firm is to achieve its long-term profit objectives because setting unrealistic target profit margins would jeopardize the firm's ability to achieve its long-term profit objectives.

The product-level target costing process introduces the cost-reduction capabilities of the firm's designers and suppliers into the target costing process. The starting point of the product-level target costing process is the current cost of the existing standard sharpener product. This cost is derived from available information on the cost of the existing product and then updated for the estimated costs of the new components and production processes to be used in the new product. The next step is value engineering, which analyzes the product design to see if its cost can be reduced further through redesign. Acme value engineers initiate a concurrent cost management project with BEM to reduce the cost of the motor assembly.

The gap between the current cost and the allowable cost determines the overall cost-reduction objective. A high probability of achievement is necessary if the discipline of target costing is to be maintained through the cardinal rule. Inability to achieve the target cost must be perceived as a major failure of the design process, not simply an outcome of setting impossible targets. Fortunately, the firm believes that it can achieve the cost-reduction objective and sets the product-level target cost at the allowable cost.

The completion of the product-level target costing process signals the shift to component-level target costing. However, the firm's suppliers have already been involved in the target costing process as their estimates and bids have been used to help set the product-level target cost. The cardinal rule plays a critical role during the component-level target costing process to help ensure achievement of the target cost. As the various suppliers indicate the prices at which they will supply their components, the drifting cost is recomputed.

Component-level target costing ends when the suppliers sign binding contracts for the components they supply. These contracts fix the purchase prices of the externally supplied components. Since Acme acquires all components externally, it can now compare actual component costs to target costs. The achievement of the manufacturing portion of the product-level target cost will become apparent only after about three months into mass production when the manufacturing process becomes stable.

INTERORGANIZATIONAL COST MANAGEMENT AT ACME

The new product requires the application of aggressive cost management throughout the value chain. Consequently, for Acme the process of component-level target costing requires considerable application of interorganizational cost management before the contracts can be signed.

The Process

The process begins with the concurrent cost management project for the sharpener assembly and electric motor and continues with the design of the other major functions. The case design creates a greater challenge than expected, and the chosen supplier has to initiate an interorganizational cost investigation. The gear assembly is less of a problem but still requires some interaction between the design teams. The cost-reduction short-fall is not that great, and an FPQ trade-off makes it possible to find a way to reduce costs to the desired level. The sharpener assembly is manufactured and assembled in-house, and by completely redesigning the assembly its costs are reduced to target levels. Consequently, the only interorganizational cost management required for these components is chained target costing. For the electric motor assembly more advanced interorganizational cost management techniques are required.

Concurrent Cost Management

The significant challenge created by the new motor assembly design places considerable stress on BEM. Acme decides that the only way to achieve the level of cost reduction the new product requires is to initiate a concurrent cost management program with BEM. Acme considers BEM a family member; on previous occasions BEM had entered into several such concurrent cost management programs. Typically, parallel engineering was utilized, with the two firms' engineers getting together early in the conceptualization process to develop a common set of specifications for the product and the major component that BEM is supplying. The two teams would then keep in contact as their designs progressed to ensure that the final solutions would be compatible.

However, for the new electric-powered pencil sharpener, it is decided that a simultaneous engineering approach should be adopted. Simultaneous engineering is considered necessary because the design of the electric motor assembly is highly dependent on the design of the sharpener assembly. It is not simply a matter of the shape of the case; the new sharpener assembly also determines the nature of the gear system and the power and hence size of the new concentric motor assembly. A simultaneous engineering project is initiated at the very start of the product development process. The two design teams meet at Acme's product development laboratory and begin joint design. The task they face is to develop new sharpener and electric motor assemblies that will fit into a contemporary shape, while still providing the functionality the customers demand.

When the two design teams begin the design process, they find, as expected, that the designs of the two assemblies are indeed too interconnected for separate design efforts to be effective. The design of the sharpener assembly is the responsibility of the Acme design team and the design of the electric motor assembly is the responsibility of the BEM design team.

The $1 cost-reduction objective for the sharpener assembly creates a significant challenge for Acme's product designers. The chief engineer is aware of the problem when the objective is set and has assigned the firm's most creative designers to the problem. The current design of the sharpener assembly relies heavily on metal. The assembly consists of four parts: the cutting cylinder, the positioning unit, the gear collar, and the automatic cut-on switch. The cutting cylinder is machined from a hard metal blank by Acme's machine shop. The machine shop also manufactures the small gear that is part of the cutting cylinder. This gear is used to turn the cutting cylinder as it rotates against the gear collar.

The positioning unit holds the pencil at the correct angle so that it is sharpened as the cutting cylinder turns. It also stops the pencil from being over-sharpened. The positioning unit consists of a metal block that has a cylindrical hole cut into it with a slit along one face. The cutting cylinder is held against the slit. As the pencil is sharpened, it slides farther down the cylindrical hole until it can go no farther. The positioning unit has a third purpose—it acts as a counterbalance to the cutting cylinder when it rotates. Counterbalancing is important because it enables the sharpening process to proceed smoothly (see Figure 15–10).

The cut-on switch is a simple micro-switch that turns on the motor when a pencil is inserted in the hole. This switch allows the sharpener to be left permanently plugged in, but it consumes power only when a pencil is sharpened. The switch is sourced from one of two local electronic parts suppliers. Since it is a custom-designed

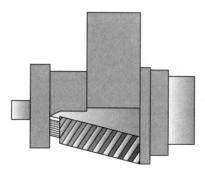

FIGURE 15–10. THE EXISTING POSITIONING UNIT

part, the two suppliers provide Acme with a complete breakdown of the manufacturing costs of the unit. The firm that provides the greatest value is usually selected, subject to maintaining a fairly balanced share of the business. In this case the two solutions are considered of equal value, and the contract is awarded to the firm that has won the fewest contracts to date. Acme and this firm then negotiate a reasonable profit margin and the price is set. In recent years, the cost of the micro-switch has fallen an average of 3% per year.

The major cost of the sharpener assembly is the material content. The sharpener cylinder is manufactured from an expensive, very hard alloy. This alloy is used to ensure that the sharpening cylinder retains its ability to cut wood for the life of the product. The labor and other manufacturing costs are relatively low. Consequently, the only way to achieve the new target cost is to design a new assembly that uses a smaller cylinder. The other major cost of the assembly is for the positioning unit. This unit is made of a less expensive alloy but is still quite expensive. The value engineering team sets out to reduce its cost in two ways. They want to reduce the diameter of the sharpening cylinder and replace the metal used in the positioning unit with plastic.

When the design team is finished, the component-level target cost of the sharpener assembly is achieved. First, the cylinder it uses is half the diameter of the old one (see Figure 15–11). This new design reduces material content by 75% and reduces machining

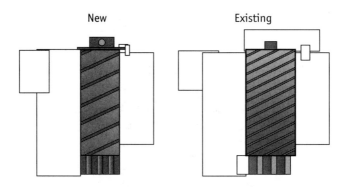

New   Existing

FIGURE 15–11. THE NEW AND EXISTING SHARPENING CYLINDER DESIGNS

time by approximately 50%. Second, the positioning unit is equivalently reduced in size and is manufactured from a very strong polymer (see Figure 15–12). This design reduces the cost of the unit by almost 60%.

The turn-on micro-switch is redesigned slightly to fit the new design. The final switch is about 25% smaller, but instead of a cost reduction, the result is increased cost. The cost rises because the electronics firm cannot modify a standard switch; instead, they have to custom design one. Developing the custom-designed switch requires the electronics firm to invest in a piece of equipment that will be dedicated to the manufacture of the new switch. Given this investment and the reduced production volume required for the custom switch, the negotiated selling price of the micro-switch is set at 50% above its target cost for the first two years of the contract. After the two years are over, the price will fall to the target level and subsequently is expected to decrease annually. These extra costs will reduce Acme's profits in those years.

The new sharpener assembly design is much lighter than its existing counterpart. The reduced weight of the rotating components means that a less powerful motor can be used. Mock-ups of the preliminary designs indicate that a 25% reduction in motor power will not alter the performance of the pencil sharpener. The

FIGURE 15–12. THE NEW POSITIONING UNIT

reduced power requirements lead to lower motor assembly costs, but the savings are not sufficient to bring the costs down to target levels.

As the design process continues, it becomes apparent that the cost-reduction challenge is greater than expected. Even with the 25% reduction in power, the new motor design is more expensive than either firm expected. As a result, the chief engineer of the project decides to increase the target cost of the electric motor assembly by $0.50 and to create a corresponding strategic cost-reduction challenge. This decision is not taken lightly. The project is approaching its feasibility review and might be cancelled if the review committee feels that the cost overrun for the product, which consists of the $0.50 increase for the motor coupled with the micro-switch's higher costs, is too great.

Fortunately, just before the committee is scheduled to meet, a serendipitous event occurs. The design team from DGI arrives for its first visit and makes suggestions to the concurrent cost management team that will lead to further cost reductions in both the motor and the sharpener assemblies. The first idea the DGI team comes up with is to replace a metal part in the motor with a plastic one. The part they identify holds the circuit board used to connect the electric power to the motor and the fuse that protects the motor against shorts. This part has no electrical role to play, and therefore the metal in the part can be replaced by a less expensive, nonconducting plastic part. The part is quite complex in shape and requires considerable machining to produce. The ability to use a molded component will reduce costs significantly. CIM is contracted to supply this part.

The second idea is to integrate the gear collar of the sharpener assembly into the case design. Given that the molding is going to be quite complex anyway, it will cost relatively little to make it slightly more complex by incorporating a nonmoving component such as the gear collar. The savings that result from these two design changes exceed the required $0.50 by an additional $0.25. The extra savings are added to the target cost of the case both to offset the additional cost of incorporating the gear collar and to reduce the cost-reduction pressure on the new supplier. The DGI design team indicates that the resulting target cost for the case is more acceptable and that it is ready to begin the formal product development process. With the target cost achieved, the designs of the electric motor and sharpener assembly are finalized.

Interorganizational Cost Investigation

The completion of the general design of the sharpener and electric motor assemblies enables the designs of the other major functions to be finalized. DGI has problems achieving the target cost of the case even with the new target cost. Three issues cause the cost over-run. First, the new, higher-quality plastic is more expensive than the plastic used in the existing product. Second, the new shape is more sophisticated and requires more expensive molds. These molds have to be amortized over their production volumes at an amortized cost of $0.05 per unit. Finally, the more complex design means that a longer cooling down period is required. This extra time reduces the capacity of the injection molding machines and leads to increased costs. Taken together, these three issues more than offset the savings from the reduced size of the case and raise its cost above its new target level. Consequently, DGI initiates an interorganizational cost investigation with Acme and CIM.

The primary problem is the inclusion of an expensive "silver" faceplate where the pencil is inserted. This faceplate has Acme's name on the front and uses silver to accent the design. It is this extra piece that has high costs. The two engineering teams get together and design a faceplate that looks similar to the original design except for the lack of silver but is actually an integral part of the main case. The resulting savings help but are still insufficient to reduce the cost of the case to acceptable levels.

The second problem is the material specified for the pencil shavings tray. The original design calls for a transparent version of the same expensive plastic as the rest of the case. A transparent, or more accurately, translucent, tray enables the user to see when the tray is full of pencil shavings. This tray is a simple part that DGI outsources to CIM. As part of the interorganizational cost investigation, CIM is called in to see what they can do to reduce the cost of the tray. A design engineer from CIM suggests using a different polymer that is lighter in color. This plastic will be much cheaper than the currently specified one and will create an attractive color difference between the case and the tray. Acme's design team agrees to the change. Consequently, the target cost for the tray is decreased to reflect the lower costs at CIM, though CIM's profits will be higher because the reduction in selling price established by Acme's new component-level target cost is less than the reduction in CIM's costs. The increased profits are a reward for CIM's innovativeness in suggesting the new polymer. The target cost of the case is not changed, as the purpose of the investigation is to help DGI achieve its cost-reduction objective.

DGI's engineers suggest a third and final modification. The original design includes suction feet. These feet are made of silicon rubber and then screwed into the base plate. The cost of these feet is high because they require both externally sourced items (the feet and the screws) and an assembly step. The solution proposed is to stick rubber feet on the base plate. These rubber feet are thin disks with an adhesive on one side and a rough gripping surface on the other. They can easily be applied immediately after the case is removed from the injection-molding machine, as part of the removal process.

The interorganizational cost investigation enables DGI to achieve its cost-reduction objective. First, the increase in the target cost of $0.25 resulting from the earlier intervention and the reduction in the component-level target cost of the tray increase the effective target cost of the case. Second, the simplifications in the design—removing the silver faceplate and the suction feet—reduce the cost of the case. Once the target cost of the case is achieved, the case design is finalized.

Functionality-Price-Quality Trade-Off

The gearing system of the existing model consists of two gears (see Figure 15–13). The smaller of these gears is attached to the motor spindle, and the other is attached to the sharpener assembly (see Figure 15–14). The greater number of teeth on the larger gear causes the sharpening assembly to rotate slower than the electric motor. This reduction in rotation speed is necessary to enable the pencil sharpener to function.

The new design consists of three gears (see Figure 15–15). The purpose of the extra gear is to increase the separation between the motor and the sharpener assembly (see Figure 15–16). This separation

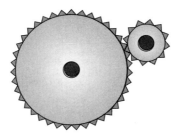

FIGURE 15-13. THE EXISTING GEAR DESIGN

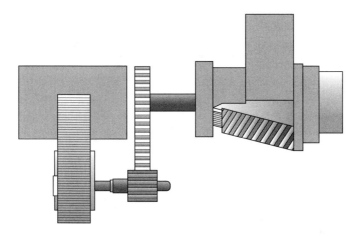

FIGURE 15-14. THE EXISTING SHARPENER DESIGN

is a problem in the new parallel layout. Without the third gear, the motor and sharpener assemblies would try to occupy the same space.

The first of the three gears is a small unit that slips over the drive shaft of the electric motor. It is made of a hard black plastic. The next gear is designed to reduce the speed of rotation to one-quarter of the motor's speed. This gear has teeth on both its outer diameter and its inner diameter. The inner diameter gear connects to a second large gear. This pair of gears further reduces the speed of rotation to one-third of the speed of the second gear. The result of the gear assembly is a 12-fold (4 × 3) reduction in rotation speed. The third gear is connected directly to the sharpener assembly and held in place by a geared portion of the case. This gear collar pro-

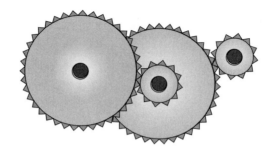

FIGURE 15-15. THE NEW GEAR DESIGN

FIGURE 15-16. THE NEW SHARPENER DESIGN

vides stability for the sharpener assembly as it rotates and causes the sharpener cylinder to counter-rotate.

The gear system is outsourced to CIM. The difference between DGI and CIM is that DGI is a major supplier that produces complex moldings that require considerable design skills on its part, while CIM is a subcontractor that produces simple components designed by its customers. The decision by Acme's chief engineer not to increase the component-level target cost of the gear system is considered quite tough by CIM's design engineers, and they expect to have great difficulties in achieving it. Acme's specifications demand very high-quality polymers to give the product a mean time between failures of 10,000 hours. Since it takes only 10 seconds to sharpen a pencil, the sharpener essentially has an infinite life expectancy. After three months of exploration CIM's engineers call for an FPQ trade-off as they cannot find a way to achieve the target cost. Acme sends in a value engineer to meet with CIM's chief engineer to discuss minor changes in the gear system specifications.

The two engineers meet and begin the trade-off analysis. They quickly identify the extremely long mean time between failures as the source of the problem. The specifications of the two large gears require polymers that are expensive both in terms of their raw material cost and the time they take to mold. Careful analysis of the specifications reveals that the same polymer is being used for all three gears. The cost of the assembly can be reduced significantly if different polymers are used for each gear. A very stiff polymer could be used for the first small gear since it is supported by the motor axle and, given its small diameter, does not have to flex under stress. The second gear requires a more flexible polymer since it takes the bulk of the strain as the pencil is inserted and the speed of rotation slows considerably. The strain is created by the third gear slowing and the first gear initially maintaining its speed. Allowing the second gear to flex slightly reduces the stress to acceptable levels. The third gear is connected to the shaft of the sharpener assembly. Hence, it can be manufactured out of a stiff polymer that does not flex.

The redesign of the gear assembly reduces its cost significantly and brings it down to target levels. One of the reasons that the cost is lower is due to a reduction in product quality; the mean time between failures of the new design is now estimated at 5,000 hours. This reduction in life expectancy is considered acceptable as it matches the estimated life of the new sharpener unit and exceeds customer expectations. These changes are not expected to alter the perceived functionality of the product in any way and are therefore approved.

Chained Target Costing

All of Acme's suppliers use target costing. Therefore all the non-commodity components outsourced to second-tier suppliers are subjected to chained target costing, as illustrated by the interactions between Acme, BEM, and CIM (see Figure 15–17). The electric motor assembly is outsourced to BEM at a target cost of $4. BEM

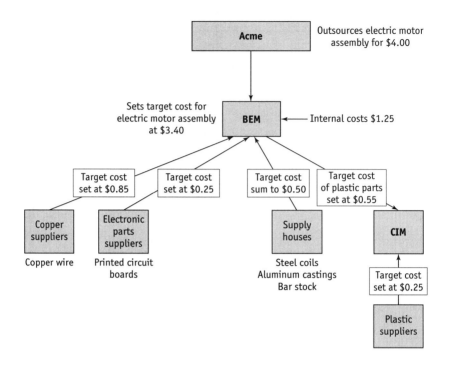

Figure 15-17. The Target Costing Chain for the Electric Motor Assembly

in turn outsources about 70% of the value-added of the motor. The primary components for the motor are copper wire, a printed circuit board, a transformer assembly, and two plastic parts. The first plastic part is used to form the copper coils and the second is the part designed by DGI's design engineers and supplied by CIM. BEM purchases the copper wire from a metal supply house and the printed circuit board from an electronic parts supplier. It manufactures the rest of the motor itself. It stamps out the transformer plates from metal coils purchased from a steel manufacturer. The armature is manufactured from aluminum castings, metal plates, and a spindle cut from bar stock. BEM develops a target cost for the motor assembly. Since the firm wants to make a 15% return on the motor, its product-level target cost is $3.40 ($4 × 0.85). This figure is then decomposed to the component level. For example, the target cost for the plastic support designed by CIM is $0.55. Since CIM has no difficulties in achieving the $0.55 target, no other interorganizational cost management techniques but chained target costing are required for that part.

Analysis of the Process

Value engineering begins from the moment the product is conceptualized and continues until it enters production. The interorganizational aspects of value engineering start when the buyer and supplier design teams begin to interact. For Acme's and BEM's teams, this interaction starts soon after the Acme design team begins to conceptualize the product. The early involvement of the BEM team means that they have both maximum freedom to influence the overall product design to help them achieve their target costs and maximum time to achieve their design objectives. DGI is involved somewhat later in the process, as the case depends on the design of the sharpener and motor assemblies. There are some aspects of parallel engineering since DGI's design team gets involved in the conceptualization stage. However, since most of their design actions occur after the product is conceptualized, the interaction is better described as an interorganizational cost investigation. CIM is a subcontractor and therefore the interaction between Acme and its design team is best described as an FPQ trade-off. Finally, the common suppliers are subjected to target costing and are not actively involved in the design process.

The degree of interaction with suppliers must be matched to the value of the item being outsourced and the level of design modifications that can be undertaken. Acme achieves this objective by choosing the nature of the interorganizational cost management techniques it uses with different levels of suppliers. For BEM, a family member that supplies the most expensive outsourced major function of the product, the relationship is very rich and concurrent cost management is appropriate. The heavy interaction between the designs of the sharpener and electric motor assemblies makes it necessary to design the two assemblies concurrently and simultaneously. Such detailed interactions are justified only if the value that can be derived from them is high enough to offset their cost. This is clearly the case with the new concentric electric motor design. It is critical to the success of the new product and, given the extreme cost-reduction objectives, only through simultaneous engineering can the motor be designed at its target cost. For example, the reduced weight of the sharpener assembly plays a critical role in the reduction in size and hence cost of the new motor. If a simultaneous approach had not been adopted, either BEM would have been directed to develop a more powerful motor or would not have been given adequate time to develop the new concentric motor.

As the value of the components and the ability to change their design decreases, so does the degree of interaction with suppliers. For DGI, the most appropriate form of interaction is an interorganizational cost investigation. Acme and DGI can find ways to reduce the cost of the sharpener without significantly changing the overall functionality of the product. However, the changes are significant and can be achieved only by the two design teams working together. For the pencil shavings tray, the involvement of a third design team is necessary, since only CIM's engineers know the range of plastics available for the tray.

For lean enterprises such as Acme and its suppliers, such interactions are especially important because of the high degree of outsourcing that they undertake and the way they outsource components. Acme views only the technology supporting the sharpening assembly as a core competence. All other technologies and related major functions are outsourced. These major functions represent approximately 85% of the total value-added of the new sharpener.

Acme outsources the major functions in their entirety instead of designing them in-house and outsourcing simple components. The decision to outsource major functions has several implications for Acme. First, it is dependent on its suppliers for technological skills and production know-how. Consequently, it cannot easily shift to another supplier of electric motors because the new firm would lack the detailed knowledge of Acme and its requirements. To educate such a firm would take a considerable amount of time. Second, a tiered supplier base naturally emerges. Since family member BEM outsources a large percentage of its value-added, it creates second-tier suppliers. BEM also uses target costing, which automatically creates a target costing chain that consists of Acme, BEM, and its suppliers.

The other firms in the supplier network outsource similarly high percentages of the value-added of their products. For Acme to be successful, its suppliers must also be successful, that is, innovative and profitable. Consequently, all the firms in the network are interdependent. Acme, as the single core firm, has created a kingdom, with itself as king. The objective of the kingdom is to take advantage of economies of scale. Acme is responsible for establishing the network protocols and ensuring that all the firms in the network operate for the good of all and not just for themselves. It is these protocols that structure the nature of the relationships between buyers and suppliers in the network. These relationships are lean, that is stable, cooperative, and mutually beneficial.

The lean relationships enable the design teams of buyers and suppliers to share their creativity and knowledge. The benefits of this sharing are well illustrated by the way DGI design engineers identify two ways to reduce costs that are not apparent to the concurrent design team. The first solution directly modifies the electric motor, the other, the sharpener assembly. The electric motor solution replaces a complex metal component with a molded plastic one, resulting in considerable savings. The second one replaces four separate components with a new, integral part of the case. Such innovations are not possible without the interactions of the design teams of all firms involved. Neither Acme's nor BEM's design teams know enough about injection molding to realize that such savings are possible.

The benefits of lean supply are further illustrated by the interactions among the various design teams at Acme, DGI, and CIM. The willingness of the three teams to get together to find innovative solutions to the cost problem enables DGI to achieve its cost-reduction objective. The resetting of the component-level target cost for the shavings tray is designed to increase CIM's profitability while reducing the pressure placed on DGI. No change to DGI's target cost result because the functionality of the product is retained (and might even be increased), and therefore Acme is willing to pay the same amount for the case.

KAIZEN COSTING AT ACME

The launch of the product is deemed a success and the new pencil sharpener is brought in at its target cost. The entry of the product into manufacturing signals the shift from target costing to kaizen costing. Acme's kaizen costing system demands six-monthly cost-reduction objectives of 2.5%. The same objective is set for every externally supplied item. The only exception is the case for the new sharpener. DGI is protected from kaizen costing pressures on that item for the next two years. This protection is the result of an agreement between the two firms to help DGI offset the high investment it had to make in specialized machinery to produce the new case. This exception is not considered a major problem. Acme does not expect to face intense price pressure in the near future.

The kaizen costing pressure that Acme places on its suppliers is transmitted down the supply chains when Acme's suppliers develop their own kaizen costing reduction factors. These supplier factors reflect the pressure placed on them by Acme and their other suppliers. Thus, the kaizen costing systems link to push the pressure deep into the supply chains.

IMPROVING THE EFFICIENCY OF THE BUYER-SUPPLIER INTERFACES AT ACME

The volume of routine transactions at Acme was too low for electronic data interchange to be justified. However, the firm had recently adopted bar-coding with some of its suppliers. The electrical industry had defined standard bar codes for some products and since many of Acme's suppliers were already using them, the firm had started to bar code some of its products and use bar-code readers on incoming shipments.

The other actions that Acme was taking to improve the efficiency of the interfaces with its suppliers was to reduce cycle times. In particular, it was working on reducing the time to process orders and make payments to its suppliers. In return, its suppliers were trying to reduce their production and delivery cycle times. Finally, Acme was experimenting with shared forecasts and other information. For example, it had just started e-mailing production schedules to its suppliers so that they could better coordinate their deliveries.

SUMMARY

While an electric-powered pencil sharpener is a simple product compared to a camera, bulldozer, or automobile, the application of interorganizational cost management at the fictitious Acme Co. illustrates the major issues that arise. The process begins with Acme using its target costing system to establish the target price of the product, its product-level target cost, and then its component-level target costs. The target costing process at Acme starts with market-driven costing to set the allowable cost of the new pencil sharpener. It continues by applying product-level target costing to create pressure on the product designers to find creative ways to enhance product functionality at the target cost. The process concludes with component-level target costing, which creates intense pressure on the suppliers to undertake creative cost reduction.

However, for Acme it is not sufficient to discipline its own design team, it must also discipline those of its suppliers. Furthermore, the creativity of the entire supplier network must be stimulated. To achieve this objective, the design teams must be encouraged to work together to achieve their design objectives. Interorganizational cost management is one of the ways in which Acme stimulates its suppliers' design teams to interact. The idea is to create a rich, interactive design process in which cost savings and functionality improvement ideas are shared.

These interactions must reflect a cost/benefit trade-off between the cost of the interactions and the magnitude of the improvements achieved. Acme incorporates this trade-off in two ways: first, in the nature of the relationships it develops with its suppliers and, second, in the type of interorganizational cost management techniques it uses. These interactions with its suppliers range from concurrent cost management with its family members to interorganizational cost investigations with its major suppliers, through simple FPQ trade-offs with its subcontractors, all the way to pure target costing with its common suppliers. Once the target cost is achieved, the pressure to reduce costs does not abate. The various firms in the supplier network have adopted kaizen costing to reduce costs during the manufacturing stage. These kaizen costing systems link to push cost-reduction pressure deep into Acme's supply chains. Finally, Acme and its larger suppliers are working to make their interfaces more efficient. They are adopting bar-coding and reducing cycle times. These actions should reduce interface costs.

At the heart of these interactions lie lean supply principles, whereby each of the firms is operating to maximize the benefit of the entire network, not just its own. The benefits of "we are all in it together" as opposed to "every firm for itself" are well illustrated by the Acme example. The core lesson is that stable, cooperative, mutually beneficial relationships provide greater competitive advantage than adversarial ones.

CHAPTER 16

LESSONS FOR ADOPTERS

INTRODUCTION

Survival strategies in today's intensely competitive environments differ from those that were effective in the past. Japanese lean enterprises have learned that adopting the generic strategy of confrontation is often the only viable way to ensure corporate survival. At the heart of the confrontation strategy lies an integrated approach toward managing the survival triplet. Inherent to this approach is aggressive cost management that begins when the product is designed and continues until the product is discontinued. Firms that find themselves facing increased levels of competition should consider developing such an integrated approach to cost management even if they have yet to adopt confrontational strategies. A critical aspect of integrated cost management is to include the firm's buyers and suppliers in the process.

At the heart of interorganizational cost management lies the view that firms should manage the supply chain for competitive advantage rather than simply to reduce costs. The aim of the approach is to manage simultaneously all three characteristics of the survival triplet across the interorganizational boundaries between buyers and suppliers. The shift to an interorganizational perspective is critical because lean producers outsource a larger proportion of the value-added of their products than their mass producer counterparts. Consequently, suppliers play a more important role in the effective management of the survival triplet for lean producers than they do for mass producers. In particular, suppliers often develop technological expertise that is critical to the buyer's success. Therefore, the buyer becomes dependent on the supplier for access to its expertise, while the supplier depends on the buyer for business. This interdependence, together with high levels of trust, leads to stable, cooperative, and mutually beneficial buyer-supplier relationships.

The objective of interorganizational cost management is to align the cost management efforts of the buyers and suppliers. When such an alignment is achieved, all the firms in the supply chain act coherently to ensure that the final product satisfies the end customer. This alignment can be achieved only if the buyers and suppliers share considerable information about product design, production processes, and production costs. The sharing of the nonproprietary portion of this information by the buyer with its other suppliers and the supplier with its other buyers contributes to the effectiveness of the supplier network. At the same time, the process of developing lean suppliers and undertaking interorganizational cost management across the supplier network reinforces confrontational competition.

Firms that have begun to convert to the lean philosophy of single-piece flow must at some point convince their suppliers and customers to adopt it as well. Only when the entire supplier network has become lean will the full benefits of the lean approach be realized. As lean supply emerges, interorganizational cost management becomes both possible and necessary. The firm must take eight major steps to develop an effective interorganizational cost management program. These steps are:

1. Identify the parts of the product that are going to be sourced externally.
2. Determine the appropriate level of the buyer-supplier relationship for each externally sourced item.

3. Rationalize the supplier base.
4. Develop appropriate buyer-supplier relationships.
5. Increase the efficiency of the buyer-supplier interface.
6. Develop the necessary skills in the techniques of interorganizational cost management.
7. Extend lean supply and interorganizational cost management both upstream and downstream in the value chain.
8. Extend lean supply and interorganizational cost management to internal suppliers.

STEP ONE

Identify the parts of the product that are going to be sourced externally.

The first determinant of whether to source a given part internally or externally is the strategic importance to the firm of the technology that underlies the part. The second is the firm's relative advantage in manufacturing that part compared to having it done by external suppliers. A technology is considered strategic when a distinctive competence in that technology is critical to the firm's success. Firms cannot afford to outsource such technologies, so they have to manufacture parts that rely on them in-house. If the firm has developed a relative advantage in manufacturing parts that do not or no longer rely on strategic technologies, it may choose to keep them in-house anyway, based on economic or quality considerations. All other parts are candidates for outsourcing.

STEP TWO

Determine the appropriate level of the buyer-supplier relationship for each externally sourced item.

The level of the supplier relationship is determined predominantly by three factors: the strategic nature of the technology that underlies the outsourced part, whether the design of the outsourced components is unique to the buyer, and whether the design of the outsourced major function is essentially independent of the design of the product (see Figure 16–1).

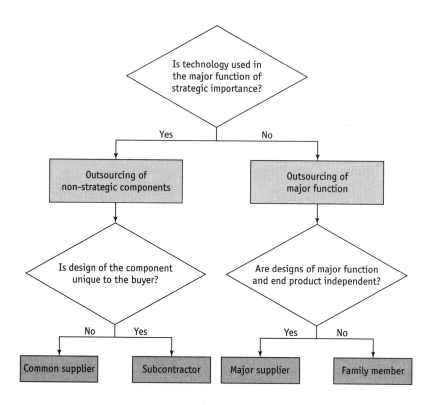

FIGURE 16-1. DETERMINING THE APPROPRIATE LEVEL OF SUPPLIER
RELATIONSHIPS

The strategic importance of the technology determines whether the entire major function or just a component is outsourced. If the technology that underlies the major function is considered strategic, the buyer should keep design and manufacture in-house and outsource only components that do not require knowledge of that technology to produce. For example, to manufacture the fan blades used in an engine cooling system requires no knowledge of the engine cooling system design. Thus, proprietary technologies lead to the outsourcing of components that are manufactured by either common suppliers or subcontractors. In contrast, if the technology is considered nonstrategic, then the firm should consider outsourcing the design of the group component or major function. For example, the technologies underlying engine cooling systems might be considered nonstrategic, and the entire major function could be outsourced.

The degree to which the design of an outsourced component is unique to the buyer determines whether a common supplier or subcontractor is utilized. A common supplier is appropriate when numerous buyers use the same component in multiple products. In this case, the buyer simply orders the component from the supplier's catalogue. In contrast, if the design of the component is determined by the design of the product, the component will be unique and a subcontractor is required. The buyer then gives the subcontractor the exact specifications for the part, and the subcontractor manufactures it to those specifications.

The degree to which the designs of an outsourced item and the product that contains it depend on each other determines whether a major supplier or family member is used. The critical factor is the value associated with joint design. If the designs are relatively independent, then the group component or major function and the product that contains it can be designed in isolation. For example, a starter motor can be designed in isolation from the engine as long as the major supplier knows the starting torque required and the maximum dimensions of the motor. Consequently, a major supplier is sufficient. In contrast, if the designs are interdependent, then the major function cannot be designed in isolation, and the buyer and supplier design teams must work together. For example, if the only way an engine cooling system can be designed to achieve the required characteristics is by simultaneously changing the design of the engine, then the two design teams must be integrated. In this case, the supplier has to be a family member.

STEP THREE

Rationalize the supplier base.

The supplier base of a lean enterprise is typically smaller than that of a mass producer, even though a higher percentage of the value-added of the products is outsourced. The first reason for this apparent inconsistency is that lean enterprises rely on single-sourcing/multi-sourcing for many of their products. Second, some of the parts that they outsource constitute significant portions of the total value-added of their products.

The single-sourcing/multi-sourcing approach that many lean enterprises have adopted consists of choosing a few suppliers to provide an entire family of parts and then selecting only one of them to supply each individual part. This approach limits the total number of suppliers quite significantly. For example, if bids for each part are elicited from the same three suppliers, then there can be only three suppliers for the entire family. In contrast, while a mass producer may obtain bids from the same or even a smaller number of suppliers for each part, a large number of different suppliers are usually considered for the parts family. Therefore, the total number of suppliers both bidding and winning orders for parts is higher. For example, if bids are elicited for each part from three suppliers out of nine suppliers, but across all bids all nine are given the opportunity to bid, then the maximum number of potential suppliers is nine (see Figure 16–2).

Furthermore, the outsourcing of research and development for major functions and group components means that the lean enterprise purchases significant portions of the value-added of a product in a single part. For example, it might buy the engine cooling system of a car as a complete system and not as a number of distinct parts such as the radiator, fan, electric motor, and other components. The number of major functions and group components is relatively small (there are approximately 30 major functions plus 100 group components in an automobile), but they represent a significant percentage of the total cost (85% for the major functions and

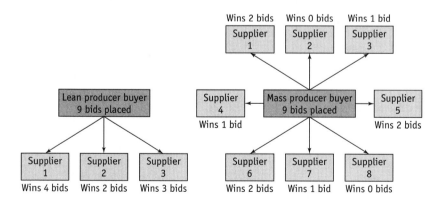

FIGURE 16–2. LEAN VERSUS MASS PRODUCER SUPPLIER MANAGEMENT

70%–80% for the group components). Therefore, only a relatively small number of parts are involved and consequently, a correspondingly small number of suppliers are required. In contrast, the mass producer typically outsources only components and therefore has a considerably larger number of parts to outsource, even though a smaller percentage of the total value-added is involved.

As the level of the buyer-supplier relationship rises, the number of suppliers that the buyer is willing to support at a given level drops because of the increasing coordination costs as the relationship becomes more sophisticated. For example, for any family of components the firm may be willing to elicit bids from three suppliers, but for major functions it may be willing to elicit bids only from a single supplier. Since there are many fewer major functions than simple components the result is a rapid reduction in the number of suppliers at each level.

STEP FOUR

Develop appropriate buyer-supplier relationships.

Several general principles govern buyer-supplier relationships in a world of lean supply. First of all, the relationships should be stable, cooperative, and mutually beneficial. In addition, the welfare of the suppliers should be taken into account when making sourcing decisions. Performance measurement and incentive schemes should be developed that reinforce appropriate behavior in the suppliers. Finally, an open relationship that supports the appropriate level of information sharing should be nurtured.

Lean enterprises enter into stable, cooperative (as opposed to short-term, adversarial), and mutually beneficial relationships with their suppliers. Instead of treating suppliers as interchangeable providers of low-cost components, lean enterprises treat them as a valuable source of innovative ideas. Mass producers that are becoming lean therefore have to change the way in which they interact with their suppliers. They must be willing to make investments in the relationship, not just the individual transactions, for example, by sending engineers to the suppliers to help develop their design and manufacturing skills. In return, suppliers must also be willing to invest in the relationship, for example, by acquiring special equipment that enables them to produce buyer-specific components at lower cost. When the relationship is short term, such investments often cannot be justified based on a single transaction.

Under lean supply, suppliers have to be protected from destructive cost-reduction pressures if they are to survive. Supplier survival is in the buyer's best interest for several reasons. First, the buyer and supplier are interdependent; having to switch to a new supplier because an existing one has gone out of business is very expensive. Second, the future benefits of all the investments made in the relationship are lost, and the new buyer-supplier relationship has to begin the investment process anew. For example, the new supplier has to be educated by the buyer's engineers and has to buy the special equipment to match the old supplier's manufacturing capabilities. Consequently, in the short term costs increase. Finally, suppliers need to generate sufficient profits to enable them to make an adequate level of investments in both the relationship and the individual transactions. If such investments are not made, the supplier will slowly cease to be competitive and the buyer will eventually suffer. To support the suppliers' ability to compete effectively the buyer must actively ensure that they can maintain adequate profitability. Among the actions that the buyer can take in this regard are setting achievable component-level target costs; relaxing component-level target costs when necessary; encouraging joint design efforts to find new, low-cost solutions; and avoiding excessive swings in volume of business awarded to the supplier.

To encourage suppliers in their journey toward lean supply, lean enterprises must create appropriate performance measurement and incentive systems. The performance measurement systems used by many Japanese buyers are relatively simple. They measure each supplier based on issues such as the number of defective parts, the percentage of on-time deliveries and proper quantities, and performance in reducing costs. These measures are designed to capture how far the supplier has come in the transition to lean supply. The scoring systems are not simply statistical exercises. They also assess the suppliers' attitude and willingness to improve.[1] The two major

---

[1] See J.P. Womack, D.T. Jones, and D. Roos. *The Machine That Changed the World*, New York: Harper Collins, 1990, p. 155.

reasons to "fire" suppliers are consistent failure to bring their performance back to acceptable levels for a significant period of time and a lack of willingness to improve.

The incentive schemes have to be designed both to encourage innovation and maintain stability. Most lean enterprises will reward the most innovative supplier by guaranteeing it business for a certain time period. For example, the buyer might award the supplier a contract for a year. Once that period is up, the component is placed up for bid again. However, such awards are made within the constraints of the stable relationship the buyer has with the supplier's competitors, which are also its suppliers. The buyer awards highly innovative suppliers sufficient additional business to encourage them to remain innovative, but not so much that the less innovative suppliers suffer considerably from the resulting decrease in business. When suppliers are lean, relatively small changes in projected volume can have significant effects on the profitability of the firm. Adopting a simple "lowest price wins" policy would subject the suppliers to excessive swings in production volume and seriously undermine their profitability.

When the buyer shares design and cost information with suppliers and vice versa, they can achieve considerable synergies. To enable such sharing to occur, open buyer-supplier relationships are nurtured. Such relationships require considerable mutual trust on the part of both firms. The buyer must trust the supplier not to share proprietary information with the buyer's competitors with which it does business. Similarly, the supplier must trust the buyer not to disseminate its proprietary information. In addition, the supplier must trust the buyer not to use its knowledge of the supplier's costs to expropriate an excessive share of the profits. Consequently, to engender trust the buyer and supplier must develop "rules of conduct" that govern how they behave, especially when business is low. These rules of conduct must be integrated into the supplier network protocols so that all the firms in the network adhere to them.

One of the risks posed to the early adopter occurs when the supplier's adversarial mass producer customers use their power to blackmail the supplier into divulging proprietary information about its other customers. Lean buyer-supplier relationships rely heavily on trust, in particular that proprietary information will not be divulged. In lean supplier networks, the supplier has access to proprietary information about all its customers. Consequently, if one of these customers forced the supplier to reveal proprietary information about its competitors, it must accept that its competitors will retaliate in the same manner. Thus, the sharing of information by all naturally reinforces the rules of conduct of lean supply.

The extent to which these general principles are applied to each supplier depends on how close the buyer-supplier relationship is and the degree to which the supplier has adopted lean thinking. The closeness of the relationship is important because it helps determine how much information sharing is required. For example, the information shared with a family member is much greater than that shared with a common supplier. The degree of leanness also helps determine the extent to which the principles are applied because many of them make assumptions about supplier behavior. For example, intensive information sharing is not advisable with a supplier that will share it with the buyer's competitors because it is still in the old adversarial model. The buyer will have to educate the supplier in lean thinking until its behavior allows both parties to benefit from a fully lean relationship.

STEP FIVE

Increase the efficiency of the buyer-supplier interface.

To increase the efficiency of its buyer-supplier interfaces, the firm must review those interfaces and see where inefficiencies can be reduced. The firm can undertake three types of initiatives. The first type requires joint efforts by the firm and its buyers and suppliers. One joint initiative is to introduce electronic commerce, with the aim of reducing transaction processing costs, increasing the accuracy of data exchange, reducing uncertainty, and improving relations. There are a variety of approaches to electronic commerce, but most center on the use of electronic data interchange and the Internet to reduce transaction processing costs. Another joint initiative is to improve the order process cycle through standardization and collaborative forecasting. This improvement is mainly intended to reduce uncertainty so that buffer inventories can be smaller. Smaller inventories lead to improved cash flow and higher asset turnover ratios.

The second type of initiatives are those undertaken by the firm primarily in its role as a buyer. These initiatives can either reduce uncertainty or lower transaction processing costs. Less uncertainty means that buffer inventories can be decreased. Initiatives aimed at reducing uncertainty include managing demand, providing adequate lead time, and reducing special orders. Initiatives to lower transaction processing costs include use of purchase contracts, payment-on-receipt, and improved accuracy of communication.

The third type of initiatives to increase the efficiency of the buyer-supplier interface are those undertaken by the firm primarily in its role as a supplier. The uncertainty reduction initiatives include shortening delivery cycle times, reducing production cycle times, and giving the buyer access to order status information. The transaction processing cost-reduction initiatives include extending supplier control over inventories and improving accuracy of communications.

Significant savings can be obtained by increasing the efficiency of the firm's buyer-supplier interfaces. These savings are easier to achieve with the richer relationships inherent to lean supply. Furthermore, concentrating outsourcing with a limited number of first-tier suppliers means that there are fewer buyer-supplier interfaces to deal with and that most of the suppliers are significant trading partners with whom the more sophisticated interface efficiency techniques can be justified. Thus, restructuring the firm's supplier base, which is an inherent part of lean supply, makes it both easier and more valuable to make the buyer-supplier interfaces more efficient.

STEP SIX

Develop the necessary skills in the techniques of interorganizational cost management.

The first phase in developing an interorganizational cost management program is to install effective target and kaizen costing systems. Sometimes firms think they already have a "target costing" system. However, often the true discipline of target costing is not achieved because target costing is almost impossible to implement in a mass production setting. The following four questions determine whether a firm is taking full advantage of target costing:

- Early in the design process, does your firm identify the target cost of products by subtracting their desired profit margin from their expected selling price?
- Does your firm specifically design new products so that they can be manufactured at their target costs?
- Are product-level target costs achieved most of the time?
- Does your firm decompose the target costs of its products to the component level and use the resulting component-level target costs as the basis for negotiations with suppliers?

If the answer to any of the above questions is no, the firm should begin to implement a full-blown target costing system before initiating any direct supplier involvement in its interorganizational cost management program.

Similarly, some firms may already have a kaizen program in place. However, it may not be fully developed for kaizen *costing*, and interorganizational kaizen costing in particular. Here the central issue revolves around setting continuous improvement cost-reduction objectives for outsourced items. The following four questions determine whether a firm is taking full advantage of (interorganizational) kaizen costing:

- Each period does your firm identify the amount by which the cost of each product's costs should be decreased to maintain its long-term profitability?
- Are these cost-reduction objectives achieved most of the time?
- Are specific cost-reduction objectives set for every component?
- Are these component-level cost-reduction objectives used as the basis for supplier negotiations?

The next phase is to assist suppliers in installing their target and kaizen costing systems. Once the buyer's and supplier's target costing systems are operational, they will be chained automatically, and the competitive pressure faced by the buyer will be transmitted to its suppliers. Similarly, the firms' kaizen costing programs will be linked, extending the pressure to reduce costs in the manufacturing phase across the entire supply chain. Inability of the supplier to achieve its target costs will trigger the need to undertake interorganizational cost management.

The various techniques that coordinate the cost management programs of the buyer and supplier, such as FPQ trade-offs, interorganizational cost investigations, and concurrent cost management, can then be used to resolve the problems. The exact technique used depends on the nature of the problem and the level of the supplier. However, if the problem requires a cost management technique that demands greater sharing of information than is typical for that level of supplier, the level of the buyer-supplier relationship should be reviewed.

STEP SEVEN

Extend lean supply and interorganizational cost management both upstream and downstream in the value chain.

Interorganizational cost management is most beneficial when all the firms in the supplier network have adopted its practices. Consequently, the firm has to find ways to encourage as many firms as possible in the network to align their cost management programs. Three classes of firms have to be convinced to adapt their cost management practices: customers, competitors, and second-tier suppliers and beyond.

Encouraging customer firms to adopt target costing can be beneficial. Target costing is one of the mechanisms of lean thinking that induces firms to replace their adversarial relationships with their suppliers with cooperative ones. While target costing will enable the customer to place considerable pressure on its suppliers to reduce costs, this pressure should be more intelligently applied than the pressure created by simply trying to get the firm to reduce its costs based on nonmarket-driven estimates.

One of the most powerful ways to convince customers to convert to interorganizational cost management is to demonstrate the benefits they can derive from the new order. The greater cost savings that can be achieved by pooling design knowledge, in particular, highlight the advantages of the interorganizational approach. The firm can also begin to act like a lean supplier and gradually begin sharing information with its customers. Caution is advised, however, because the customer initially will be tempted to use the information to extract additional short-term profits from the firm instead of taking a long-term perspective.

On the surface, the conversion of competitors may seem like a suicidal act. Why would a firm ever volunteer to help its competitors learn to become more efficient? The answer lies at the network level. It is very difficult for suppliers to serve both lean and mass producer customers simultaneously, with the lean customers working in cooperative mode and the mass producers in adversarial mode. The two approaches require very different levels of trust and openness. It is difficult to sustain an open relationship with one customer when all the other customer relationships are closed, because open relationships require a different culture than closed ones. For example, a mass producer might subject its supplier to excessive volume swings, making it difficult for the supplier to maintain appropriate profitability and service levels to its lean customers. A single lean firm cannot accept responsibility for the overall profitability of its suppliers, just its share. Consequently, it is only when all customers are lean that the supplier can derive the full benefits of lean supply.

The extension of the discipline of interorganizational cost management further upstream requires extending the process beyond the first-tier suppliers to second-tier and beyond. This extension occurs in two ways. First, the first-tier suppliers train their suppliers (and so on) and second, the buyer educates the subsequent tiers. The extension into the second tier normally is spearheaded by the first-tier suppliers. However, sometimes the buyer will initiate the educating of the second-tier suppliers. Beyond the second tier, the firms are often quite small and relatively unsophisticated. Their education is typically driven by their major customer.

The primary purpose of the interactions between the buyer and supplier design teams is to find ways to reduce costs and increase the level of supplier innovation. The buyer benefits from its investment in the relationship through the lower prices it pays in the long run for supplied components, as do the supplier's other customers. When all the customers are lean, then each firm invests its share and reaps the benefits from all the investments. Thus, every lean customer is willing to make investments based on the combined benefit stream. However, when many of the customers are mass producers operating in adversarial mode, only the lean customers make the investment and the mass producers get a free ride. The problem is that the failure of the mass producers to invest reduces the overall benefits that can be achieved. The lean customer now reaps the benefits of only its own investments and therefore is willing to undertake only investments that are justified in their own right (see Figure 16–3).

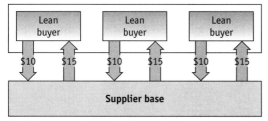

A) All buyers are lean and willing to invest in improvements in supplier efficiency; the investments are justified.

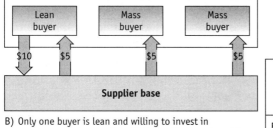

B) Only one buyer is lean and willing to invest in improvements in supplier efficiency; the investment is not justified.

FIGURE 16–3. JUSTIFYING INVESTMENTS IN INNOVATION AND
IMPROVEMENTS

STEP EIGHT

Extend lean supply and interorganizational cost management to internal suppliers.

The discipline of interorganizational cost management can also be applied to internal suppliers. However, additional problems have to be overcome first. For example, internal suppliers are often protected by "must buy internally" rules. These rules reduce the buyer's ability to encourage the adoption of lean thinking on the part of the supplier because the threat of changing suppliers is negated. In addition, other buyers are often loath to share information with and educate suppliers that are beholden to a competitor. Consequently, the full effectiveness of lean supply can be lost.

The political pressures and the difficulty of achieving the full benefits make it inadvisable to try to convert internal suppliers early in the adoption process. Only when the benefits from the conversion of external suppliers has been demonstrated will it usually be possible to encourage internal suppliers to adopt the lean philosophy. For this reason, converting internal suppliers is often the last step on the road to implementing lean supply.

SUMMARY

Interorganizational cost management is a powerful mechanism to reduce costs by coordinating the buyer and supplier cost management programs where necessary. Making the buyer-supplier interface more efficient ensures that the transaction costs are kept low. Target costing systems communicate the competitive pressures from buyers to suppliers, but isolate the design teams. This isolation is beneficial if the suppliers can achieve their cost-reduction objectives, but becomes a problem when they cannot. Thus, target costing serves to discipline the firms in the supplier network while the other three techniques—FPQ trade-offs, interorganizational cost investigations, and concurrent cost management—create the mechanisms that coordinate the buyer and supplier design teams. Finally, kaizen costing can be used interorganizationally to transmit cost-reduction pressures to suppliers for existing products and the outsourced items they contain.

There are eight major steps to implementing an interorganizational cost management program. These steps deal with the outsourcing decision, the development of lean suppliers skilled in cost management, and the creation of a lean supplier network. They do not represent a general cookbook solution to interorganizational cost management, however. Each firm has to apply the general principles as deemed appropriate, given its particular situation.

PART 4

CASE STUDIES

CHAPTER 17

CITIZEN WATCH COMPANY, LTD.: COST REDUCTION FOR MATURE PRODUCTS

INTRODUCTION

Citizen, founded in 1930, was the world's largest watch manufacturer, producing over 146 million units in 1990. Citizen comprised Citizen Watch Company, Ltd., which was responsible for manufacturing, and Citizen Trading Company, Ltd., which was responsible for marketing and sales. In addition to watches, Citizen manufactured and sold numerically controlled production equipment, flexible disk drives, liquid crystal displays for televisions and computers, dot matrix printers, and jewelry.

Citizen's non-watch products resulted from more than 20 years of carefully planned diversification. In 1990, almost half of Citizen's revenues were generated by the sale of products other than watches (see Exhibit 17–1). All of the non-watch products relied heavily upon tech-

Professor Robin Cooper prepared this case as the basis for class discussion rather than to illustrate either effective or ineffective handling of an administrative situation. The assistance of Ms. May Mukuda of KPMG Peat Marwick is gratefully acknowledged.

EXHIBIT 17-1. 1988-1990 REVENUES BY MAJOR PRODUCT LINES
(IN MILLIONS OF YEN)

	1988	1989	1990
Watches	161,745	164,186	200,835
Clocks and jewelry	35,580	38,606	41,940
Information and fine mechanics	84,374	112,428	147,166
Other	19,057	19,193	19,215

nology that was critical to watch manufacture. For example, the decision to enter the flexible disk drive market in 1984 reflected the firm's ability to miniaturize electromechanical products. This expertise allowed Citizen to be the first firm to break both the "1 inch" and "3/4 inch" flexible disk drive barriers. Developing such thin disk drives was considered critical if the firm was to establish a strong foothold in the notebook computer disk drive market. Similarly, the liquid crystal display products (such as liquid crystal televisions, introduced in 1984) reflected the firm's expertise in producing LCD watches, which began with the introduction of digital watches in 1974.

THE WATCH INDUSTRY

From about 1970 to 1990, the watch industry underwent a number of significant changes. Historically, the industry was dominated by the Swiss. Prior to the emergence of electronic versions, watch movements were tiny mechanical devices that required considerable skilled labor to manufacture. The Swiss had gained world dominance through a long history of technological developments that allowed them to be the low-cost producers of mechanical watch movements. At the heart of these developments was the ability to manufacture watch components, in volume, to the high tolerances required to produce accurate timepieces. These production processes relied upon a mixture of craft and mass production techniques. The high skill and capital investment required to produce mechanical watch movements led to the consolidation of movement manufacture into a very small number of companies, each specializing in a limited number of parts. In contrast, the manufacture of the watch case and the assembly of the completed watch, which was manually intensive and required a relatively low-skill work force, was done by a large number of small firms.

The Japanese watch industry, however, was vertically integrated. The difference between the structure of the Japanese and Swiss industries reflected Japan's lack of experience in precision mechanics. As the fledgling Japanese industry developed, it proved that the best way to mass produce quality watches was through vertical integration and concentration of the industry. In 1970, the Japanese industry contained only four firms: Citizen, Seiko, Orient, and Ricoh.

The National Aeronautics and Space Administration's (NASA's) development of the digital electronic watch allowed mass production techniques to be applied throughout movement manufacture, thereby removing the need for a highly skilled labor force. The Swiss industry's unique mix of both centralized and decentralized firms was poorly configured to adapt to the new technology, which changed both the movement and case design. This structural handicap, particularly relating to movement production, coupled with both a reluctance to switch to a new technology that invalidated their historical competitive advantage and a lack of true mass production experience, caused the Swiss to hesitate before adapting to electronic movements. This hesitation created an opportunity for the Japanese watch industry to break the dominant position of the Swiss.

The Japanese quickly adopted the new technology. Their vertical integration and heavy mass production experience had created a work force capable of switching from mechanical to electronic production relatively easily. This ease of transition, combined with a strategic disadvantage in the mechanical movement market, caused the Japanese industry to view the new technology as an opportunity, not a threat. The application of true mass production procedures to watch manufacture, and rapid advances in electronics, allowed the cost of digital watches to fall rapidly. Whereas the first digital watches sold for ¥100,000, by 1990 they were selling for under ¥1,000.

The digital watch craze was short-lived, however, because Japanese consumers felt that digital watches looked inexpensive. Consequently, quartz analogue watches rapidly came to dominate the industry. These watches, while identical in appearance to mechanical ones, were about 50 times more accurate and could be mass produced. Highly skilled workers were not required and production volumes soared. World capacity soon exceeded demand and prices fell dramatically. The impact on the industry was enormous. As the selling price of electronic watches fell below that of mechanical ones, the Swiss industry collapsed.

Japanese watch firms, while in better shape than their Swiss counterparts, faced a future of low profits. Realizing that the only way to survive was through volume, Citizen adopted an aggressive strategy of continuous price reductions matched by equivalent cost reductions. This strategy depended upon the average consumer increasing the number of watches he or she owned. This strategy proved successful: by 1990 the average Japanese adult owned three watches, compared to only one in 1970.

Despite success in changing consumer buying behavior, the watch industry continued to experience downward price and profit pressures. At Citizen and its primary competitor, Seiko, a culture of continuous expansion and cost reduction evolved. Until 1985, Seiko was larger than Citizen. Seiko had dominated primarily because of its decision to adopt quartz technology somewhat earlier than Citizen.

Citizen had chosen not to adopt quartz technology because in 1970 it had entered a joint venture with Bulova, a Swiss firm, to produce Accutron watches. These watches relied upon miniature tuning forks for their accuracy. Because the Accutron technology was protected by patent, Seiko was forced to find an alternative technology: it chose quartz. Over the next three years, the inherent superiority of the quartz technology became apparent and Citizen was forced to shift from Accutron to quartz technology. The delay, however, had caused Citizen to lose significant market share to Seiko.

In 1979, Citizen adopted a new strategy of selling watch movements as well as completed watches. This decision created a major conflict within Citizen. Citizen Watch Company, the manufacturing arm, favored this decision because it would significantly increase its scale of production. Citizen Trading Company, the trading arm that sold completed Citizen watches, opposed the strategy because it felt that the new strategy would create additional competition for its products. Because the highest profit margins were on completed watches, the Trading Company argued that the new strategy would cause overall profits to fall. At Citizen, the parent company (and hence the dominant one) was Citizen Watch Company; Citizen Trading Company was a subsidiary of the watch company. Consequently, after considerable debate, the new strategy was adopted.

At Seiko, in contrast, the parent company was the trading arm. Consequently, Seiko chose not to follow Citizen's lead. Citizen's decision to sell movements was extremely successful and in 1986 Citizen overtook Seiko in watch movement production worldwide. By 1990, Seiko, accepting the inevitable, began to sell watch movements.

MANUFACTURING PROCESS

The Tanashi plant, built in 1935, was Citizen's primary watch movement manufacturing facility. Located in a suburb of Tokyo, it was responsible for producing approximately 20% of all watch components and all domestic watch movement assembly. The other 80% of components' manufacture was undertaken at 10 other sites spread throughout Japan. Complete watch assembly was undertaken at three domestic and three overseas facilities. In addition, the Tanashi plant designed all of the specialty tools and dies required by the firm. The tiny size of the components used in watch movements had required Citizen to develop an expertise in small die manufacture. This expertise had allowed it to profitably sell dies to other companies. Other products produced at Tanashi included flexible disk drives and liquid crystal displays.

The Tanashi plant contained two distinct manufacturing areas dedicated to watch movement production: component production and assembly. Several different technologies were used in the component production area, including wire turning, pressing, and plating. Wire turning machines were used to produce mainly pins and pinions. The press facility produced some five billion pressed parts per year, primarily wheels, springs, and levers. The plating department was responsible for all nickel plating operations for rust protection operations.

The assembly area assembled watch movements in a highly automated and clean room environment. The Tanashi plant and associated plants of subsidiary companies contained 40 automated assembly lines. Each line was dedicated to a major family of movements, which on average contained more than three different movements. The average line assembled 35 components into a movement using 130 robots. Production ran 24 hours per day. Daily output per line was about 550,000 units. The high robot-to-component ratio reflected the use of robots to perform 100% testing of every movement after each assembly operation and to oil the movements at numerous stages in the assembly process.

Through its automation and kaizen (continuous improvement) programs, Citizen had significantly reduced the cost of watch movement production. Much of this reduction had been accomplished by designing movements with fewer components and by achieving very high-quality production standards. The culmination of this automation/parts reduction program was the introduction, in 1980, of the Caliber 2000 line of products. This line contained 38 different models, was used in low- to mid-range watches, and in 1990 accounted for approximately two-thirds of Citizen's unit production. It was expected to remain in production until changes in market demand made the line obsolete. Citizen management did not expect this line to become obsolete in the near future. The long product life cycle of the Caliber line indicated the maturity of quartz watch technology.

Current defect rates were well below 1 per 1,000 movements produced. These rates had been achieved by automatically stopping any assembly operation that was out of tolerance. With 100% automatic testing after each operation, only one defective movement could be produced before that operation and hence the line would automatically stop. The cause of the out-of-tolerance condition was then analyzed and the problem corrected.

THE COST MANAGEMENT SYSTEM

The cost management system at Tanashi was originally installed in 1964, and was continually updated over the next 25 years to adapt to changing conditions in the production areas. A major change was implemented in 1987 when the movement product and completed watch assembly areas were split into separate divisions and treated as independent profit centers. At the same time, the way indirect costs were assigned was changed. Previously these costs were allocated according to headcount; starting in 1987 they were allocated according to the number of units produced.

The cost system identified three major categories of costs: direct and indirect production costs and common indirect costs. *Direct production* costs encompassed three categories: parts production, movement assembly, and royalties. Parts production costs were split into direct material and labor costs. Direct material consisted of raw material and purchased parts. The purchase prices of these two types of material inputs were negotiated every six months. For each product, the cost system computed a material cost equal to the standard quantities of material consumed, after allowing for standard yield, multiplied by the actual material prices specified by contract.

The direct labor expenses associated with parts production were charged to products based upon the standard time they took to be produced. The parts production process was divided into three areas that represented the major subassemblies of a watch movement: gear train, base plate, and printed circuit board. Each of these major areas was further divided into numerous cost centers, each representing an operation required to manufacture the subassembly. For example, the printed circuit board area contained three centers relating to soldering: placement of solder, soldering the chips, and soldering other parts. In total, there were 59 such production cost centers for parts.

These 59 cost centers represented the smallest unit of cost control at the factory. Each center had a group leader who was responsible for that center's labor costs. The typical group leader had a high school education and approximately 25 years of experience. The labor costs for each center were directly charged to that center at the negotiated rate (labor rates were negotiated every three months). The direct labor hour standards for each component represented the average time required to produce the part over the previous three months, adjusted for any expected savings.

Direct material and labor expenses associated with movement assembly were treated virtually the same as they were for parts production. Any part of the movement that was subcontracted was charged directly to the movement at its negotiated price. Like other material contracts, these were negotiated every six months. The labor costs were directly charged to each assembly line and then to the model using standard hours, again based upon the previous three months' actuals. Royalty expenses were charged directly to the products to which they related.

The *indirect production* costs were also split into four categories: research and development, tooling, quality assurance, and administration. The expected costs for each of these four categories over a six-month period were divided by the number of units produced to give an estimated cost per unit. The number of units varied for the three cost categories because different models were involved. For example, research and development expenses were charged to the type of movement to which they were related and then divided by the expected production volume of that type of movement.

The *common indirect expenses* included a pro-rated share of both the expenses of corporate headquarters in Tokyo and the firm's technical laboratory at Tokorozawa, the administration expenses of Tanashi, and interest charges. Headquarters and laboratory expenses were pro-rated between operating divisions based upon their sales volumes. They were then allocated to manufacturing areas responsible for different product lines within Tanashi based upon headcount. These costs were then allocated to individual products based upon the number of units produced. Tanashi administration expenses, which included executive salaries, secretarial, and computer services, were treated similarly, except that the initial proration to the facility was not required. Interest expenses were charged to product lines based upon the level of their inventories and accounts receivable and then to products based upon the number of units produced.

The product costs reported by the cost system were used primarily to support product-related decisions such as product introduction, discontinuance, cost reduction, and redesign. Cost-plus pricing was rarely used at Citizen because most products were sold into competitive markets where the competitors had similar product offerings. Occasionally, Citizen would bring out a watch or movement for which there was no direct competitive offering. In these cases, where there was no market price, the selling price was determined using a "to be accepted" market price. This price was determined by market savings and analysis that consisted of an evaluation of the attractiveness of the product and a comparison with other watches and other consumer products.

Reported product costs played an important part in product introduction because products would be introduced only if they could be sold at a profit. Once a new product had been designed, a market analysis was undertaken. This analysis identified the likely selling price of the new product and its potential sales volumes. The next step was to estimate the full cost of production. This cost estimate used the same definitions of cost as the cost system. If this estimate was accurate it would equal the reported cost of the product after it went into production. This cost estimate included allowances for both production volume and learning curve effects.

The final step was to estimate the profitability of the new watch, which was determined by subtracting the expected costs from the selling price and multiplying the result by the anticipated volume. If the watch was profitable it was introduced and orders accepted from Citizen Trading Company and other customers. If the watch was unprofitable, then the selling price, production cost, and design were reviewed. If there was no way for the product to be made profitable it was never introduced. The only exceptions to this rule were products that were considered strategically important to Citizen's corporate image, such as the perpetual calendar watch.

A similar process was used for established products to determine if they should be subjected to specific cost-reduction efforts, redesigned, or discontinued. The firm monitored the rate at which selling prices were falling on all its products. When the selling price of a product was expected to fall below its cost in the near future, the product was subjected to an intense specific cost-reduction analysis. This analysis consisted of identifying the major cost components of the product to determine if they could be produced at a lower cost. For example, if the largest costs were associated with machining, then ways to replace the machined parts with stamped or plastic components were explored. If the cost reductions identified by the analysis were insufficient to reduce costs so that the product would remain profitable, then complete product redesign was explored. If even complete redesign was unable to make the product profitable, it was usually discontinued.

THE COST-REDUCTION PROGRAM

The cost-reduction program at Citizen encompassed the entire production chain, including subsidiaries and outside suppliers. For subsidiaries, the firm knew the material, labor, and overhead content of the purchased parts or subcomponents. The corporate technical staff would provide engineering support to help the subsidiaries find ways to become more efficient. The technical staff would visit the subsidiaries to observe the production process and make suggestions on how it might be improved. For external suppliers, the process focused on steady cost reduction. Citizen's current target was 3% per annum. All external suppliers were expected to deliver at least this level of annual cost reduction. If a supplier was able to exceed the 3% target, then it retained the surplus. If a supplier was unable to achieve the 3% target, there was no punishment, but Citizen's engineers would assist it in achieving the 3% the following year.

The maturity of quartz watch technology made it very difficult to remove significant costs by improving product designs. Consequently, the firm identified its major cost-reduction opportunity as becoming more efficient in the production process. Considerable effort was made to remove the direct labor content of products by increasing the number of machines, on average, run by a single employee.

Labor content was reduced primarily in two ways: either production engineering would change the way the product was produced or the work force would find ways to become more efficient. In the early 1990s, about 80% of all cost reductions were expected to be achieved by production engineering changes. Only 20% was expected from the work force, because it had already spent years becoming more efficient and management believed that any remaining savings opportunities were limited.

The major way to reduce labor was by altering the time it required to operate or support the production machines. There were two major approaches to machine-time reduction. First, ways to increase the running speed of the machines were identified; increasing the running speed allowed more parts per hour to be produced. Second, ways to increase the number of machines a single employee could operate were identified.

The success of this program was illustrated by the turning machine department. The 150 turning machines in the department were operated by 15 people during the day shift and only two people on the night shift. The high ratio of machines to people had been achieved by paying considerable attention to what events caused downtime and eradicating them. The 15 people on the day shift were primarily involved with setting up the manual machines, troubleshooting, and keeping the machines loaded with wire. Only two people were required on the night shift because high-volume components that did not require changeovers were produced at night. The only task of the night shift was to keep the machines running. If a machine broke down or drifted out of tolerance, it was left for the day shift to troubleshoot.

Group leaders were responsible for labor content reduction. Each of the 59 group leaders was required to set cost-reduction targets every three months. These targets were submitted to the administration department, which consolidated the targeted reductions and, if they were sufficient firm-wide, accepted them. If the overall reductions were not satisfactory, they were sent back to the group leaders for more aggressive targets. This process of adjusting the targeted savings could go several rounds before an acceptable overall target was reached.

Individual group leaders' cost-reduction targets were reviewed by the 14 managers to whom they reported. These managers had all previously been group leaders and, because of their prior experience and relationship with the current group leaders, were able to evaluate the appropriateness of the individual target reduction objectives. The final plans were reviewed by two general managers. The emphasis of the review was not on the individual targets but on the division-wide savings level. Citizen felt it was more important to achieve its overall target than worry about whether one center should achieve 6% cost reductions as opposed to 5%.

The target labor reductions for each group were included in the standards every three months. For expected savings that were due to changes in the production process, the savings were not included in the standards until the month after which the change was expected to occur. For example, if a process change was planned to be implemented in the second month of a three-month cycle, the standard would be adjusted for the third month. Therefore, if all went according to plan, there would be no positive or negative variance from the process change. Only if the savings were different from expected would a variance occur.

The success of cost-reduction efforts was measured using an achievement ratio, which was obtained by dividing actual labor hours by standard labor hours. Achievement ratios were computed monthly for each group and semiannually for each product. The expected value of the achievement ratio was 100%, reflecting the incorporation of the cost-reduction targets into the standards on a monthly basis.

If the achievement ratio for a group was above 101%, then a review was triggered. At this review, the group leader would discuss ways to ensure that the following month's achievement ratio would fall to 100%. The standard was not changed for the first month that the achievement ratio was over 100%. This created additional pressure on the group to achieve its cost-reduction targets. If the ratio remained above 100% for a second month in a row, then the standard was adjusted in the third month to reflect the failure to achieve the desired cost reductions. In effect, the cost-reduction target for the group was revised downward. Even though the target was revised, the review continued of why the targeted savings were not achieved and how they could subsequently be achieved. There was no direct reward or punishment associated with over- or under-achieving. The reasons behind the failure to reach an achievement ratio of 100% were discussed thoroughly and fully analyzed. If the reason was based on the manager's ability, the results would be reflected in his or her personal evaluation and promotion potential.

To achieve continuous direct labor cost reduction, the involvement of the entire work force was required. Even incremental improvements in efficiency were considered important. To create incentives for the work force to identify savings, picture boards were placed throughout the factory. These boards contained pictures of before and after improvements, and identified the group and individual who identified the savings and the degree of savings. For example, one set of before and after pictures covered a reduction in the time required to read a set of meters. The person reading the meters determined that the time he required to read them could be reduced by shifting them. Prior to moving them, it required 2 minutes and 58 seconds to read each meter. After they were moved, it required only 1 minute and 30 seconds.

Considerable effort had been focused on reducing the indirect costs, both production and common, at Tanashi. The long-term objective was to reduce these costs by 30% and to use the freed-up resources in other functions. Several approaches were used. The first was to identify unnecessary activities. The workload of each indirect person was reviewed to see if the position could be eliminated or the duties reduced. This analysis typically resulted in a new job description, which was prepared by the cost center group to which the indirect person belonged and reviewed by the general managers. At the heart of this cost-reduction exercise was the belief that if the work did not go away there would be no long-term savings. The second approach was to identify the necessary indirect activities, and where possible automate them so that they could be performed less expensively.

The result of these labor-content reduction programs was to considerably reduce the number of people involved in watch movement production. In 1972, 2,952 people were required; by 1980 it was down to 2,520, and by 1990 it had fallen to 1,542, which was an overall reduction of almost 50%, though the number of units produced and subcontracting to subsidiaries must be taken into consideration. The displaced work force had guaranteed lifetime employment, so Citizen was responsible for finding them new positions within the firm. Fortunately, the diversification program was able to absorb all of the displaced work force.

CHAPTER 18

KAMAKURA IRONWORKS
COMPANY, LTD.

INTRODUCTION

Kamakura Ironworks is a family-run firm located in Tochigi-ken, a distant suburb of Tokyo. The firm was founded in 1910 as a blacksmith shop; it was incorporated in 1950 as the Kamakura Ironworks Company, Ltd., with capitalization of only ¥200,000. Over the years it has increased its capitalization several times, most recently in 1975, when its capitalization was increased to ¥100,000,000. The firm has remained relatively small; 1993 sales were nearly ¥6 billion and profits were approximately ¥35 million.

The firm had 21 major customers, including Yokohama Corporation (40% of sales), Isuzu Motors (20%), Hino Motors (15%), Jidosha Kiki

Professor Robin Cooper of the Peter F. Drucker Graduate Management Center at The Claremont Graduate School and Professor Takeo Yoshikawa of Yokohama National University prepared this case as the basis for class discussion rather than to illustrate either effective or ineffective handling of an administrative situation.

Company (10%), and Yamaha Motors (5%). The majority of its customers are either automobile manufacturers or suppliers to that industry. Other customers included Iseki, Kayaba Industries, and Shinryo Heavy Equipment.

Despite the high percentage of sales represented by a few customers, Kamakura was an independent company. It did not belong to a keiretsu; it sold products to firms that belonged to a number of vertical keiretsu, including the Toyota group, the Tokyo Motors group, and the group to which Isuzu belonged, and to horizontal keiretsu, including the Mitsubishi Group.

PRODUCTS

Kamakura produced three major product lines: hot forgings, cold forgings, and finished products. The last two product lines were fairly recent additions: cold forgings were introduced in 1985 and finished products in 1987. In 1993, Kamakura produced approximately 1,250 different products. The hot forging department produced approximately 80% of the firm's total product output, which included mainshafts, counter shafts, gears, sleeves, camshafts, yokes, and brackets. The cold forging department produced approximately 10% of the firm's products, including camdisks, torqued pins, gears, flanges, shafts, and fly weights. The finishing operation department produced the remaining 10% of the products, including driver couplings, hold fly weights, flanges, and pulleys. Kamakura produced 450 products for its largest customer, Yokohama; in addition, the firm also produced 90% of the molds that Yokohama required.

Forging is a process by which metal ingots are forced under great pressure into specially shaped molds. In hot forging, the metal is heated to 950°C before being pressed. In cold forging, the metal is first coated with a lubricant so that it does not catch on the sides of the mold, and then is pressed into the mold at room temperature. The advantage of cold forging over hot forging is that more precise tolerances can be achieved because the metal does not contract on cooling after forging.

Finished products are forgings that have been further processed; they are usually ready for use by the customer. Finishing processes include drilling, tapping, polishing, degreasing, and painting. Finished products manufactured by the firm include driver cup rings, fly weight holders, mirror stays, and flanges.

Kamakura had invested heavily in the equipment required to finish its products. In 1993, it had over 82 finishing machines in three plants, all located in Tochigi-ken, including numerically controlled lathes, drilling and tapping machines, and automatic painting furnaces.

Due to the fundamental differences in the production processes for forging and finishing, top management decided to treat the forging and finishing facilities as separate profit centers. This allowed the firm to calculate accurate cost and profit figures for each department and facilitated performance evaluation of each department in addition to the planning and control operations of the firm. Transfer prices between the two facilities were set so that both facilities made the same percentage profit on the labor and overhead costs of each product. For example, if a product cost ¥200 to forge and ¥400 to finish (for a total labor and overhead cost of ¥600), and if it sold for ¥900, then the transfer price would be ¥300, which would give the forging facility a profit of ¥100 (or 50%) and the finishing facility a profit of ¥200 (again, 50%). Splitting profits equally between the forging and finishing facilities was introduced on a trial and error basis and had worked well. Consequently, the firm saw no reason to switch to a market-based transfer pricing system or any other approach.

The move to introduce finished products was driven by three factors. First, Kamakura's customers wanted to reduce their logistics costs by decreasing the number of layers in their supply chains. Shifting to firms that both forged and finished parts was considered advantageous because it meant that only one firm was responsible for processing finished parts. Second, it allowed Kamakura to gain a better understanding of post-forging processing, allowing it to design forgings that were easier and more efficient to finish. Third, it allowed Kamakura better access to technology.

CORPORATE STRATEGY

Kamakura specialized in producing low-volume products. This strategy was adopted because most of the firm's customers could produce forgings in high volumes in-house. It was not unusual for a part that was initially outsourced to Kamakura because of its low volume requirements to be taken in-house when its volume increased, or for a part initially produced in-house to be outsourced to Kamakura when its volume requirements declined.

As a result of its strategy, Kamakura relied upon manually intensive production processes that could be cost-justified for low-volume production. Kamakura's low-volume strategy made it difficult for the firm to migrate towards advanced manufacturing technologies, such as robotics and flexible machining systems. These technologies were extremely expensive and could only be justified by production volumes that were higher than those produced by Kamakura.

Kamakura had built a reputation as a high-quality, low-cost producer among the 460 forging companies in Japan. For example, as part of its vendor certification procedure in 1989, Yokohama undertook a minimum cost investigation (MCI) of the way Kamakura controlled costs. MCIs were multilevel supplier meetings in which engineers from Tokyo Motors, Yokohama, and Yokohama's suppliers met to discuss how to design and manufacture a new part. The advantage of the MCI approach was that the parts could be designed so that all of the steps, from raw material to finished product, could be made more efficient. Engineers at Kamakura would design a forged part so that the amount of machining required at Yokohama to complete it was reduced; Yokohama was willing to pay more for such a component because it cost Yokohama less to complete it.

Because Kamakura had been identified as a superior supplier by Yokohama, Kamakura employees were invited to give a presentation on their value engineering techniques. Value engineering techniques were used at Kamakura only on new products. The production process of established products was only rarely modified. In most cases, management did not believe that the improvements were cost-justified. Although most product designs were provided by the customer, Kamakura personnel would review the submitted designs and, if appropriate, suggest how they could be improved to make them easier to forge or less expensive to finish. These reviews were conducted by multifunction teams drawn from marketing, production, engineering, production control, and quality assurance. Kamakura held technical exchange meetings with its customers four or five times a month. Most of its customers, including Yokohama, were not knowledgeable about forging technology. Kamakura would often get involved in the design process by requesting functional specifications from customers and then working with their engineers to design the appropriate part.

COST REDUCTION

Large customers placed heavy pressure on Kamakura to become more efficient and reduce its selling prices. Several customers, especially those in the automobile industry, required that Kamakura reduce its selling prices from 1% to 5% per year.

In order to make Kamakura a low-cost producer, top management had developed a hands-on, team-oriented approach. Managers at Kamakura were expected to spend their time in the plant advising and helping the workers, not sitting at their desks being administrators.

Reflecting this philosophy, managers' offices at Kamakura were small and sparsely furnished, even by Japanese standards.

Kamakura had a well-established kaizen program, which was begun in 1980 to improve production processes. For example, throughout the factory, "before and after" photographs illustrated the improvements that resulted from employee suggestions.

Kamakura had also introduced a preventative maintenance program designed to focus employee attention on reducing the cost of equipment maintenance. As part of this program, every worker was expected to make at least one maintenance reduction suggestion each month.

As part of its overall cost-reduction program, the firm had implemented a total quality control program in 1980 and the Kamakura Plant Maintenance program (KPM) in 1988. As a result, Kamakura's defect rate decreased by more than 50%.

Top management considered employee morale extremely important. If employees became dissatisfied with Kamakura, they could move to one of the smaller firms that surrounded the Kamakura factory in the Kanagawa area. Fortunately, employee morale at Kamakura was high and turnover was low. Kamakura provided employees with lifetime employment and the average employee could be expected to work there for 30 years. There were usually many applicants for each new position Kamakura created.

PRICING

Selling prices for most of Kamakura's products were established either by the market or by customers' target costing systems. For example, Yokohama and Isuzu (the firm's two largest customers) had well-established target costing systems that were used to identify the target price for most of the components they purchased from Kamakura.

For new products, the customer would either identify the target price using its target costing systems or would ask Kamakura to bid for the work. The approach used depended upon the nature of the new product. When the new product was similar to existing products, then the target price would be set based upon the price of the existing part. If a part was different from existing products, then a bid would be requested. When asked to bid on a new product, Kamakura would determine the expected cost of the new product using its price estimation system. The firm's bid would be based upon the expected cost of the part, the customer in question, and general market conditions. Even for these products, the customer would usually compare Kamakura's bid price with the price generated by its target costing system.

Often, Kamakura's bid would be considered too high by the customer and the two firms would enter into price negotiations. The primary purpose of these negotiations was not to allow Kamakura to set prices but to allow it to explain why it could not produce the product at the desired target price. Kamakura's objective for these negotiations was to get the customer to make some price concessions. Major customers like Yokohama (and even minor customers) dominated these negotiations and, after listening to Kamakura's arguments, would set the selling price. However, Kamakura had considerable leverage in these negotiations because of its three areas of strength relative to other suppliers: its high technological capacity, high quality standards, and reputation for delivering products on time.

A customer's target prices were not immutable even when the product was similar to an existing one because often the customer did not take into account factors such as the quality of the product. If Kamakura could demonstrate that by increasing the product's quality it could reduce the customer's overall costs (by reducing defects and rework), then the customer would be willing to increase the selling price accordingly.

Only rarely would Kamakura agree to sell a new product at a loss. It was more likely to refuse to manufacture a part than accept an unprofitable contract. Most of Kamakura's customers accepted this constraint; because they understood Kamakura's cost structure, they would rarely press for an unprofitable price. As a result, it was not unusual for customers to be willing to pay as much as two or three times the target costs in the early years of production. This would typically occur when production volumes were less than expected or when production techniques became more complicated than expected. When Kamakura's management considered a product's production volume to be too low to be economical (under 60% of full production volume), Kamakura would press for a higher price to cover the higher costs associated with low production volumes. Customers such as Yokohama would be willing to pay the additional amount because it could expect prices to fall in the future as production volumes increased and as costs decreased through kaizen techniques.

COST ESTIMATION

Kamakura was expected to share most of its cost information with its customers. For example, Yokohama used a formal cost estimation document that had to be returned with each bid. This document required Kamakura's bid to be divided into eight categories: material cost, mold cost, facility fees, labor costs, heat treatment costs, shot blast costs, management fees, and profit.

Facility fees represented the majority of production costs. These fees included the depreciation charge for the equipment used to produce the product; utilities, oils, and rags; the cost of the machine operators; and machine operating costs (including energy costs). Equipment depreciation was computed using the expected machine hours for the life of the machine and the machine hours dedicated to the product. The conversion charge was negotiated with the customer and represented a markup over direct labor costs.

Management fees included building depreciation expenses, which were calculated by multiplying the number of operating hours by a charge rate; factory overhead, which included indirect workers such as salespeople and internal office staff; miscellaneous expenditures; and plant management salaries. The management fee was budgeted at 8% and profit at 7% of the calculated product costs. Calculated product costs included direct material, direct labor, and direct other costs plus overhead.

In theory, if every customer agreed to pay the selling price determined by this estimation procedure, then Kamakura would earn a pretax profit of 7%. However, actual profitability during the early 1990s was running at about 2%. The 5% difference was mainly attributed to overly optimistic estimates for products that experienced a decrease in production volume or that were subjected to price cutting; to decreased efficiency; to a shortening of product life cycles; or to products taking longer than expected to machine.

KAMAKURA'S COST SYSTEM

The firm's cost system calculated product costs in virtually the same way as did the cost estimation system. The cost system was not a formal system that was run throughout the year. Rather, it was run once a year at budget time to determine the profitability of all products and to create the overhead rates used during the year to estimate the profitability of new products.

When a new product was introduced, these rates were used to calculate its production costs. It generally took six months before the production process completely settled down and the machine and labor hours stopped decreasing. However, most of the learning occurred in the first two months. The long-term profitability of the product could be established after two months, when reported costs were relatively stable.

If at the end of the two-month period the product was unprofitable, then the firm would take action to make it profitable. If the actual product costs (e.g., direct material costs, direct labor costs, other direct costs, and overhead costs) were higher than expected, the firm would try to renegotiate the selling price with the customer. If conversion costs were too high, this meant that the product was taking too long to machine and the firm would explore ways to reduce processing time.

Product costs were no longer calculated after the first two months because management felt that there was little point in reporting the same number month after month. The production process was still monitored but only physical characteristics were measured; these characteristics were the quantities of material input, labor hours, and machine hours consumed. The material consumed was determined from the number of blanks that were released into the production process. Comparing the number of blanks released to the number of units of finished products allowed the yield to be calculated. The yield rate was calculated every hour because Kamakura believed that this was the best way to control the quantities of material consumed.

The actual labor and machine hours required to produce each product were monitored hourly by plotting the number of units actually completed compared to the standard rate of production for the part. If run times were too long, ways to improve the manufacturing process to shorten run times were identified and implemented as part of the firm's kaizen activities.

No form of financial variance analysis was used at Kamakura to monitor production efficiency. The physical measures and their graphical plots were considered sufficient to monitor both product costs and the efficiency of the production process.

EXPENDITURE CONTROL

Once a week, actual spending was checked against budget to ensure that production costs were under control. These weekly analyses, which were prepared by the production manager, were combined into a monthly report that was circulated throughout the firm (see Exhibit 18–1).

The budgeting process began with a mid-term plan covering a three-year period, divided into monthly periods. This plan was supported by the departmental plans of the firm's six departments (quality assurance, heat-process forging, production, technology, operations, and administration) that described the expected monthly spending patterns for the same period for each department. The departmental plans in turn were supported by mid-term project plans that covered the subdepartments in each department. Subdepartments were responsible for distinct tasks (e.g., the production department was divided into three subdepartments: production management and first and second production).

EXHIBIT 18-1. KAMAKURA'S EXPENDITURE CONTROL REPORT

Line item	Planned	Actual
Sales	******	******
Material	******	******
All other production costs	******	******
Pollution costs	******	******
Labor costs	******	******
Welfare	******	******
Management costs	******	******

Project plans were supported by section plans. Sections were cost centers responsible for the tasks performed in each subdepartment. For example, the first production subdepartment contained two sections (forging and molding) and the second production subdepartment contained the machining process and inspection sections. Feedback was offered daily at the morning assembly on whether each section was performing according to plan. This feedback focused mainly on quantities of material input, the yield rate, labor and machine hours consumed, and production volumes. One of top management's expectations was that every department would make a profit. If a department was not making a profit, it was expected to find ways to improve its profitability.

INCENTIVE SCHEMES

Kamakura used two employee incentive schemes. The first rewarded superior performance based upon section profitability. The second rewarded superior performance based upon section sales.

Each section's profitability was monitored monthly. If a department was profitable, then a percentage of its profits was awarded to the indirect overhead personnel. If a department was continuously profitable, the award (which came in the form of a biannual bonus) amounted to between 7% and 8% of wages. The exact amount of the award was determined by the director responsible for the section and had to be approved by the president. A second smaller award was given every 10 days if a section achieved its target volume; this award was used for section parties and outings.

Most improvements to profitability were the result of intrasection efforts. For example, forging could help finishing by redesigning molds so that less metal had to be removed to finish the part. When such intrasection efforts resulted in profitability improvements, both sections would benefit equally under the incentive scheme.

When improvements were introduced, the profitability expectations for the participating sections were not updated immediately. Instead, a two-month study was initiated to set the new profit targets for the section. Thus, any improvement increased the sections' incentive awards. Based on Kamakura's evaluation system, departmental improvements affected an employee's promotional considerations and the amount of his or her bonus.

CHAPTER 19

KOMATSU, LTD. (A): TARGET COSTING SYSTEM

INTRODUCTION

Komatsu, Ltd. was one of Japan's largest heavy industrial manufacturers. Founded in 1917 as part of the Takeuchi Mining Co., Komatsu Ironworks separated from its parent in 1921 to become Komatsu, Ltd. By 1991, Komatsu was a large international firm with revenues of ¥989 billion and net income of ¥31 billion. The company was organized along three major lines of business: construction equipment, industrial machinery, and electronic-applied products. Together these three lines of business generated about 80% of corporate revenues. Other operations, which accounted for the remaining 20% of corporate revenues, included construction, unit housing, chemicals and plastics, and software development. Construction equipment and industrial machinery were considered

Professor Robin Cooper of The Peter F. Drucker Graduate Management Center at The Claremont Graduate School prepared this case as the basis for class discussion rather than to illustrate either effective or ineffective handling of an administrative situation. The assistance of Ms. May Mukuda, KPMG, is gratefully acknowledged.

core businesses while electronic-applied products and other operations were considered new businesses.

In 1989, the company adopted a "3G" strategy of *growth, globalization, and group diversification.* The growth objective required all divisions to expand aggressively, with 1995 sales expected to reach ¥1.4 trillion. The globalization objective was to achieve worldwide production by the year 2000. In 1993, the firm's equipment was used in over 160 countries and was manufactured on three continents in 11 countries. The group diversification objective sought to aggressively develop three new business areas: electronics, plastics, and robotics. By the year 2000, the firm expected all nonconstruction products, including these three areas, to account for 50% of group revenues.

Construction Equipment

Komatsu was the world's second-largest manufacturer of a complete line of construction equipment. The firm's product line contained over 300 models, including bulldozers, hydraulic excavators, wheel loaders, and dump trucks. With a more than 30% share of the domestic excavator market, Komatsu was the largest player in the Japanese market. There were four other major players in the excavator market: Hitachi, with just under 30% of the market; Kobelco, with about 15%; Caterpillar Mitsubishi, with about 12.5%; and Sumitomo, with under 10%. Only Komatsu and Caterpillar Mitsubishi produced both bulldozers and excavators. The other three firms produced only excavators.

The number of competitors in the excavator market reflected the large market for those products in Japan. In the early 1990s, Japan represented over 50% of the world market for excavators; this was due to the mix of construction projects in that country. Most Japanese construction projects were in urban settings and were relatively small in size. Excavators were more practical than bulldozers for such applications because they were more versatile and less expensive. For example, excavators could perform applications such as digging, carrying, moving, and loading dirt, while bulldozers could only move dirt.

THE PRODUCT DEVELOPMENT PROCESS AND DESIGN FOR MANUFACTURABILITY COST STUDIES

The product development process at Komatsu lasted two years on average. If the redesign was relatively minor, the process might take as little as six months, while complete redesigns might take as long as three years. The process contained four major stages: product planning, design, trial production (including testing), and preparation for full production.

The Product Planning Stage

The product planning process, which was last updated in 1981, began with the preparation of a long-range development plan. This plan, prepared at the same time as the firm's long-range production and sales plans, described the mix of products that Komatsu expected to sell over the next five to ten years. For products that had yet to be designed, the plan described their functionality in conceptual terms only. The conceptual designs of these products were then developed before they entered the design stage. These conceptual designs consisted of detailed descriptions of the structure of the major subassemblies.

The Design Stage

The objective of the design stage of product development was to prepare the product for prototype production. The design phase consisted of three major steps: first, a conceptual drawing of the product; second, layout drawings for the product; and third, detailed parts drawings. During the first step, the first of four design-for-manufacturability studies (the A study) was conducted. The A study evaluated the feasibility of achieving the target cost and the overall manufacturability of the design (Exhibit 19–1 outlines the major objectives of the A study).

The A study culminated in a meeting attended by the product manager, the design managers, and the production managers of the plants at which the product would be produced. If concerns about the product's design were voiced at this meeting, further analysis of its design was undertaken. Once the product passed through this evaluation stage, layout drawings were produced.

The layout drawings contained a more detailed description of the product and its subassemblies. The completion of the layout drawings allowed the second, or B, study to be conducted. This study evaluated in more detail the firm's ability to achieve the target cost (Exhibit 19–2 outlines the major objectives of the B study).

Once the product passed this hurdle, the preparation of the parts drawings was approved. The parts drawings allowed the third, or C, study to be undertaken. The purpose of this study was to ensure that the product could indeed be built at the target cost and to confirm the actual

EXHIBIT 19-1. PURPOSE OF THE A STUDY

- Evaluation of prospects to achieve the cost target (planning and coordination departments and purchasing department)
- Evaluation of number of basic specifications and fastening capability of attachments (planning and coordination department of each plant)
- Evaluation of manufacturing possibility through current facilities and current techniques and confirmation of incorporating production technology and research outcomes into products (manufacturing departments)
- Evaluation of timing required for implementation of new techniques and new facilities (manufacturing departments)
- Evaluation of whether main components and parts should be manufactured in-house or through outside contractors (manufacturing department and purchasing department)
- Evaluation of problems associated with purchasing parts (purchasing department)
- Evaluation of problems with the transportation of products (purchasing department)
- Evaluation of periods required for solution of the two preceding problems (purchasing department)

EXHIBIT 19-2. PURPOSE OF THE B STUDY

- Follow up A study manufacturability study results (various related departments)
- Evaluation of interchangeability and common ratios of use (planning and coordination department of each plant)
- Evaluation of VE improvement plan (planning and coordination department of each plant, manufacturing departments, and purchasing department)
- Evaluation of work lines for main parts (manufacturing departments)
- Extraction of items to improve process capability in producing main components and main parts (manufacturing departments and purchasing department)
- Evaluation of time required for mass production preparation (manufacturing departments)
- Selection of suppliers/subcontractors (purchasing department)

manufacturing process and the facilities at which the product would be manufactured (Exhibit 19–3 outlines the major objectives of the C study). After the C study, a meeting of the development committee authorized prototype production. This committee consisted of the directors of the three technical divisions, the executive managing director of the corporation, the managing directors of both the domestic and overseas sales divisions, and the manager of related departments.

The Trial Production Stage

The objective of the trial production stage was to finalize the design of the product. Trial production consisted of producing prototypes of each product, and was conducted at the plants at which the product was to be

EXHIBIT 19–3. PURPOSE OF THE C STUDY

- Extraction of manufacturing process improvement items (manufacturing departments and purchasing department)
- Evaluation of facilitating measures for work and assembly (manufacturing departments and purchasing department)
- Confirmation of specifications for purchasing parts (purchasing department)
- Extraction of mass production preparation items (manufacturing departments and purchasing department)

EXHIBIT 19–4. PURPOSE OF THE D STUDY

Manufacturing departments and purchasing department shall, during the processes of trial-manufacture and quality confirmation, evaluate the process capability and other necessary matters and, if there is any discrepancy, issue a trial-manufacture problem document.

manufactured. The completion of trial production allowed the final, or D, study to be carried out (Exhibit 19–4 summarizes the major objectives of the D study). This study examined the ease of production and assembly of the new product and confirmed its quality. If any problems were encountered, a trial-manufacture problem document was issued. This document identified all of the problems that had to be resolved before mass production could commence (e.g., design changes to improve the ease of manufacturability and reduce assembly time). In addition, expected production costs were reestimated at this time. After trial production was completed, the prototypes were subjected to a series of comprehensive tests designed to ensure the quality and durability of the final product. Any problems encountered during this testing phase were fixed before the product was prepared for full production.

The Preparation for Full Production Stage

Once the product achieved the desired quality targets, results of the trial production, estimates of final target costs, and the various studies were provided to the marketing committee for final approval to move into mass production. The marketing committee was the most senior committee in the firm. It consisted of the president, executive managing director, the managing directors of the technical and sales divisions, the plant managers, and the product manager. Once approved by this committee, the product was readied for full production. The production drawings were prepared and the pre-production plans were developed. As part of the pre-production plans, any potential problems identified in the D study were confirmed and rectified. After this step, the product was released for mass production.

Reducing the Time to Market

Players in the highly competitive market for excavators and bulldozers had begun to compete on the basis of the time it took to get new products to market. Part of Komatsu's plan to improve its design for manufacturing was to change its relationship with its suppliers. In 1993, Komatsu manufactured about 30% of its products, designed and subcontracted another 50%, and purchased from outside suppliers the remaining 20%. The firm set target costs for the subcomponents manufactured by its suppliers and expected its suppliers to find ways to achieve these targets. Though target costs were supposed to be negotiated with suppliers, Komatsu management was concerned that in reality these negotiations were relatively one-sided. Additionally, management felt that the suppliers were brought into the negotiations too late in the design process. To allow the suppliers to have greater input into the design process, Komatsu initiated periodic meetings between the suppliers' research and development staff and its own. The aim of these meetings was to integrate the research and development efforts of the two groups, allow suppliers to provide input much earlier in the design process, and help ensure that target cost negotiations were more substantive.

TARGET COSTING

Throughout the product development process, target costs played a critical role in ensuring that the product would be profitable when released for mass production. The preliminary target costs used in the long-range development plan for major subassemblies, such as the engine, power train, and cooling system, were developed from prior experience with similar subassemblies and discussions with production and engineering.

These preliminary target costs or target values, as they were known, were used to help identify when the application of cost-reduction techniques was required. Three different cost-reduction techniques were used at Komatsu: design analysis, functional analysis, and productivity analysis. Design analysis was used to identify the approximate structure of the major subassemblies in new products; the other two techniques were used to identify target costs for the subassemblies. Design analysis involved identifying alternative designs for major subassemblies and selecting between them. Once the design approach for the major subassemblies was identified, their target costs were determined using either functional or productivity analysis, depending on who was responsible for designing the subassembly. Functional analysis, a procedure for identifying the target cost of a subassembly based upon its functional characteristics, was used for parts designed and produced outside of Komatsu (such as cooling systems, hydraulic devices, and electrical subassemblies) because this procedure did not rely upon detailed knowledge of the production process. Productivity analysis, a procedure for identifying the target cost of a subcomponent based upon its manufacturing process, required more in-depth knowledge of the production process and was therefore used for subassemblies designed by Komatsu (such as vehicle mainframes, buckets, and gears) and either manufactured by Komatsu or by one of its subcontractors.

Design Analysis

Product engineers were expected to identify several design alternatives for each major subassembly of a new product. Two factors were taken into account when choosing between these alternatives: quality and cost. A new design alternative was only adopted if it achieved both the desired levels of quality and cost. Frequently, one of the alternatives proposed produced a higher quality product but at a higher cost. The product engineers then explored ways to manufacture the higher quality alternative at a lower cost. If a cost-effective way to implement the new alternative was identified, then it was adopted; otherwise, the alternative was abandoned or subject to further study for future applications.

The process of design analysis at Komatsu can be illustrated by a change in the way the engine and torque converter, transmission, and steering clutch and brakes were positioned in the firm's larger bulldozers. In the old design, these three modules were physically separate. This approach, however, required 86 hours to mount and dismount these modules during maintenance. Komatsu's customers had identified this mount/dismount time as a critical factor when they selected a bulldozer.

Design analysis identified two different ways to position the three components. The first approach integrated the three modules into two, one consisting of the engine and torque converter and the other the transmission and steering clutch and brake modules. The integration of the transmission and steering clutch and brake modules into a single module reduced the mount/dismount time to 44 hours. The second approach also integrated the three modules into two, but this time the torque converter, transmission, steering clutch and brakes were integrated into a single module. This approach had the advantage of removing the need to change the oil, thereby reducing the mount/dismount time to 33 hours (see Exhibit 19–5). Unfortunately, both of the new design alternatives were more expensive than the old design; the fastest design was also the most expensive.

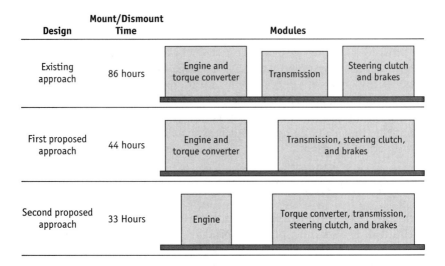

Design	Mount/Dismount Time	Modules		
Existing approach	86 hours	Engine and torque converter	Transmission	Steering clutch and brakes
First proposed approach	44 hours	Engine and torque converter	Transmission, steering clutch, and brakes	
Second proposed approach	33 Hours	Engine	Torque converter, transmission, steering clutch, and brakes	

EXHIBIT 19–5. DESIGN ANALYSIS EXAMPLE

This conflict between quality and cost was resolved by changing the way the ripper mounting bracket was attached to the bulldozer. Bulldozers were used for a number of tasks, and changeable attachments increased their versatility. For example, rippers were used for breaking up hard surfaces while dozers were used for removing loose material. The ripper mounting bracket enabled the ripper to be attached to the mainframe. The new approach allowed the mounting bracket to be welded, as opposed to bolted, to the mainframe. Welding was cheaper than bolting and the savings equaled the additional cost of adopting the alternative design of the engine, transmission, and torque converter.

Welding, while less expensive than bolting, required that every bulldozer have a mounting bracket attached. Previously, Komatsu was able to sell bulldozers with or without an attached mounting bracket. The effective cost savings from adopting the new attachment approach and welding the mounting bracket thus depended on the percentage of bulldozers that were ordered with mounting brackets. This mounting ratio varied depending upon the size of the bulldozer: the larger the bulldozer, the higher the ratio. When the mounting ratio was taken into account, the new approach was cheaper for large bulldozers but more expensive for small ones. Consequently, the new configuration of the engine, transmission, and converter and the welded ripper mounting bracket approach was adopted for large bulldozers but not for small ones.

Functional Analysis

The process of functional analysis at Komatsu can be illustrated by the development of the target cost of an excavator cooling system. The process began with an analysis of the functions of the cooling system and how they were achieved. The primary function of the cooling system was identified as its cooling capacity; secondary functions included how quickly it started cooling after the engine was first switched on and how stable a temperature it maintained.

The determinants of cooling capacity were ranked in the order of their importance. The most important determinant of cooling capacity was identified as the surface area of the radiator. The second most important determinant was the size of the fan, followed by the rotation speed of the fan, the volume of water in the system, and the ambient air temperature.

The functional analysis began by plotting the cooling capacity versus the radiator surface area for all existing products that used the same type of cooling system. This information was maintained in functional tables. From this plot the average and minimum lines for existing equipment were determined. The average line was determined using linear regression and the minimum line was drawn so that it passed through the most efficient cooling systems. The required cooling capacity for the new model was used to identify the minimum cooling area required according to the best designs. The minimum cooling area was that which generated the desired cooling capacity on the minimum line (see Figure 19–1).

The target cost for the cooling system was determined by a similar process, using surface area versus cost information for existing products. This information was maintained in functional cost tables. A graph of the

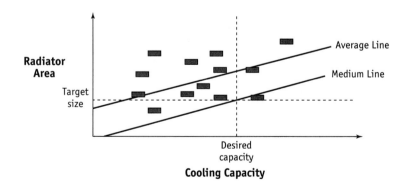

FIGURE 19–1. COOLING CAPACITY VERSUS RADIATOR CAPACITY

cost of cooling systems against their surface area was plotted for all existing models using the same cooling technology. The average cost per surface area was determined using linear regression. The minimum cost line was again drawn passing through the most cost efficient designs. The minimum surface area identified from the cooling capacity/radiator surface area analysis was used to identify the minimum cost of the new cooling system. This minimum cost for the minimum radiator surface area became the target cost for the radiator (see Figure 19–2).

The same techniques were used to generate target costs for the other major components of the cooling system. For example, the target cost of the fan in the cooling system was determined by plotting the size of fan against cooling capacity, identifying the average and minimum lines for the relation between fan size and cooling capacity. The minimum fan size-to-cooling capacity line was used to identify the minimum fan size. A plot of the cost of fans versus fan size was used to determine the minimum cost/size line and hence the target cost of the fan. This process was repeated for all major components of the cooling system.

The functional analysis approach was modified for components such as shafts, where the function could be approximated by a simple physical measure such as the weight of the component. The function of the shaft was to connect the rotating output of the transmission to the wheels; the weight of the shaft identified the torque that it was able to handle. A shaft weight/cost table was used to develop a plot of the weight of shafts in existing products against their cost. From this plot, the average and minimum shaft weight/cost lines were identified and hence the target cost of the shaft. The target cost was the shaft cost predicted by the minimum cost line.

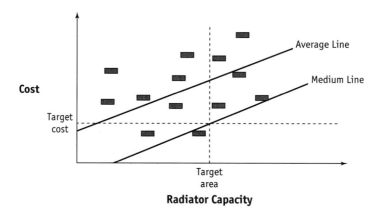

Figure 19–2. Radiator Capacity Versus Cost

Productivity Analysis

Productivity analysis was used for major subassemblies designed by Komatsu. At the heart of this analysis was a set of tables that identified the cost of each production step as a function of its physical characteristics. For example, information was maintained about the cost of each type of material, the weight required by each design, the cost per meter of welding, and the length of weld required by each subassembly.

In productivity analysis, the major steps in the production process of the new subassembly were analyzed and the sum of their costs compared to the subassembly's target cost. If the expected cost was too high, the section leaders responsible for each step in the production process were asked to identify a cost-reduction target for each step.

Ultimate responsibility for these cost-reduction targets lay with the product manager, who was responsible for ensuring that the new product successfully entered production. If the initial aggregated cost reductions were insufficient to allow the subassembly to be manufactured for its target cost, then the product manager and the production staff negotiated to increase the expected productivity savings. The final aggregation of the negotiated cost-reduction targets provided the latest estimate of the subassembly's target cost.

The process of productivity analysis at Komatsu can be illustrated by the redesign of a mounting socket in the mainframes of the firm's bulldozers. In the old design, the mounting socket consisted of a hole drilled through the body of the mainframe. This design was simple to manufacture but had the drawback of creating a stress zone around the hole. To ensure that the mounting socket was strong enough, that section of the mainframe had to be manufactured out of expensive, high-grade materials. Productivity analysis had identified the reduction of the level of high-grade material in the mainframe as one way to reduce costs. The new design consisted of welding to the vehicle mainframe a mounting bracket that contained the mounting socket hole. The new mounting unit was designed to reduce the strain imposed on the mainframe so that normal-grade steel could be used.

CHAPTER 20

MIYOTA COMPANY, LTD.

INTRODUCTION

I have a very high level of autonomy as the president of Miyota.
I set my own targets and try to ensure that Miyota is profitable,
thus contributing to the Citizen Group. If our parent, Citizen,
knew every detail of our costs, I would be nothing more than a
cost center manager.

— *Kazuo Tanaka, President, Miyota Co., Ltd.*

Miyota Co. Ltd. (Miyota), founded in 1959, was a wholly-owned subsidiary of Citizen Watch Company, Ltd. In 1995, its sales were just over
¥36 billion. Originally dedicated to watch assembly for Citizen, over the

Professor Robin Cooper of The Peter F. Drucker Graduate Management Center at The
Claremont Graduate School prepared this case as the basis for class discussion rather
than to illustrate either effective or ineffective handling of an administrative situation.

years Miyota diversified along technology lines by specializing in miniature mechatronic (the fusion of mechanical and electronic technologies)
products. By 1995, Miyota produced four major product lines. The first,
accounting for approximately 30% of sales, was completed watches sold
under the Citizen name brand. The second, accounting for approximately
20% of sales, was watch movements and parts sold to Citizen (Miyota
supplied approximately 50% of Citizen's watch component requirements). The third product line was quartz oscillators, used in watches and
other synchronized electronic applications such as telephones, televisions,
video cassette recorders, and personal computers. High-frequency oscillators, a relatively new product for Miyota, accounted for 9% of sales; low-
frequency ones, first introduced in the mid-1970s, accounted for 18%.
Fourth, Miyota produced viewfinders for camcorders, which accounted
for approximately 23% of sales. These viewfinders were miniature television cathode ray screens. Miyota was the sole producer of camcorder
viewfinders for the Citizen Group.

Miyota sold all of its products to Citizen except for the viewfinders,
which it sold to the major camcorder producers such as Sony and Victor.
Miyota did not sell viewfinders to Matsushita, because that company was
a direct competitor in that market.

Citizen

Founded in 1930, Citizen was the world's largest watch manufacturer,
producing over 200 million units in 1994. Citizen comprised Citizen
Watch Company, Ltd., which was responsible for manufacturing, Citizen
Trading Company, Ltd., which was responsible for marketing and sales,
and other subsidiary companies. In addition to watches, Citizen manufactured and sold numerically controlled production equipment, flexible
disk drives, liquid crystal displays for televisions and computers, dot
matrix printers, and jewelry.

Citizen's non-watch products resulted from more than 20 years of
carefully planned diversification. In 1995, 56% of Citizen's revenues were
generated by the sale of products other than watches. All of the non-
watch products relied heavily upon technology that was critical to watch
manufacture. For example, the decision to enter the flexible disk drive
market in 1984 reflected the firm's ability to miniaturize electromechanical products.

This expertise allowed Citizen to be the first firm to break both the
"1 inch" and "3/4 inch" flexible disk drive height barriers. Developing
such thin disk drives was considered critical to establishing a strong

foothold in the notebook computer disk drive market. Similarly, the liquid crystal display products (such as liquid crystal televisions, introduced in 1984) reflected the firm's expertise in producing LCD watches, which began with the introduction of digital watches in 1974.

Citizen's primary watch movement manufacturing facility was the Tanashi plant, built in 1935. Located in a suburb of Tokyo, it produced approximately 20% of all watch components and all domestic watch movement assembly combined. The other 80% of watch components were manufactured at 10 other sites spread throughout Japan. Complete watch assembly was done at three domestic and 15 overseas facilities. Miyota sold six different watch movements and four watch parts to the Tanashi plant.

THE COST-REDUCTION PROGRAM

Citizen's cost-reduction program for watch movements encompassed the entire production chain, including subsidiaries and outside suppliers. Corporate technical staff provided engineering support to help the subsidiaries find ways to become more efficient. The technical staff would visit the subsidiaries to observe the production process and make suggestions on how it might be improved. For external suppliers, the process focused on steady cost reduction. Citizen's current target was 5% per annum. All external suppliers were expected to deliver at least this level of annual cost reduction. If a supplier was able to exceed the 5% target, then it retained the surplus. A supplier was not penalized if it didn't achieve the target, but Citizen's engineers would assist it in achieving the target the following year. As a subsidiary, Miyota was held to the same 5% cost-reduction targets as the group's independent suppliers.

The Tanashi-Miyota Negotiations

Miyota retained a high degree of autonomy from Citizen and acted more like an independent supplier; for example, unlike many subsidiaries of other Japanese companies, Miyota did not share detailed cost information with its parent. Miyota negotiated all prices and other contractual relations with Citizen at arm's length. Both sides characterized these negotiations as tough but cooperative. Given Miyota's high level of autonomy, it viewed the negotiations as critical to its success. As Kazuo Tanaka, Miyota's president, described it:

Citizen derives great advantage from treating each subsidiary as an independent company even though they are wholly owned. Treating them as independent companies puts teeth into the negotiations. If Miyota was totally controlled by Citizen, I would be very disappointed and would have little incentive to work hard. As president of Miyota, I want to set my own target costs and profits as well as contributing to Citizen. I call the relationship between Citizen and Miyota supportive autonomy. I can call on Citizen for help but if I do a good job, they leave me alone. This freedom creates a stimulating environment for Miyota. We have to find our own ways to achieve our objectives.

Cost-reduction negotiations were both long term, which dealt with the next three to five years, and short term, which dealt with the next six months. Senior management of both firms conducted the long-term negotiations; lower-level managers negotiated the short-term objectives, which were then ratified by top management at both firms. The long- and short-term cost-reduction objectives helped Citizen achieved its desired level of profits. Every year, the long-term objectives were modified to reflect changing conditions in the industry (see Exhibit 20–1). Citizen made the long-term objectives more aggressive if it felt its long-term profitability was threatened, and loosened them if it seemed likely that its long-term profit objectives would be met. Citizen made its short-term cost-reduction objectives more aggressive if it felt it might not achieve the current year's profit objective.

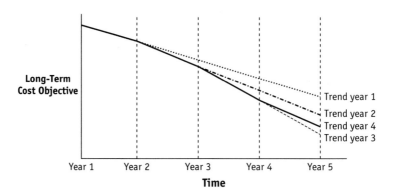

EXHIBIT 20–1. SETTING LONG-TERM COST-REDUCTION OBJECTIVES

Each year Citizen's top management reviewed competitive conditions and set the group's long-term cost-reduction objectives. These objectives were transmitted to the Tanashi plant, which then informed Tanaka. Tanaka would then meet with Citizen's senior managers about the objectives. At these meetings, Tanaka would not argue about the aggressiveness of the targets, but instead would just listen. He believed he was responsible for achieving Citizen's cost-reduction objectives as well as maintaining Miyota's profitability. No contracts for long-term cost-reduction objectives were ever established at these meetings. Both parties knew what was expected and that was considered sufficient.

Tanaka would be held responsible if Miyota failed to deliver the long-term cost-reduction objectives. If Miyota failed to deliver the long-term cost-reduction objectives for a period of three to five years, then Tanaka would be fired. Miyota's success in achieving the objectives was not measured on a part-by-part basis. Therefore, it did not matter if five watch movements and parts were below their cost-reduction targets and five were above; the only thing that mattered was the overall savings.

The short-term cost-reduction negotiations occurred within the framework of the long-term cost-reduction objectives. Although the two sets of negotiations were obviously interrelated, they could be different in the short term. For example, Citizen might negotiate a short-term cost-reduction objective that was higher or lower than the current long-term one. But over time the short-term negotiations had to achieve the long-term cost-reduction objectives. Thus, the short-term objectives oscillated around the long-term ones (see Exhibit 20–2). Prior to the dramatic

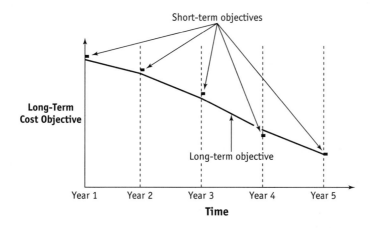

EXHIBIT 20–2. SETTING SHORT-TERM COST-REDUCTION OBJECTIVES

appreciation of the yen against the dollar in 1994, the short-term cost-reduction objectives had been 3%. Typically, Miyota's overall short-term cost-reduction target was between 2.5% to 3.5% each year, but had averaged the required 3% over recent years.

The 5% cost-reduction target was the group's current short-range and long-range objective. Tanashi engineers were aware that cost-reduction potentials were different for each type of movement and part supplied. Therefore, they would request a cost reduction for each part ranging from 3% to 7%. The exact cost-reduction target for each part and subassembly was based upon the history of negotiations for that movement or part between Tanashi and Miyota. If Miyota felt that it could not achieve Tanashi's objective for a given movement or part, it would negotiate to have that objective relaxed. Given the lack of information sharing between the two firms, there was no way that Miyota engineers could determine if Tanashi engineers were making trade-offs across movements and parts. All that Miyota saw was the final cost-reduction objectives. However, during the negotiation process Miyota personnel were able to estimate the expected cost-reduction objective for each of the 10 watch movements and parts it sold to its parent. Officially, it only knew the total cost-reduction objective.

Movements and parts recently transferred from Citizen Watch to Miyota were exempted from this cost-reduction program. Parts were transferred from Citizen to Miyota for two reasons. First, Citizen's direct labor force often had too much work; outsourcing movement and parts manufacturing reduced the overload. Second, Miyota's direct labor was less expensive than Citizen's. When Citizen transferred the sourcing of parts and assemblies to Miyota it would use the standard costs, as reported by Citizen's standard cost system, as the basis for setting the transfer price (which was equal to or less than Tanashi's standard cost) between the two firms. No formal profit figure was built into these transfer prices, but since Miyota's cost were typically lower than Citizen's, the transferred parts usually generated a profit. After two to three years, it would allow the transfer prices for those parts, and assemblies were negotiated in the normal manner.

Although Citizen did not have direct access to detailed cost information from Miyota, Tanashi engineers believed that they could accurately estimate the cost of Miyota's products using information from the negotiations and factory visits. These cost estimates enabled Tanashi engineers to place considerable short-term pressure on Miyota to reduce costs. The first source of cost estimate information was Citizen's own cost system. Citizen Watch produced parts and subassemblies that were similar to many of the parts supplied by Miyota. Because the Tanashi engineers knew the exact costs of these parts, they used them to accurately estimate the cost of similar parts supplied by Miyota. The second source of information for estimating the costs of Tanashi-supplied parts came from the multiple sourcing of parts. Most of the other components that Miyota sold to Tanashi were also produced by other subsidiaries or by external suppliers. These multiple sources created a competitive market that generated arm's-length prices for these parts. Citizen's engineers used these prices as a basis for developing their cost estimates.

Miyota engineers would push harder to have the cost-reduction objectives relaxed when they were considered unachievable and less hard when considered achievable. Thus, the intensity of the short-term negotiations gave Citizen a sense of how well Miyota was achieving its cost-reduction objectives. In addition, Miyota's profitability was determined by the relationship between Citizen's cost-reduction objectives and the amount of costs that Miyota could take out of the parts and assemblies it sold to Citizen. If Miyota could take more costs out than required by Citizen, its profitability would increase (see Exhibit 20–3). If it could not take out sufficient costs, its profitability would suffer (see Exhibit 20–4). Thus, Citizen's top management could monitor how well Miyota was performing overall by simply looking at its profitability.

Citizen's top management used these two sources of information, the intensity of short-term negotiations and Miyota's profitability, to help set Miyota's long-term cost-reduction objectives. Its aim was to create a reasonable degree of pressure on Miyota to maximize its ability to reduce

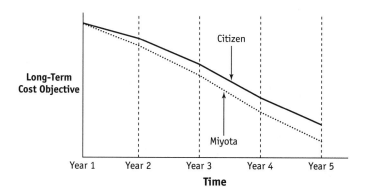

EXHIBIT 20–3. THE RELATIONSHIP BETWEEN MIYOTA'S
           PERFORMANCE AND CITIZEN'S COST-REDUCTION
           OBJECTIVES: MIYOTA'S PERFORMANCE EXCEEDS
           CITIZEN'S OBJECTIVES

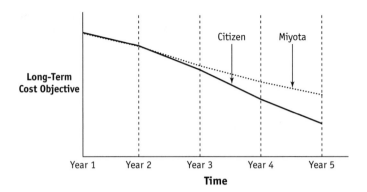

EXHIBIT 20-4. THE RELATIONSHIP BETWEEN MIYOTA'S
             PERFORMANCE AND CITIZEN'S COST-REDUCTION
             OBJECTIVES: CITIZEN'S OBJECTIVES EXCEED
             MIYOTA'S PERFORMANCE

costs; Citizen viewed impossible targets as pointless. The reasonableness of the long-term cost-reduction objectives (which were based in competitive reality), not a lack of power or autonomy, explained why Tanaka felt he did not have to negotiate them.

CHAPTER 21

OLYMPUS OPTICAL COMPANY, LTD.(A): COST MANAGEMENT FOR SHORT-LIFE-CYCLE PRODUCTS

INTRODUCTION

Olympus, which consisted of Olympus Optical Company, Ltd., and its subsidiaries and affiliates, manufactured and sold opto-electronic equipment and other related products. The firm's major product lines included cameras, video camcorders, microscopes, endoscopes, and clinical analyzers. Olympus also produced microcassette tape recorders, laser-optical pickup systems, and industrial lenses. Olympus was founded in 1919 as Takachiho Seisakusho, a producer of microscopes. The brand name Olympus was first used in 1921 and became the firm's name in 1949. The first Olympus camera was developed in 1936, and by 1990 Olympus was the world's fourth-largest camera manufacturer.

This case was prepared by Professor Robin Cooper of The Peter F. Drucker Graduate Management Center at The Claremont Graduate School as the basis for class discussion rather than to illustrate either effective or ineffective handling of an administrative situation. The assistance of Professor Regine Slagmulder of the University of Ghent and of Ms. May Mukuda, KPMG Peat Marwick, is gratefully acknowledged.

Olympus had six divisions plus a headquarters facility. Four divisions—consumer products, scientific equipment, endoscopes, and diagnostics—were responsible for generating revenues (Exhibit 21–1 shows 1995 financial results). The other two divisions were responsible for corporate research and production engineering, respectively. Headquarters was responsible for corporate planning, general affairs, personnel, and accounting and finance.

The consumer products division manufactured and sold 35mm cameras, video camcorders, and microcassette tape recorders. In 1995, the division employed 3,900 people (29% of the total Olympus work force) and generated revenues of ¥73 billion (29% of group revenues). Cameras were by far the firm's most important consumer product, accounting for ¥62.8 billion in revenues. Cameras were sold worldwide, with approximately 70% sold outside of Japan.

The consumer products division consisted of six departments: division planning, quality assurance, marketing, product development, production, and overseas manufacturing. Responsibility for the division's production facilities was centered at the Tatsuno plant, which opened in 1981 and was the firm's main camera production facility. Tatsuno was responsible for trial production of experimental products, introductory production of new products, and, to a limited degree, camera and lens production. Five other domestic manufacturing facilities reported to

EXHIBIT 21–1. OLYMPUS OPTICAL 1995 FINANCIAL RESULTS

	Yen (millions)			US Dollars (thousands)
	1995	1994	1993	1995
Net sales	252,097	239,551	267,718	2,801,078
Net income	3,101	556	3,805	34,456
Net income per share:				
Total assets	442,367	434,704	439,716	4,915,189
Working capital	205,256	202,070	164,712	2,280,622
Shareholders' investment	182,418	183,039	145,775	2,026,287

Notes:

1. Net income per share is shown in yen and US dollars.

2. For the reader's convenience, US dollars amounts were translated from yen at the rate of ¥90=$1.

3. Fully diluted net income per share assuming full dilution is not presented because it is not significant.

4. The above figures were based on accounting principles generally accepted in Japan.

Tatsuno. These facilities were all located in Japan and were responsible for plastic molded parts, lenses, camera assembly, and die casting. Overseas production facilities located in Hong Kong and China reported to the overseas manufacturing department.

THE 35MM CAMERA MARKET

Five Japanese firms dominated the world's 35mm camera market: Asahi Pentax, Canon, Minolta, Nikon, and Olympus. Canon and Minolta were the largest of the five firms, each with approximately 17% of the market compared to Olympus' 10%. There were two major types of 35mm cameras: single lens reflex (SLR) and lens shutters (LS) or compact cameras. SLR cameras, first introduced in 1959, used a single optical path to form the images for both the film and the viewfinder, allowing the photographer to see exactly what a picture would look like before it was taken. This ability allowed SLR cameras to take advantage of interchangeable lenses. Because of this feature SLR cameras rapidly gained a dominant share of the professional photographic market. As their price fell, they also came to dominate the high-end amateur market.

The low-end amateur 35mm market continued to be dominated by cameras with two separate optical paths. This market was divided into two segments. One segment contained very inexpensive cameras produced primarily by film manufacturers. The economics of this segment was driven predominantly by film, not camera, sales. The cameras in this segment primarily used the disc or 110mm film formats, though film producers had started to sell 35mm cameras that included new single-use versions. The other segment consisted of 35mm cameras that were less expensive than SLR cameras. This segment had undergone a dramatic change in the 1980s with the introduction of compact cameras.

Compact cameras, as suggested by their name, were smaller than SLR cameras. The first compact camera, the "XA," was introduced by Olympus in 1978 when miniaturized electronic shutters allowed the size of non-SLR cameras to be significantly reduced. The size of SLR cameras could not be equivalently reduced because their single optical path required a retractable mirror. This mirror was positioned between the lens and the film when in the down position and reflected the image into the viewfinder. When the shutter was pressed, the mirror retracted up into the body of the camera, allowing the image to expose the film. The retractable mirror, which was approximately the same size as the image, required SLR cameras to remain relatively bulky. Cameras with two optical paths, however, did not require a retractable mirror and therefore could be reduced to quite small sizes. For example, the Olympus Stylus, which was ergonomically designed to fit the hand, was only 4.6" long by 2.5" wide by 1.5" deep and weighed 6.3 ounces.

The early compact cameras were relatively unsophisticated and posed little challenge to the SLR market. However, as advances in electronic control systems allowed auto-focusing and automatic exposure features to be added at relatively low prices, the compact camera began to be viewed as a serious alternative to SLR cameras. The introduction of zoom auto-focus compact cameras in the mid-1980s removed the last major advantage of SLR cameras, that is, variable focal length lenses. Sales of SLR cameras plummeted.

The shift in consumer preference to compact cameras adversely affected Olympus in particular, because the firm historically had relied heavily on SLR sales and had failed to develop a leadership position in the compact camera arena. In the mid-1980s, Olympus' camera business began to lose money and by 1987 its losses were considerable. Top management ascribed these losses to a number of internal and external causes. The major internal causes were poor product planning, a lack of "hit" products, and some quality problems. While Olympus' overall quality levels were above average for the industry, certain products that relied on completely new technologies had rather high defect rates. These quality problems had caused Olympus' reputation to suffer. Externally, two factors were identified as primary contributors to losses: the appreciation of the yen from over 200 to the dollar in 1985 to around 130 in 1990 and an extended low-growth period for the industry that had caused prices (hence profits) to drop.

STRATEGIC CHANGE AT OLYMPUS

In 1987, Olympus' top management reacted to the losses by introducing an ambitious three-year program to "reconstruct" the camera business. At the core of this program were three objectives: first, to recapture lost market share by introducing new products; second, to dramatically improve product quality; and third, to reduce production costs via an aggressive set of cost-reduction programs.

Recapturing Market Share

To recapture market share, Olympus developed a new strategy of rapidly introducing, producing, and marketing new 35mm SLR and compact cameras. The firm's strategy in the SLR market was to differentiate its products from competitors' by the innovative use of technology. For compact cameras, Olympus' strategy was to develop a full line of low-cost cameras with particular emphasis on zoom lens models. Rapid introduction was considered important because it would allow the firm to react in a timely fashion to changes in the competitive environment. One of the key elements in improving the firm's ability to react rapidly was a plan to reduce to 18 months the time required to bring new compact cameras to market. The equivalent benchmark when the OM10 SLR camera was developed in 1980 was 10 years.

New products were introduced via the firm's extensive product planning process. At the heart of this process was the product plan, which identified the mix of cameras that the firm expected to sell over the next five years. The information required to develop this plan came from six sources: Olympus' corporate plan, a technology review, an analysis of the general business environment, quantitative information about camera sales, qualitative information about consumer trends, and an analysis of the competitive environment. As part of the three-year reconstruction program, the information collected to support the product plan was extended considerably from pre-1987 levels. In particular, the amount of qualitative data captured was increased. To ensure that all this new information was appropriately incorporated into the product plan, more extensive reviews of the plan were introduced.

The *corporate plan*, which was developed by Olympus' senior management, identified the future mix of business by major product line, the desired profitability of the corporation and each division, and the role of each major product line in establishing the overall image of the firm. It provided division management with a charter by which to operate.

The *technology review* had two sections. The first consisted of a survey of how current and future technological developments were likely to affect the camera business. For example, digital image processing was reaching the stage where electronic still cameras were rapidly becoming both technically and economically feasible replacements for conventional cameras that relied on chemical film for image capture. Olympus was in the forefront of electronic still image capture and in 1990 had introduced its first electronic camera. The second part of the review sought to determine whether Olympus had developed any proprietary technology that could be used for competitive advantage. For instance, Olympus had developed an advanced electronic shutter unit that combined auto-focus control and the lens system, which allowed the size of the camera to be smaller. This shutter unit allowed the firm to develop "small in size" as a distinctive feature of its cameras.

The *analysis of the general business environment* consisted of estimates of how changes in the environment would affect camera sales and the profitability of the business. Factors included foreign exchange rates, how cameras were sold, and the role of other consumer products. How cameras were sold was especially critical, because during the 1980s the percentage of the firm's cameras sold via specialty stores had decreased steadily from 70% to 40%. This change in retail distribution demographics had reduced the average wholesale prices of cameras because the bulk of cameras was now sold through discount houses and mass merchandisers, where profit margins were lower. The role of other consumer products was important because some of them competed for the same segment of the consumer's disposable income. For example, consumer research had shown that many consumers were trying to choose between buying a compact disc player or a compact camera. Therefore, Olympus viewed compact disc players as competitive products.

Quantitative information about the world's 35mm camera market was collected from three primary sources. The first was export and domestic market statistics for cameras published by Japan's Ministry of International Trade and Industry. These statistics included the number of units and dollar sales for each type of camera (e.g., zoom, SLR, and compact) for the entire Japanese camera industry. The second, published by the Japan Camera Industry Association, was statistics on camera industry shipments, which captured the number of units and dollar value of each type of camera shipped from the manufacturers to each major overseas market (e.g., the United States and Europe). The third source consisted of third-party surveys, commissioned by Olympus, of retail sales by type of camera in each major market.

Olympus collected *qualitative information* from seven major sources. First, the company collected questionnaires from recent purchasers of Olympus cameras. These questionnaires, included with every camera sold, captured information about the purchaser's age, income range, lifestyle demographics, and the other cameras the consumer considered before making the purchase. Second, group interviews were conducted by survey firms two to three times a year in each of the major markets to spot changes in consumer preferences for cameras. Third, surveys were conducted in Roppongi, the trendy fashion center of Tokyo; historically, these interviews had proven to be good predictors of future changes in the lifestyle of the Japanese population as a whole.

Fourth, professional photographers were interviewed to provide insights into both the leading edge of camera design and ways to improve the ease-of-use of compact cameras. Fifth, the Olympus sales force interviewed camera dealers. In addition, Olympus helped pay the salaries of "special salespeople" who worked behind the counters at very large camera stores. These individuals supplied Olympus with feedback about how their cameras were being received by consumers compared to competitive offerings. Sixth, members of the product planning staff would spend some part of the year behind the counter selling cameras, thus becoming familiar with the reactions of both consumers and dealers. Finally, members of the planning staff would attend industry fairs and conventions to obtain additional feedback on industry trends.

The *competitive analysis* was based on any information Olympus could gather about its competitors' current and future product plans. Sources of competitive information included press and competitor announcements, patent filings, and articles in patent publications. This information was used to predict what types of products competitors would introduce in the short and long terms and what their marketing plans were.

The information collected from all these sources was integrated into the preliminary product plan. This plan was the responsibility of a manager in the product planning section. Olympus differed from most other Japanese camera companies in the way it developed its product plan.

First, the product planning function was part of sales and marketing, not research and development, as it had been prior to 1987. Second, the purpose of the product plan review was to balance the demands of a consumer-oriented market with the realities of research and development and production. Third, the firm had a stated objective of trying to design global products. Twice a year, the persons in the firm responsible for worldwide marketing met with the product planners to ensure that proposed products could be sold successfully in all the world's major markets.

Once the preliminary plan was completed, it was subjected to an exhaustive review to ensure its practicality. The review covered issues such as the expected sales volume and profit for each camera model and the load such sales would place on the division's production and research and development resources. A team composed initially of research and development and product planning personnel conducted the review. Subsequently, as the product plan approached acceptance, production personnel were added to the review team. Once the review was completed, a general meeting was held to formally accept the plan. This meeting was attended by division management, by the heads of the marketing, research and development, and production functions, and by the managers of the product planning section. If the product plan was accepted at this meeting, it was then implemented.

Improving Product Quality

Olympus' quality improvement program focused on two areas: the introduction of new products and the manufacturing process in general. The

aim of the quality improvement program was to enable the firm to produce the highest-quality products in the industry. Olympus cameras were
historically above average in quality, but management felt that it was
important to be the best. Highest quality was considered important
because it would help the firm recapture its lost market share by improving the reliability of the firm's products from the customer's perspective.
In addition, improved product quality was expected to reduce production
costs through decreased disruptions to the production flow.

Reducing Production Costs

To bring its high production costs into line, Olympus developed an
aggressive cost-reduction program that focused on five objectives: to
design products that could be manufactured at low cost, to reduce unnecessary expenditures, to improve production engineering, to adopt innovative manufacturing processes, and to shift a significant percentage of
production overseas.

Designing High-Quality Products at Low Cost

At the heart of the program to design low-cost products was the firm's
target costing system. The first step in setting target costs was to identify
the price point at which a new camera model would sell. For most new
products, the price point was already established. For example, in 1995
the simplest compact cameras were sold in the United States at the $80
price point, down from $100 in 1991. The actual selling prices for a given
camera varied depending on the distribution channel (e.g., mass mer-
chandiser versus specialty store). Thus, cameras at the $80 price point
would sell for between approximately $70 and $100. The appropriate
price point for a camera was determined by its distinctive feature (e.g., it
might be magnification capability of the camera's zoom lens or the camera's small size). The relationship between distinctive features and price
points was determined from the competitive analysis and technology
review used in the development of the product plan. The product plan
thus described cameras only in terms of their distinctive features. Other
features were added as the camera design neared completion.

The price point at which a camera with given functionality was sold
tended to decrease over time with improvements in technology. Price
points were typically held constant for as long as possible by adding functionality to the cameras offered. Typically, a given type of camera would
be introduced at one price point, stay at that price point for several years

but with increasing functionality, and then as the functionality of the next higher price point was reached, drop to the next lower price point. The natural outcome of this process was to generate new price points at the low end. For example, the price point for the simplest compact camera was $150 in 1987 and $80 in 1995. At the high end, technology also generated new price points. As the functional gap between the capabilities of compact and SLR cameras closed, it became possible to introduce compact cameras at higher prices. For example, Olympus created a new price point of $300 when it introduced the first compact camera with 3X zoom capability in 1988.

The growing number of price points required camera manufacturers to expand their product offerings to maintain a full line. The decision to be full-line producers was based on two strongly held beliefs: that Japanese consumers trade up over time and that only by offering a full line could a firm obtain a balanced position in the entire market. A firm trying to compete in only the low end of the market would not have access to the high-end technology that would rapidly come to define the low-end market, and a firm selling only at the high end would not have the loyalty of consumers who were trading up.

The proliferation of products due to the increase in the number of price points was further aggravated by Olympus' decision to introduce multiple models for some price points. This change in strategy was prompted by the observation that market share associated with some price points was considerably larger than others. For high-volume price points, it was possible to identify different clusters of consumer preferences and profitably produce and market cameras designed specifically for those clusters. Under the new strategy, the number of models introduced at each price point was roughly proportional to the size of the market. Thus, the expected market share of each camera model offered was approximately the same unless it was designed to satisfy a low-volume strategic price point.

Once the price point of a new camera was identified, the free on board (FOB) price was calculated by subtracting the appropriate margin of the dealers and the U.S. subsidiary plus any import costs, such as freight and import duty. Target costs were established by subtracting the product's target margin from its FOB price. The product's target cost ratio was calculated by dividing the target cost by the FOB price. Every six months, the divisional manager set guidelines for acceptable cost ratios. These guidelines were developed in tandem with the division's six-month profit plans. In 1996, the divisional manager had identified the acceptable cost ratios as 85% for Tatsuno manufactured products and 60% for products manufactured overseas.

The target ratio for a given camera was set based on the historical cost ratios of similar cameras, the anticipated relative strength of competitive products, and the overall market conditions anticipated when the product was launched. Once the target cost ratio was established, it was converted into yen by multiplying it by the target FOB price. This yen-denominated target cost was used in all future comparisons with the estimated cost of production to ensure achievement of the target cost.

As part of the program to design low-cost products, target costs were set assuming aggressive cost reduction and high quality levels. A target cost system existed prior to 1987, but it was not considered effective. As part of the three-year program to reduce costs, the target cost system was improved and more attention was paid to achieving the targets. Aggressive cost reduction was achieved by applying three rationalization objectives. First, the number of parts in each unit was targeted for reduction. For example, the shutter unit for one class of compact camera was reduced from 105 to 56 pieces, a 47% reduction that led to a 58% decrease in production costs. Second, expensive, labor-intensive, and mechanical adjustment processes were eliminated wherever possible. Finally, metal and glass components were replaced with cheaper plastic ones. For instance, replacing metal components that required milling in an SLR body with plastic ones that could be molded reduced the SLR body costs by 28%. Similarly, replacing three of the glass elements with plastic ones in an eight-element compact camera lens reduced the lens cost by 29%

During the design phase, the anticipated cost ratio of new products was monitored on a frequent basis, typically two to three times before launch. The FOB price of a new product was sensitive to both market conditions and fluctuations in foreign exchange rates. Olympus sold 70% of its cameras overseas, and the FOB price of a product was the weighted average yen price. Since the FOB price for cameras sold overseas was designated in the appropriate foreign currency, fluctuations in the exchange rates caused the FOB price to change when measured in yen.

If the FOB priced changed sufficiently during the design phase to cause the anticipated cost ratio for the camera to fall outside the acceptable range by about 10%, then the target cost of the camera was reviewed and usually revised to bring the anticipated cost ratio back into the acceptable range. If the FOB price was falling, the result was a lower target cost that was harder to achieve. If it was rising, the result was higher profits, which were used to increase promotions and advertising fees as well as reduce prices to overseas subsidiaries.

The target cost was based on the price point for the distinctive feature of the camera. Research and development was responsible for identifying the other features of the camera (e.g., the type of flash and shutter units). Feature identification was an iterative process in which the cost of each new design was estimated and compared to the product's target cost. Production engineering developed estimated costs of production in collaboration with production. Research and development reviewed these estimates and revised them as deemed appropriate. Most revisions resulted in lower estimated costs. The research and development group identified additional ways to reduce the cost of the product either through minor product redesign or a more efficient production process.

Approximately 20% of the time, the estimated cost was equal to or less than the target cost, and the product design could be released for further analysis by the production group at Tatsuno. The other 80% of the time, further analysis was required by the research and development group. First, marketing was asked if the price point could be increased sufficiently so that the target cost was equal to the estimated cost. If the price could be increased, the product was released to the production group. If the market price could not be increased sufficiently, then the effect of reducing the functionality of the product was explored. Reducing the product's functionality decreased its estimated cost to produce. If these reductions were sufficient, the product was released to production.

If it was not possible to raise the price or reduce the production cost enough to reduce the estimated cost below the target cost, then a life-cycle profitability analysis was performed. In this analysis, the effect of potential cost reductions over the production life of the product was included in the financial analysis of the product's profitability. In 1990, Olympus expected to reduce production costs by about 35% across the production lifetime of its products. The product was released if these life-cycle savings were sufficient to make the product's overall profitability acceptable. If the estimated costs were still too high, even with these additional cost savings included, the product was abandoned unless some strategic reason for keeping the product could be identified. Such considerations typically focused on maintaining a full product line or creating a "flagship" product that demonstrated technological leadership.

Once a new product had passed the research and development design review it was released to Tatsuno production for evaluation. The Tatsuno design review consisted of evaluating the research and development design to determine where and how the new product would be produced. To make these decisions, a detailed production blueprint was developed. This blueprint identified both the technology required to produce the camera and the components it contained. Using this blueprint and cost estimates from suppliers and subsidiary plants, the production cost of the product was reestimated. If this cost was less than or equal to the target cost, the product was submitted to the division manager for approval for release to production.

If the estimated production cost was too high, then the design was subjected to additional analysis. Frequently, relatively minor changes in the product's design were all that were required to reduce the cost estimate to the target cost level. As long as these changes did not change the product's price point, then the functionality was changed and the product was submitted for approval. If the design changes would change the price point, the product was returned to the research and development group for redesign.

The estimated production cost used in the evaluation of the product was the expected cost of production three months after it went into production. The initial cost of production was higher than this target cost due to the work force's lack of experience with producing the new camera. As the work force gained experience, production costs would fall below target costs. Thus, the cost system would report negative variances for the first three months. In subsequent months the variances were expected to be positive. After the product was in production for six months, the target cost was changed to reflect any expected savings in the next six months due to the firm's cost-reduction programs.

Reducing Unnecessary Expenditures

The program to reduce unnecessary expenditures contained four components:

- It analyzed fixed expenses and curtailed any unnecessary expenditures.
- It analyzed and improved the procedures surrounding new product launching to reduce launch costs.
- It lowered the cost of purchased parts by implementing strict controls to ensure that target costs were met, widening the sources of procurement to obtain lower costs, and identifying multiple suppliers for each component to create competitive pressures.
- It strengthened and integrated its existing cost-reduction programs.

The first program focused on production costs, the second on the costs of defects, the third on capacity utilization costs, and the fourth on overhead expenses. The *production cost control and reduction program* focused primarily on removing material, labor, and some overhead costs from products; the division's profit plan identified cost-reduction targets for these costs for each product. These targets were considered challenging though achievable. The standards were set every six months and included the anticipated reductions that would be achieved in the next six months. Progress toward achieving these cost-reduction targets was monitored using variance analysis. Material price, work improvement, and "budgetary other" cost variances were computed weekly and accumulated monthly.

The material price variance was computed for each product by comparing the actual material cost to the standard material monthly target. This target was the average of the material costs for the previous six months adjusted for any anticipated changes in material costs in the upcoming month. The work improvement variances were the difference between the actual labor hours and the standard labor hour monthly target and between actual machine-hours and the standard machine-hour monthly target. Their target was calculated by assuming that labor cost reductions would occur evenly over time. To these linear cost reductions were added any specific reductions due to planned changes in the production process. The actual "budgetary other" costs, which included general expenses of the factory, were compared to budgeted costs to determine the other budgetary variance.

The second cost control and reduction program focused on the *costs of defective production*. To give these costs high visibility, they were not included in the standard costs and hence were not covered by the production cost control and reduction program. The cost of defects program consisted of setting cost of defects targets for each production group every six months. Groups were responsible for segments of the production process (at Tatsuno there were 10 groups).

Cost-reduction targets were identified for each product the group produced. Division management negotiated with the group leaders to set cost-reduction targets for each product the group produced. The group leaders recommended their cost-reduction targets, then divisional management reviewed these recommendations. If the overall reductions were sufficient to achieve the division's cost-reduction objectives, divisional management accepted the targets. If the overall savings were insufficient, the targets were renegotiated until the savings were acceptable.

The team leader and foreman in each group met daily to discuss their progress at achieving their reduction targets. Group and team leaders held weekly meetings to report on progress. If a group did not meet its weekly objectives, the group leader was expected to explain why the group had failed and what corrective actions would be taken. A request to engineering for assistance might be included in these actions. Occasionally, if a group consistently failed to meet its objectives, management would send in engineering—a serious blow to the group's reputation.

The third program focused on managing the costs associated with *capacity utilization*. The division's long-range management plan included estimates on the amount of overtime, actual working hours, operation days, and attendance rates. These estimates and the expected workload for each cost center were combined to give a capacity utilization cost budget for each center. This budget, which consisted of overall attendance rates and direct labor hours by cost center, was set every six months and updated each month. The updated monthly budget was used to compute a daily variance, which was reported to management weekly and accumulated monthly. The variance captured the over- or underutilization of direct labor capacity at the standard distribution rate of processing costs.

The final program focused on *overhead* expenses. These expenses included items such as the personnel expenses of support and administration, depreciation of factory buildings, and computer costs. The long-term management plan contained targeted levels for these expenses. Monthly budgets for these expenses were prepared taking into account the production volume for the six-month period, the introduction of new products, and any planned cost-reduction actions by the groups. Division management approved the resulting budget after any necessary adjustments were made. Each month, the budget was compared to actual and multiple cost center variances. Costs subjected to separate variance analysis included machine repair costs, machine maintenance costs, expenses of repair and maintenance personnel, and miscellaneous expenses. These variances were computed monthly because management felt that these expenses could not be controlled in a shorter time frame.

The four cost control and reduction programs each generated variances, which were combined in a monthly cost report. This report provided division management with important insights into the success of the cost control and reduction programs.

Improving Production Engineering

Olympus achieved the desired improvements to production engineering through a three-phase approach. This approach shortened production lead times by decreasing batch sizes. In the production area, for example, batches were halved and moved to a zero inventory system. Improving communications between sales and manufacturing reduced introduction times for new products and production lead times in general. For example, the MRP system was used to check inventory levels twice a day as opposed to once a week. Finally, office automation improved the level of general administrative support provided to both marketing and sales.

Adopting Innovative Manufacturing Processes

The program to introduce innovative production technologies focused on increasing the level of automation in manufacturing, particularly in the assembly, lens production, electronic parts mounting, and molding processes. In all these processes, the level of automation was significantly increased. For example, in assembly four major processes were automated in the three-year period after the new strategy began: the assembly of the film winding and shutter units, the adjustment and inspection processes for the focusing unit, the alignment and related inspection processes, and the transportation system for assembled parts.

Similarly, the molding, lens processing, and IC mounting stages of production underwent complex changes. All told, the program initiated some 23 different automation projects.

Shifting to Overseas Production

The cost reductions that the aggressive application of target costing and production cost reduction achieved were further augmented by shifting some of the manufacturing processes to lower-cost areas of the world. Olympus was the last of the camera firms to open such overseas facilities. Other manufacturers had opened such facilities in the late 1970s and early 1980s. Cost analyses at Olympus had indicated that the potential savings from shifting production offshore was about 15%. In 1988, the firm opened production facilities in Taiwan, Hong Kong, and Korea, and in China in 1989. The firm anticipated offshore production to reach ¥10 billion by 1991 and to expand rapidly thereafter.

The New Cost-Reduction Effort

The 1987 program to reconstruct Olympus' camera business achieved most of its objectives. The program to introduce new products was relatively successful at recapturing lost market share. The firm increased camera sales volume by almost 70% to ¥50 billion from ¥30 billion and almost doubled its market share for compact cameras. Unfortunately, the program was not as successful for the SLR product line. The firm continued to lose market share from 1987 through 1990, but with the introduction of a completely new camera, the IS-1, the firm hoped to turn the situation around.

The combined results of the cost-reduction program were impressive. By the end of 1990 every measure of productivity at Tatsuno had improved.

For example, overall production had increased by 50%, the production cost ratio had fallen by 20%, the production value per employee had risen 70%, and gross added value per person had increased over 125%. Simultaneously, the work-in-process inventory had not increased despite the higher activity level and the fact that lead time had almost halved.

Despite the success of the 1987 plan, top management at Olympus determined that additional cost reductions would be necessary in the coming years. In particular, they were worried by three trends that together would place significant pressure on the firm's profitability. These trends were an increased proliferation in products required to satisfy consumer demand in the domestic market, an additional shortening of the product life cycle to less than a year, and reduced selling prices. The decision to introduce a new program was driven in part by the observation that the savings from the 1987 plan had gone down in recent months.

At the heart of the new plan were two important concepts. The first was innovations in technology, and the second was functional group management. Innovations in technology consisted of applying new production technology—primarily automation—to all stages of production. Separate automation projects were initiated for camera assembly, lens processing, molding, and electrical components. The most ambitious of these projects was a fully automated robotic assembly line designed to assemble cameras. This line was undergoing evaluation at Tatsuno before being released to other assembly facilities.

Functional group management consisted of dividing the production process into a number of autonomous groups. Ten such groups were identified at the Tatsuno plant. These groups were given full management responsibility for their area of responsibility or cost center and were expected to manage it as if it were a separate company. Thus each group would effectively become a separate profit center. Top management felt that holding the groups responsible for their profitability would promote greater pressure to reduce costs and hence increase profitability than would any conventional cost-reduction program. By 1990, senior management had yet to operationalize the function group management concept but believed that it was going to play a critical role in the firm's future.

APPENDIX

The Evolution of the Cost System

From 1970 to 1990, the firm's cost system had undergone three major changes. Prior to 1976, there was only one overhead rate at the Tatsuno plant. The system directly traced some material costs to products, but all other costs were allocated. These allocated costs were divided into two categories: processing and overhead. Processing costs included the indirect material, direct and indirect labor, and direct expenses of the production process. Direct labor was allocated because the direct labor wage rates varied by individual, and it was considered too expensive to assign the cost directly to products. The overhead costs contained the indirect material, indirect labor, and indirect expenses associated with support and administration. The processing overhead costs were combined and divided by the number of direct labor hours to give an average allocation rate. The reported cost of a product was given by the sum of the direct material charge and the direct labor hours that the product consumed multiplied by the allocation rate. Such a simple system was considered adequate because there were only small differences in the cost structure of the products. In addition, the level of automation was small, as was depreciation. The stated objective of this system was to differentiate material cost from other expenses and provide mechanisms for total cost reduction.

In 1977, the cost system was updated. The overhead costs were split into two categories: procurement costs and other costs. Procurement costs were those costs associated with obtaining raw material and purchased parts. They included the personnel expenses of the procurement section, transportation charges, car fares, and other miscellaneous expenses. A single allocation rate was determined for processing costs and some of the other costs. A separate rate was determined for procurement costs and the allocated expenses of the administration and production technical sections. The costs of these two sections were allocated to the production and procurement sections based on head count. The procurement costs were allocated to products based on the sum of the direct material charge plus the allocated processing costs. The primary purpose of this system was to draw attention to the procurement costs, which had grown substantially over time. This increase was due both to an increase in production capacity, which was accompanied by a corresponding increase in the volume of procured parts, and by an increase in the ratio of procured to internally manufactured parts. The other important change in the system was its focus on the cost of quality. The cost of defects was isolated from the standard costs to give it more visibility. Separate variances were computed for standard production and defects.

In 1983, the cost system was again updated. The general structure was maintained, but now multiple allocation rates were computed for processing costs. The production process was split into 10 different cost centers and different overhead rates were computed for each center.

Examples of the cost centers included camera final assembly, electronic flexible board assembly, lens processing, and lens assembly. In addition, the firm had begun to enter into OEM contracts with other firms that would produce components for Olympus. The support and administration costs for the OEM production were significantly different from Tatsuno production. To capture this difference, the two overhead cost allocation rates were computed, one for general suppliers and the other for OEM suppliers. These two rates replaced the single procurement rate computed in the prior system. The treatment of other costs as partially related to processing and partially related to procurement was suspended, and all other costs were allocated as part of the support and administration costs. The primary purpose of this system was to provide improved control over production and support and administration costs.

CHAPTER 22

OMACHI OLYMPUS COMPANY, LTD.

INTRODUCTION

Omachi Olympus Co., Ltd. (Omachi) was a wholly-owned subsidiary of Olympus Optical Co., Ltd. (Olympus). Omachi produced complex, curved, plastic moldings primarily for camera products made by Olympus' consumer products division. The firm was located in Omachi City, in the Nagano Prefecture some 150 miles from Tokyo.

Omachi employed approximately 150 workers—a mix of full-time, part-time, and Olympus Optical employees. Most Omachi employees worked full time and enjoyed lifetime employment. Omachi's part-time employees were employed by the hour; their contracts were renewed every three months and they did not have lifetime employment. The Olympus employees located at Omachi were primarily production engi-

Professor Robin Cooper of The Peter F. Drucker Graduate Management Center at The Claremont Graduate School prepared this case as the basis for class discussion rather than to illustrate either effective or ineffective handling of an administrative situation.

neers assigned to Omachi for several years at a time; they helped Omachi engineers find ways to reduce costs.

The firm managed its headcount by first pulling in work from its subcontractors and then by reducing the size of the part-time labor force. Omachi wanted to keep as many people as possible gainfully employed and not violate the firm's lifetime employment practices. The part-time employees were less skilled than their full-time counterparts and consequently were paid less; however, both part-time and full-time employees received the same benefits.

OLYMPUS OPTICAL COMPANY

Olympus Optical Company, Ltd., and its subsidiaries and affiliates manufactured and sold opto-electronic equipment and other related products. The firm's major product lines included cameras, video camcorders, microscopes, endoscopes, and clinical analyzers. Olympus also produced microcassette tape recorders, laser-optical pickup systems, and industrial lenses. Olympus consisted of six divisions plus a headquarters facility. Four of the six divisions—consumer products, scientific equipment, endoscope, and diagnostics—were responsible for generating revenues. The other two divisions were responsible for corporate research and production engineering, respectively. Headquarters was responsible for corporate planning, general affairs, personnel, and accounting and finance.

The consumer products division manufactured and sold 35mm cameras, video camcorders, and microcassette tape recorders. In 1995, the division employed 900 people (18% of the total Olympus work force) and generated revenues of ¥53 billion (31% of Olympus Optical's revenues). Cameras were by far the firm's most important consumer product, accounting for ¥45 billion in revenues. Cameras were sold worldwide, with approximately 75% sold outside of Japan. The division consisted of six departments: division planning, quality assurance, marketing, product development, production, and overseas manufacturing. Responsibility for the division's production facilities was centered at the Tatsuno plant, which opened in 1981 and was the firm's main camera production facility. Tatsuno was responsible for trial production of experimental products, introductory production of new products, and, to a limited degree, camera and lens production. Tatsuno was approximately 30 miles from Omachi, for which it was responsible.

PRODUCT MIX

Omachi produced three major types of products: molded parts, assemblies of molded parts, and molds for some of the simpler parts it produced. The plant ran non-stop year round with only three breaks: New Year, Golden Week, and summer vacation. The only exception was the prism section; due to demand, this section worked 24 hours a day, 365 days a year. The night shift for the prism section was fully automated and ran without manual intervention. In contrast, the molding section's night shift consisted of 3 employees.

Omachi's product mix had changed quite rapidly over the years. Olympus Camera's shift from metal to plastic parts caused the number of auto-lathe-press (ALP) parts to decrease rapidly from 1980 to 1988. In 1995, no ALP parts were produced. Plastic molding commenced in 1978 and by 1981 dominated ALP production. In 1995, the firm produced over 600 different moldings per month, requiring quite complex scheduling and production control. These 600 moldings were used in 21 different Olympus cameras.

Assemblies were introduced in 1982 and after 1987 grew rapidly; in 1995 they accounted for about 50% of sales revenues. Assembled products included viewfinder units for compact cameras and some flexible circuit boards. Viewfinder assembly was shifted to Omachi from Tatsuno when viewfinders became 100% plastic. Because nearly all of the parts for the viewfinder were manufactured at Omachi and dust in the viewfinder created quality problems, it made sense for Omachi to manufacture parts as well as assemble the viewfinders.

Omachi began to produce molds in 1993. By 1995, Omachi produced only relatively simple molds; Tatsuno still produced the more complex ones. The introduction of mold production at Omachi was a move designed to make the firm more independent of its parent and to reflect restructuring of Olympus Camera. Olympus Camera expected to move up to 60% of its domestic production capacity overseas, primarily to China. This restructuring was expected to create a 30% reduction in production volume at Omachi. To keep the work force gainfully employed, Olympus Camera shifted simple mold production from external subcontractors to Omachi. Shifting mold production to Omachi was initiated because the quality of the finished products depended upon the quality of the molds. If Omachi engineers designed the mold, then yields were typically higher because they understood more about molding than subcontractors. Thus, having mold production and molding at the same facility provided better control over the quality of products.

RELATIONSHIP WITH OLYMPUS OPTICAL'S CONSUMER PRODUCTS DIVISION

As part of its overall planning procedure, Olympus' consumer products division set Omachi's five-year long-term plan. In addition, the division produced a rolling three-year mid-term budget. The division also set six-month budgets every six months. Unlike the other plans, which were at the business-line level, the six-month budgets were at the product-line level (cameras, camcorders, binoculars, and pearlcorders). After the division set the six-month budgets, profit objectives for the divisions and subsidiaries were set. Achieving the profit objective was considered more important than meeting the sales objective. However, keeping revenues high and hence production at capacity—thereby keeping the work force occupied—was also considered critical.

Using these six-month budgets, the marketing department developed a division-wide sales plan at the individual-product level. After adjusting for inventory changes, the sales plan was used to develop the production plan. The section of the production plan that related to Omachi was negotiated with Tatsuno; only after it was accepted was it shown to Omachi. Production plans consisted of existing and new products. For existing products, the standard cost was expected to be 3% lower than in the previous budget (this 3% was applied to all components). Therefore, Omachi's selling prices were automatically reduced by 3% every six months.

The 3% cost-reduction target was the same for all subsidiary companies that reported to Tatsuno, and was based on historical trends. The 3% target was considered fairly easy to achieve in good times, but could be very hard to achieve when sales were down. Omachi had difficulty in recent years achieving the target because of decreasing production volumes as Olympus moved its production offshore.

Using simulations, Omachi developed a profit budget based on the production volumes in the six-month budget, the target selling prices set by Tatsuno, and their expected costs. Omachi set final unit prices for its products from this budget; if these were higher than the prices set by Tatsuno, Omachi would request that the target costs be relaxed.

Olympus built a 3% profit target into the Omachi budget. Omachi faced intense competition from outside suppliers and was not expected to generate higher profits because, as a wholly-owned Olympus subsidiary, it did not have to stand on its own. Therefore, its profitability, though low by industry standards, was considered acceptable. Because Olympus had shifted production offshore, Omachi lost economies of scale as its production volumes decreased. Consequently, Omachi had increasing difficulty maintaining its profitability target. If Omachi became unprofitable, Tatsuno had agreed to cover the losses by making a total cost allowance that would enable Omachi to break even. When Tatsuno made such an allowance, it was forced to find other ways to reduce costs (e.g., by increasing labor efficiency to bring in-house some previously outsourced components, or by reducing material costs. In this context, material costs included both materials that were used in the camera and those consumed in the production process, such as cooling chemicals, jigs, and tools).

Most years, Omachi achieved its 3% overall profit target. Of the 600 components manufactured in 1995, 60% had cost ratios (Omachi cost/Olympus target cost) of under 97%, which therefore exceeded the firm's 3% profit target. The other 40% had cost ratios above 97%. This 60%/40% mix was relatively stable. For example, when Omachi began producing components for three new Olympus products in 1994, the average cost ratio for two of these products was under 97%.

TARGET COSTING

Olympus' consumer products division used its target costing system to set the cost of manufacture of a new product and its components. The components' target costs were Omachi's selling prices. The first step in setting target costs was to identify the price point at which a new camera model would sell. For most new products, the price point was already established. For example, in 1994 the simplest compact cameras were sold in the United States at the $100 price point. The actual selling prices for a given camera varied depending upon the distribution channel (e.g., mass merchandiser versus specialty store). Thus, cameras at the $100 price point would sell for between approximately $85 and $125. The appropriate price point for a camera was determined by its distinctive feature (e.g., magnification capability of the camera's zoom lens, or the camera's small size). The relationship between distinctive features and price points was determined from the competitive analysis and technology review used in the development of the product plan. The product plan thus described cameras only in terms of their distinctive features. Other features were added as the design neared completion.

A camera's target cost was based on the price point of its distinctive feature. Research and development was responsible for identifying other features (e.g., the type of flash and shutter units). Feature identification was an iterative process in which the cost of each new design was estimated and compared to the product's target cost. Approximately 20% of the time, the estimated cost was equal to or less than the target cost and the product design could be released to Tatsuno's production group for further analysis. The rest of the time, further analysis was required by the research and development group. First, marketing was asked if the price point could be increased sufficiently so that the target cost was equal to the estimated cost. If the price could be increased, the product was released to the production group. If the market price could not be increased sufficiently, then the effect of reducing the product's functionality was explored. Reducing the product's functionality decreased its estimated cost to produce—if these reductions were sufficient, the product was released to production.

If it was not possible to increase the price or to lower the production cost enough to reduce the estimated cost below the target cost, then a life cycle profitability analysis was performed. In this analysis, the effect of potential cost reductions over the product's production life was included in the financial analysis of the product's profitability. In 1995, Olympus expected to reduce production costs by about 35% across the production lifetime of its products. A product was released if these life cycle savings were sufficient to make its overall profitability acceptable. If the estimated costs were still too high even with these additional cost savings, the product was abandoned unless there was some strategic reason for keeping it (such as maintaining a full product line or creating a "flagship" product that demonstrated technological leadership).

Once a new product had passed the research and development design review it was released to Tatsuno production for evaluation. The Tatsuno design review consisted of evaluating the research and development design to determine where and how the new product would be produced. To make these decisions, a detailed production blueprint was developed. This blueprint identified the technology required to produce the camera and its components. Using this blueprint and cost estimates from suppliers and subsidiary plants (such as Omachi), the product's production cost was reestimated. If this cost was less than or equal to the target cost, the product was submitted to the division manager for approval for release to production.

If the estimated production cost was too high, the design was further analyzed. Frequently, only minor changes in the product's design were required to reduce the cost estimate to the target cost level. As long as these changes did not change the product's price point, then the functionality was changed and the product was submitted for approval. If the design changes would change the price point, the product was returned to the research and development group for redesign.

Usually, Omachi accepted Olympus' target costs for the components it manufactured. Only if a simulation showed that a target cost was unachievable would Omachi negotiate with Olympus (for example, if a new product required more technical work or was unusually complex). Ordinarily, Olympus would agree to temporarily relax the target cost to give Omachi time to reduce the cost of the components so that they would be profitable at the target cost when it was finally invoked. When a component's target cost was increased to allow Omachi to remain profitable, then Tatsuno engineers had to find equivalent cost reduction elsewhere in the camera design. Only by finding such savings could the camera's overall target cost be achieved.

If Olympus was unwilling to relax the target cost of a new component sufficiently to guarantee Omachi an acceptable profit level, then Omachi could refuse to make the part. This option was considered critical to maintaining the balance of power between Tatsuno and Omachi. Without it, Omachi risked failing to make its 3% profit objective.

Olympus' target costing system was not as draconian as it might sound. Considerable negotiation went into setting the target costs for new components. If a new component was launched in time to be incorporated into the next six-month plan, then Omachi and Tatsuno would negotiate the component's target cost. If the component was introduced too rapidly to be incorporated into the six-month plan, then Omachi would put it into production; if it could not be manufactured for its target cost, then Tatsuno would pay Omachi the full production cost (i.e., more than the component's target cost). The next six-month plan would reflect the negotiated selling price for the component, which might still exceed its target costs.

If Omachi thought a new component's target cost was too low, it negotiated with Tatsuno to either change the component's specifications or to get the target cost increased. If Omachi expected to exceed its 3% profit target, then it might accept a target cost that was below its production costs.

The Olympus engineers at Omachi supported the negotiations. Because a design was considered fixed in most cases, the engineers used value engineering to try to reduce the costs of the product. For example, they might change the production steps so that either cycle time or material consumption was reduced. Cycle time might be reduced by decreasing the amount of material in the stems that were attached to the finished parts, so the reduced material content cooled more rapidly. Material costs could be reduced by using less expensive polymers. Alternatively, engineers might increase the yield of good parts by reducing the amount of dust that was in precision optical components or by decreasing the number of parts ruined when they were cut off their stems (by using a curved cut rather than a straight cut, or by changing the size of the stem to reduce the risk of dimpling in large parts).

A recent innovation reduced costs by doubling up on the molds, which allowed twice as many parts to be produced in a cycle. This approach was particularly effective because most of the cycle time was spent letting the polymers cool sufficiently so that the part could be ejected without deforming. However, the additional molds meant extra expense. Consequently, this technique was used only for small components with long cooling times, such as lenses and prisms. It could not be used for large components because the double molds were too heavy for the injection machines.

PLANNING AT OMACHI

Tatsuno provided Omachi management with three major pieces of information: the sales volume by product, the target costs of all new components, and the cost-reduction plan (3%) for all existing products. Omachi used this information to determine its production volumes for each product; these volumes were derived from the sales volumes by including an allowance for yield. Material costs were determined from these production volumes using the actual cost at the end of the last six-month period, and for new products, using their target costs.

The production volumes were also used to estimate the headcounts in the production hour plan. This plan identified the number of days and hours per day worked, allowing total production hours to be determined.

The process plan was established next—this captured the processing costs per hour and other expenses such as personnel, equipment leases, and maintenance costs (personnel expenses included both salaries and wages plus benefits). Finally, all of these plans were consolidated into the six-month Omachi profit plan. In addition, a monthly plan was developed that was not based solely on the six-month plan. These monthly plans were adjusted for the actual performance achieved in the previous month in order to keep the monthly plans as realistic as possible.

COST SYSTEM

Omachi's cost system was based upon the cycle time to mold a part. Each molded product had a standard production time—the time it took the machine to complete a production cycle from closing the press, adding the pellets, melting the plastic, letting it cool, opening the press, and ejecting the part. This cycle time was used to allocate both overhead and all labor costs to the products. Material costs were added to the cycle time cost to give total product costs. A single cycle time rate of ¥26 per hour was used throughout the facility.

"Actual" costs were determined by replacing the standard cycle times with actual cycle times. No attempt was made to change the rates to reflect actual costs. Thus, the variances from standard to actual captured only changes in cycle times, not in spending levels.

VARIANCE ANALYSIS

Both Olympus and Omachi performed monthly variance analysis to see how close to plan Omachi was performing. The major difference between the two sets of variances was that Olympus ran them on total production cost because it was not concerned about performance at the individual-product level. In contrast, Omachi ran variances at the product level because it was concerned about how close to standard it was achieving on each product. Product-level variance analysis allowed Omachi engineers to better focus additional cost-reduction efforts on products that were having manufacturing problems or were not meeting their cost-reduction objectives.

Olympus held production conferences every other month to discuss production variances in order to determine how close to plan they were and what actions should be taken if performance was below expectations. These meetings had been held monthly, but experience had shown that a longer interval made trends easier to spot. Individuals from Olympus, its subsidiaries, and its subcontractors attended these conferences. The Tatsuno Cost Result was generated from the conference, which summarized production results of all subsidiaries and subcontractors over the last two months.

After three months, the six-month plan was reforecast to see how close the firm expected to come to plan at the end of the six-month planning period. These reforecasts, called Terminal Forecasts, included detailed countermeasures on how to get back on track with the six-month plan.

THE RELATIONSHIP BETWEEN OMACHI AND TATSUNO

The relationship between Tatsuno and Omachi was basically friendly—both firms worked together to achieve their joint objectives. However, both firms agreed that the negotiations were very tough, with neither side readily conceding. Tatsuno would also subject Omachi to increased quality control if it felt that Omachi was not doing an adequate job. In turn, Omachi would ask for relief if it felt that a drastic change in its production plan was caused by an error on Tatsuno's part as opposed to a change in sales volumes due to market conditions. To maintain this relationship, frequent meetings were held to ensure that the firms were in sync.

CHAPTER 23

TOKYO MOTOR WORKS, LTD.: TARGET COSTING SYSTEM

INTRODUCTION

In terms of worldwide production, Tokyo Motor Works, Ltd. (TMW) was by 1990 one of the world's top ten automobile manufacturers. In 1990, TMW produced just over 2 million vehicles, supplying approximately 4% of the world's demand for cars and trucks. Of these vehicles, slightly over 1.2 million were passenger cars. TMW, founded in 1945, produced vehicles at 20 plants in 15 countries and marketed them in 110 countries through 200 distributorships and over 6,000 dealerships.

The domestic Japanese passenger automobile market was characterized by intense competition. The largest manufacturer was Toyota. Nissan was second with approximately 25% market share, followed by Honda, Mazda, and TMW (each with 9%), and finally Isuzu, which had a 3% market share. In an attempt to increase its market share in the expanding but fiercely contested domestic market, TMW had recently implemented a plan to achieve annual domestic sales of 1 million cars by 1994, and to obtain the number one rating in terms of customer satisfaction. At the core of this strategy lay its target costing system and the design of products that were engineered around clearly defined concepts chosen to offer customers automobiles that matched their lifestyles.

The range of product offerings that automobile firms felt obliged to produce had been steadily increasing since the 1950s. Despite this pressure, TMW had chosen to systematically reduce the number of distinct models it would introduce in the 1990s. This decision reflected two additional trends. First, the differences between consumers in the three major markets—Japan, North America, and Europe—were decreasing and second, the costs associated with introducing new models were increasing. The decrease in differences among consumers in the three major markets reduced the need to develop models specific to a single market. The increased costs associated with launching new models made it difficult to make acceptable profits if the number of new models introduced each year was too large. The reduced requirement for market-specific models coupled with the increased costs of launching each model suggested to TMW's top management that overall profitability would be increased by reducing the number of distinct models supported, but maintaining the same level of overall effort to market the remaining models.

INTRODUCING NEW PRODUCTS

TMW, over the years, had developed a formal procedure to introduce new products. One of the major elements of this procedure was a sophisticated target costing system that relied heavily upon consumer analysis. In this system, a target selling price for each new model was first established; second, a target margin was determined based upon corporate profitability objectives; and finally, the model's target cost was identified as the difference between the target selling price and the target margin. Once the target cost of the new model was established, value engineering was used to ensure that the new model, when it entered production, could be manufactured at the desired target cost.

As the conceptual design of the new model progressed, additional consumer analysis and financial analysis were undertaken. Consumer analysis was used to obtain a better idea of the price range over which the model would sell and the level of functionality that the consumer expected. The financial analysis consisted of a rough profitability study in which the profitability of the highest-volume variant of the new model was estimated using historical cost estimates and the latest estimate of that variant's target price. This target price was determined by taking into account a number of internal and external factors. The internal factors considered included the position of the model in the firm's product matrix and the strategic and profitability objectives of top management for that model. The external factors considered included the corporation's image and level of customer loyalty in the model's niche, the expected quality level and functionality of the model compared to competitive offerings, the model's expected market share, and, finally, the expected price of competitive models.

Cost Planning

Cost planning at TMW was primarily a program to reduce product costs at the design stage. TMW first set its cost planning goals and then set out to achieve those goals through aggressive design changes. To correctly assess the gains made, the exact amount of cost reduction achieved through design changes was estimated after excluding all other factors that affected costs, such as increases in material and labor prices. The target costing system was at the heart of the cost planning process.

The first stage of target costing was designed to determine whether the new model could be manufactured at an acceptable profit. The process began by developing an order sheet detailing the characteristics of the 20 to 30 major functions of the proposed model. Examples of the major functions identified included the engine, air conditioner, transmission, and sound system. The characteristics of each major function were chosen to satisfy the collection of consumer mind-sets for which the model was designed. For example, the engine specified for an SF would be a high-performance one, while for the Celestieal it would be smaller, less powerful, and less expensive. The current cost of the model was determined by summing the current manufacturing cost of each major function of the new model. This current cost was compared with the model's allowable cost to determine the level of cost reduction required to achieve the desired level of profitability.

The measurement process started with cost tables, used to estimate the current cost of existing models. These cost tables were kept up-to-date for changes in material prices, labor rates, and production volume levels that helped determine both depreciation and overhead charges. The estimated cost of the existing model was used as the basis for estimating the cost of the new model without additional savings. Comparison of this estimated cost to the vehicle's target cost gave the desired level of savings, or cost planning goal, as it was called.

The allowable cost of the new model was determined by subtracting its target profit margin from its target price. The target margin was determined by careful consideration of available information on the consumer, the firm's anticipated future product mix, and its long-term profit objective. Each new model's target margin was established by running simulations of the firm's overall profitability for the next 10 years if it were to sell the models identified in the future product matrix at their expected sales volumes. The simulations started by plotting the actual profit margins of existing products. The desired profitability of planned models was then added and the firm's overall profitability determined over the years at various sales levels. This predicted overall profitability was compared to the firm's long-term profitability objectives set by senior management. Once a satisfactory future product matrix was established that achieved the firm's profit objective, the target margins for each new model were set.

To help minimize the risk that the firm would not achieve its overall profitability targets, the simulations explored the impact on overall profitability of different price/margin curves for different product mixes. For example, historically higher margins have been earned on higher-priced vehicles. However, with the reduced product offering and the increased profitability expected, the future curve might be higher. Alternatively, since there was no guarantee that the existing relationship between price and margin would remain unchanged, simulations were also run to explore the impact of fundamentally different relationships between selling price and margins.

The primary use of target costing was to bring the target cost and the estimated cost of a product into line by better specification and design. Simply estimating the cost of new products was not the purpose of the target costing system. Its ultimate goal was to enable a product to attain its profit targets throughout its life.

- Specifications like size (length, width, wheelbase, and interior space), weight, mileage, engine (type, displacement, and maximum power), transmission (gear and moderation ratios), chassis (suspension and brake types), and body components;
- Development budget;
- Development schedule; and
- Retail price and sales targets.

New models basically maintained the same product concept as their predecessors. The development plan might define some specifications for the new model, but styling was left unspecified; usually no more than a vague image was mentioned.

The price increase for an added function was not always equal to its selling price as a stand-alone option. The incremental price for a given increase in functionality might be lowered because of the firm's strategy for the vehicle model in question and because of the pricing strategies of competitors. As functions were added to the standard version the selling price was increased until it reached the upper limit for that class of vehicle. This upper limit was the maximum selling price that the firm believed it could set for the new vehicle. When this limit was reached, the only potential benefit from adding functionality was in increased sales.

The uncertainty associated with market conditions when the product was introduced some four years after the design project began forced the firm to delay setting the functionality of the standard version as long as possible. Therefore, the target price and margin for the product, and thereby the associated target unit price, were set quite some time before product launch.

The exact functionality of the standard version was only set when factors such as competitive offerings, foreign exchange rates, and user demand were better understood. Changing the functionality of the standard version allowed TMW to increase the probability that the new model would achieve its desired level of profitability. Similarly, the actual selling price was not fixed until just before the product was launched. Delaying these two critical decisions reduced significantly the uncertainty faced by the firm. For example, the incremental value assigned to an air bag in the US market might have been $450 but the competition had set the incremental value at $700 (in which case, TMW might increase its price by the difference). Similarly, if the competitive prices were lower, TMW would drop its prices to match.

The goal of cost planning was to refine the unit profit needed to achieve the profit target and thus the amount to be trimmed from the new product's cost through cost planning activities. Rather than adding together all of the costs for a new model, TMW's approach to cost planning was to sum the differences in cost between new and current models. There were several advantages to this approach. First, cost planning could begin even before blueprints for the first test model were drawn. Second, estimating the total difference, instead of the total cost, tended to be less troublesome and more accurate, and finally, it helped the related divisions understand cost fluctuations. The differences approach was considered more accurate because the typical new model was heavily based upon existing designs. Trying to estimate the cost of a new vehicle from scratch would, in management's opinion, introduce more errors than using existing data and modifying it accordingly. The approach was more helpful to the design divisions because it highlighted the areas of the new model that were different from existing designs. It was these new designs that required most of the work in the design divisions.

The estimated cost of a new model was therefore described as the cost of the current model plus the cost of any design change. Thus, for every increment in the functionality of a new model there was an estimated incremental price and cost. This approach therefore allowed the firm to measure the incremental profitability of each new function it built into a new model of vehicle.

Value Engineering

Once the performance specifications and the cost reduction targets were distributed to the design division, value engineering began. The designers' top priority was to create high-quality, high-performance products that satisfied the customer. At the same time, they were expected to attain their cost targets.

Each design division becomes responsible for attaining its respective cost reduction goal. The specifics of parts, materials, and machining processes were left to their discretion. Exceptions were made for large, especially costly parts. The chief engineer would sometimes specify cost-reduction targets for specific parts to the related divisions. These specific parts cost-reduction targets were set at the same time as the divisional targets. For example, consider a part that is estimated to cost ¥8,000. If it is judged that a cost break on this particular part will contribute significantly to attaining the target goal for the entire model, the chief engineer may ask the related design division for a parts-specific cost reduction of perhaps ¥1,000.

Value engineering and the identification of a target price were an interactive process. When the allowable costs were considered to be too far below the estimated cost the appropriate price range and functionality were reviewed until an allowable cost that was considered achievable was identified. The first step in the value engineering stage was to prepare a detailed parts list for the new model. This parts list included all of the components required in the new model divided by functional lines. This listing was analyzed to see which components would likely be sourced internally versus externally. Suppliers, both internal and external, were provided with a description of each component and potential production volumes. Suppliers were expected to provide price and delivery timing estimates for each component.

After the first value engineering stage was completed a major review of the new model was undertaken. This review included an updated profitability study and an analysis of the performance characteristics of the model. In the profitability study the expected profitability of the model, given by the target price minus its draft target cost, was compared to the latest estimates of the capital investment and remaining research and development expenditures required to complete the design of the product and allow production to commence. In the performance analysis, factors such as the quality of the hardware, engine capacity, exhaust emissions, and safety were considered. If both the financial and performance analyses were considered acceptable, the project to introduce the new vehicle was authorized and the model was then shifted from the conceptual design to the product development stage.

The next step in the development of a new model was to produce the engineering drawings for trial production. Value engineering was used at this stage of product development to determine allowable costs for each of the components in every major function of the automobile. This estimation was achieved by identifying a cost-reduction objective for each component. There were several ways that cost-reduction objectives for components were identified. First, competitors' products were purchased, disassembled, and analyzed. From this analysis, ideas for cost reduction were sometimes generated.

Second, the parts suppliers were asked to generate cost-reduction ideas. An incentive plan was used to motivate the suppliers. For example, if a cost-reduction idea was submitted by Yokohama (a supplier of hydraulic systems) and accepted by TMW, Yokohama would be awarded a significant percentage of the contract for that component for a specified time period, say 50% for 12 months. This incentive scheme was viewed as particularly important because even if a cost reduction could not be achieved for this model, it signaled to the suppliers that when the next model was developed this component would be subject to cost-reduction pressures. In addition, TMW would share information about the innovation with its other suppliers, which typically were Yokohama's competitors. For example, TMW held technical exchange meetings with its suppliers several times a month, and asked its suppliers that had developed innovative techniques to share them with both TMW and its related companies. This information sharing allowed competitors to match relatively rapidly Yokohama's costs. Once competitors' costs are reduced, the target selling price rapidly falls to match the underlying production costs.

Most of the time, it is up to suppliers' engineering staff (such as Yokohama) to continuously innovate and find ways to manufacture its products so that they can be sold at target prices and make adequate returns. In theory, TMW is not interested in the level of Yokohama's profit margins, only its ability to provide products at the target price. Thus, if Yokohama finds a way to significantly reduce the cost of one of its products it can make a high return on that product. However, since there is considerable sharing of production information between Yokohama and TMW, it does not take long for the target price to reflect the new production cost.

Third, ways to increase the commonality of parts across variations and models were identified. For example, the same seats might be used in two different models. Fourth, ways to reduce the number of components in each model were identified. For example, originally the kick plates used to protect the door were held in place by plastic nuts. Recently, a way to mold the plastic interior of the door so that no nuts were required had been developed.

Accounting was not involved in the value engineering process, which was the responsibility of the cost design and engineering department. The primary function of accounting was to set the final target cost for each model variant and ensure that the vehicles were manufactured for that amount. As the vehicle entered production, accounting would monitor all component and assembly costs and if these were not in line with the final target costs then they would notify cost design and engineering that the final target costs were not being met. When the target costs were exceeded, additional value engineering was performed to reduce costs back to the target levels. Thus, the fourth and final value engineering stage ensured that the actual component and assembly costs were equal to their final target costs. When the value engineering process was completed, the product was ready for mass production.

From Cost Planning to Mass Production

Since the main concern of cost planning was design, cost planning was effectively finished when the project entered the mass production stage. Unless something unusual happened, Tokyo Motors rarely failed to attain its cost planning goals. Follow-up studies were undertaken for about a year after start-up to ensure that mass production was going forward at the planned standard cost. The standard cost and target cost for a product were not identical. The target cost was established before all of the details of production were known; therefore, it did not reflect the current conditions such at the going rate for labor and materials or the specific plant in which the vehicle would be manufactured. In contrast, the product's standard cost was adjusted for all these factors.

The essential point was that target cost in cost planning and standard cost for mass production were treated as different standards with different functions. In cost planning, costs were estimated from the cost tables as the sum of the differences between the current and new models, though at this point the planners do not know on which lines the model's production will occur.

Standard cost at the mass production stage changed depending upon the specific production line upon which the product was manufactured and the prevailing conditions at the time. For instance, production on lines working below capacity pushed costs up, while production on lines working at close to full capacity led to the best cost performance. At the cost planning stage, it was difficult to imagine the details of line conditions for every part and thus accurately to reflect these conditions in cost estimates. At the mass production stage, the lines that worked best under the current circumstances were chosen for production of the new model. ("Best" in this context means at the optimum for the entire company, which was not always optimal for the new model.) Once the lines were chosen based on these criteria, the standard cost was calculated. The production division then began its effort to maintain or even improve on the standard cost. Such improvements were under the auspices of the firm's kaizen program.

CHAPTER 24

TOYO RADIATOR COMPANY, LTD.

INTRODUCTION

The Highest Technology Begets the Highest Quality

Low Cost is Born Out of Originality and Ingenuity

— Company mottos

Toyo Radiator Company, Ltd. (Toyo) was founded in 1936 as a radiator supplier to the fledgling Japanese automobile industry; it was independent from the major keiretsus. Over the years, Toyo diversified into all arenas of heat-exchange applications. By 1995, it sold heat-exchange products for use in automobiles, heavy construction and agricultural vehicles, air conditioners for home and office, and freezers. Its product lines included radiators, oil coolers, inter-coolers, evaporators, and condensers. In 1995, it was one of the world's largest independent heat-exchange equipment manufacturers for construction equipment.

Headquartered in Tokyo, Toyo operated a technical research center and four production facilities. The technical research center, located at Hatano in the Kanagawa prefecture, was responsible for the firm's research and product development. It was split into three major groups: (1) the research group, which conducted basic research, in particular, the replacement of traditional copper products with aluminum and plastic; (2) the development group, which developed and tested new products; and (3) the experimental group, which evaluated new products and rigorously tested them for durability and performance.

The four production facilities were located in Nagoya, Higashiura, Yokaichi, and Hatano. The Nagoya facility, opened in 1940, produced small-scale copper and brass radiators for passenger vehicles. Higashiura, opened in 1985, manufactured mainly aluminum radiators for use in passenger and mini-recreational vehicles. Yokaichi, opened in 1969, produced evaporators and condensers for air conditioners and freezers. It also produced aluminum radiators for motorcycles and charged air coolers, the firm's latest products.

The Hatano facility produced large-scale radiators for construction equipment such as road rollers, power shovels, and bulldozers. Hatano consisted of two major plants, the original Hatano plant, opened in 1960, and the Togawa plant, opened in 1981. There were four major customers for Hatano products: the Mitsubishi Group (Shin Caterpillar Mitsubishi, Mitsubishi Motor Corporation, and Mitsubishi Heavy Industries) purchased over 50% of Hatano's output; the Komatsu Group (Komatsu Ltd., Komatsu Forklift Co. Ltd., and Komatsu Mec Corporation) accounted for another 30%; Hitachi Construction Machinery Co. Ltd., Sumitomo, and several other smaller customers accounted for the remaining sales. Toyo dominated the construction equipment segment of the heat-exchange market with an 80%-90% share of the Japanese domestic market.

Toyo recognized 24 major customers (see Exhibit 24–1), with the largest six accounting for approximately 60% of sales. Toyota was the firm's largest customer, accounting for 18% of sales. Honda and Mitsubishi Motor Corporation were the second and third largest customers, each accounting for over 12% of 1993 sales. Komatsu was the fourth largest customer at 6%, followed by Sharp and Matsushita, each at just over 5%.

The largest competitor for Hatano's products was U.S.-based Modine, which manufactured and sold heat-transfer equipment. One of Modine's major product lines was heat exchangers for cooling all types of engines, transmissions, and auxiliary hydraulic equipment, as well as air conditioning equipment used in cars, trucks, and farm and construction machinery and equipment. It also produced heat exchanges for heating and cooling equipment for residential and commercial buildings. As part of an expansion strategy, Modine was entering into partnerships with its customers where it assumed more responsibility for overall cooling design in return for long-term agreements as a supplier. In addition, Modine was

Exhibit 24-1. Toyo Radiators: 24 Major Customers by Sales

- Toyota Motor Co., Ltd.
- Mitsubishi Motor Corp.
- Honda Motor Co., Ltd.
- Matsushita Electric Industrial Co.
- Komatsu Ltd.
- Sharp Corp.
- Shin Caterpillar Mitsubishi Ltd.
- Yammar Diesel Engine Co., Ltd.
- Daikin Industries, Ltd.
- Mitsubishi Electric Corp.
- Mitsubishi Heavy Industries, Ltd.
- Daihatsu Motor Co., Ltd
- Suzuki Motor Co., Ltd.
- Komatsu Mec Corp.
- Mazda Motor Corp.
- Toyoda Automatic Loom Works, Ltd.
- Hitachi Construction Machinery Co., Ltd.
- Seirei Industry Co., Ltd.
- Komatsu Forklift Co., Ltd.
- Yutani Heavy Industries, Ltd.
- Kubota, Ltd.
- Toyo Umpanki Co., Ltd.
- Iseki & Co., Ltd.
- Honda Access Corp.

selling an increasing number of assembled cooling system modules, which were expected to become more important as Modine added the expertise to manufacture entire cooling systems.

Komatsu, Ltd.

Komatsu, Ltd. was one of Japan's largest heavy industrial manufacturers. It was the world's second-largest manufacturer of a complete line of construction equipment. The firm's product line contained over 300 models, including bulldozers, hydraulic excavators, wheel loaders, and dump trucks. With a more than 30% share of the domestic Japanese excavator market, Komatsu was the largest player in the Japanese market. There were four other major players in the excavator market: Hitachi, with just under 30% of the market; Kobelco, with about 15%; Shin Caterpillar

Mitsubishi, with about 12.5%; and Sumitomo, with under 10%. Only Komatsu and Shin Caterpillar Mitsubishi produced both bulldozers and excavators. The other three firms produced excavators and other construction equipment, but not bulldozers.

Komatsu had been a Toyo customer since 1955. Toyo had developed a special line of oil coolers for Komatsu using a proprietary stacked fin approach. These oil coolers used air as the heat-exchange medium, as did the plate-fin and drawn-cup style coolers used in construction machinery. Other products, such as the plate type and concentric oil coolers used in construction machinery, used water as the heat-exchange medium. Toyo sold two types of radiators and five types of oil coolers to Komatsu.

KOMATSU-SUPPLIER RELATIONS

In 1995, Komatsu manufactured about 30% of its products, designed and subcontracted another 50%, and purchased the remaining 20% from outside suppliers. In recent years, Komatsu's interaction with its major suppliers had changed. Players in the highly competitive market for excavators and bulldozers had begun to compete on the basis of time-to-market for new products. Unfortunately, Komatsu's existing supplier relations did not allow it to significantly decrease the time it took to bring new products to market. To achieve this objective, Komatsu implemented a new simultaneous engineering program to develop major components and subassemblies for its new products that were manufactured by its major suppliers. This program formed the basis for new relationships between Komatsu and its major suppliers.

To allow its suppliers greater input into the design process, Komatsu held periodic meetings between the suppliers' research and development staff and its own. These simultaneous engineering meetings were meant to integrate the research and development efforts of the two groups, allow suppliers to provide input much earlier in the design process, and help ensure that target cost negotiations were more substantive.

The Old Approach to Supplier Relations

Prior to this new approach to supplier relations, Komatsu would tell Toyo to produce a radiator (and other components) with a given cooling capacity. Komatsu left it up to Toyo to develop the components using whatever technologies it thought appropriate. Thus, Komatsu would study its user requirements, develop the concept for its next generation of bulldozers and excavators, and ask Toyo to produce the required heat exchangers.

Toyo designed the parts and submitted a blueprint for Komatsu's approval. Once Komatsu's specifications were met, Toyo's sales department and Komatsu's purchasing department studied Toyo's expected costs and negotiated each part's selling price. However, this approach did not leave Toyo enough time to improve its designs. Until it received Komatsu's work order, Toyo did not know what level of performance was required for the new heat-exchanger unit. Therefore, if the new model required increased heat-exchange capacity and improved performance (e.g., in terms of noise level), often the only feasible solution, given the time left, was to simply increase the size of the unit. Unfortunately, increasing the size often meant increasing the cost.

Komatsu realized it needed a new approach to supplier relationships when the improved performance that it demanded for its A20 and A21 power shovels would have required an increase in radiator size of approximately 36%. This increase would have pushed Toyo's costs above far their target levels, resulting in losses for the firm. The only way to avoid such cost increases was to have a joint research program to develop a new generation of more efficient engine cooling systems.

The New Approach to Supplier Relations

The simultaneous engineering approach adopted by Komatsu for the A20 and A21 power shovels was designed to provide suppliers such as Toyo with advance notice about performance requirements for components for the new models. Under this new approach, negotiations between Toyo and Komatsu began much earlier, while the product was still being designed. If the estimated the cost of manufacture appeared too high, Toyo's engineers tried to find ways to relax Komatsu's specifications so that the part could be manufactured for less. Changes in specifications for Toyo parts were only allowed if they did not compromise the functionality of the final Komatsu product.

One immediate outcome of the decision to adopt simultaneous engineering was a reduction in the number of Komatsu suppliers. Under the old approach, Toyo would supply only the radiator. Other companies would produce the other components for the engine cooling system, such as condensers, fans, and electric motors. Komatsu would assemble the final system. This multi-supplier approach, however, did not allow the increased design efficiency that Komatsu considered necessary for it to remain competitive. Consequently, Komatsu decided under the new program to design and produce both the radiator and the fan in a single integrated package.

A major benefit from this integration was realized almost immediately. To achieve the increased performance, the airflow around the radiator had to be improved. Conventional fans pushed the air horizontally, causing a portion of the airflow to be directed at the engine where it was reflected back into the air stream, thus reducing the overall flow of air that was cooling the engine. By introducing a "mixed flow" fan, the airflow was directed around the engine, where it was more effective in cooling the engine (see Exhibit 24–2). This allowed a smaller radiator to be utilized in the A20 and A21 models.

Product Development Under the New Approach

Under the new simultaneous engineering approach, Toyo began designing the cooling systems for the A20 and A21 models 24 months before the prototype was developed, instead of 12 months in the old Komatsu design process. The first two years of the simultaneous engineering design project for the A20 and A21 models was the prototype stage. In this period, Komatsu engineers worked on developing the general designs of the new construction vehicles based upon customer requirements. For example, for the A20 and A21 line of power shovels, customer requirements included simplified maintenance, noise reduction, improved operator friendliness, and increased functionality, including a higher-horsepower engine and more powerful hydraulics.

Simultaneously, Toyo engineers designed a new heat exchanger. At the heart of this new design was the specially developed fan that both increased effective airflow around the engine and reduced the noise level. The new radiator-fan package also increased parts commonality across all of the

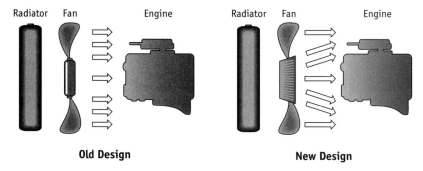

Exhibit 24–2. Improving Airflow Around Engine

firm's construction equipment products. One of the innovations was a common mounting approach in all vehicles that used the new cooling system; this spurred an increase in parts commonality across the firm's different customers for heavy industrial engine cooling system—and lower costs overall.

Toyo and Komatsu engineers updated each other on their progress so that they shared a common objective. Both groups worked to improve the overall future performance of their products, not just those currently under development. These overall improvements were guided by anticipated changes in customer requirements (e.g., in the power shovel market, there was a trend towards increased engine power).

In the third year, joint research was formalized in the product development phase of new product introduction. The two groups focused on solving issues that were specific to the new Komatsu models. While general engineering still continued, engineers at both firms tried to resolve issues specific to the new models. For example, Komatsu engineers tried to improve operator friendliness, reduce noise, and increase the functionality of the new models. At the same time, Toyo engineers worked on the new high performance fan and increased standardization of parts to be installed on the chassis. At periodic intervals, prototypes were developed for testing and to ensure that both groups' efforts were compatible.

At the end of the fifth year of product development, the products entered the review phase, where any residual engineering problems were resolved. For example, Komatsu's engineers identified the open issues for the A20 and A21 models as operator friendliness, which still was considered inadequate, and the power of the engine and the hydraulic equipment, which were still considered too low. For Toyo's engineers, the main issue during the review stage of these models was equipment planning to ensure that there would be adequate capacity the following year to start manufacturing the cooling systems.

COST MANAGEMENT UNDER THE NEW APPROACH

Toyo and Komatsu used two cost management techniques to create internal cost reduction pressures: target costing and cost balance verification. Both techniques were applied during the product design stage.

Target Costing

Komatsu's target costing system was designed to establish both the target cost of Komatsu's new products and the target prices of all components purchased from outside suppliers. The preliminary target costs used in the long-range development plan for major subassemblies, such as the engine, power train, and cooling system, were established using prior experience with similar subassemblies and discussions with production and engineering. These preliminary target costs, or target values as they were known, helped identify when cost reduction techniques were required.

Komatsu used functional analysis to set the final target costs for subassemblies designed and produced by firms such as Toyo. This process began by identifying the critical functionality of the engine cooling system, its cooling capacity. Next, the primary determinant of the cooling capacity was identified, which was radiator size. Functional tables were used to develop scatter diagrams of cooling capacity against radiator size for all radiators Komatsu purchased (see Exhibit 24–3). The frontier of the more efficient design was identified as the line that passed through the three most efficient designs. The target radiator size was determined by finding the size of radiator that was required on the minimum line to give the desired cooling capacity. The target size was then adjusted to reflect the actual size that could be manufactured; for example, Toyo could manufacture radiators that were 830 mm and 880 mm in height.

Next, cost tables were used to create a scatter diagram of the cost to manufacture against size of all radiators Komatsu purchased (see Exhibit 24–4). Constructing the minimum cost line, which passed through the three most effective designs, allowed the target cost of the new radiator to be determined. This cost resulted from an independent, double minimum procedure. It represented the minimum cost of the minimum radia-

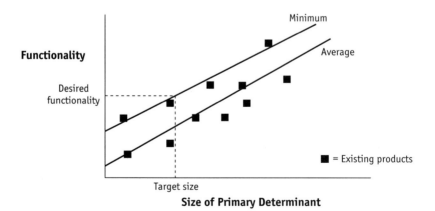

EXHIBIT 24–3. TARGET COSTING VIA FUNCTIONAL ANALYSIS: DETERMINING TARGET RADIATOR SIZE

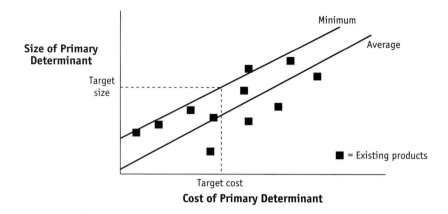

EXHIBIT 24-4. TARGET COSTING VIA FUNCTIONAL ANALYSIS:
DETERMINING TARGET RADIATOR COST

tor area given the desired cooling capacity, and was designed to represent a significant but achievable challenge to the suppliers. The functional analysis procedure was repeated for each subassembly component, such as the electric motor and fan, to obtain their target costs.

The A20 and A21 models presented a severe challenge. In particular, the fan's airflow volume was expected to increase 36% while simultaneously reducing noise levels by 5%. It was decided that increasing the size of the fan from 830 mm to 880 mm was necessary if the required cooling capacity was to be achieved. This size increase required reallocating the target costs, or value targets as they were called, for components in the cooling system. These reallocations reflected performance changes needed in the various components in the cooling system once the radiator's size was increased. If a component's performance had to be increased, its target cost was usually increased; if its performance requirements were decreased, so was its target cost. The increases in target costs for parts had to be offset by decreases in target costs for other parts so that the overall target cost of the overall engine cooling system remained constant. Reallocation of target costs in this manner forced the engineers to decide where to focus their cost-reduction efforts. Under the old approach, the expansion of the radiator size by 36% would have led to an equivalent increase in cost. However, Komatsu's customers were not willing to pay that much extra for the increased performance, so Komatsu set Toyo's target cost at 118% of the old cost.

This new target cost meant that Toyo had to develop a new cooling system with adequate cooling capacity, but with costs that were sufficiently low to allow it to make an adequate profit at Komatsu's target cost. The increase in Komatsu's target cost also meant that Komatsu's engineers had to look elsewhere for the additional 18% that had been added to the cost of the radiator over its cost in the old A20 line. Fortunately, if the increased functionality was sufficiently great, the selling price of the new power shovel might be increased by 5%, thus reducing the required cost reductions to 13%.

The new cooperative relationship changed the way Komatsu approached target costing. Under the old approach, the target cost was an internal rather than an external objective. Toyo would submit a bid for a component and then Komatsu would add up all of the bids for a subassembly's components and compare the total with its target cost for the subassembly. With this approach, the firm's ability to achieve the target cost was tested only after the prototype was completed. It was often too late at that stage of the product design process to change the design enough so that the target cost could be met. If the bids were too high, Komatsu negotiated with the suppliers to reduce them until the subassembly could be purchased for its target cost. Though target costs were supposed to be negotiated with suppliers, Komatsu management was concerned that, in reality, these negotiations were relatively one-sided.

Under the new approach, Komatsu told Toyo the target cost for each of its components and then expected Toyo to find a way to achieve them. From Komatsu's perspective, the important issue was to design the cooling system so that it could be purchased for its target cost. If multiple firms were involved in delivering the cooling systems, then Komatsu split the cooling system's target cost among the suppliers based on the parts they produced. If a supplier produced more than one component for the cooling system, Komatsu would develop target costs for each of these components, to provide guidance to suppliers such as Toyo. However, once the individual component target costs were accepted, the supplier was held to the overall sum of all of the components that it supplied for the new model, not the target costs for individual parts. In effect, Komatsu managed suppliers to a single target cost for each specific cooling system, leaving the suppliers' engineers to decide how much each component would cost and hence where to focus their cost-reduction efforts.

Negotiations only occurred if Toyo decided it couldn't meet Komatsu's target cost for a new model and still make an adequate profit (i.e., if Toyo could not make the parts at the target cost that had been established by Toyo's target costing system). This new approach meant that Toyo knew much earlier in the design process what its selling prices (and hence target costs) had to be in order for it to make an adequate profit. If Toyo saw a potential problem with Komatsu's target costs (i.e., its selling prices), it could negotiate with Komatsu to relax them.

The amount of cost information shared between the firms was significant. Komatsu had access to all of Toyo's cost information for Komatsu-related products, even to the level of the price paid for a single bolt used in a component of a Komatsu product. This sharing of cost information allowed Komatsu to find new ways to reduce costs. For example, it might increase discounts by purchasing the bolt centrally and having its manufacturer deliver the bolts directly to all in the Komatsu group and its major suppliers that used the bolt.

At times, this sharing of cost information and Komatsu's knowledge of Toyo's profits led to a conflict of interest—pressure built within Komatsu to reduce target costs where Toyo's profits were known to be high. However, the two firms shared a common goal—getting costs as low as possible—which ensured that these conflicts rarely become serious. To reduce the incidence of such conflicts and to let Toyo make as much profit as possible, Komatsu did not set its target costs for Toyo manufactured parts based upon its knowledge of Toyo's costs.

Cost Balance Verification

Even with the 18% increase in the cooling system's target cost, Toyo could not manufacture the new cooling system at an adequate profit. There were significant engineering problems in obtaining improved fan performance. Toyo's early attempts to deliver the increased airflow were not particularly successful and the firm encountered many problems in the research stage. The bench tests at Toyo indicated insufficient airflow, which would have caused engine overheating. The new fan design resolved the problem; however, though the functionality and quality requirements were met, the cost was above Toyo's target cost.

To reduce further the cost of the new cooling system, Komatsu and Toyo initiated a cost balance verification (CBV). The CBV was meant to help Toyo manufacture the new cooling system and sell it at Komatsu's target cost while still making the desired profit. The CBV focused on two areas of cost reduction: reducing costs through product redesign using value analysis, and evaluating individual parts that cost too much.

Value analysis was used to improve a vehicle's value through functional improvements and to reduce costs without changing the product's functionality. The value analysis program applied to the A20 and A21 engine cooling systems found one major way to increase the functionality and *three* ways to reduce costs.

Functionality was improved by changing how the air cooler was installed, which improved the system's cleaning performance. Construction equipment typically operated in very dirty conditions. The air sucked in by the cooling system often contained grass and other contaminants, which clogged the radiator and necessitated periodic cleaning. The objective of the new design was to create a radiator that was both easier to clean and less prone to clogging. Because the new approach was expected to be more expensive than the old approach (and was), the new product's target cost was modified accordingly.

The first cost-reduction approach was used to eliminate parts without changing the functionality of the air cooling system (for example, reducing the number of brackets required to mount the radiator).

The second cost-reduction approach was used to eliminate major components through product redesigns while maintaining cooling capacity. The old cooling system design had separate fans and motors for both the radiator and the condenser. Toyo's new design for the A20 and A21 models placed the condenser in front of the radiator instead of behind it and used only one fan and motor for increasing the airflow (see Exhibit 24-5). In the past, the radiator-fan and condenser-fan subassemblies were supplied by different firms, making it impossible for the new design to be developed. Under the new approach, Toyo was responsible for delivering, though not necessarily manufacturing, the entire cooling system. For example, while another supplier produced the condenser, Toyo was

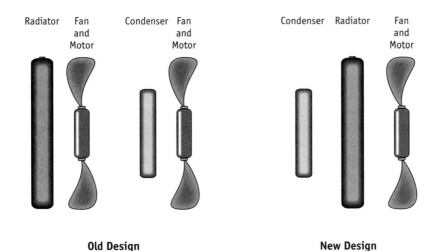

Old Design   **New Design**

EXHIBIT 24-5. REDUCING COST OF RADIATOR AND CONDENSER

responsible for mounting it in the cooling system. Thus, Komatsu and Toyo could negotiate with each other to combine the radiator and condenser subassemblies into a single unit, thereby reducing the cooling system's overall cost. The redesign also achieved more than just a simple cost reduction. Because the savings were greater than required by Komatsu's target costing, Toyo was able to spend more on the system's overall functionality and still make an adequate return.

Finally, a system to control the level of heat generation was developed, which allowed for a lower cooling capacity design. This reduction in required cooling capacity was critical because it allowed the size of the radiator to remain at 830 mm. Toyo would have preferred to use the old A20 line but was limited to radiators that were 830 mm in height. Toyo developed a 830 mm prototype that had an acceptable cooling capacity, so it negotiated with Komatsu to change the specifications of the radiator from 880 mm to 830 mm. The two redesigns—the combined condenser-radiator package and the smaller radiator—made it possible to bring the A20 and A21 cooling systems in at their target costs. Under the old approach, the reduction in radiator size would not have been possible because Toyo would not have had time to test the smaller design.

Toyo used four major cost-reduction approaches to analyze parts with cost problems. First, Toyo analyzed the cost and functionality of these parts; those that cost a lot but added little functionality were targeted for elimination. For example, a water-level gauge was eliminated once it was determined that it served no useful purpose. Second, Toyo sought to reduce the cost of parts by changing their shape. For example, a deep draw pressing technique was developed that allowed complex parts to be manufactured at lower cost. Pressing required a high initial up-front cost for the die but was cheaper per unit than the welding approach it replaced. Third, Toyo changed how it mounted the wire net that was used to make the spinning fan safer. This allowed standardized parts to be used across models, thus reducing costs. Finally, Toyo analyzed parts used for noise insulation and decided to explore whether to reduce noise at the source or simply insulate against the noise. This comparison allowed Toyo to eliminate and simplify parts, again reducing costs. For example, some components had been protected by a heavy frame; by installing cushions, which were much cheaper, Toyo eliminated these frames.

The larger 880 mm radiators required for the new A20 and A21 created a serious problem for Toyo because they would have to be manufactured on the production line used for Komatsu's PC300 series. Because the PC300 series was a low-volume model—the A20 and A21 were high-volume models—it would be expensive for Toyo to transform the PC300 line into a high-volume line.

THE NATURE OF THE
KOMATSU-TOYO RELATIONSHIP

Toyo and Komatsu viewed themselves as independent, despite some mutual shareholdings and employees assigned long-term at the other company. Toyo saw Komatsu as a very important customer with whom it was willing to share extensive cost and technical information. Komatsu saw Toyo as part of a cooperative group that consisted of Komatsu and a few dozen select suppliers. Cost information was shared extensively within this group—suppliers outside the group were treated more conventionally (i.e., using the old supplier approach). Both firms thought of their relationship as akin to a strong friendship.

Certain Toyo design engineers worked for two days every two weeks at Komatsu as "guest" engineers. The joint technical design meetings were typically held during these visits. Guest engineers were assigned for three years at a time, and had been introduced around 1985. Under the old approach to supplier relations, these engineers were design-oriented. Under the new approach, they were expected to be both design- and cost-oriented. This shift in orientation significantly changed the nature of the discussions between Komatsu and guest engineers. Previously, these discussions focused on research and development already in process; now, they focused on setting the direction of future research and development.

Under the new approach, Komatsu test engineers were often asked to visit Toyo to explain Komatsu's test procedures and evaluation criteria. No Komatsu personnel were specifically assigned to Toyo, so they were not viewed as guest engineers. Instead, Komatsu engineers visited Toyo to discuss specific design issues, increasing the probability that a solution Toyo proposed would be approved by Komatsu. Toyo developed its own simulation program to test prospective designs, reducing the chances that Komatsu's prototype would show Toyo's heat-exchange solution to be inadequate. Toyo engineers could also borrow Komatsu's prototypes for testing. In the past, Komatsu would test Toyo's designs on its prototypes; the resulting delays and reduced information available to Toyo engineers lengthened the development process. Now, the entire process could be completed in less time.

Komatsu and Toyo had developed six important insights from their interactions for the A20 and A21 models:

1. A joint analysis of the appropriate research and development issues was beneficial.
2. It was more appropriate for Komatsu's research and development center than for Toyo's to conduct basic research into heat-exchange problems.

3. Synchronizing Toyo's product engineering efforts with Komatsu's development plan was beneficial.
4. Periodic technical exchange meetings were critical to the new product design process.
5. Bench simulations of cooling system performance were critical to the rapid product development process.
6. Expanding the design engineers' responsibilities to include cost was a critical step in achieving increased cost-reduction objectives.

CHAPTER 25

YOKOHAMA CORPORATION, LTD. (A): THE YOKOHAMA PRODUCTION SYSTEM

INTRODUCTION

Yokohama Corporation, Ltd., was created as a joint venture between a Japanese automobile manufacturer and the Japanese government. Yokohama was founded in July 1939 and began production in late 1942. The objective of the firm was to manufacture hydraulic systems for automobiles and trucks and associated equipment under license from a German firm. The venture was successful and within a few years had diversified into other automotive products, including fuel pumps and transmission systems.

Yokohama was first listed on the Tokyo Stock Market in 1955. Firm ownership changed over the years and in 1993 only three major shareholders remained: Kanagawa Motors, Tokyo Motors, and The Industrial Bank of Japan.

Professor Robin Cooper of the Peter F. Drucker Graduate Management Center at The Claremont Graduate School and Professor Takeo Yoshikawa of Yokohama National University prepared this case as the basis for class discussion rather than to illustrate either effective or ineffective handling of an administrative situation.

The firm's international expansion began in the mid-1970s with the incorporation of Siam Yokohama Company, Ltd., in Thailand. Further expansion followed rapidly with the opening of Yokohama USA Co., Ltd., in 1975, Yokohama Pty., Ltd., in Australia in 1978, and Yokohama GmbH in 1988. By 1992, the firm had 13 overseas affiliates, 7 liaison offices, and a worldwide service network of over 100 distributors and 2,000 service representatives. In 1992, the firm had sales of nearly ¥260 billion and employed just under 7,000 individuals.

Yokohama was split into three corporate divisions: injection pump, air conditioning, and hydraulics & pneumatics. The injection pump corporate division contained two major business areas, diesel fuel-injection systems and control systems. The diesel fuel-injection systems area produced a range of products that were used in diesel engines: in-line, distributor-type, and camshaftless fuel-injection pumps, as well as electronic diesel engine control systems and numerous smaller products (e.g., injectors, governors, and timing devices).

The control systems area produced a range of products that were used in automobiles. Products included an electronically controlled transmission system, electronically controlled gasoline injection systems, fuel injectors, and fuel pumps. The electronically controlled transmission system was a good example of the type of innovative product development that Yokohama considered its strength. The specially developed electronic circuits allowed manual transmissions to be automated without major modifications. The advantage of this approach was that it combined the fuel efficiency of a manual transmission with the ease of operation of an automatic one.

Yokohama's air conditioning corporate division produced a full range of air-conditioning products for the automotive industry. Yokohama pioneered the development of automotive air-conditioning in Japan when it began production of air-conditioners in 1958. Automobile heater production began the following year and since then the firm diversified into air-conditioning products for construction equipment, agricultural equipment, and industrial equipment. In addition, the firm also produced chlorofluorocarbons (CFCs) recovery and recycling equipment as part of its program to first reduce and then eliminate the environmental effects of CFCs on the ozone layer.

The hydraulics and pneumatics corporate division consisted of two business areas: hydraulics and pneumatics and new products. The hydraulics and pneumatics division produced both hydraulic and pneumatic products. Hydraulic products included hydraulic equipment for vehicles (such as gear pumps, control valves, and air brakes) and centralized lubrication systems. Hydraulic products, which were usually custom-designed, were used in agricultural and industrial equipment such as bull-dozers and excavators. Pneumatic products included air brakes for trucks and air line systems to generate the air pressure used for pneumatic suspension systems and pneumatic doors in buses. The new products area produced products that were used primarily outside the automotive industry. This division developed products based upon proprietary technologies that the firm had developed. Products included hybrid ICs; sensors; actuators; industrial robots; IC card reader/writers; computer software and hardware; and heating, ventilating, and air-conditioning systems. These products were evolved from applications developed inside Yokohama for its own use. For example, the IC card reader/writers were used throughout Yokohama's factories to keep track of important production information.

Yokohama had five manufacturing facilities in Japan: Ranzan, Ibaraki, Chiba, Hiroshima, and Maebashi. The original production facility, the Ranzan plant, was opened in 1940 to produce hydraulic products. In 1992, it manufactured four major product lines, including electronic fuel-injection control systems, in-line injection pumps, automatic timing devices, and fuel-injection nozzles. The Ranzan plant produced products for the injection pump and hydraulics and pneumatics divisions. The Ibaraki plant was built in 1965 to manufacture injection nozzle holders for the injection pump division. The Chiba plant was built in 1970 to manufacture air-conditioning equipment for the air conditioning division. The Hiroshima plant was built in 1982 and manufactured injection nozzles for the injection pump division. Finally, the Maebashi plant was built in 1990 and was responsible for the manufacture of electronic and hydraulic systems for the firm's hydronics business area or division. The hydronics division manufactured and sold products for both the hydraulics and pneumatics and new products areas.

COMPETITIVE ENVIRONMENT

Yokohama's major automotive customers included Tokyo Motors, Hino, Mazda, and Toyota. In addition, the firm sold its products to several other Japanese automotive firms, to European automotive firms such as Volvo and Volkswagen, and to Korean automotive firms such as Hyundai. Its other major customers included Komatsu, Fuji Heavy Industries, Control Systems Company, Ltd., and the Korean firm Daewoo Heavy Industries.

The firm competed with a number of large Japanese firms. In the injection pump market, the firm's major competitors were Zexel, Nippon Nozzle Co., Yanma Diesel Co., and Tokyo Diesel Co. In the hydraulic and pneumatic systems market, its main competitors were Zexel, Shimazu Manufacturing Co., and Kayaba Industries. In the electronic devices market, Yokohama's main competitors were Japanese Electronic Control Systems Co., Ltd., and Nippon Denso.

Competition in all markets was intense. Yokohama's competitors were typically able to match its technological capability. Consequently, no firm was able to maintain any real degree of technological leadership for any length of time. Given the number of relatively equivalent competitors, the firm's customers wielded considerable power. Most customers had developed target costing systems to set the selling prices of Yokohama's products. Over time, customers' power, coupled with the downward price pressure that their target costing systems had placed on selling prices, led to decreased profitability for Yokohama. For example, Yokohama's profits in 1980 were nearly ¥9 billion; by 1986, they had fallen to under ¥6 billion, and by 1991 to ¥4 billion.

The decreased prices were aggravated by two other factors: the contraction in product life expectancies from about four years in 1970 to approximately two years, and the transfer of considerable design activities from the customers to Yokohama. The shortened life cycles made it even more difficult for Yokohama to recoup the cost of its R&D efforts because lifetime production levels were necessarily smaller. The transfer of design activities also proved difficult because it increased the firm's upfront development costs. Previously, the customer had designed the product and provided Yokohama with the product's specifications; now, Yokohama engineers had to design products as well as manufacture them. Taken together, these two changes meant that higher development costs had to be recovered on sales of fewer units.

To return profitability to its traditional levels, Yokohama began to implement a new strategy, which had three elements. First, the firm increased its product design and planning efforts to reduce product costs. Second, it approached its customers and proposed new approaches to the design, manufacture, and processing of existing products. Third, the firm identified new products that it could produce at competitively low costs and aggressively bid for contracts to produce them. Under this new strategy, Yokohama resolved that any new product that was not going to generate an adequate profit margin across its life would not be introduced.

CUSTOMER RELATIONSHIPS

Many customers, such as Tokyo Motors, multi-sourced products, typically buying from at least two different suppliers. Yokohama tried to remain competitive by finding new ways to add value to its products. Yokohama viewed its negotiations with Tokyo Motors and other major customers as being defined by a quality-function-price (QFP) trade-off. This trade-off meant that Yokohama would explore ways to provide its customers with products whose quality, functionality, and price—though below the levels originally requested by the customer—were acceptable. Successfully achieving this trade-off allowed Yokohama to find solutions to a customer's product requirements that generated adequate returns.

Most of Yokohama's customers used target costing systems to set the prices at which they were willing to purchase products. The margin that Yokohama earned was not factored into the prices set by these systems. Instead, the target costing systems calculated the maximum purchase price that the customer was willing to pay for a part while still making a targeted return on the sale of its products. Most major customers usually would not agree to long-term changes to target prices. However, they would sometimes allow the prices to rise above the target for the first few years after introduction to allow Yokohama time to find ways to reduce their costs sufficiently to make an acceptable return at the target costs.

Most of the time, it was up to Yokohama engineers to continuously innovate and find ways to manufacture its products so that they could be sold at the target prices and make adequate returns. In theory, the customer was not interested in the level of Yokohama's profit margins, only in its ability to provide products at the target price. Thus, if Yokohama found a way to significantly reduce the cost of one of its products, it could make a high return on that product. However, because there was considerable sharing of production information between Yokohama and its customers, it did not take long for the target price to reflect the new production cost. In addition, Yokohama's customers would share information about the innovation with their other suppliers, who typically were Yokohama's competitors. This sharing allowed the competitors to match Yokohama's costs. Once the competitor's costs were reduced, the target selling price rapidly fell to match the underlying production costs.

The target costing systems were coupled to strong supplier-customer relationships that often spread over several layers of the parts supply chain. For example, it was not unusual for engineers from Tokyo Motors, Yokohama, and Yokohama's suppliers to meet to discuss how to design and manufacture a new part. The advantage of these multilevel supplier meetings, or minimum cost investigations (MCI) as they were called, was that a part could be designed so that each step—from raw material to finished product—could be made more efficient. For example, engineers at Kamakura Ironworks, which supplied Yokohama with metal forgings, would design a forged part so that the amount of machining required at

Yokohama to complete it was reduced. Yokohama was willing to pay more for such a component because it cost less to complete it.

MCI meetings were initiated by Tokyo Motors as part of its cost-reduction program. MCI was a technique developed by the Jamco Consulting Company to help firms reduce costs. It consisted of five major steps:

1. Gathering cost information about each function of a product.
2. Searching for ways to minimize costs.
3. Proposing alternative ways to reduce costs and proposing guidelines for developing inexpensive products.
4. Performing feasibility studies for the proposals in step 3.
5. Developing an implementation plan for the cost-reduction proposals approved in step 4.

The major difference between target costing and MCI was that under MCI, Tokyo Motors was aware of the profit margins made by both Yokohama and Kamakura. The MCI process began with a target cost for a part set by Tokyo Motors' target costing system. Yokohama would request an MCI meeting if it believed that it could not manufacture the part profitably at its target price. The MCI meeting allowed everyone involved to make suggestions about how to minimize the cost of production. The advantage of MCI over other techniques was that it brought together representatives from all three firms. By getting everyone into the same room, low-cost solutions could be identified that would not have been apparent if the three firms had tried to solve the problem independently. Despite this advantage, MCI was not popular with Tokyo Motors' suppliers because they felt Tokyo Motors had too much leverage in the negotiations.

Yokohama was protective of Kamakura in the MCI negotiations. To protect Kamakura from excessive downward price pressures, Yokohama would often intercede on Kamakura's behalf in the MCI negotiations. One of Yokohama management's objectives was to create a corporate culture that enabled it to say "no" when it could not identify a way to make a product profitably. It was trying to instill the same culture at Kamakura to help protect that firm from excess supplier pressure. Yokohama's management believed that developing such a culture was critical to its survival because it ensured that the firm did not become dependent on its customers.

Often, the negotiations between Yokohama and its customers would not focus on the price of a part but on its specifications. If Yokohama could demonstrate, using a QFP trade-off, that relaxing either the quality or the functionality of the product would not result in end products with lower quality or functionality, then Tokyo Motors would often accept the change in product specifications in lieu of increased prices. Yokohama viewed these QFP trade-offs as critical to its survival. For example, Yokohama might find a way to produce a part by pressing as opposed to machining it. The pressed product would be less expensive to produce but it would be inherently lower in quality.

Yokohama occasionally refused to sell products at the target price identified by the customer. Several forces drove this decision. First, Yokohama had to remain profitable in order to survive. If it accepted too many unprofitable contracts it would become insolvent. Second, Yokohama dealt with a sufficient number of customers such that losing a single order from any one of them did not place the firm at significant risk. Third, if the same product was supplied to other firms, then an effective market price for that product existed. If Yokohama sold that product to another customer below its effective market price, there was a substantial risk that once the new price leaked out, it would rapidly become the market price for that product. If the revenue gained by selling the product at the reduced price to the new customer was less than the revenue lost by the decreased selling price for existing products, Yokohama would be worse off by accepting the new customer's price.

If a product was sold only to one customer, such as Tokyo Motors, Yokohama would offer it a preliminary breakdown of the cost structure of the product. This cost breakdown allowed Tokyo Motors to determine the profit margin that Yokohama *expected* to earn on this product. If the margin was too low, it would provide Yokohama with a rationale for using QFP to negotiate some change in either the target price or the specifications of the product. Actual profitability information was shared with Tokyo Motors or other customers. Typically, only Yokohama knew its actual profit margins.

Because of its small size and limited engineering capability, Yokohama rarely manufactured commodity products. It avoided such products because the ability to negotiate QFP trade-offs with them was limited. Sometimes, however, it was not possible to avoid manufacturing commodity products. Automobile air-conditioners were a good example of a commodity product that Yokohama produced. There were over 30 competitors in the air-conditioner industry; the leader in volume and price was Nippon Denso. All of the other competitors were effectively forced to follow Nippon Denso's price leadership. However, even under these conditions, Yokohama often found ways to negotiate. In particular, if it could develop a quality, cost, or delivery time advantage, it could use this advantage to negotiate the conditions of the order.

Another opportunity to negotiate occurred when Yokohama was heavily involved in designing and scheduling a product. Under these conditions, it was difficult for competitors to intervene because Yokohama was acting like a captive supplier. If Yokohama was unable to meet the target price under these conditions, the customer was often forced to accept a higher price that provided Yokohama with an adequate return. However, even under these conditions, only a temporary reprieve was given; in the long run, Yokohama was expected to sell the product to the customer at the target price.

Major customers had substantial bargaining power over Yokohama during pricing negotiations. Yokohama managed to remain profitable by taking advantage of QFP trade-offs. It was also protected somewhat by its strong reputation and good relations with well-established customers; however, these benefits were not always sufficient. For example, Tokyo Motors' parts design department was highly supportive of Yokohama. The engineers in that department wanted to maintain good relations with Yokohama and were more accommodating about price and functionality than other Tokyo Motors departments, such as purchasing. Occasionally, purchasing would intervene in negotiations between Yokohama and parts design and force a contract to go to a competitor with a lower bid.

YOKOHAMA'S COST REDUCTION PROGRAMS

At the heart of Yokohama's survival was the ability to manufacture products at low cost. To help it achieve this objective, the firm had developed an integrated set of cost-reduction programs, the most important of which were the Yokohama Production System (YPS) and value engineering (VE) programs. These two programs were designed to operate together to make all aspects of the production system more efficient. The YPS was designed to improve the efficiency of the work force and the VE system was structured to find ways to design less-expensive products.

Yokohama Production System

The YPS, introduced at Yokohama in 1987, integrated just-in-time (JIT) production and a kanban system to pull the orders through the plant, total quality management (TQM), the Yokohama Preventative Maintenance system (YPM), and value engineering. The YPS was as much a philosophy of cost reduction as it was a formal system. The process began with the education of the work force. There were no formal classes; workers were educated on an as-needed basis. The major objective of these education programs was to create a "force for change." More specifically, the objective was to foster changes that led to cost reduction.

The YPS consisted of three distinct cost-reduction pathways. The objective of the first pathway was to reduce costs by using capital investments to reduce head count. The objective of the second pathway was to reduce costs via improved inventory management. The objective of the third pathway was to reduce costs by identifying process improvements that reduced head count.

The first pathway, capital investment, began with a request for equipment acquisition. The request was prepared with the assistance of a technical support group specially convened for the request process. The members of this group were drawn from several functions, including the production, design, and equipment departments. Once the requisition was approved, the equipment was purchased and installed. The quality assurance support group was responsible for helping the work force learn how to produce high-quality products using the new equipment.

The capital investment requests formed the basis for Yokohama's large-scale kaizen program. This program was the responsibility of the heads of the production and design departments. The primary objective of this program was to encourage the introduction of advanced manufacturing technologies, such as robotics, flexible machining, and transfer technology. The firm wanted to encourage the introduction of these new technologies because top management felt that they would lead to improved quality, reduced costs, and more timely delivery. The large-scale kaizen program also helped reduce lead time, one of the objectives of the inventory control pathway, by introducing machines that could produce products at a faster rate and had faster set-up times.

The second pathway, inventory control, had two objectives: the first was to introduce small-lot manufacturing and the second was to introduce the philosophy of manufacturing one unit at a time. Small-lot manufacturing required reducing set-up times and hence costs. Reduced set-up times were achieved, for example, by changing machines or machine layouts, introducing flexible robots that required less set-up time, and developing or identifying tooling that could be set up faster. The technical support departments were heavily involved in set-up-time reduction and assisted the work force in developing ways to reduce set-up times.

Manufacturing one unit at a time reduced defects and improved lead times by making the production process flow more smoothly. The end result of small-lot production and manufacturing one unit at a time was reduced lead time. The large-scale kaizen program also provided some opportunities to reduce lead time, primarily by reducing set-up times. As lead time was reduced, the firm could shift to balanced production volumes, which, theoretically, allowed all of the machines to be kept busy all of the time. Under balanced production, each machine was expected to complete its task at the same time. When this condition was met, inventories were reduced even further and, theoretically, all production resources were fully utilized.

The use of balanced production volumes was combined with a kanban system that pulled the products through the plant. This combination allowed orders to be processed after they had been received from the customer, thus avoiding the buildup of excessive inventories of finished parts. Instead, where possible, raw material was converted into work-in-process assemblies that were common to multiple products. These assemblies were converted into finished goods when the customers' orders were received.

The final stage in the inventory control pathway was the implementation of flexible manufacturing and advanced inventory control procedures. The objective of introducing these two approaches was to reduce the finished goods inventory to an absolute minimum.

The third pathway, reduced head count, started with Yokohama's small-scale kaizen program. This was a typical Japanese kaizen program where the work force was responsible for both making and implementing the cost-reduction suggestions. The primary objective of the program was to reduce the amount of lost production time. Production time could be lost for several reasons, including waiting for work to arrive, machine downtime, and rework. The objective of the reduction in lost time was to create a smoothly running production process. The adoption of manufacturing one unit at a time in each process was a critical step in the development of smoothly running processes because it reduced the throughput time of the production process. For example, if one component was produced in batches of four units, the throughput time was necessarily longer than if a single unit was produced at a time. Throughput-time reduction was considered important because the only way to achieve it was to improve the quality of the production process. Actions taken under this program included improved machine layout, job standardization, and worker education. The long-term outcome of reduced throughput time was decreased work force requirements.

Each of the three cost-reduction pathways played a critical role in helping Yokohama to achieve its cost-reduction targets. It was the integration of these three pathways that, in top management's opinion, allowed the firm to take maximum advantage of its cost-reduction activities.

Value Engineering

VE techniques were applied widely at Yokohama. The origins of VE at Yokohama could be traced back to the formation of an industrial engineering department in 1946 and the quality control department in 1956. The primary objectives of the industrial engineering department were to learn how to improve the way products were manufactured, to establish an efficient production system, and to introduce a continuous improvement program. The primary objectives of the quality control department were to introduce quality control techniques to the firm and in particular to improve the quality of the firm's high-volume products.

VE proper began at Yokohama after several employees attended a VE workshop in 1964. The core lesson of this seminar was that the first step in eliminating problems was to identify their sources. This philosophy appealed to the attendees and they rapidly adopted VE as a cost management tool.

The first formal VE activity at Yokohama consisted of a small study group that met regularly. The size of this group increased rapidly and eventually a permanent VE task force was introduced. This permanent task force was staffed by individuals devoted full-time to VE activities.

There were certain limitations to a permanent VE task force. First, only the members of the task force, and not the workers as a whole, developed significant interest in the application of VE techniques. Second, several of the task force members became overzealous and this created barriers to the successful spread of the techniques. Third, interest in cost management was not sustained across the different facilities, in part because of the lack of involvement of nonteam members. Finally, the cost-reduction ideas generated by the VE groups, which were located in the plants, took too long to disseminate to all the facilities.

In 1977, the VE project management system was introduced to overcome these limitations. Under this system, VE project teams were established at each facility. The objective of this approach was to develop support for VE activities at all levels of the firm, especially the work force. The new system was successful; VE activities spread more widely throughout the firm and the commitment of the work force to their success increased significantly. Over time, VE activities became an integral part of the firm. To ensure continued success, the results of VE activities were shared within and across facilities. Each VE project was carefully evaluated to ensure that it was indeed beneficial.

The project management system that evolved at Yokohama contained two major systems, first- and second-look value engineering. First-look VE was applied during the product design process; second-look VE was applied during the production stage. A zero VE stage was identified during product planning, but no systematic project management system was developed for this stage.

The VE Implementation Process

The VE implementation process began with the development of the product plan. This plan was prepared by R&D based upon customer, market, and environmental requirements. Customer requirements only considered the purpose of a product, not the underlying functions that had to be performed if the product was to achieve its purpose. From these requirements, the conceptual design of the new product was developed. These conceptual designs were subjected to a design review before the requirements were converted into functional specifications. Functional specifications identified the functions that the product had to perform in order to achieve its purpose. From the functional specifications, function family trees were drawn (these were diagrams that related the product functions together in logical ways). The product's functions were evaluated based upon cost, capacity, performance, technological feasibility, environmental factors, and regulatory constraints. If the product was deemed successful, its product plan was developed.

From the product plan, target costs were established, basic product functions identified, and the development plan prepared. The target cost was determined by subtracting the desired margin, as identified in the divisional plan, from the target selling price set by the customer's target costing system.

The basic functions identified were those functions that were essential for the product to perform in order to achieve its primary purpose. The development plan identified the steps that were to be taken to bring the product into production.

The next step was to develop the research/experimental design. The experimental design allowed the firm to manufacture a number of trial products. Once the trial products had been manufactured, a second design review was undertaken. The primary purpose of this review was to ensure that the previous design steps had been properly executed. After this review was completed, the material, labor, and other product-related expenses were estimated and expected variances from target costs determined. The trial products were also tested for reliability. Once they were deemed satisfactory, they were sent to the customer for evaluation along with any relevant test results.

If the customer was satisfied with the design and it passed the reliability tests, it was analyzed to ensure that the product could be efficiently mass produced. From this analysis the final design of the product was established. The cost of this final design was estimated and the variances from target costs determined. If the costs of this design were considered too high (i.e., if they significantly exceeded the product's target cost), a first-look VE project was initiated.

Once the estimated cost of the product was accepted, the production design was established. This design was subjected to a third round of cost estimation and variance analysis. The design was also subjected to a process review in which the quality of the design and the procedures to ensure that the final product met the required quality standards were established.

The product was now subjected to a third design review. After this review was completed, experimental production commenced. Experimental production consisted of manufacturing prototypes that were used to confirm the functionality of the design and the appropriateness of the design for mass production. The analysis of the prototypes provided information that was used to fine-tune the product's design and ready it for mass production. The product was then released for experimental mass production.

The first few months of experimental mass production were used as the basis for estimating the product's cost for a fourth time, and variance from target costs were determined. The analysis was also used to help fine-tune the production process. For example, even if the trial product achieved the required quality level, the mass-produced version might not be acceptable and modifications to the product's design or its production process might be required. The product, which was now nearly ready for mass production, was subjected to a fourth and final design review. Once this review was completed, the product was released for mass production.

Before mass production could begin, the product's production plan had to be developed. This plan, which defined its production schedule, was based upon the latest customer information. Once this plan was developed, mass production began. At about the same time, a review of the effectiveness of the VE process was conducted. The primary purpose of this review was to ensure that the product was properly designed and that each step in the design process had been well-managed. After the product had been in mass production for a year or two, a review was conducted to determine if additional VE activities were required. Typically, additional VE activities were required if the product's DQC (delivery times, quality, and cost) was considered unacceptable. If the product's DQC was unacceptable, a second-look VE project was initiated. If additional VE activities were not required, then no redesign actions were taken and mass production of the product continued.

The outcome of the second-look VE project was a redesigned product whose DQC was acceptable to both the customer and Yokohama management. This redesign was subjected to a round of cost estimation and variance analysis reviews similar to those performed during the original design stages. If the product redesign was acceptable, it was released for experimental mass production. The purpose of the experimental mass production was to iron out any problems in the product's design and in its tooling and production processes. The final design review was then conducted and if the design required additional work, another second-look VE project was initiated. If no additional design work was required, the redesigned product was released into production. As before, once the product entered into mass production, a review of VE activity was conducted.

Company Descriptions

Citizen Watch Company, Ltd.

This company was the manufacturing arm of the world's largest watch producer, Citizen, founded in 1930. It was not only responsible for manufacturing watches but was also strategically diversified into products that required expertise in watch technology: numerically controlled production equipment, flexible disk drives, liquid crystal displays for televisions and computers, dot matrix printers, and jewelry. The non-watch products consisted of almost half its revenues in 1990.

Higashimaru Shoyu Company, Ltd.

This manufacturer of soy sauce was formed in 1942 by the merger of the Kikuichi Shoyu Goshi Gaisha and Asai Shoy Gomeri Gaisha. Higashimaru produced light and dark soy sauce (80 types), Japanese-style porridge, Japanese-style salad dressing, sweet sake, soup stocks, and noodle sauces. This variety of products, with the light soy sauce being most important, generated approximately ¥21 billion of sales in 1992 and employed 510 people.

Isuzu Motors, Ltd.

Isuzu originated in 1916 with Tokyo Ishikawajima Shipbuilding and Engineering Co., Ltd. manufacturing automobiles. Based on units produced, Isuzu was the ninth-largest automobile company in Japan in 1992 with 10 large domestic competitors. The 4% market share of Isuzu was misleading because it did not reflect the firm's specialized market strength in trucks and buses due to the higher-volume passenger car market. Isuzu had 10% market share in heavy- and light-duty trucks and 11% share in the bus market.

JKC

JKC was founded in 1955 when it became independent of Diesel Kiki Co., Ltd. Its products were directly related to the three basic functions of a vehicle: driving, turning, and stopping. They included brakes, clutches, steering systems, and pumps. Among its major customers were Isuzu, Toyota, Nissan, and Komatsu. Its annual production was approximately ¥22 trillion.

Kamakura Iron Works Company, Ltd.

Kamakura, founded in 1910 as a blacksmith company, was a family-run firm located in a distant suburb of Tokyo. The firm has remained relatively small with 1993 sales of nearly ¥6 billion and profits of ¥35 million. The firm has been a supplier of automotive parts, with 21 major customers, including Yokohama Corporation (40% of sales), Isuzu Motos (20%), Hino Motos (15%), Jidosha Kiki Company (10%), and Yamaha Motors (5%). The majority of its customers have been either automobile manufacturers or suppliers to that industry. Other customers have included Iseki, Kayaba Industries, and Shinryo Heavy Equipment. Although large portions of the revenues were from vertically integrated companies, Kamakura was an independent company and did not belong to a keiretsu.

Kirin Brewery Company, Ltd.

Kirin originated as the Spring Valley Brewery in Yokohama in 1870, when W. Copeland, an American, established Japan's first brewery. The firm was diversified into a wide range of products—biotechnology-based pharmaceutical products, new hybrid vegetable varieties, and optical sensing systems—using its beer manufacturing technologies. They also produced products derived from by-products of the brewing process such as carbonated drinks, yeast-related feed for fish and livestock, and yeast-derived natural seasonings. With these products, Kirin generated ¥1,800 and ¥90 billion in sales and operating profits, respectively.

Komatsu, Ltd.

Founded in 1917 as part of the Takeuchi Mining Co., this firm was one of the largest heavy industrial manufacturers in Japan. It was organized into three major lines of business—construction equipment, industrial machinery, and electronic-applied products—which accounted for 80% of total revenues. The remaining 20% consisted of construction, unit housing, chemicals and plastics, and software development. These products together generated revenues of ¥989 billion and net income of ¥31 billion, making Komatsu a large international firm. Since 1989, the company has been aggressively diversifying and expanding globally.

Kyocera Corporation

Kyocera was founded in 1959 by its chairman, Dr. Kazuo Inamori, and seven of his colleagues as the Kyoto Ceramics Company, Ltd. It considered itself to be a "producer of high-technology solutions," specializing in developing innovative applications of ceramics technology. Kyocera established a strong reputation for innovation among major technical leaders in the semiconductor and electronic industries by taking on technically impossible jobs. The firm had sales of ¥453 billion and net income of ¥27 billion in 1992.

Mitsubishi Kasei Corporation

Formerly known as Mitsubishi Chemical Industries, Ltd., this company was Japan's largest integrated chemical company with ¥710 billion in revenues and ¥5 billion in net income. Its three major groups were carbon and inorganic chemicals, petrochemicals, and functional products. The first two groups consisted of high-volume and mass produced products, whereas the functional products were relatively low in volume with high value-added. The firm had successfully implemented the strategy to diversify by adding functional products to the firm's traditional product offerings.

Miyota Company Ltd.

Miyota Co. Ltd. (Miyota), founded in 1959, was a100%-owned subsidiary of Citizen Watch Company, Ltd. In 1995, its sales were just over ¥36 billion. The firm was originally dedicated to the assembly of watches for its parent, but over the years it diversified along technological lines by specializing in miniature mechatronic (the fusion of mechanical and electronic technologies) products. By 1995, Miyota produced four major product lines: completed watches, watch movements and parts, quartz oscillators, and viewfinders for camcorders.

Nippon Kayaku

Juntaro Yamamoto in 1916 founded this first manufacturer of industrial explosives in Japan. In 1992, the firm had five major lines of business—pharmaceuticals, sophisticated products, agrochemicals, dyestuffs, and explosives and catalysts—that were organized into pharmaceuticals and fine chemicals. Nippon Kayaku had sales of ¥117 billion and net profit of ¥2.8 billion in 1992. The firm's growth was achieved both through internal expansion and through several acquisitions and mergers.

Nissan Motor Company, Ltd.

This firm, founded in 1933, considered itself the most highly globalized of the Japanese automobile companies with 36 plants in 22 countries and marketing in 150 countries through 390 distributorships and over 10,000 dealerships. In 1990, Nissan was the world's fourth-largest automobile manufacturer, producing just over 3 million vehicles, about 10% of the world's demand for cars and trucks. Nissan had a stated policy of globalization through a five-step process that emphasized localization of production, sourcing, research and development, management functions, and decisions.

Olympus Optical Company, Ltd.

As part of Olympus, Olympus Optical Company manufactured and sold opto-electronic equipment and other related products. Originally Takachiho Seisakusho, Olympus was founded in 1919 as a producer of microscopes. Major product lines were cameras, video camcorders, microscopes, endoscopes, and clinical analyzers. By 1995, Olympus was the world's fourth-largest camera manufacturer, with consolidated revenues of ¥252 billion and ¥3 billion in net income.

Omachi Olympus Co., Ltd.

Omachi Olympus Co., Ltd. (Omachi) was a 100%-owned subsidiary of Olympus Optical Co., Ltd. (Olympus). It specialized in producing complex curved plastic moldings primarily for incorporation into the camera products that were made by the Consumer Products Division of its parent. The firm was located in the city of Omachi, which was in the Nagano Prefecture some 150 miles from Tokyo.

Shionogi & Co., Ltd.

This firm was founded as a wholesaler of traditional Japanese and Chinese medicines by Gisaburo Shiono in 1878. Shionogi was a research-and-development-oriented pharmaceutical manufacturer with 12.4% of sales dedicated to R&D. Shionogi's strategy focused on selling its products to hospitals and universities. The majority of its revenues were generated through pharmaceutical products; however, it also had other business such as animal health products, agrochemicals, industrial chemicals, diagnostics, and cosmetics. It was recognized around the world for the quality of its antibiotics and other pharmaceutical products with ¥225 billion in sales in 1992.

Sony Corporation

Sony, on of the world's largest electronics companies, started as Tokyo Telecommunications Research Institute and generated revenues by repairing broken radios and manufacturing short-wave converters in its earlier years. The company's first really successful product was Japan's first magnetic tape recorder in 1950. The company continued to grow rapidly, and by 1960 it became a truly international firm with Sony Corporation of America and Sony Overseas, S.A., in Switzerland, followed by Sony UK and Sony GmbH in 1968 and 1970, respectively.

Sumitomo Electric Industries, Ltd.

This firm was founded in 1897 as a manufacturer of bare copper, Sumitomo Copper Rolling Works. Since then, Sumitomo Electric Industries (SEI) has continued to produced electric wires and cables and was the world's third-largest manufacturer of these products. The firm has adopted a diversification program since 1931, taking advantage of the distinctive competencies in the manufacturing of electric wires and cables. SEI's top management considered the firm to be one of the most highly diversified in Japan.

Taiyo Kogyo Co., Ltd. (The Taiyo Group)

This firm was founded in 1947 by Kuniyasu Sakai and Hiroshi Sekiyama as The Taiyo Painting Company. As the firm grew and the Japanese economy expanded, it diversified from painting into metal stamping and electronic equipment. The Taiyo Group's Bunsha philosophy was to have small companies with highly autonomous managers to avoid bureaucracy. This philosophy was based on Sakai's notion that "when a company gets too large it cannot respond in time." He focused on the flexibility of the small firms as a powerful form of cost management.

Tokyo Motor Works, Ltd.

Tokyo Motor Works, Ltd. (TMW), when measured in terms of worldwide production, was by 1990 one of the world's top 10 automobile manufacturers. The firm, which was founded in 1945, by 1990 produced just over 2 million vehicles, supplying approximately 4% of the world's demand for cars and trucks. Of these vehicles, slightly over 1.2 million were passenger cars. TMW produced vehicles at 20 plants in 15 countries and marketed them in 110 countries through 200 distributorships and more than 6,000 dealerships.

Topcon Corporation

Topcon was originally founded as the Tokyo Optical Company, Ltd., in 1932. It diversified along its core competencies in advanced optics and precision equipment processing. By 1992, Topcon sold four major product lines: surveying instruments, medical and ophthalmic instruments, information instruments, and industrial instruments. The surveying instruments business unit contributed approximately 36% of sales; medical and ophthalmic instruments, 28%; information instruments, 13%; and industrial instruments, 23%. Topcon specialized in high-technology, high-margin, low-volume products. To rely continuously on high technology for profit, Topcon invested heavily in research and development.

Toyo Radiator Co. Ltd.

Toyo Radiator Co. Ltd. (Toyo) was founded in 1936 as a radiator supplier to the fledgling Japanese automobile industry. Toyo was not associated with and was independent of any of the major kieretsus. Over the years it diversified into all the arenas of heat-exchange applications, and by 1995 it sold heat-exchange products for use in automobiles and heavy construction and agricultural vehicles, air conditioners for home and office, and freezers. Its product lines included radiators, oil coolers, intercoolers, evaporators, and condensers. In 1995 it was one of the world's largest independent heat-exchange equipment manufacturers for construction equipment.

Toyota Motor Corporation

Toyota Motor Corporation (Toyota) started as a subsidiary of the Toyoda Automatic Loom Works, Ltd. It was founded in 1937 as the Toyota Motor Company, Ltd. It changed its name to the Toyota Motor Corporation in 1982 when the parent company merged with Toyota Sales Company, Ltd. In 1993 Toyota Motor Corporation was Japan's largest automobile company. It controlled approximately 45% of the domestic market. Over the years, Toyota had changed from a Japanese firm into a global one. In 1993 a considerable part of the firm's overseas markets were serviced by local subsidiaries that frequently designed and manufactured automobiles for local markets.

Yamanouchi Pharmaceutical Company, Ltd.

This firm was founded in 1923 to manufacture and sell pharmaceutical products. In 1992 Yamanouchi was Japan's second-largest pharmaceutical drug company in terms of net profit and was highly respected both in Japan and internationally. A.T. Kearney designated this company as one of the best-performing companies in the world in 1990. This company had a strong corporate philosophy of "Creating and Caring...for Life." In 1992 the consolidated sales were ¥357 billion and the net income was ¥33 billion; pharmaceutical products accounted for 73% of sales, nutritional products, 17% and food and roses, 10%. In 1989 as part of its diversification strategy, Yamanouchi acquired the Shaklee Group, where the bulk of its nutritional products were sold.

Yamatake-Honeywell Company, Ltd.

Founded in 1906 as a small trading company, this firm has grown into a group of six companies with consolidated 1993 sales of ¥196.8 billion and pretax income of ¥14.5 billion. In 1993, the group consisted of Yamatake & Co., Ltd., Yamatake Keiso Co., Ltd., Yamatake Engineering Co., Ltd., Yamatake Control Products Co., Ltd., Yamatake Techno-systems Co., Ltd., and Yamatake-Honeywell Co., Ltd. Yamatake-Honeywell comprised four divisions that carried out research and development for control and automation: industrial systems, building systems, control products, and factory automation systems.

Yokohama Corporation, Ltd.

Yokohama was founded in July 1939 as a joint venture between a Japanese automobile manufacturer and the Japanese government. The objective of the firm was to manufacture hydraulic systems for automobiles and trucks and associated equipment under license from a German firm. Firm ownership changed over the years and in 1993 only three major shareholders remained: Isuzu Motors, Nissan Motors, and The Industrial Bank of Japan. By 1992, the firm had 13 overseas affiliates, seven liaison offices, and a worldwide service network of over 100 distributors and 2,000 service representatives with sales of ¥257 billion and 6,800 employees. Yokohama was split into three corporate divisions: injection pump, air conditioning, and hydraulics and pneumatics.

GLOSSARY OF TERMS

ACTIVITY-BASED COSTING (ABC). A highly accurate product costing methodology that assigns costs to products based on the activities required to produce the product. ABC traces costs to products using many different activity measures that reflect the quantities of input consumed to manufacture the product.

ALLOWABLE COST. The difference between the target selling price and the target profit margin.

AMOEBA MANAGEMENT SYSTEM. A system developed at Kyocera that organizes the firm into a large collection of quasi-autonomous profit centers or highly independent pseudo firms responsible for selling a number of products both internally and externally.

AUTOMATED INVENTORY REPLENISHMENT. The supplier takes responsibility to maintain the inventories of its parts at the buyer, and the buyer's systems send a refill order automatically.

BAR CODING. A machine-readable way to identify products.

BARON. One of the core firms in a barony.

BARONY. A supplier network with multiple core firms.

BATCH-AND-QUEUE. An approach to task completion that consists of making a large number of similar items and then queuing that batch before the next step in the process.

BUNDLED TARGET COSTING. When a single supplier is responsible for multiple components for a product, the individual component-level target costs can be bundled. The supplier is then held accountable for the total cost of all of the components, not their individual costs.

BUNSHA PHILOSOPHY. An approach to managing firm size used by the Taiyo Kogyo Group founder Kuniyasu Sakai, who believes strongly that small firms are inherently more efficient and effective than large firms. Bunsha, meaning "to divide," refers to the spinning off of new venture firms from the parent firm.

CARDINAL RULE OF TARGET COSTING. Rule that says that the target cost can never be exceeded.

CHAINED TARGET COSTING. When the buyer's target costing system provides the target selling prices for the supplier's target costing system, the two target costing systems are said to be chained.

COMMON SUPPLIER. A firm that sells commodity-like products that have established market prices.

CONCURRENT COST MANAGEMENT. When the buyer outsources research and development of a major function to the supplier, the two firms can undertake concurrent cost management by coordinating their cost management programs in the conceptual design phase. The advantage of concurrent cost management is that coordinated cost management can begin earlier in the design process.

CONFRONTATION. A competitive strategy that assumes sustainable, product-related competitive advantages are unlikely to be developed. Confronting competitors head on is achieved by rapidly matching the cost/quality/functionality improvements other firms initiate while nurturing the ability to create temporary competitive advantages.

CORE FIRM. A firm that wields significant power in a supplier network. The power is derived from the disproportionately high share of the total demand for goods and services produced by the core firm.

COST BALANCE VERIFICATION. The term used by Komatsu for interorganizational cost investigations.

COST-DOWN PROGRAMS. A disciplined companywide cost-reduction campaign with a primary focus on finding ways to design costs out of products before they enter production. These programs also include methods for improving efficiency in the manufacturing process.

COST LEADERSHIP. A generic competitive strategy that requires the firm to establish itself as the lowest cost producer in an industry. Traditionally, cost leaders offer products that are low in price and functionality.

COST-REDUCTION OBJECTIVE. The difference between the allowable cost and the current cost.

COST TABLES. Databases that capture the cost and other part characteristics that can be used to help estimate costs of new parts.

CURRENT COST. The cost of a future product, assuming that it is manufactured today from existing components using existing production processes.

DESIGN FOR MANUFACTURE AND ASSEMBLY (DFMA). A simultaneous engineering process that optimizes the relationship between materials, manufacturing technology, assembly process, functionality, and economics. It seeks to ease the manufacture and assembly of parts or eliminate them.

DIFFERENTIATION. A generic competitive strategy that relies on the provision of unique product offerings that closely satisfy customers, requirements. The differentiator's product offerings are usually high in both functionality and price.

DRIFTING TARGET COST. The estimate of what the product cost would be if the product were manufactured at any point during the product design process, given confirmed cost savings.

ECONOMIES OF SCALE. The reduced unit costs associated with manufacturing products in higher volumes.

ECONOMIES OF SCOPE. The reduced unit costs associated with producing a range of similar items.

ELECTRONIC COMMERCE. The ability to transact business electronically.

ELECTRONIC DATA INTERCHANGE. The electronic transmission of standard business documents in a predefined format from one company's business computer application to that of another company with which it is doing business.

EXPECTED SELLING PRICE. The price used in the product pricing methods associated with a cost-plus approach. It becomes the dependent variable and is determined by adding a target profit margin to the expected product cost.

FAMILY MEMBER. A firm that designs and sells major functions.

FIRST-TIER SUPPLIER. A firm that supplies its outputs directly to a core firm.

FUNCTION TABLES. Databases that capture the physical dimensions of parts and their functionality.

FUNCTIONAL ANALYSIS. A cost estimation process that uses function tables and cost tables to predict the target cost of an item whose design and manufacture have been outsourced.

FUNCTIONAL GROUP MANAGEMENT SYSTEM. The Olympus Corporation's term for a bottom-up approach to identifying and achieving cost-reduction targets that are carried out by self-directed work teams.

FUNCTIONALITY-PRICE-QUALITY (FPQ) TRADE-OFF. A cost management technique where the buyer and supplier get together to determine if small relaxations in the buyer's quality and functionality (and rarely, price) specifications can be used to enable the supplier to achieve its target costs.

GROUP COMPONENT. A subassembly that performs a specific task, for example, a starter motor.

HORIZONTAL COORDINATION. The processes that operate among firms in the same tier to maintain the effectiveness of a supplier network.

ITEM-SPECIFIC KAIZEN COSTING. Kaizen costing whose cost-reduction objectives are for a specified item.

INTERORGANIZATIONAL COST INVESTIGATION. A cost management technique whereby the design teams of all the firms in a target costing chain work together to identify ways to reduce costs so that all the firms in the chain can achieve their target costs.

INTERORGANIZATIONAL COST MANAGEMENT SYSTEM. A cost-reduction program initiated by a core firm and carried out across the entire value chain. These systems contribute to the blurring of organizational boundaries as firms share information and resources to improve the efficiency of interfirm activities.

JUST-IN-TIME (JIT). The ordering and delivery of parts as they are needed in the production process to achieve minimum inventory and waste.

KAIZEN. A Japanese term that stands for continuous improvement. As applied in cost management practice, the term refers to a total commitment on behalf of the work force to finding new ways to reduce costs and increase efficiency in the manufacturing process.

KAIZEN COSTING. The application of kaizen techniques to reduce the costs of existing components and products by a pre-specified amount. Its objective is to reduce a product's cost through increased efficiency of the production process.

KANBAN. A small card attached to boxes of parts that triggers upstream activities.

KEIRETSU. A federation of firms joined in a relationship based on their common traditions and business dealings. Keiretsu can be vertical, between a manufacturer, its component/material suppliers, and its distribution partners, or horizontal, usually centered around a financial institution that holds equity stakes in the participants while it meets their financing needs.

KING. The single core firm in a kingdom.

KINGDOM. A supplier network with a single core firm.

LEAD TIME. The time between placing an order and receiving the goods.

LEAN ENTERPRISE. A new organizational form originating in Japan. It employs lean production methods such as just-in-time production, total quality management, team-based work arrangements, supportive supplier relations, and improved customer satisfaction. The lean enterprise is capable of producing high-quality products economically in lower volumes and bringing them to market faster than mass producers.

LEAN SUPPLIER NETWORK. A constellation of lean buyer-supplier relationships organized around one or more lead firms. Transactional network protocols emerge within the network to support sustained interaction among member firms based on lean supply principles. These protocols help to lessen excessive competition among member firms and thus reinforce the development over time of cooperative relationships critical to network-based competitive advantage.

LEAN SUPPLIER RELATIONSHIP. The relationship between a lean buyer and supplier, characterized as stable, cooperative, and mutually beneficial.

LEAN SUPPLY. Occurs when a lean enterprise supplies another lean enterprise using a just-in-time philosophy.

LINKED KAIZEN COSTING. When the cost-reduction objectives of the buyer's kaizen costing system become inputs to the supplier's kaizen costing system, the two systems are said to be linked.

MAJOR FUNCTION. Part of an end product that performs a distinct secondary function, for example, an engine cooling system.

MAJOR SUPPLIER. A firm that designs and manufactures group components.

MASS PRODUCER. A firm that relies on mass production manufacturing techniques similar to those pioneered by Henry Ford, among others.

MAXIMUM ALLOWABLE PRICE. The highest price the customer is willing to spend for the product irrespective of its quality and functionality.

MAXIMUM FEASIBLE VALUES (of a survival triplet characteristic). Determined by the capability of the firm, maximum feasible values are the highest values for product characteristics a firm can achieve without violating the minimum or maximum values of the other characteristics.

MINIMUM ALLOWABLE VALUE (of a survival triplet characteristic). Determined by the customer, the minimum allowable level is the lowest value of each product-related characteristic that the customer is willing to accept.

MINIMUM COST INVESTIGATIONS. The term used for interorganizational cost investigations by Isuzu.

NETWORK INFRASTRUCTURES. Any arrangement that improves the collective capabilities of a supplier network. Examples include technical seminars and training programs, consulting, and interorganizational problem solving.

NETWORK PROTOCOLS. These rules of conduct extend the behavior developed between individual buyers and suppliers to the level of the network as a whole. Their primary purpose is to ameliorate the negative consequences of excessive competition among firms in the network.

OPERATIONAL CONTROL. Method for obtaining feedback on how well costs are being controlled. Assigning responsibility to individuals for costs they control makes responsibility centers the primary unit of analysis to evaluate how well costs are controlled, through the use of variance analysis.

OVERHEAD-SPECIFIC KAIZEN COSTING. Kaizen costing in which the cost-reduction objectives are specified for indirect costs.

PARALLEL ENGINEERING. An approach to concurrent cost management in which the buyer's and supplier's design teams rarely interact. The buyer provides the supplier with high-level specifications, and then the two design teams work essentially in isolation to complete their designs, as long as they can deliver the desired functionality and quality for both the end product and the outsourced major function at their specified target costs.

PAY-ON-RECEIPT. The buyer pays the supplier upon receipt of the goods. No statements or invoices are prepared by the supplier.

PERIOD-SPECIFIC KAIZEN COSTING. Kaizen costing in which the cost-reduction objectives are for a specified time period.

PRODUCT COSTING. A systematic cost accounting method for assigning appropriate costs to products during the manufacturing process to determine product costs and monitor profitability.

PRODUCT-SPECIFIC KAIZEN COSTING. Kaizen costing in which the cost-reduction objectives are for a specified product.

PRODUCTIVITY ANALYSIS. A detailed cost estimation process that decomposes the cost of an item into production steps and then computes the expected cost of the item. Included in the estimates are aggressive cost-reduction objectives.

QUALITY FUNCTION DEPLOYMENT. A visual decision making procedure for multiskilled project teams. It develops a common understanding of the voice of the customer and a consensus on the final engineering specifications of the product, which has the commitment of the entire design team.

REPUBLIC. A supplier network with no core firms.

SECOND-TIER SUPPLIER. A firm that supplies its outputs directly to a first-tier supplier.

SIMULTANEOUS ENGINEERING. An approach to concurrent cost management whereby the buyer's and supplier's design teams interact continuously during the conceptual design stage. The purpose of this interaction is to find innovative design solutions that provide the desired level of functionality and quality for both the end product and the outsourced major function at their specified target costs.

SINGLE-PIECE FLOW. An approach to task completion that consists of completing each product or design in its entirety without any queues.

STRATEGIC COST-REDUCTION CHALLENGE. The difference between the allowable and product-level target costs.

SUBCONTRACTOR. A firm that manufactures simple components designed by the buyer.

SUPPLIER ASSOCIATION. A mutually beneficial grouping of key suppliers linked together to form a strategic alliance.

SUPPLY CHAIN. The suppliers involved in the manufacture of a single component used in an end product. The chain begins with the supplier that is producing the simplest component that can be identified with the end product and ends with the firm that manufactures the end product.

SURVIVAL TRIPLET. Three product-related characteristics—cost (price), quality, and functionality—that must be managed to ensure that products remain within their survival zones.

SURVIVAL ZONE. Area defined by the gaps between minimum and maximum price, functionality, and quality. Only products that fall inside their survival zone can be successful.

SUSTAINABLE COMPETITIVE ADVANTAGE. The ability to sustain product-related or other competitive advantages and thus generate high profit margins for a lengthy period of time.

TARGET COSTING. A structured approach to determining the cost at which a proposed product with specified functionality and quality must be produced to generate the desired level of profitability at its anticipated selling price. A product's target cost is determined by subtracting its target profit margin from its target selling price and adjusting for the strategic cost-reduction challenge.

TARGET COSTING CHAIN. The chain created by a set of chained target costing systems. The firm at the top of the chain in characterized by an inability to legislate prices to its customers, but it can legislate prices to the next firm in the chain. The chain ends with a supplier that is unable to legislate prices to its suppliers while it is being legislated by its buyers.

TARGET COST-REDUCTION OBJECTIVE. The difference between the current cost and the target cost.

TARGET PROFIT MARGIN. The target profit margin is set based on corporate profit expectations, historical results, competitive analysis, and, in some cases, computer simulations. Target profit margins applied in target costing procedures ensure that products will be sold at a minimum acceptable profit.

TARGET SELLING PRICE. The selling price of a new product determined primarily from market analysis. It is used to determine a target cost, which is applied during the design phase of new product development. It is also used as the basis for determining the purchase price of components and raw materials acquired externally.

TEARDOWN ANALYSIS. A method used to analyze competitive product offerings in terms of materials and parts used as well as ways in which they are manufactured.

TEMPORARY COMPETITIVE ADVANTAGE. An advantage achieved over one's competitors that is not expected to last for long.

THIRD-TIER SUPPLIER. A firm that supplies its outputs directly to a second-tier supplier.

TOTAL QUALITY MANAGEMENT (TQM). An integrated approach that focuses on designing quality into products and ensuring that the production process is as defect-free as possible.

VALUE-ADDED. The difference between the selling price and the cost of the raw material and the selling price of a product.

VALUE ENGINEERING (VE). A systematic interdisciplinary examination of factors affecting the cost of a product so as to devise a means of achieving the required standard of quality and reliability at the target cost.

VERTICAL COORDINATION. The processes that maintain the effectiveness of a supplier network that operates among firms in different tiers.

ZERO DEFECTS (ZD). A quality program with the objective of reducing defects to zero.

Selected Bibliography
and References

Selected Bibliography on Interorganizational
Cost Management

Cooper, R. *When Lean Enterprises Collide: Competing Through Confrontation.* Boston: Harvard Business School Press, 1995.

This book introduces a new theory of competition, the confrontation strategy, in which sustainable competitive advantages cease to exist and lean enterprises become locked in relentless, head-on competition. These firms engage in a competitive game of constantly introducing new products with the desired levels of quality and functionality at the lowest cost. Cooper shows that the key to success in such a competitive environment is the careful balance of the three elements in the "survival triplet"—price/cost, quality, and functionality—with an emphasis on aggressive cost management across the supply chain. Eight integrated cost management techniques are described, including interorganizational cost management techniques such as target costing, quality-function-price trade-offs, and minimum cost investigations. The crucial role these techniques play in supporting the confrontation strategy is demonstrated using vignettes from practice. The evidence on which the insights in this book are based is drawn from an in-depth field study of the strategy and cost management practices of 20 Japanese firms.

Cooper, R., and T. Yoshikawa. "Inter-Organizational Cost Management Systems: The Case of the Tokyo-Yokohama-Kamakura Supplier Chain." *International Journal of Production Economics,* Vol. 37, 1994, pp. 51–62.

This article documents the use of interorganizational cost management systems in three Japanese firms in a single supply chain in the automobile industry. The findings from the exploratory field research show how these firms have blurred their organizational boundaries to improve the coordination of their activities and become more efficient by sharing detailed product design and cost information. Downward cost pressures on the entire supply chain are achieved through the application of interorganizational cost management techniques such as target costing, quality-function-price trade-offs, and minimum cost investigations. The article concludes that the success of these systems depends heavily on the development of cooperative, trusting relationships among the three firms in the supply chain. One drawback of the use of interorganizational cost management systems is that they create a pathway for technological diffusion that makes it harder for each firm to achieve a sustainable competitive advantage.

Dyer, J. H., and W. G. Ouchi. "Japanese-Style Partnerships: Giving Companies a Competitive Edge." *Sloan Management Review,* Fall 1993, pp. 51–63.

This article focuses on Japanese-style partnerships, which are characterized by the long-term nature of buyer-supplier relationships, frequent communication, mutual assistance, a focus on total value chain costs, the willingness to make dedicated investments, intensive sharing of technical and cost information, and the creation of a high degree of goal congruence and trust. The article discusses three major benefits that can be derived from such relationships. First, using fewer direct suppliers leads to lower transaction and production costs due to economies of scale and experience curve effects. Second, customized investments in physical and human assets create significant switching costs and help reduce costs and improve quality. Third, these partnerships provide incentives for the suppliers to continue to innovate and reduce costs, for example, by using a two-vendor policy, providing assistance to the weaker of two suppliers to maintain competition, and applying experience-curve-based pricing. The success of Japanese firms in developing such cooperative relationships is attributed to the high level of intercompany trust, created through stable, long-term employment, employee transfers between companies, face-to-face contact, minority ownership, and specialized investments.

Hines, P. *Creating World Class Suppliers.* London: Pitman Publishing, 1994.

This book starts by explaining the essential characteristics of the lean production system. It then extends the internal process requirements for the achievement of world-class performance to the external management systems, called network sourcing. Hines describes the history of lean supplier networks as they developed in Japan. Examples of innovative Japanese and Western firms in different industries are used to demonstrate how firms can capitalize on the development of cooperative and mutually beneficial buyer-supplier relations for gaining competitive advantage. In particular, the book discusses how supplier associations can be powerful tools for disseminating new technology up and down the supplier network. The last part of the book is concerned with identifying what Western and Japanese firms can learn from each other with regard to supplier development. It concludes by describing a road map for the creation of supplier associations outside Japan.

Lamming, R. *Beyond Partnership. Strategies for Innovation and Lean Supply,* New York: Prentice Hall, 1993.

The purpose of this book is to document and analyze how lean buyer-supplier relationships operate in the automotive industry. Lamming starts with a historical perspective, describing the transformation of the automotive industry from "craft" and "mass" to "lean" production, and the roles of component suppliers within it. The book provides statistics on the automotive assembly and components industries worldwide and summarizes literature about technological innovation and strategic collaboration. Lamming introduces a four-phase model of customer-supplier relations as they evolved over the years, ranging from traditional, stress, resolved, to partnership. Lamming's central argument is that buyer-supplier relations under lean supply go beyond Japanese-style partnerships in that they are based on collaboration between truly equal partners. The book concludes with some guidelines for moving to a lean supply strategy.

Lewis, J. D. *The Connected Corporation.* New York: The Free Press, 1995.

In this book, Lewis argues that effective customer-supplier alliances are powerful tools for building competitive advantage as they unlock a capacity for improvement and innovation that outweighs the short-term cost savings offered by arm's-length competitive bidding. Best-practice examples from Western companies such as Motorola, Chrysler, and Marks & Spencer are used to show how the right kind of cooperation and information sharing can yield significant cost savings for both buyers and suppliers. Instead of simply setting specifications for parts and then squeezing suppliers to meet them at the lowest prices, firms should form close partnerships with a limited number of suppliers. Being part of a stable and trusting relationship encourages the suppliers to make suggestions for improvements and investments tailored to the purchasing firm's needs. The book discusses a number of practical issues related to developing successful customer-supplier partnerships, such as partner selection, practices for fostering joint creativity, supply base management, and methods for monitoring performance of the alliance.

Other Readings on Interorganizational Cost Management

Carr, C., and J. Ng. "Total Cost Control: Nissan and Its U. K. Supplier Partnerships." *Management Accounting Research,* Vol. 6, 1995, pp. 347–365.

Dyer, J. H. "Dedicated Assets: Japan's Manufacturing Edge." *Harvard Business Review,* November-December 1994, pp. 174–178.

Dyer, J. H. "How Chrysler Created an American Kereitsu." *Harvard Business Review,* July-August 1996, pp. 42–56.

Kamath, R. R., and J. K. Liker. "A Second Look at Japanese Product Development." *Harvard Business Review,* November-December 1994, pp. 154–170.

McMillan, J. "Managing Suppliers: Incentive Systems in Japanese and U. S. Industry." *California Management Review,* Summer 1990, pp. 38–55.

Munday, M. "Accounting Cost Data Disclosure and Buyer-Supplier Partnerships—A Research Note." *Management Accounting Research,* Vol. 3, 1992, pp. 245–250.

Richardson, J. "Parallel Sourcing and Supplier Performance in the Japanese Automobile Industry." *Strategic Management Journal,* Vol. 14, 1993, pp. 339–350.

Background Readings

Competition

Cusumano, M. A. *The Japanese Automobile Industry.* Cambridge, MA: Council on East Asian Studies, Harvard University, 1985.

D'Aveni, R. *Hypercompetition.* New York: The Free Press, 1994.

Meyer, C. *Fast Cycle Time.* New York: The Free Press, 1993.

Porter, M. *Competitive Advantage of Nations.* New York: Free Press, 1990.

Stalk, George, Jr., and Thomas M. Hout. *Competing Against Time.* New York:, The Free Press, 1990.

Thomas, P. R. *Competitiveness Through Total Cycle Time.* New York: McGraw-Hill, 1990.

Williams, J. R. "How Sustainable Is Your Competitive Advantage?" *California Management Review,* 34, Spring 1992, p. 51.

Lean Production and the Lean Enterprise

Fruin, W. M., and T. Nishiguchi. "Supplying the Toyota Production System" in B. Kogut, ed., *Country Competitiveness: Technology and the Organizing of Work.* New York: Oxford University Press, 1993.

Harrison, B. *Lean and Mean: The Changing Landscape of Corporate Power in the Age of Flexibility.* New York: Basic Books, 1994.

Krafcik, J. F. "Triumph of the Lean Production System." *Sloan Management Review,* Fall 1988, pp.41–52.

Morales, R. *Flexible Production.* New York: Polity Press, 1993.

Womack, J. P., and D. T. Jones. "From Lean Production to the Lean Enterprise." *Harvard Business Review,* March-April 1994, pp. 93–103.

Womack, J. P., and D. T. Jones. *Lean Thinking.* New York: Harper Collins, 1996.

Womack, J. P., D. T. Jones, and D. Roos. *The Machine That Changed the World.* New York: Harper Collins, 1990.

Product Development

Clark, K. B., and T. Fujimoto. *Product Development Performance.* Boston: Harvard Business School Press, 1991.

Clark, K. B., and S. C. Wheelwright, eds. *The Productivity Development Challenge.* Boston: Harvard Business School Press, 1994.

Imai, K., I. Nonaka., and H. Takeuchi. "Managing the New Product Development Process: How Japanese Companies Learn and Unlearn" in K. B. Clark et al., eds., *The Uneasy Alliance: Managing the Productivity-Technology Dilemma.* Boston: Harvard Business School Press, 1994.

Odagiri, H., and A. Goto. "The Japanese System of Innovation: Past, Present, and Future" in R. Nelson, ed., *National Innovation Systems.* New York: Oxford University Press, 1993, pp. 76–113.

Ward, A., J. K. Liker, J. J. Cristiano, and D. K. Sobek II. "The Second Toyota Paradox: How Delaying Decisions Can Make Better Cars Faster." *Sloan Management Review,* Spring 1995, pp. 43–61.

Supply Chain Management

Burt, D. N. "Managing Suppliers Up to Speed." *Harvard Business Review,* July-August 1989, pp. 127–135.

Davis, T. "Effective Supply Chain Management." *Sloan Management Review*, Summer 1993, pp. 35–46.

Harland, C. M. "Supply Chain Management: Relationships, Chains and Networks." *British Journal of Management,* Vol. 7, Special Issue, March 1996, pp. S63–S80.

Lee, H. L. "Managing Supply Chain Inventory: Pitfalls and Opportunities." *Sloan Management Review,* Spring 1992, pp. 65–72.

Saunders, M. *Strategic Purchasing and Supply Chain Management.* London: Pitman Publishing, 1994.

Supplier Relations

Bensaou, M., and N. Venkatraman. "Configurations of Interorganizational Relationships: A Comparison Between U. S. and Japanese Automakers." *Management Science,* Vol. 41, No. 9, September 1995, pp. 1471–1492.

Cusumano, M. A., and A. Takeishi. "Supplier Relations and Management: A Survey of Japanese, Japanese-Transplant, and U.S. Auto Plants." *Strategic Management Journal*, Vol. 12, 1991, pp. 563–588.

Helper, S. "How Much Has Really Changed Between U. S. Automakers and Their Suppliers?" *Sloan Management Review*, Summer 1991, pp. 15–28.

Helper, S. "Strategy and Irreversibility in Supplier Relations: The Case of the U.S. Automobile Industry." *Business History Review*, Vol. 65, No. 4, Winter 1991, pp. 781–784.

Helper, S. "Incentives for Supplier Participation in Product Development: Evidence from the U.S. Auto Industry" in T. Nishiguchi, ed., *Managing Product Development*, New York: Oxford University Press, 1996, pp. 165–189.

Helper, S., and M. Sako. "Supplier Relations in Japan and the United States: Are They Converging?" *Sloan Management Review*, Spring 1995, pp. 77–84.

Lyons, T. F., A. R. Krachenberg, and J. W. Henke. "Mixed Motive Marriages: What's Next for Buyer-Supplier Relations?" *Sloan Management Review*, Spring 1990, pp. 29–36s.

Sheth, J. N., and A. Sharma. "Supplier Relationships: Emerging Issues and Challenges." *Industrial Marketing Management*, No. 26, 1997, pp. 91–100.

Technology Diffusion

Okimoto, D. *Between MITI and the Market*. Stanford: Stanford University Press, 1989.

Samuels, R., Jr. "Pathways of Technological Diffusion in Japan." *Sloan Management Review*, Spring 1994, pp. 21–34.

Networks

Byrne, J. A. "The Horizontal Corporation." *Business Week*, Dec. 20, 1993, pp. 76–81.

Davidow, W. H., and M. S. Malone. *The Virtual Corporation*. New York: Harper Collins, 1992.

Dyer, J. H. "Specialized Supplier Networks as a Source of Competitive Advantage: Evidence from the Auto Industry." *Strategic Management Journal*, Vol. 17, 1996, pp. 271–291.

Gerlach, M. L. "The Japanese Corporate Network: A Blockmodel Analysis." *Administrative Science Quarterly*, Vol. 37, March 1992, pp. 105–139.

Powell, W. W. "Neither Market nor Hierarchy: Network Forms of Organization" in B. M. Staw and L. L. Cummings, eds., *Research in Organizational Behavior*, Vol. 12. Greenwich, CT: Jai Press, Inc., 1990.

INDEX

The IMA Foundation for Applied Research, Inc. (FAR) is the research affiliate of the Institute of Management Accountants. The mission of the Foundation is to develop and disseminate timely management accounting research findings that can be applied to current and emerging business issues. For further information on IMA, contact:

The IMA Foundation for Applied Research, Inc.
10 Paragon Drive, Montvale, NJ 07645-1760
Telephone: 800-638-4427, ext. 278; telefax: 201-573-9507
E-mail: jpirard@imanet.org.

Productivity, Inc. publishes books that empower individuals and companies to achieve excellence in quality, productivity, and the creative involvement of all employees. Through steadfast efforts to support the vision and strategy of continuous improvement, Productivity delivers today's leading-edge tools and techniques gathered directly from industry leaders around the world. Productivity also offers a diverse menu of consulting services and training products that complement the exciting ideas from our books. Whether you need assistance with long-term planning or focused, results-driven training, Productivity's experienced professional staff can enhance your pursuit of competitive advantage. For further information about Productivity, Inc. and to obtain our free catalog, contact:

Productivity, Inc.
P.O. Box 13390, Portland, OR 97213-0309
Telephone: 503-235-0600; telefax: 503-235-0909
Sales Department: 800-394-6868
E-mail: service@productivityinc.com